LOST AT SEA

The strange route of the Lena Shoal junk

LOST AT SEA

The strange route of the Lena Shoal junk

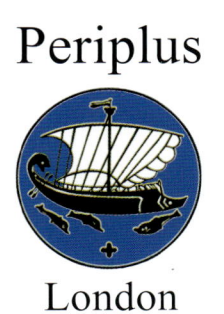

Periplus

London

© Periplus Publishing London Ltd 2002
© English and French translation: Periplus Publishing London Ltd 2001

All rights reserved. No part of this publication may be reproduced, stored in a retrieval system, or transmitted in any form or by any means, electronic, mechanical, photocopying, recording or otherwise, without the prior permission of the copyright owner.

First published in 2002 by
Periplus Publishing London Ltd
98 Church Rd
London SW13 0DQ

Publisher: Danièle Naveau
Managing editor: Nick Easterbrook
Production manager: Sophie Chéry
Translation from French into English: Josephine Bacon (Pholiota Limited)
With thanks to John Crick for his collaboration to the translations.

English language editions
Hardback   ISBN 1-902699-13-0
Softback   ISBN 1-902699-35-1

French language editions
Hardback   ISBN 1-902699-12-2
Softback   ISBN 1-902699-36-X

Printed and bound in Italy by Graphicom.

The archaeological excavation of the Lena Shoal Junk was conducted
in close collaboration with the National Museum of the Philippines
and with generous support from the HILTI Foundation

FOREWORD

The discovery of a wreck north-east of the Phillipine island of Palawan in February 1997 is testimony to the interconnection of earlier cultures and of the trading relationship between Filipinos and the peoples of other regions in South-East Asia.

Committed to protecting and preserving the material culture of the past through its underwater archaeology section, the National Museum of the Philippines collaborated with the Far Eastern Foundation for Nautical Archaeology (FEFNA) headed by Franck Goddio to salvage the wreck. The archaeological excavation, undertaken at a depth of 48–50 metres below the surface, brought to light remnants of a Chinese trading vessel and an array of magnificent artefacts that are solid evidence of a flourishing maritime trade around the turn of the sixteenth century.

The Lena Shoal junk carried with it a valuable cargo from China, Siam and Annam, some of which would have been destined for the distant ports of Hormuz and Aden, while some would have been bartered for exotic products in the Moslem sultanates of the Philippines, Borneo or the Moluccas.

High quality ceramics such as blue and white wares, ewers, boxes and inkstands, and other merchandise such as iron and tin ingots, copper utensils and cooking pots comprise some of the more than 3,000 artefacts retrieved from the site.

The Lena Shoal wreck with all the information contained therein is an affirmation of the presence of a civilised Filipino society that participated actively in maritime trade, long before Spaniards set foot in the archipelago. It attests to an ancient culture of which contemporary Filipinos can be proud.

Gabriel S. Casal
Director of the National Museum of the Philippines

1997 MISSION PARTICIPANTS

Mission directors

Franck Goddio: Director of the Institute of Underwater Archaeology (IEASM)
Director of the Far Eastern Foundation for Nautical Archaeology (FEFNA)

Gabriel S. Casal: Director of the National Museum of the Philippines

IEASM – FEFNA

Cécile Bernardo
Jean-Paul Blancan
Bernard Camier
Nicolas Day
Florenio Frayre
Patrick Gay
Bruno Giossa
Jose Gregorio
Jean-Jacques Groussard
Alaa El Din Mahrous Mahmoud
Pascal Morrisset
Frédéric Osada
Alain Petton
Nicolas Ponzone
Ashraf Abd El Raouf
Roland Savoye
Gérard Schnepp
Pablo Rodriguez
Jean-Claude Roubaud
Philippe Rousseau
Eric Smith
Rolando Tayag
Arturo Tolico
Daniel Visnikar

National Museum of the Philippines

Wilfredo F. Ronquillo, Director of the Archaeology Department
Euzebio Dizon, Director of the Underwater Archaeology Department

Larry Alba
Rodolfo Agnasin
Eduardo Bersamira
Eduardo Conese
Antonio Malones Jr.
Dante Posades

TABLE OF CONTENTS

Chapter I	**The wreck on the Lena Shoal**	1
	Franck Goddio, Director of the European Institute of Underwater Archaeology	
	1 The development of Chinese maritime commerce	1
	2 Navigation to the Phillipines in the fifteenth century	4
	3 Discovery of the site	12
	4 The archaeological excavation	14
	5 Vestiges of the hull	22
	6 Packaging and distribution of the artefacts	28
Chapter II	**Maritime trade in China during the middle Ming period**	43
	Peter Lam, Director of the Art Museum, The Chinese University of Hong Kong	
	1 Foreign trade policy of the Ming dynasty	43
	2 The tributary trade system	46
	3 Private trade and smuggling	50
	4 China and the Philippines	51
Chapter III	**Industrial ceramics in China**	59
	ceramic production at Jingdezhen from the 10th to the 16th century	
	Stacey Pierson, Curator of the Percival David Foundation of Chinese Art	
	1 The industrial complex	59
	2 The ceramics	62
Chapter IV	**Traditions and transitions**	71
	Chinese ceramics at the end of the 15th century	
	Monique Crick, Consultant on Chinese Art and Far Eastern Ceramics	
	1 Blue and white porcelains, *qinghua*	72
	2 Monochrome porcelains	86
	3 *Fahua* porcelains	86
	4 Celadon-glazed stoneware	86
	5 Conclusion	89
Chapter V	**Connoisseurship and commerce**	91
	Rosemary Scott, Senior Academic Consultant, Asian Art Departments, Christie's	

Chapter VI	Typology		97

Porcelains and ceramics
Monique Crick

	1	Ewers, bottles and *kendi*	98
	2	Jars and lids	107
	3	The boxes	116
	4	Rimmed dishes	122
	5	Large saucer-shaped dishes	136
	6	The bowls	168
	7	Monochrome white porcelain, enamelled porcelain and *fahua* stoneware	186
	8	Vietnamese porcelain	192
	9	Chinese stoneware	198
	10	Thai stoneware	210
	11	The martaban jars	222
	12	Terracotta and ceramics of indeterminate origin	230

Other artefacts
Franck Goddio

	13	Iron artefacts	235
	14	Bronze artefacts	237
	14.2	**Cannon** written by *Javier López-Martín*	239
	15	Copper artefacts	242
	16	Tin goods	248
	17	Plant and animal remains	248
	18	Glass beads	249
	19	Stone and shell goods	252

Lacquerware
Rosemary Scott

	20	Lacquerware	256

Conclusion	*Franck Goddio*	259
Appendices		263
Selected bibliography		273
List of plates		281
Photographic credits		287

Fig. 1. Detail of map of Asia (VE94). Reproduced by permission of the Controller of Her Majesty's Stationary Office and the United Kingdom Hydrographic Office.

THE WRECK ON THE LENA SHOAL
Franck Goddio

1. The development of Chinese maritime commerce

There is proof of the existence of a sea route along which goods were traded between the Mediterranean basin and China as early as the Han dynasty (second century BC – third century AD). Second century Roman coins, Hellenistic intaglios, Chinese brass and Indian jewellery have all been found during excavations at Oceo, a port in the south of the Indo-Chinese peninsula which was at its busiest between the sixth and eleventh centuries AD.

During the Eastern Han dynasty (25 BC–220 AD), Chinese silks reached the Roman Empire via the high seas, which hastened the development of ports such as Guangzhou on the south coast of China. Towards the end of the third century AD, China improved its relations with its neighbours along the South China seaboard. From the fifth and sixth centuries, large colonies of foreigners from the countries engaged in trading were established in China. Some merchants came from as far away as the Middle East.

The reunification of the Chinese states under the Sui dynasty (581–618) and the prestige of the Tang Empire (618–907) facilitated sea trading around the South China Sea and the annals of the Tang dynasty mention the fact that Chinese junks frequently sailed to the Moluccas.[1] At the time, trade was also particularly brisk with the Islamic world and the kingdom of Srivijaya. The port of Guangzhou experienced intense activity and became a large and prosperous cosmopolitan city. Luxury products such as incense, ivory, camphor, tin, spices and precious woods were brought in from various trading posts, and ships sailed with cargos of ceramics and silks.

This flourishing trading port was attacked by Arab and Persian pirates in 778. Then, in 878, the army of the rebel Huang Chao again attacked the city, with the resulting massacre of 200,000 Muslims, Christians, Jews and Zoroastrians.[2] These events contributed massively to the port's decline. The destruction of Siraf in 977, which caused a major decline in trade in the Persian Gulf only exacerbated the slowdown in activity of this great port.

Although sea trade between the Persian Gulf and South China had existed since ancient times, it was only under the Song dynasty (960–1279) that it expanded considerably,[3] thanks to the use of large junks that were capable of protracted sea voyages and the development of navigation techniques such as the compass and the axial rudder.[4] Political and economic circumstances favoured this development. Invasions of the land-bound north and north-east of the Empire made trade with central Asia difficult and caused the Chinese population to move southwards to the coast, where trade was more important than in the agricultural regions of the north and centre.

The emergence of a trading class changed society in the urban centres which became less aristocratic in character and more oriented towards trade and crafts. The state favoured this change in the economy by reforming the taxation system, making it more flexible and attempting to standardise the copper coinage, before introducing paper money in the early eleventh century.

The period of commercial expansion, which lasted from the eleventh to the thirteenth centuries, was made possible by the development of a huge network of navigable waterways covering 50,000 km, based on the Yangtze River and its tributaries and the construction of canals.

Maritime trade further increased when the Song imperial family withdrew to the South, abandoning their capital, Kaifeng, after its capture by the Djurtchets. Hangzhou was made the imperial capital in 1127. Henceforward, sea trading became more important than land-based trading. The building of large junks capable of braving the high seas seems to have begun in the later ninth or early tenth century. Shipyards were constructed in the Yangtze estuary, which was large enough to be the perfect interface between river and sea navigation.[5]

The seafarers of the Empire sailed in imposing, four to six-masted vessels, learning from the Arab and Persian navigators, who had been the first to take advantage of the trade winds, buying and selling their wares in the southern regions of the Chinese world. The trade winds (north-east winds blowing south-eastwards in winter and south-west winds blowing north-eastwards in summer) had always governed navigation in these regions.

---

[1] The annals of the Tang Dynasty (618–906), mention these isles under the name of "Mi-li-kü".

[2] J. Dars, *La marine chinoise du Xe siècle au XIVe siècle*, Etudes d'histoire maritime 11, Economica, Paris, 1992, p. 389.

[3] J. Gernet considered this to be one of the most important developments in the history of Asia. See *Le monde chinois*, A. Colin, Paris, 1972, p. 765.

[4] The existence of the compass is documented from the beginning of the 12th c. The Chinese author Zhu La mentioned it in 1119 under the name zhinanzhen: "The needle which shows south".

[5] Gernet, 1972.

The number of Chinese vessels increased during the Song dynasty, thanks to the opening of numerous shipyards at Guangdong, Fujian and Zhejiang, where numerous sea-going junks were built. Trade between the Empire of the Middle and the lands of South-East Asia, known as the "Nanhai trade", thus took on considerable importance.

The routes taken by the junks can be retraced thanks to written Chinese sources of the period. Of course, the Chinese placenames are different to those used currently, and complex research is often required in order to correctly identify the names of the trading posts at which the junks called on their first trading missions. Several large ports vied for the Nanhai trade but Quanzhou in the province of Fujian, was the most important. The development of this city can be followed from the ninth century AD. In 834, an imperial edict ordered that all the foreign merchants who frequented the ports of Guangzhou, Quanzhou and Yangzhou should be treated hospitably and be permitted to trade freely.

The presence of a large Muslim community in Quanzhou is proved by the existence of its Ashab mosque, founded in 1009; at the time, there were five other Islamic places of worship in the city.[6]

Under the Song dynasty, Quanzhou and Guangzhou traded mainly with the countries of South-East Asia, the lands bordering the Indian Ocean, and the Middle East.

Until the late eleventh century, the absence of a customs post at Quanzhou forced merchants to perform the administrative formalities in Guangzhou.

In 1087, a customs post was opened at Quanzhou, manned by a government-appointed inspector. Conditions for visitors to the city were improved, inns were opened and measures taken to facilitate trade. Foreign merchants settled in the city and formed an influential community. Quanzhou eventually became the largest port in China. Communications with the imperial capital, Hangzhou, were good and the port played an essential role in the Nanhai trade as well as in relations with countries bordering the Indian Ocean and the Middle East.

Upon his arrival in China, Marco Polo[7] was astonished at the port of Zaitun (Quanzhou) "to which all the vessels of India come with much costly merchandise and many precious stones of great value and many large, good pearls, and through which passes such a great abundance of merchandise and precious stones that it is a wonderful sight to behold. We have been told that for every ship laden with pepper and bound for Alexandria or elsewhere to be transported to Christendom, more than a hundred enter this port".

In the early fourteenth century, the Arab traveller Ibn Battuta states that Zaitun was the largest port in the world,[8] accommodating countless small junks and hundreds of gigantic ships.

---

[6] Chen Da-sheng and L. Kalus, *Corpus d'inscriptions Arabes et Persanes en China: I, Province du Fujian*, Bibliothèque d'études Islamiques, Vol. VIV, Paris, 1991.

[7] Marco Polo, *Le devisement du monde. Le livre des merveilles. La Découverte*, Éditions François Maspero, Paris, 1980.

[8] C. Defrémery and B.R. Sanguinetti, *Voyages d'Ibn Battuta*, Paris, 1854.

Fig. 2. River boats. Detail of *Riverside Scene at the Qingming Festival in Kaifeng* by Zhang Zeduan, Northern Song dynasty, 12th c. Collection of the Palace Museum, Beijing.

Fig. 3. River boat by a bridge. Detail of *Riverside Scene at the Qingming Festival in Kaifeng* by Zhang Zeduan, Northern Song dynasty, 12th c. Collection of the Palace Museum, Beijing.

2. Navigation to the Philippines in the fifteenth century

Under the Song and Yuan dynasties, long-haul voyages were deliberately encouraged by the government, although restrictions were sometimes imposed such as those relating to the export of certain metals.[9] Borneo[10] was a major crossroads on the maritime trading routes and a favourite destination for junks during the Song dynasty. This fact is confirmed by the Chinese coins and Song ceramics found there, especially at the site of Kota Batu in Brunei.

In fact, China seems to have established regular trading relations with the Philippines archipelago from the late twelfth century. One of the main navigation routes between China and Borneo was via the internal sea of the Philippines archipelago. Chinese merchants could not have avoided bartering with the islands past which they sailed. There is much archaeological evidence of trade between the Empire and the archipelago, starting during the Tang dynasty.

Although Palawan is not mentioned specifically, there is archaeological evidence to show that ships sailed the length of this large island during the Song dynasty.[11]

Hongwu (1368–98), the first Ming emperor, played a crucial role in the huge increase in Chinese sea trade thanks to his energetic action to rid the Chinese coasts of the pirates that plagued them and his impressive policy of reforestation that would eventually result in a major ship-building programme.

After the short-lived reign of his grandson, Jianwen, his brother Yongle (1403–24) came to the throne and introduced a remarkable expansion policy for navigation. He constructed a massive fleet consisting of ships, some of which, namely the treasure ships, were of impressive size. Within the space of a few years, between 1405 and 1421, he ordered six different expeditions to set sail on the China Sea bound for the Indian Ocean. These huge trans-oceanic expeditions, most of them commanded by Admiral Zheng He, were the Far Eastern counterpart of the Portuguese and Spanish voyages of discovery of the fifteenth and sixteenth centuries. They visited in succession, Malacca, Ceylon, Calicut, Hormuz, and Aden. In 1433, a seventh expedition reached the east coast of Africa. These expeditions were an opportunity for trading and the treasure ships brought back lavish gifts from the kings and princes of the visited regions as tributes to the emperor. Malacca was one of the principal ports for the redistribution of products from the Chinese Empire to the Indonesian archipelago and the Islamic world. Numerous Arab ships plied between this great trading port and along the Malabar coast to Calicut, Aden and Hormuz. In the course of his expeditions, Zheng He founded an official and permanent trading-post in the port.

Trade between China and the Philippines experienced further considerable expansion under the Ming dynasty. These countries even exchanged ambassadors, such as the ambassador who was received in 1372 by the Emperor Hongwu. In the late fifteenth century, government-run trade was gradually taken over by the Chinese shipowners. In the reign of the Emperor Chenghua (1465–87) several shipowners supplied and provisioned ships for large trading operations in the ports of South China, which became a hive of activity. Malacca, Korea, then Manchuria, were regular ports of call for the merchants, while Chinese influence in Borneo and the Philippines increased perceptibly. By the turn of the fifteenth century, almost all the sea trade with the Philippines was in the hands of the Chinese. Several original Chinese writings deal with the Nanhai sea trade, explaining the navigation routes, the countries to which Chinese goods were exported and the opportunities for barter in exchange for local goods. Sometimes information is given about the goods that were the most sought after, region by region.

2.1 Manufactured goods for export and goods imported into China

The *Chu-fan-chi*[12] (Description of the Barbarian Peoples) written by Zhao Rugua is a document that is essential reading in order to understand the traditional Nanhai trade. The author was the Inspector of Foreign Trade in the province of Fujiang, under the Southern Song dynasty (in the early thirteenth century). This document describes the lands and peoples with whom the Chinese merchants traded and provides valuable information about the products that were sold or bartered in exchange for goods which were much in demand in China. If goods for export, such as silks and certain types of ceramics, changed with the fashions of the times, or due to regulations imposed on foreign trade, such as the ban on the export of metals, for example, it can also be assumed that the goods brought back from these lands by the Chinese merchants were probably the same as they had been in the fifteenth century, when the Lena Shoal junk sailed.

---

[9] Many edicts prohibiting the export of metals were passed by emperors over the centuries. See on this subject W. Rockhill, "Notes on the Relations and Trade of China with the Eastern Archipelago and the Coast of the Indian Ocean during the Fourteenth Century", *T'oung Pao*, vol. XVI, Leyden, 1913.

[10] The annals of the Song dynasty (960–1279), the *Song shi* and *Song hui yao* mention Borneo under the name of "P'o-ni".

[11] Goddio and Dupoizat, 1993.

[12] Zhao Rugua, *Chu-fan-chï*, translated by F. Hirth and W. Rockhill, Imperial Academy of Sciences, St. Petersburg, 1911.

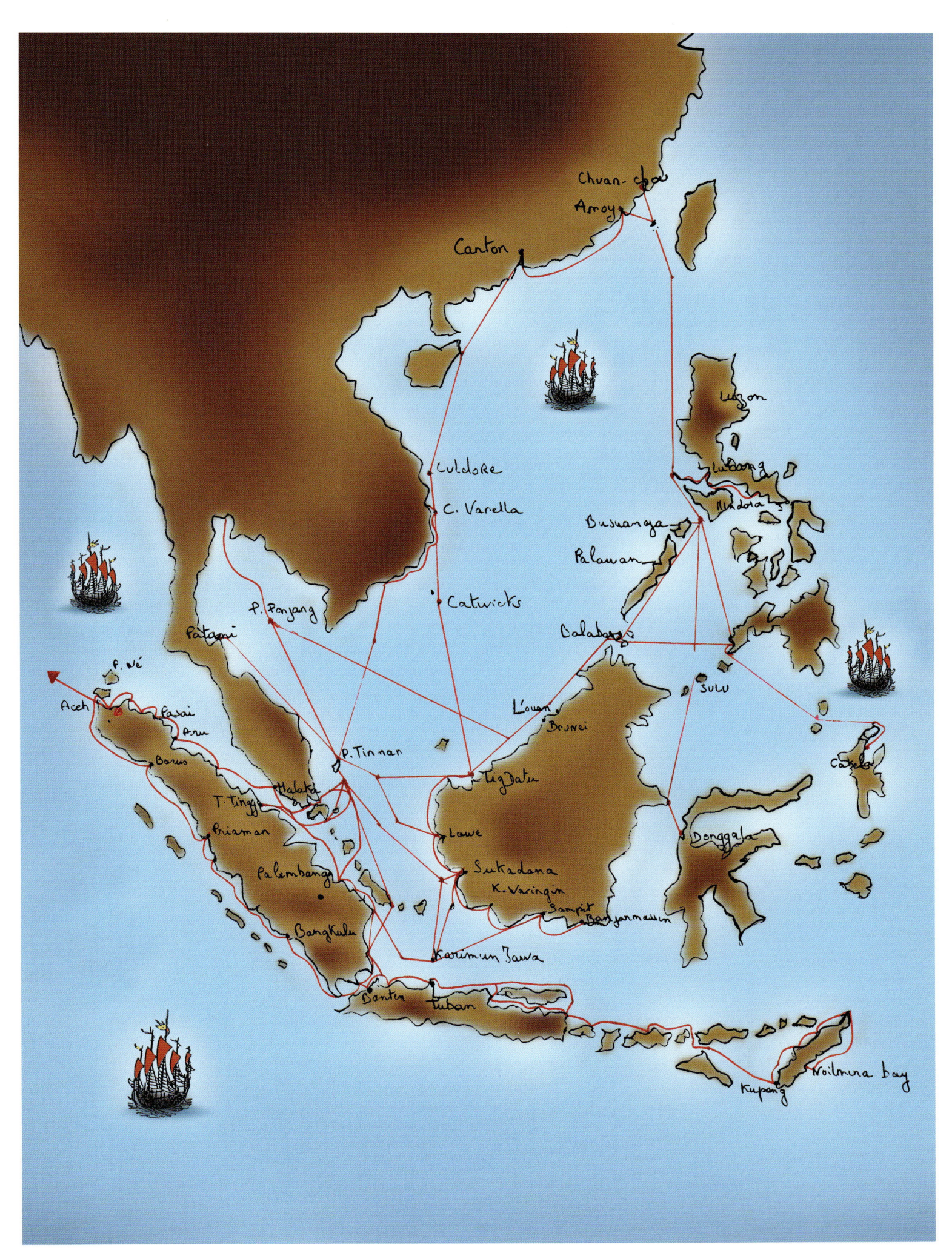

Fig.4. Map of maritime routes employed by junks in the 15th century.

The long list of these products is interesting. It includes spices such as cloves, nutmeg, cardamom and pepper; fragrant incense and medicines such as camphor, frankincense, myrrh, benzoin, ambergris, areca nut, aloes, rhinoceros horn, civet, musk, asa-fœtida, beeswax, hornbill beaks and seahorses; and luxury items such as fine pearls, precious stones, kingfisher feathers, tortoiseshell and ivory; precious woods such as sandalwood, ebony, gharuk, laka and sapan; and exotic foods such as swallows' nests from the caves of Niah, sea cucumbers and jakfruit.

Nutmeg and cloves originated from the Moluccas in Indonesia. In 1605, the Dutch took over the monopoly of nutmeg and cloves by chasing away the Portuguese who had already settled in the Moluccas. In order to maintain this monopoly and to avoid allowing cultivation to expand to other islands, they limited their production to two islands belonging to the Moluccas, Ternate and Tidore. There they installed an authoritative customs policy. Because the two islands were easy to supervise, they were able to achieve their aim of eliminating all of the other plants from the remaining islands of the archipelago, and held their monopoly status for a century and a half.

Cloves were also used by the Chinese as they were well known for their medicinal properties long before the Christian era, around the third century BC. Around 200 BC, cloves were imported to China from Java for the court of the Han dynasty (206 BC–220 AD), so that courtisans could purify their breath before standing in front of the Emperor.

The Portuguese discovered the Moluccas in 1511 and soon snatched them from the natives. They then started to limit the repartition of clove plants. In 1605, the Dutch took control of the Moluccas until the eighteenth century, and control on production was made even tighter in order to maintain prices artificially.

2.2 Maritime routes

One of the most important sources of descriptions of the maritime routes used in the fifteenth century by Chinese sailors is the *Shun Fêng Hsiang Sung*.[13] This anonymous compilation was written c. 1430,[14] but in its present form it contains material added in 1571. Apart from the fact that it provides interesting information about the theory of navigation, the document lists 100 different maritime routes and offers relevant information about certain localities. It lists which maritime routes to follow, including those from South China to the Indonesian archipelago, the Malabar Coast, Yemen, the Red Sea, the Sunda Islands and the Sulu Sea. This guide also offers a compilation of various nautical instructions including the observed heights of the stars[15] (which should match the zeniths of the stars mentioned) and estimated nautical distances in *keng* (a measurement of time of about 2.4 hours; if matched with the speed of a junk, this would produce a distance of 10 nautical miles per *keng*, an average speed of about four knots).

The *Shun Fêng Hsiang Sung* shows that if navigators left from the southern ports of the Middle Empire, they had a basic choice between two main routes, the western route along the Chinese coast to the Malay peninsula and into the Indian Ocean, or the eastern route, crossing the South China Sea to the islands of Luzon and Mindoro, with an extension along the east coast of Palawan, ending either at Balambagan, Borneo and Java or the archipelagos of the Celebes or the Moluccas. Of course, there were many variations on these routes.

One important fact should be noted: there is no mention anywhere of a route along the west coast of Palawan (where the junk in question was found). It does not feature among the main routes nor any of the secondary variations. The "Palawan Passage", as it is now called on marine charts, seems not to have been mentioned at all until the late sixteenth century. Pedro Fidalgo's voyage on a junk, illustrated in a map by Fernão Vaz Dourado dating from 1571,[16] alludes to this passage, though there is a lack of topographical precision. In fact, the passage was still little known to Europeans even as late as the end of the eighteenth century.[17]

The presence of submerged rocks just below the surface and the rarity of suitable sheltered anchorages in which a ship could take refuge during the storms that

---

[13] *Shun Fêng Hsiang Sung*, Laud MS, Or. 145, Bodleian Library, Oxford.

[14] J. Needham, *Science and civilisation in China*, Cambridge University Press, Cambridge, 1971.

[15] It is interesting to note that many of the texts that deal with maritime navigation mention that sailors steered by the stars and spoke of the star zeniths they observed. Yet the observed height of a star cannot provide a direction to follow, even less indicate a position. Only when the stars are at their zenith can they give a mariner information about his latitude in that he can relate it to the celestial pole, since the declination of each star is more or less constant over time.

[16] A. Kacmerer, "La découverte de la Chine par les portugais", *T'oung Pao*, 1944.
Map by Fernão Vaz Dourado in the Arquivo Nacional da Torre do Tombo, Casa Forte No. 70. This map contains a long caption in the area of the China Sea, referring to a barrier of islands of which the southernmost are in the position of the islands of Balabac and Palawan. The caption reads, "The coast of Luzon and adjacent islands; it is through here that Pedro Fidalgo passed from Borneo on a Chinese junk; the storm forced him to sail the length of the island, from whence he made for Lamao".

[17] In 1999, the IEASM conducted an excavation on the *Royal Captain*, a British East India Company ship which foundered in 1773 on a then uncharted reef beside the notorious Palawan Passage. Cf. F. Goddio and E.J. Guyot de Saint Michel, *Griffin, on the route of an Indiaman*, Periplus Publishing London Ltd, London, 1999, §6; and F. Goddio, *Dossier Histoire et Archéologie: No. 113*, Archéologia, Quetigny/Turin, February, 1987.

上有石壁似船帆樣單庚十更取單戌嘮梅山一小平生是崑
崙對開有淺打水三托單申二十更取西蛇龍山辛酉二十五
更取林嘮咭山在馬戶邊辛酉十五更取苧盤是也

瞞咖喇往舊港

開船用辰巽五更取射箭山打水二十托辰巽三更取崑宋巽
西邊有淺打水四五托巽巳單巳五更取吉里問山夜不可行
丙巳單巳四更取鬼巽東南過西南恐犯牛屎礁水漲不見對
過是卅巴港口有仁義礁單巽四更取卅巴門過單丙巳丙巳
十更取鱷魚巽單巳四更取佛寺巽西邊過單巳四更取單巽

raged during the monsoon rendered this route dangerous. It would be a mistake, however, to draw the conclusion that this route to the west of Palawan was unknown in the fifteenth century. In 1988, we mentioned the probability of a route to the west of this large island, following the discovery of a late sixteenth-century Chinese junk. An archaeological excavation was conducted on this junk by the European Institute for Underwater Archaeology (IEASM)[18] which revealed that the ship had foundered with its cargo of Chinese export goods, and thus must have been on its way from China. Of course, a single example such as this would not be enough to confirm the existence of a known commercial route. We concluded in the excavation report:[19] "If similar wrecks are discovered in future in the vicinity of this passage, the theory that the traditional Nanhai trade also used a route west of Palawan would have additional support".

Since then, the IEASM has discovered four ships that were on their way from China with their cargos, but were wrecked near the reefs which mark this passage. It has conducted archaeological excavations on them[20] and found that the wrecks date respectively from the eleventh, twelfth, thirteenth, fifteenth and sixteenth centuries.

There is thus a strong probability that the route was known and in use – even in frequent use – from the eleventh century. The fact that the itinerary is not clearly indicated in any Chinese route guide so far discovered remains a mystery.

---

[18] F. Goddio, *Discovery and archaeological excavation of a 16th century trading vessel in the Philippines*, Manila, 1988.
[19] Ibid.

[20] F. Goddio, *Weisses Gold*, Steidl Verlag, Göttingen, 1997. Goddio et M-F. Dupoizat, "Investigator shoal wreck, Southern Song-Yuan dynasty", *Archaeological Report*, Paris, 1993.

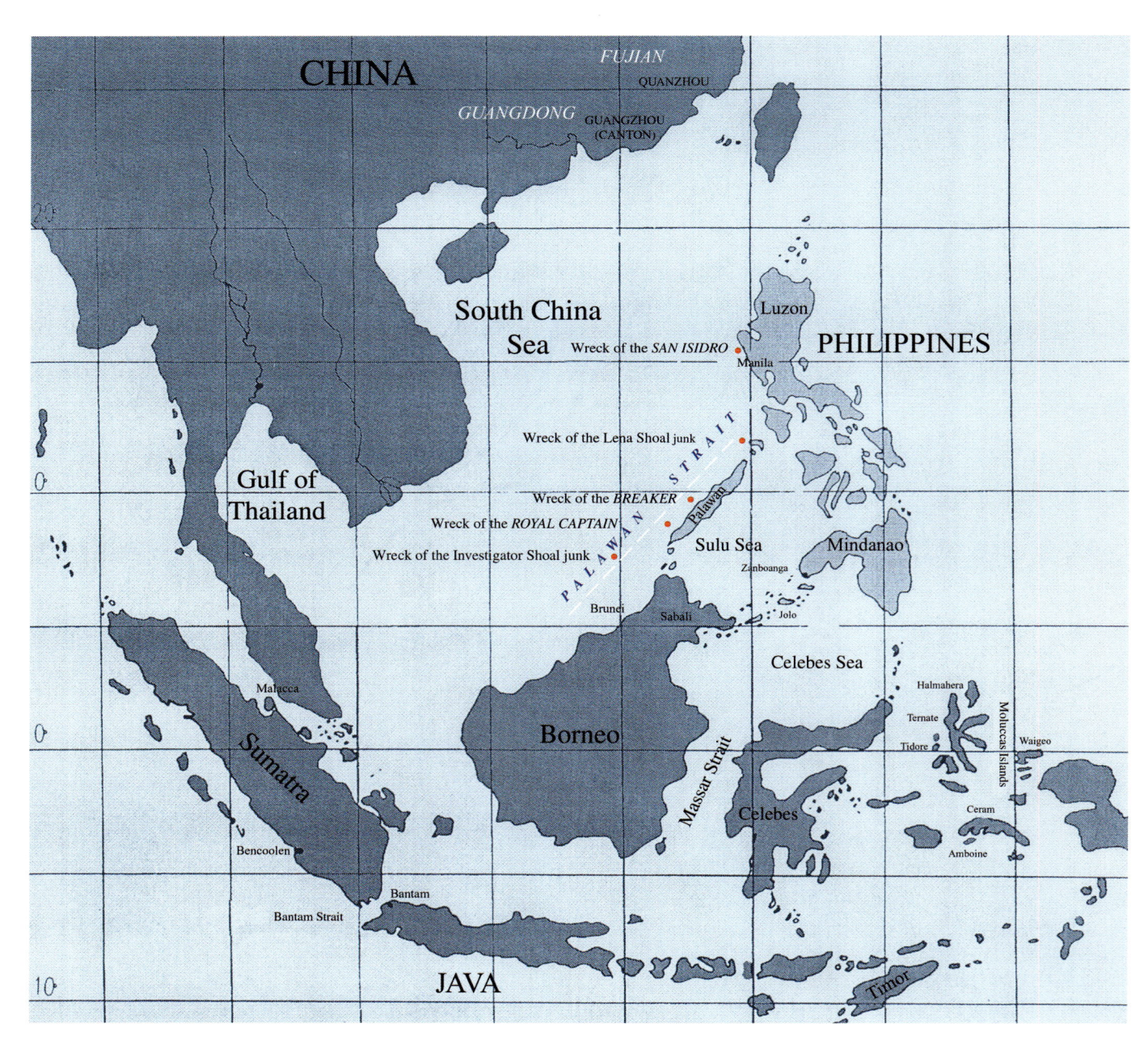

Fig. 6. Map showing the positions of wrecks discovered by l'IEASM in the vicinity of the island of Palawan.

Fig. 7. Map AC 4058, reproduced by permission of the Controller of Her Majesty's Stationary Office and the Hydrographic Offices of France and the UK.

Fig. 8. Map Casa No. 70 from the Atlas de Fermão Vaz Dourado, 1571.
Reproduced by permission of the Instituto dos Arquivos Nacionais/Torre do Tombo, Lisbon.

11

3. Discovery of the site

On 1 March, 1996, the *Kaimiloa*, a research vessel, was sailing along the west coast of Palawan, en route to an archaeological site at which it was to perform a magnetic survey. The position of the deposit had been indicated to the National Museum of the Philippines by fishermen who had found shards of ceramics in their nets. The research team consisted of the crew plus a member of the National Museum and four members of the IEASM.

The *Kaimiloa* had just reached the Bay of Quezon on the east coast of Palawan when she received a radio message from the museum. She was to leave as soon as possible for a point at sea off the island of Busuanga, north-west of Palawan. The latitude and longitude of the site were specified but we knew no more than that, as the message then became garbled. The *Kaimiloa* changed course and six hours later, by early afternoon, she was at the site.

When we arrived, we found that great confusion reigned. Twelve pirogues had gathered at this remote spot on the high seas. A coastguard cutter was also present and seemed to have them under guard. As we approached, our team saw that the pirogues were equipped with snorkelling equipment.

The coastguard informed us of the situation. An archaeological site had been discovered by a fisherman a few weeks previously. The coastguard had been alerted to the pillaging and had intervened during the previous week, confiscating the objects raised to the surface by the illicit treasure-seekers. They had informed the museum and had handed over the confiscated material.

Although they had been warned off, the pillagers returned on a daily basis. Coastguard headquarters had thus decided on a pre-emptive strike and the museum requested us to become involved.

We decided to perform a reconnaissance dive. The sight that met our eyes on the bottom was a disaster. The sand was covered with a layer of shards of stoneware jars, blue and white porcelain and celadon ware, to a thickness of nearly 20 cm. The area covered by these freshly broken fragments was 20 m long and 15 m wide. Craters gave it the appearance of a lunar landscape. Crowbars, wooden flippers, ropes, snorkelling tubes and even a pair of wooden diving goggles had been abandoned or lost at the site. The ground was also littered with elephant tusks.

A report was made to the coastguard and to the museum, and when the coastguard mentioned that the divers claimed to have seen huge bones, the museum's representative explained to them that these were ivory tusks. Upon examination, the ceramics discovered proved to be of excellent quality and dated from the years 1480–90.

Photo 1. The IEASM research vessel, *Kaimiloa*, used for magnetic surveying.

The damage done to the site appeared at first sight to be irreparable but by the following morning, a measure of calm had at least been restored. The pirogues had made themselves scarce under threat of serious punishment by the coastguard officer. An expert survey of the site was completed in less than a week. The damage done was considerable, although the robbers appeared to have failed to penetrate right through the tumulus. In addition to the obvious damage, they had managed to destroy a lot of material that lay under the sand by probing with crowbars in various places. An archaeological excavation was recommended on what remained of the wreck and the *Kaimiloa* was to return to Manila as an expedition had to be organised.

The deposit lay at a depth of 48 m and the excavation required major logistical support. Time was short; we were convinced that the pillaging would start again shortly after our departure, as the coastguard cutter was unable to visit the site on a daily basis.

Organising such a major mission in just a few days is no easy task. No ship of suitable size was available in Manila, so we chartered a 50 m barge, the *Thania*, and a little support tugboat only 28 m long, the *African Queen*. The barge was fitted out with mobile living accommodation for the site, two compartments for bedrooms and one for the bathrooms. It was also provided with a decompression chamber, powerful 125 KVa electric generators and several tonnes of equipment.

We got a crew together in Manila in the space of a few days. The ship was provisioned with fuel, water and food. Only one week after the *Kaimiloa*'s return, our little flotilla was ready for departure.

The *Thania* left the port of Manila, towed by a high seas tugboat and followed by the *African Queen*; *Kaimiloa* acted as scout and a large motorised pirogue, the *Lucky Mariner*, which was to serve as a liaison ship between the islands of Busuanga and the site, brought up the rear.

Travelling on the various vessels of the expedition were 12 members of the IEASM, six representatives of the National Museum of the Philippines and 19 crew members.

Upon arrival at the wreck site, a reconnaissance dive was arranged. The site had suffered new depredations and all the elephant tusks we had seen the previous week had disappeared. We realised that the information indicating that these were not the bones of mythical beasts who haunted the site, but were in fact ivory, had spread rapidly, and the pillagers, who had previously been afraid to touch them, had unfortunately drawn the correct conclusions from their new-found knowledge.

In four days, we anchored the barge firmly over the site and got all our equipment up and running. We also set up large canvas awnings to protect us from the burning sun.

Photo 2. The barge *Thania* anchored by six anchors over the site.

4. The archaeological excavation

The first task that awaited us, after constructing the underwater grid, was the most unpleasant one. We had to collect, shard by shard, the remains of the extensive carnage inflicted by the robbers.

The baseline of the grid was at a 90° angle to the numbers in ascending order. The mesh of the grid was one metre, so the shards collected over each square metre were placed in a plastic box and raised to the surface. There they were sorted by the material of which they were made – porcelain, stoneware, terracotta, etc. The shards were packed in nylon nets labelled with the reference number of the square in which they had been found. The labelled nets were then placed in tanks of fresh water in order to enable the ceramics to release the salts they had absorbed during their long stay in the sea. This task alone took the team one week to complete.

The proper excavation could now begin. Across the front of the grid, at right angles to the main baseline, our equipment removed the thick layer of sand that had fortunately hindered the local divers. The sediment was dislodged with the help of vacuum cleaners using suction over a section 20 cm in diameter to remove the top layers of sand and 10 cm in diameter when the archaeological level was reached. The ends of the hoses were fitted with sieves to catch any items that might have escaped the notice of the divers.

The archaeologists working on the bottom used nylon nets of various meshes, each with a polyester label attached to the handle with a plastic tie. The labels were pre-printed in indelible ink with the excavation identification code of the National Museum and a square representing the equivalent grid square.

Each item discovered was placed individually in a

Photo 3. The tumulus of the junk lay at a depth of 48 m.

Photo 4. Condition of the site during archaeological excavations.

LOST AT SEA

Photo 5. A label is completed by the diver at the time of discovery and is attached to a recovery net. Another label is attached to the object at the time it is recorded.

The nets were collected in plastic crates that were weighted down with lead and raised to the surface. Once on board, the object was rinsed in seawater and replaced in its net. The label was then marked with the date of the discovery and the object was placed in the first desalination tank.

This tank was filled with a mixture of 50 per cent fresh water and 50 per cent seawater, in order to prevent deterioration that might be caused by too sudden an osmosis. Once the object had spent five days in this bath, it was submerged, still inside its net, in a fresh tank of unsalted water. Measurement of the salinity of the bath indicated when the object was ready to be removed and dried without it suffering any harm. A more complete desalination would be performed, using distilled water, once on dry land. The organic matter would therefore be preserved in a wet environment.

The object was then described, measured and inventoried, and a second label bearing the inventory

nylon net and the diver wrote the following information on the label:

- reference number of the square in the grid, identified by two letters and two figures,
- position of the object within the square, shown by a cross in the pre-printed square and represented by coordinates (x,y),
- depth in cm of the object beneath the sediment or elevation of the object within the hull, where the hull was present,
- identification code of the researcher who discovered the object.

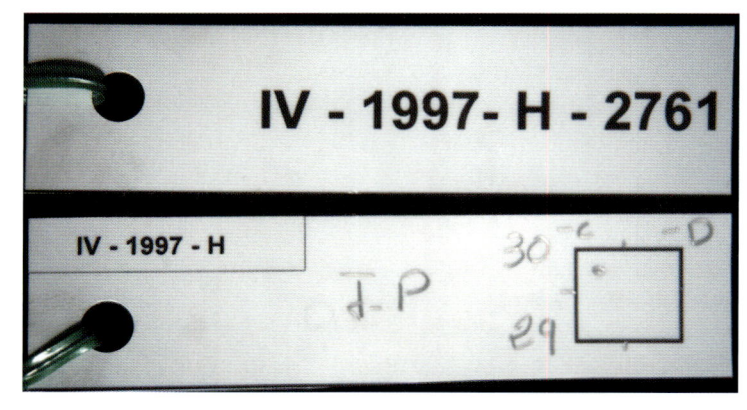

Photo 6. Close-up of labels. The lower is attached by the diver on finding an object; the upper when the find is recorded.

aPhoto 7. Recording search information on the database.

16

Photo 8. The porcelains are placed in plastic crates for recovery to the surface.

number of the Museum was attached to the net. This label was also pre-printed by computer on polyester paper in indelible ink. This prevented numbers being missed out or misread. Information about the object was then entered into the database. In view of the large number of operations that needed to be performed between the discovery of the artefact and the final stage of its restoration, the rigorous application of this procedure ensured that there was a minimum loss of the information collected on the bottom and at the surface. The final marking was performed in India ink on a thin sliver of white lacquer.

Life on board was governed by a strict routine. The divers went down to the site in pairs, wearing double tanks of compressed air. Work on the bottom was very carefully timed: 45 minutes were allowed in the morning and 40 minutes in the afternoon. In view of the various decompression stages, the return to the surface lasted for more than one hour. It would have taken even longer if we had not been breathing pure oxygen at a 6 m depth.

A succession of nets was raised to the surface and a team was constantly working on the bottom for at least ten hours a day. The site was so exciting that each diver awaited his turn impatiently, despite the 48 m depth which made the dives tiring. As soon as each diver resurfaced, he would make a detailed report of the excavation. This information was recorded in a log that included the position of the artefacts discovered, marked on a map with a millimetre grid. This map of the excavation gradually began to show the state of the site once the sediment had been removed. It was a valuable aid that pointed to the direction in which the excavation should proceed and it proved to be an indispensable tool for assisting the divers in making their reports. The archaeological material was hoisted to the surface in a large basket capable of holding up to four plastic crates.

The site soon proved to be very rich in material. Huge quantities of all types of ceramics were unearthed, including porcelain of various qualities, stoneware, earthenware and terracotta. Bracelets and bronze gongs, elephant tusks, lead ingots, iron ingots and pans and several unusual objects were found among the ceramics. The junk's cargo provides a surprising retrospective view of the ceramics produced in China, Annam and Siam in the late fifteenth century. It also provides interesting information about life and trade of the period.

When the excavation season came to an end, all of the vestiges of the hull and the lumps of iron that had become welded together were again covered by sand by reversing the suction action of the vacuum cleaners. The wreck was thus covered by a uniform, 150 cm layer of sand so as to protect it from the action of the elements and from human curiosity.

Photo 9. Rolls of porcelain bowls.

Photo 10. Piles of plates being discovered.

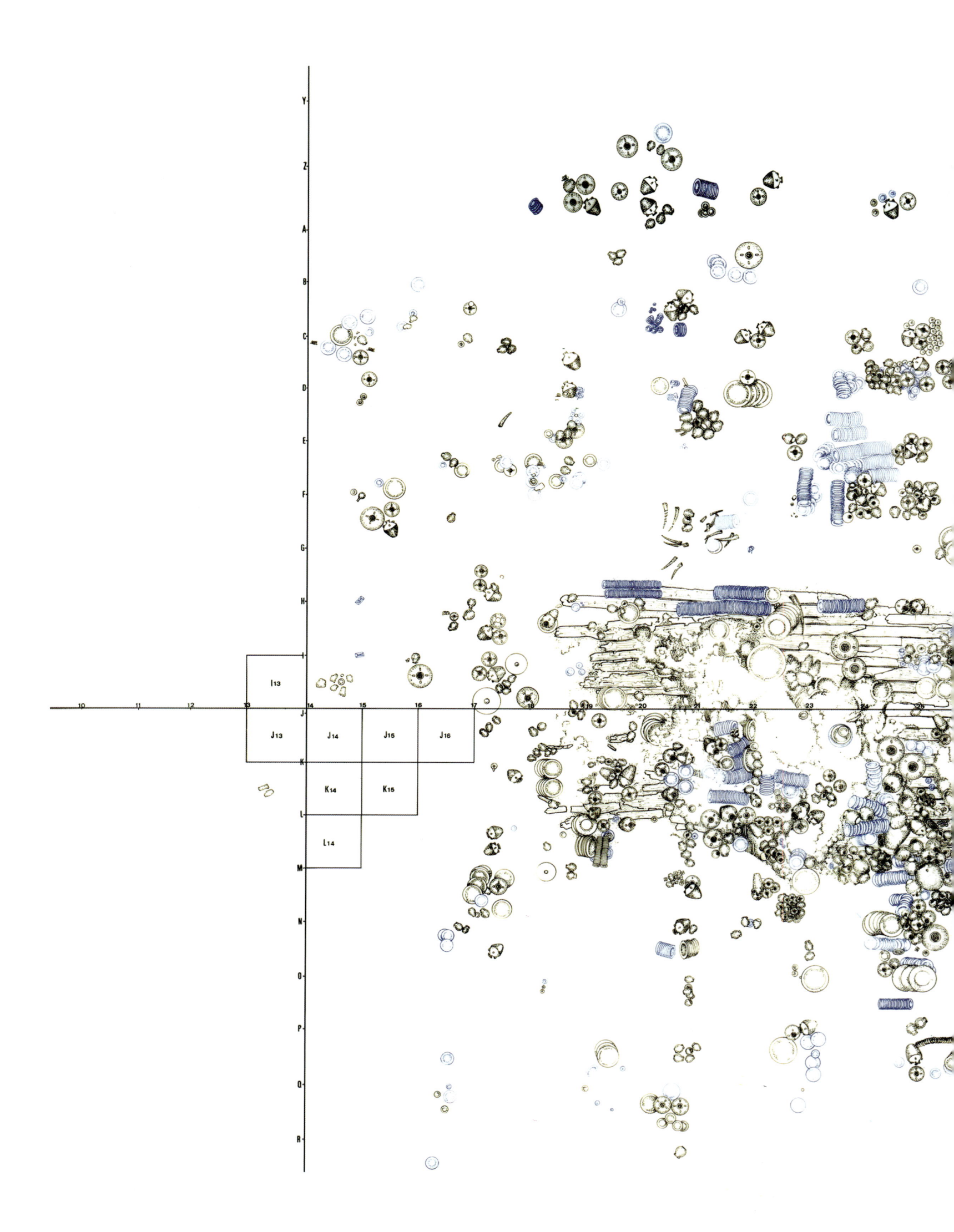

Fig. 9. Diagram of the grid laid over the Lena Shoal wreck site showing the location of the various artefacts.

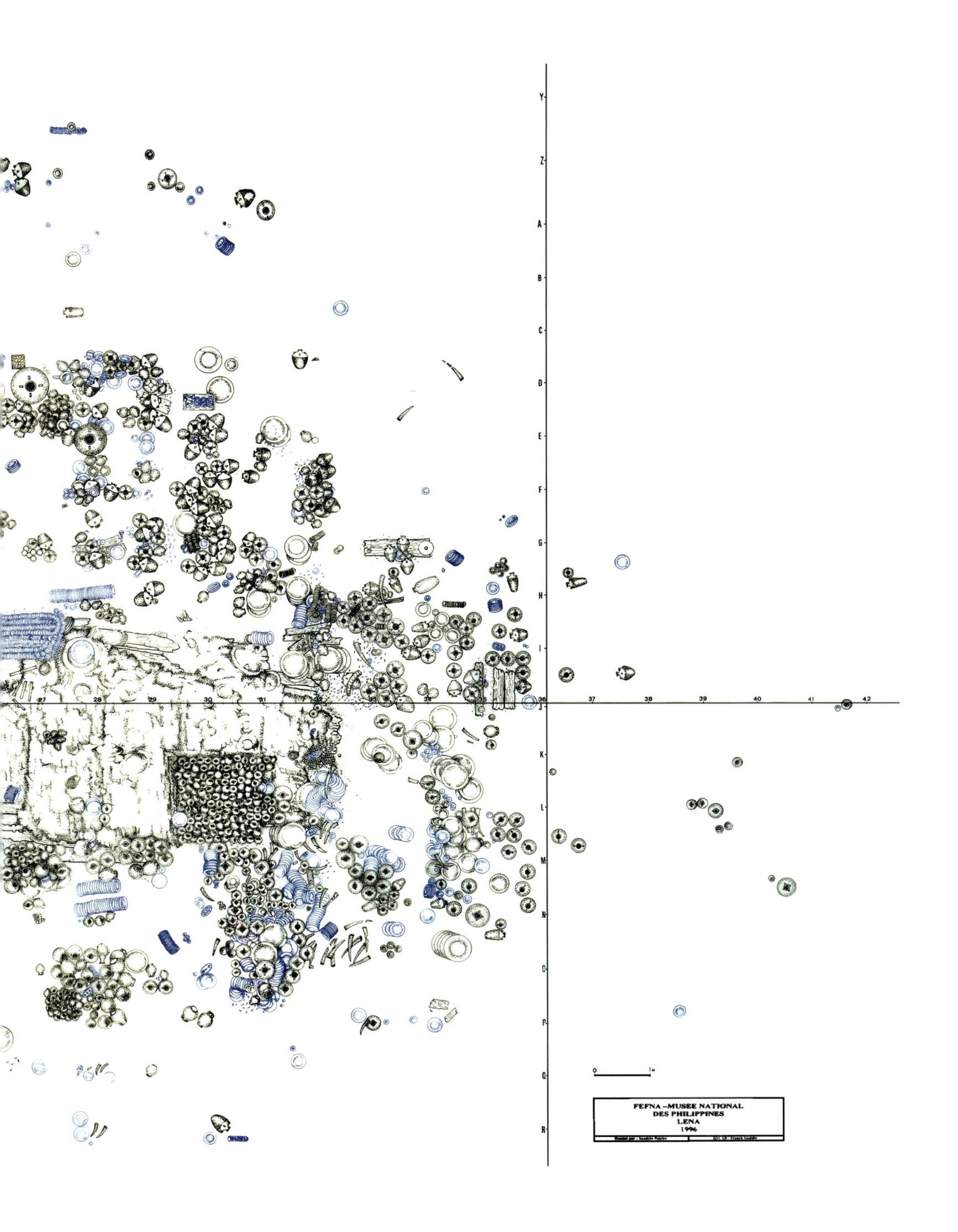

FEFNA – MUSEE NATIONAL
DES PHILIPPINES
LENA
1996

5. Vestiges of the hull

The excavation revealed a part of the bottom of the ship's hull. It had been preserved thanks to an accumulation of iron ingots and the protection provided by a layer of sand of an average thickness of one metre. Vestiges of wood were partially visible over a length of 18.3 m and a maximum width of 5 m.

The hull lay on an east-west axis and was almost flat on the sea-bed. The eastern tip lay at a depth of 48.4 metres, the western tip at 48.3 m and the middle of the wreck was at 48.3 m. The highest parts, where the metal accretions were found, were at references 23 and 29 on the baseline, and lay at a depth of 47.1 m. The remains thus appeared to be aligned on the K line.

A study of the bottom of the hull was unfortunately hampered by the presence of this large amount of metal accretions. The iron ingots loaded had become welded to each other and constituted huge accretions which in turn had become attached to the wood. They were extremely hard and could not be cut away and removed, so they concealed a large proportion of the bottom of the hull, especially the central part. Metal bars from this ballast that had fallen away towards references 18.3 and 32.2 blocked access to the keel, so only the planking was accessible for examination purposes.

At reference 23, we found partially preserved planking streaks over a maximum 5 m width. At reference points 19-K and 20-K we discovered double planking on the hull. These lining planks were lap-jointed.

This type of double-lined construction was mentioned by Marco Polo: "the hull consists of a double row of two superimposed planks throughout the length of the ship, and these were meticulously caulked with tow on both sides and attached to each other by strong iron nails".[21]

So little of this double lining was accessible to us that we were unable to determine the way in which the inner lining was attached to the outer lining.

The accretions only enabled us to observe a single lining element along its total length. Planking streak No. 4 between reference points 19.5 and 24 was 4.5 m long and

---

[21] Marco Polo, op. cit.

Photo 11. Remains of the bottom of the hull. It is possible to discern the double-lined construction.

20 cm wide with a thickness of 4.2 cm. The poor state of preservation of the planking at the points below 21 and the fact that it was absent at points above 32 made it impossible to check whether the planking varied in width from the centre to the extremities of the ship.

Fig. 10. Section of planking on the Lena Shoal wreck.

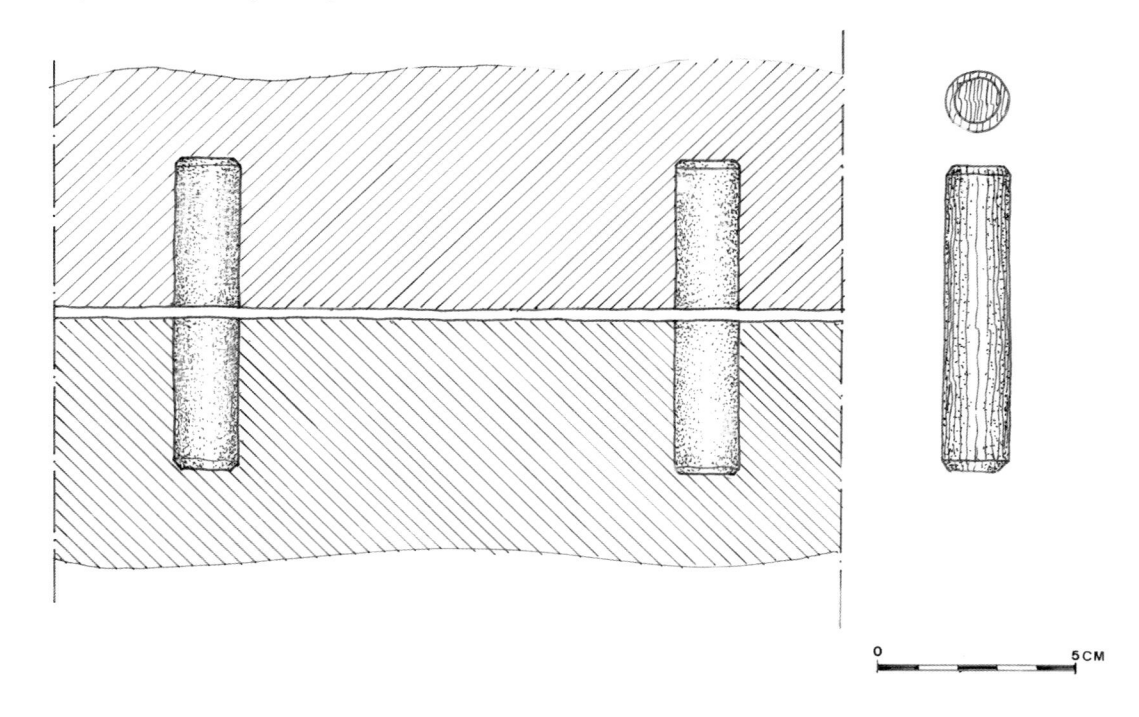

Photo 12. The best preserved section of the hull's bottom.

A plank was attached at its edge to the adjoining planks with pegs 8 cm long and 1.6 cm in diameter. Spacing between the pegs varied from 11 to 12 centimetres. The pegs were arranged symmetrically on each side of the planking.

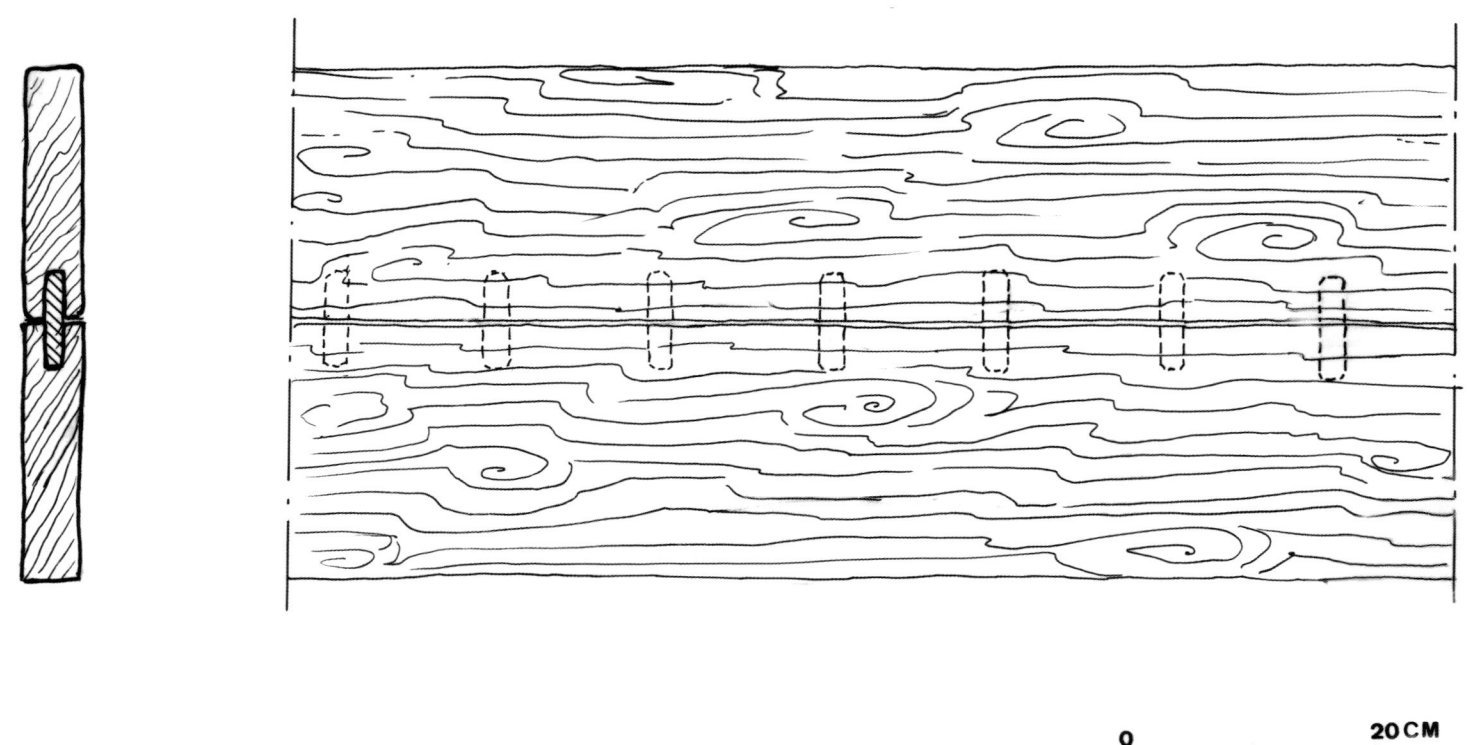

Fig. 11. Fastening between two rows of planking.

Photo 13. A split between the planking reveals the lateral fastenings.

The parts of a planking streak were joined by Jupiter joints 40 centimetres long. The wood used for the planking was a variety of *Shorea sp.*, a wood of average density belonging to Dipterocarpaceae. The pegs were from a tree of the palaquium species. The tree belongs to *Sapotaceae sp.*

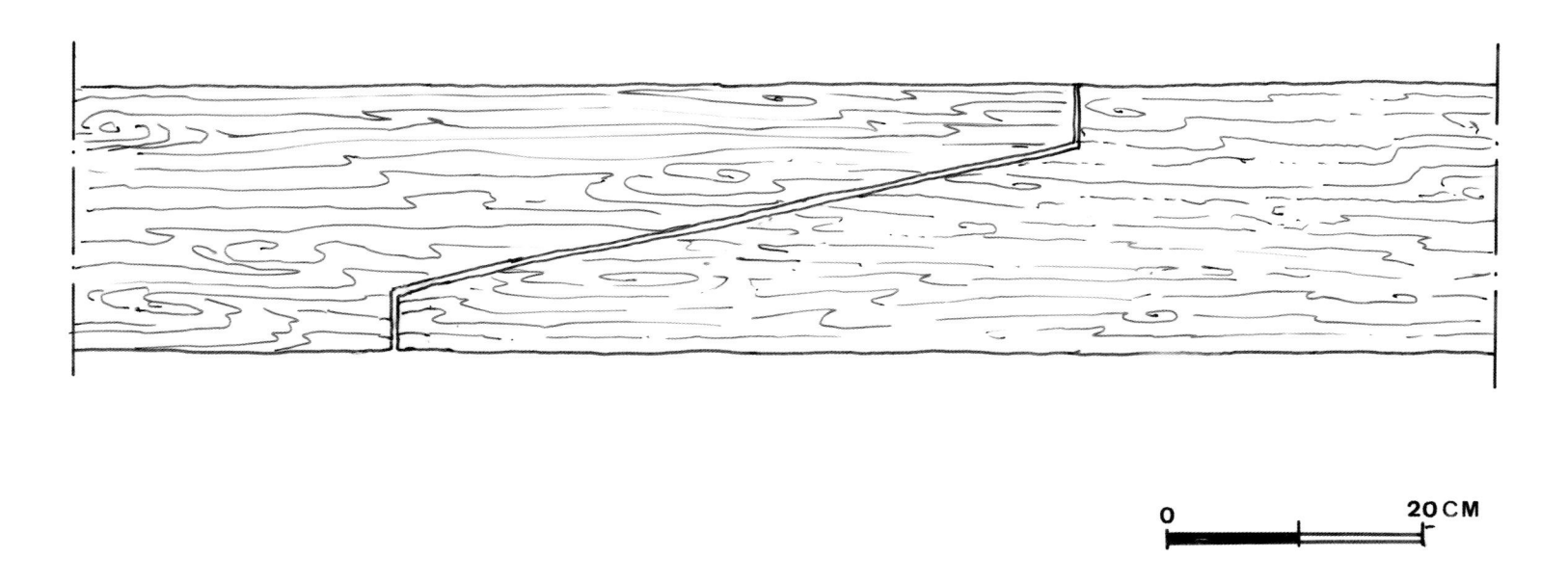

Fig. 12. Diagram of a Jupiter joint.

Photo 14. Sections of a planking streak meeting in a Jupiter joint.

The absence of remains of a ribbed frame is consistent with what is known of the structure of this type of vessel, thanks to writings[22] and to other archaeological finds. The hold was divided into bulkheads by vertical load-bearing partitions, serving as frames, which constituted the transverse frame of the ship.[23] As the partitions of this ship had not been preserved, we can only presume that they were made of a wood that was less resistant to marine woodworm and immersion than the wood of the planking. However, at reference points 29K, 29L, 30K and 30L there was a cargo of almost 300 small, green-glazed, globular jars that had been fired in the kilns of Sawankhalok. They filled a rectangular space free of any iron accretion. The space appeared to be the vestige of a half-bulkhead in the hold, because it was clearly separated and was aligned with the axis of the part of the bottom of the hull that had been preserved. The bulkhead measured about 150 cm across.

The planimetry photographs and the map showed traces of this partitioning in crossways strips in several locations. It was indicated by variations in the levels of the surface of the ferrous accretions and the alignment of some of the artefacts. The sectioning was particularly visible between the following map references:

a. 32.2 and 31;
b. 31 and 29.5: the half-bulkhead in the hold containing the round jars;
c. 29.5 and 28;
d. 28 and 26.8;
e. 26.8 and 25.3. The mark of a load-bearing bulkhead can be seen at reference 25.3 at planking streaks 8, 9 and 10.

Vestiges of the bottom of the hull were visible from map reference 18.3 to reference 32, a length of 13.7 m. If the bulkheads in the hull of the wreck are assumed to be 140 cm wide, this would indicate that about 10 bulkheads have been preserved.

In estimating the total overall external length of the ship, it is tempting to apply the proportions and characteristics of the junk found at Quanzhou, which is far better preserved and whose hull was reconstructed.[24] The hull had 13 bulkheads, including the forward bulkhead, and the overall external length was 34 m. Its front projection, including the thirteenth bulkhead, was of a length equivalent to five of its bulkheads amidships.

If these proportions and characteristics were applied to the Lena wreck, it would result in a total overall length of about 24 m. The junk shipwrecked on the Lena Shoal must thus have been a relatively small ship with a tonnage of about 100 tons.

---

[22] In his book, *The Description of the World. The Book of Marvels*, Marco Polo states, "Certain vessels, and these are the largest of them, also have thirteen bulkheads, that is to say internal compartments, made of strong planks that are well joined. Thus, should misadventures befall the vessel, and it is pierced in several places... the skipper will find the place in which the ship had been damaged and the goods contained in the bulkhead which is flooded will be removed and placed in others; for water cannot pass from one to another, they are so firmly closed".

[23] The hull of the vessel excavated in 1974 near the port of Quanzhou was divided into thirteen bulkheads of varying capacity, divided into sections by twelve cross-partitions. *Wenwu*, No. 10, Beijing, October, 1975.

[24] idem.

Photo 15. A section of the Lena Shoal junk's hull.

6. Packaging and distribution of the artefacts

The distribution of the artefacts was surprising in that they appeared to have been widely scattered all around the preserved bottom part of the hull. However, it should be noted that it was not possible to count or remove ceramics and other artefacts from inside the hull due to the thick metal accretion that covered a large part of it. The distribution diagrams are thus distorted in these particular areas. On the other hand, they reflect the true situation as regards the areas free of such accretions.

Density of porcelains

The diagram of the density of the Chinese porcelain of all shapes and sizes clearly illustrates the importance of these goods in the cargo of the junk. The porcelain was distributed throughout various parts of the ship. The collapse of the hull and the action of the currents dispersed the porcelain over an even larger area at the bottom of the hull.

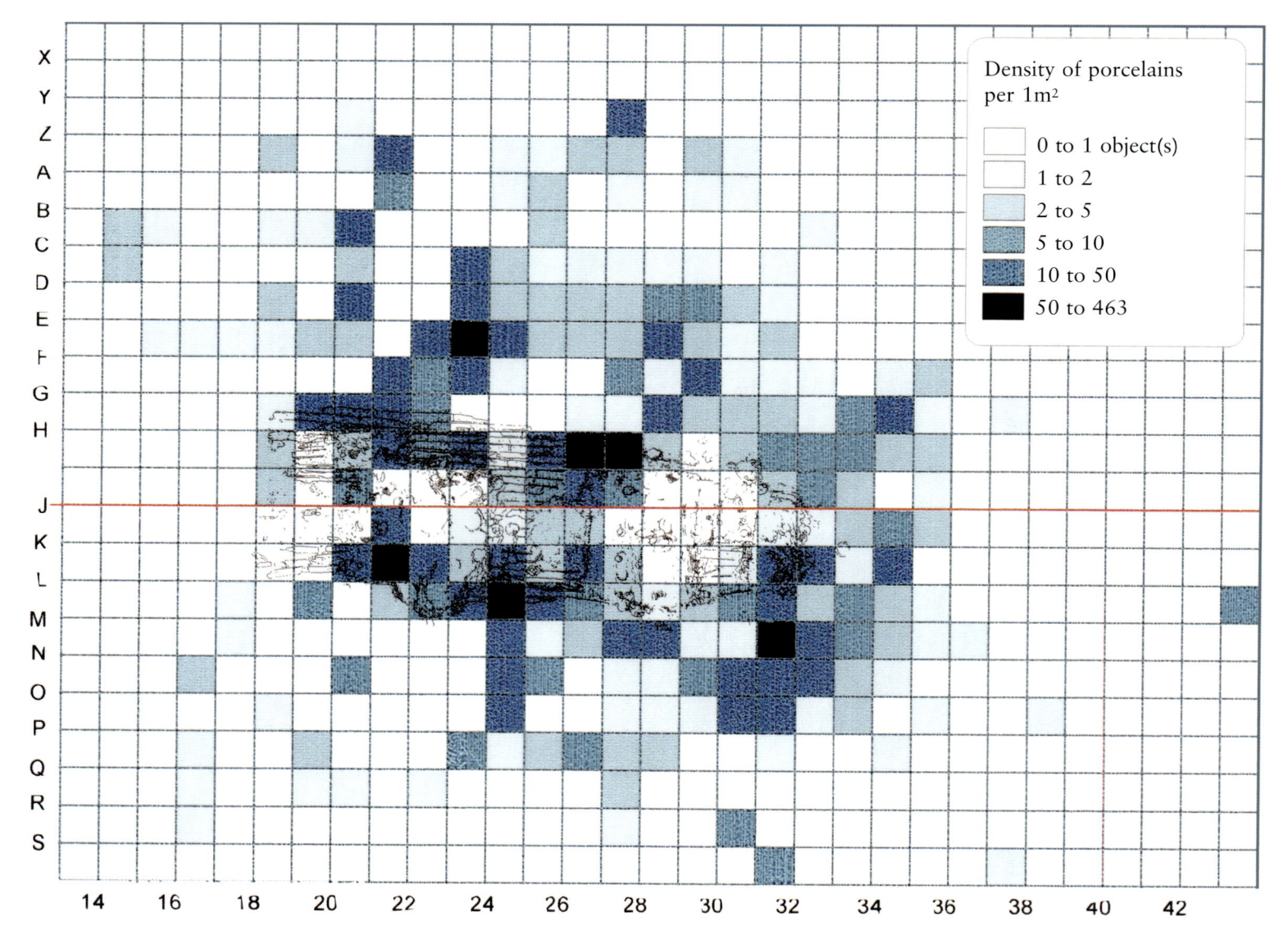

The wreck on the Lena Shoal

Photo 16. Piles of porcelain bowls at 25-H

Density of porcelain bowls

Certain shapes, however, were found in their original position. These were mainly bowls, which were concentrated in 25-H, 25-I, 26-H, 26-I and 27-H. They had been packed in tubular fashion, stacked one upon the other in similar shapes, regardless of surface design.

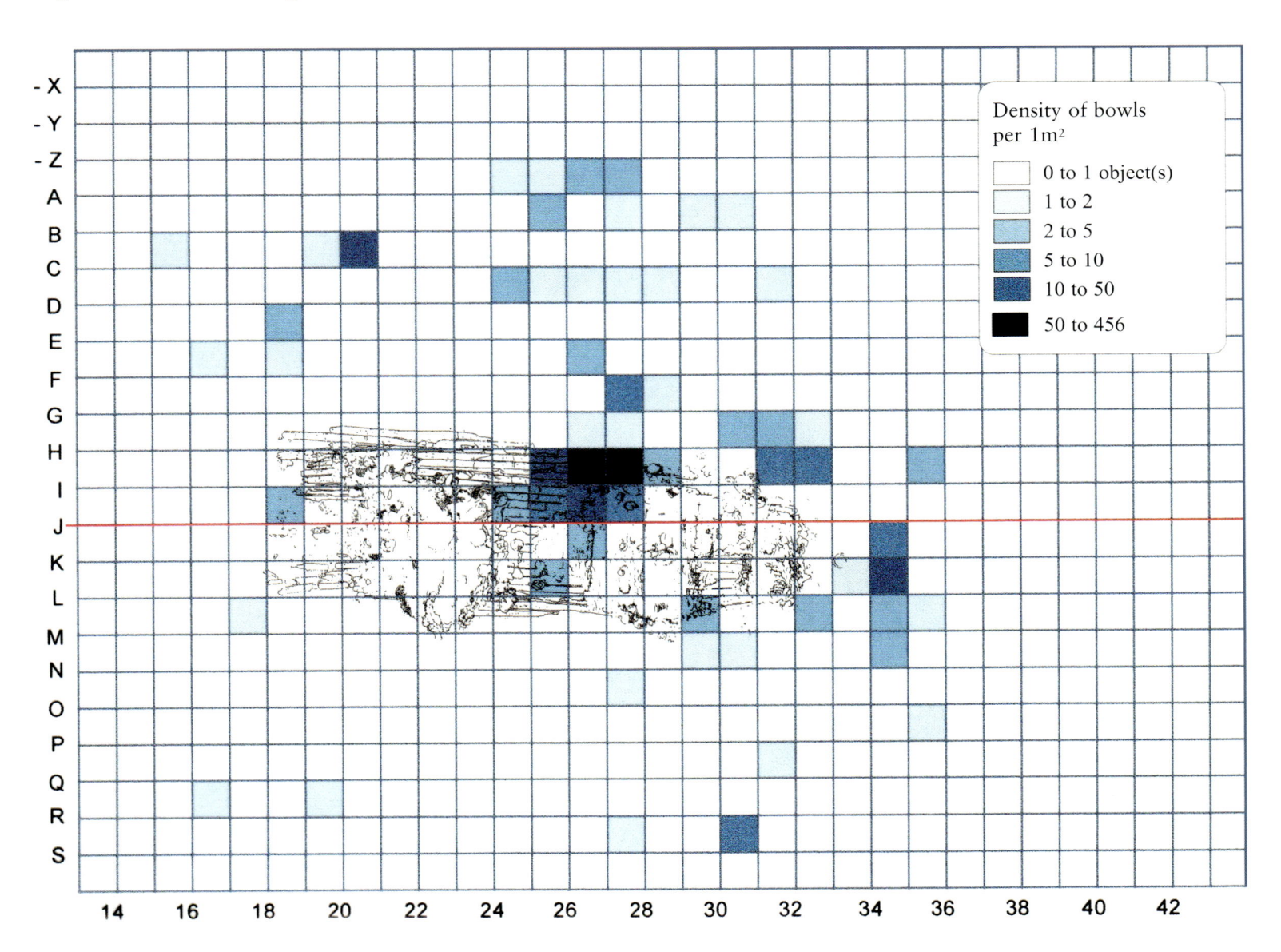

Density of bowls per 1m²

- 0 to 1 object(s)
- 1 to 2
- 2 to 5
- 5 to 10
- 10 to 50
- 50 to 456

29

LOST AT SEA

Photo 17. Piles of stacked dishes at 24-L.

Density of porcelain plates and dishes
The same applies to the dishes found at 19-G, 19-H, 20-G, 20-H, 21-G, 21-H, 22-G, 22-H and 23-G, which were arranged on the planking and also piled up in matching sizes and shapes, regardless of pattern.

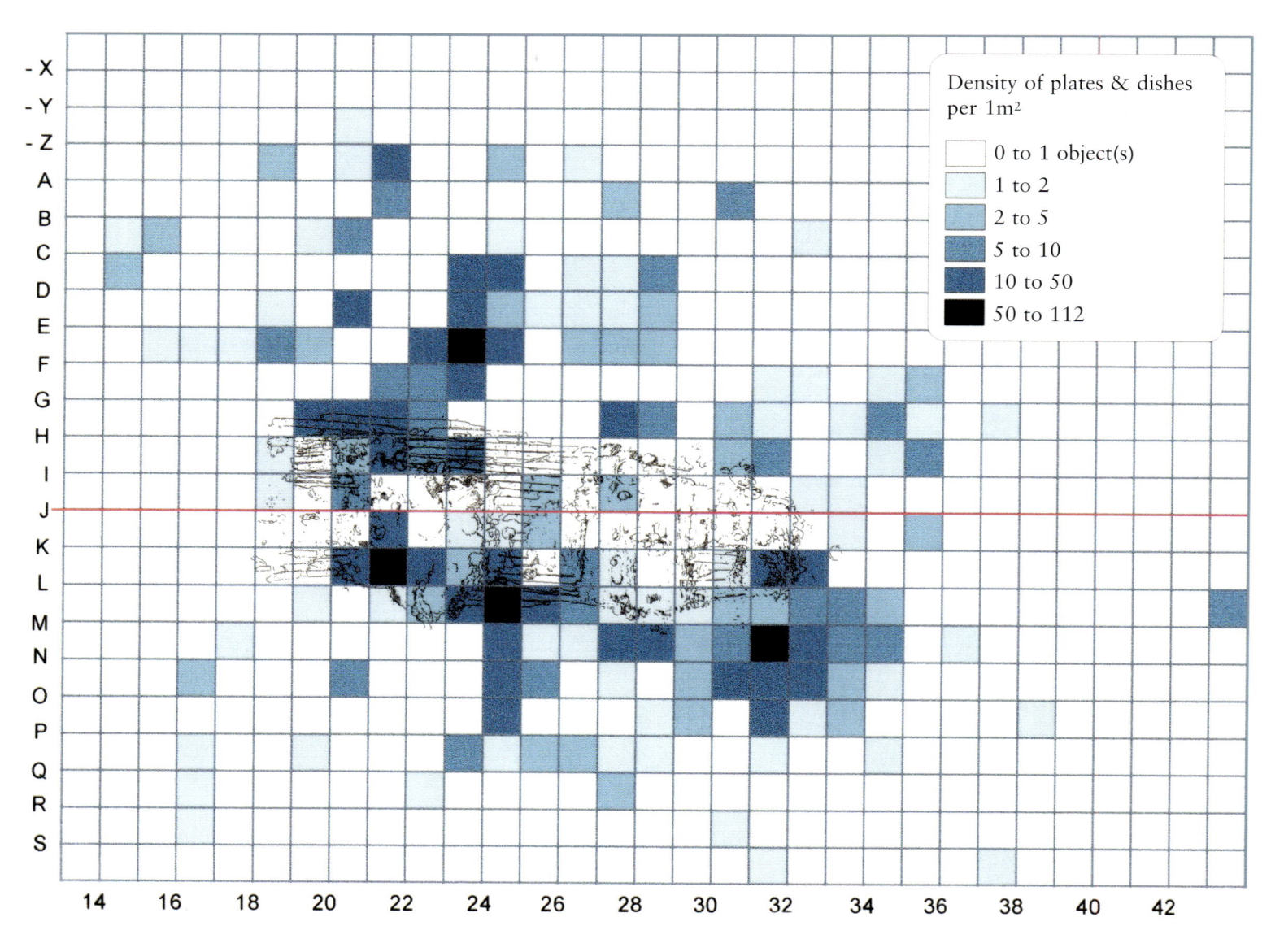

Photo 18. Piles of porcelain dishes lying directly on the wooden hull at 23-H.

LOST AT SEA

Long piles of plates and tubes of bowls were discovered in numerous places on the excavation site. The length of these heaps, which were sometimes more than 2 m long, suggests that these ceramics had not been crated. This supposition is corroborated by the arrangement of the piles of ceramics still in place on the wood of the wreck. If they had been crated they would have been found in a condition that would favour conservation of the packaging between them and the structure of the ship, and yet no trace of packing wood was identifiable. It is therefore highly unlikely that they had been crated.

Only two crates were unearthed and they were standing on the sand in quite a good state of preservation despite the fact that they were a long way from the bottom of the hull. The remains of one crate were found at 29-D which contained double-lidded boxes and little pitchers in the form of pairs of mandarin ducks. The wood of the crate was made of pine, probably Scot's pine (*Pinus sylvestris*). The remains of the other crate, also pine, were found at 26-C and contained brass bracelets. It should also be noted that the ceramics found on this junk were never found packed into jars, unlike those found on other wrecks in Asian waters.[25] It would appear that the goods were either stacked straight into the hold without packaging or in baskets of organic matter which have completely disintegrated. Traces of rice husks were also identified in the bowls found at 26-H, which had clearly been used as packing material.

---

[25] Goddio, 1997.

Photo 19. The remains of a packing case containing porcelain pitchers of high quality.

Density of small globular Sawankhalok jars with green glazing (kiln of Si Satchanaloi)

Another remarkable feature of this wreck as regards the packaging of the cargo was the surprising accumulation of little, round, green-glazed Sawankhalok jars from the kilns of Si Satchanalai.[26]

Of these jars, 287 were found stacked inside a half-bulkhead of the hold at 29-K, 29-L, 30-K and 30-L. In this case, it would appear that the objects had been placed exposed in the hold, piled on top of each other without any packaging, their shape being particularly suited to this arrangement.

The fact that almost all these little jars remained intact throughout their adventures shows that this arrangement worked well. The density of distribution of these spherical jars also indicates they had been stored in various parts of the ship.

---

[26] Cf. Typology 10.1.

Photo 20. Small, globular jars from Sawankhalok.

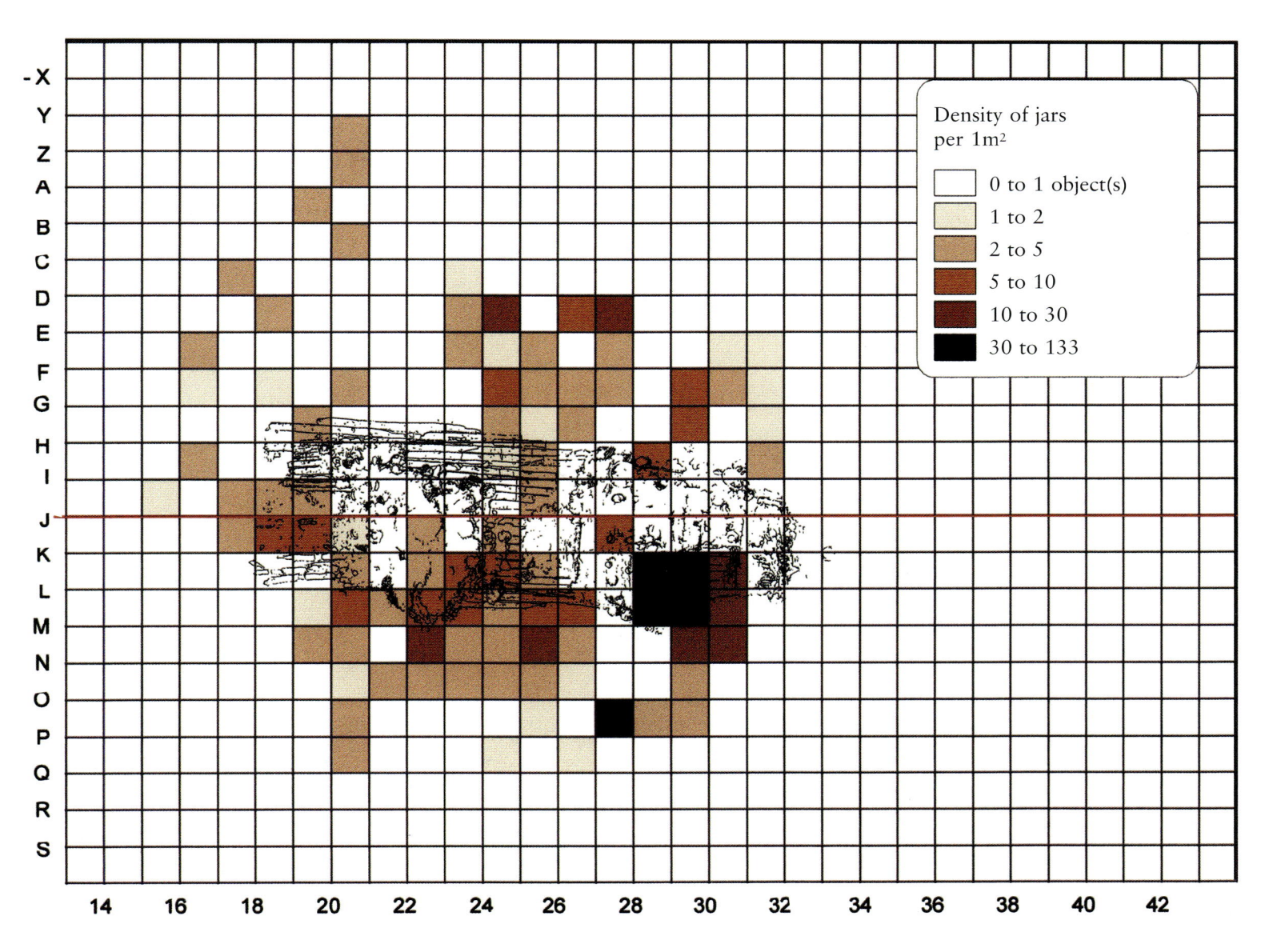

LOST AT SEA

Density of small ovoid jars
(kiln of Tao Maenam Noi)

It is interesting to note that while a large number of these small spherical jars were placed in a half-hold, the small oval jars from Sawankhalok, products of the kilns of Tao Maenam Noi,[27] were fairly uniformly distributed throughout the ship rather than being concentrated at a specific point, as can be seen by the diagram indicating their position. Some had been filled with small coloured glass beads of various sizes.[28]

---

[27] Cf. Typology 11.3.
[28] Cf. Typology 15.

Photo 21. A jar from the kilns of Tao Maenam Noi.

34

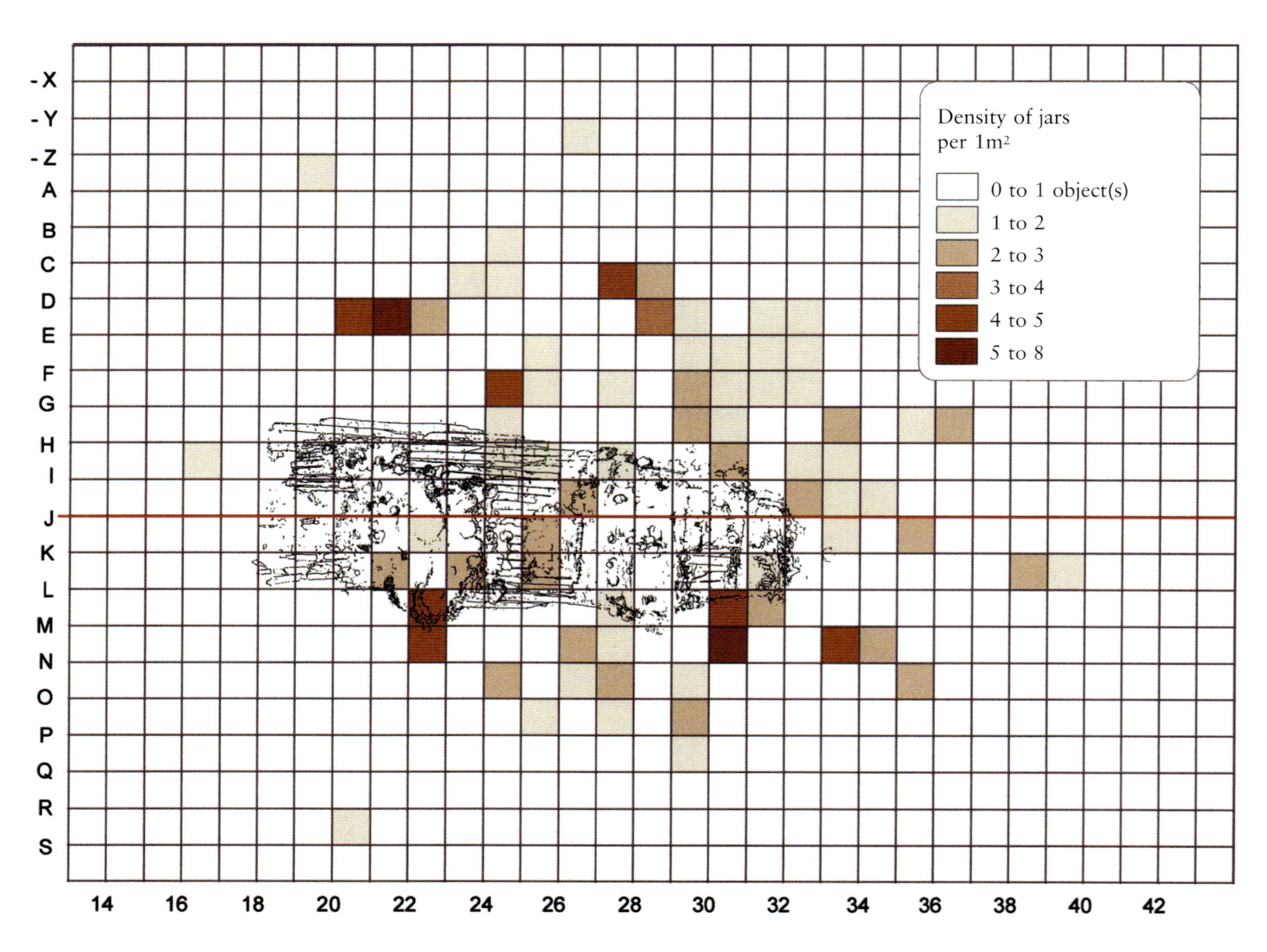

The wreck on the Lena Shoal

Photo 22. Glass beads found inside a jar.

Photo 23. Detail of glass beads.

Position of glass beads in small ovoid jars (kiln of Tao maenam Noi)

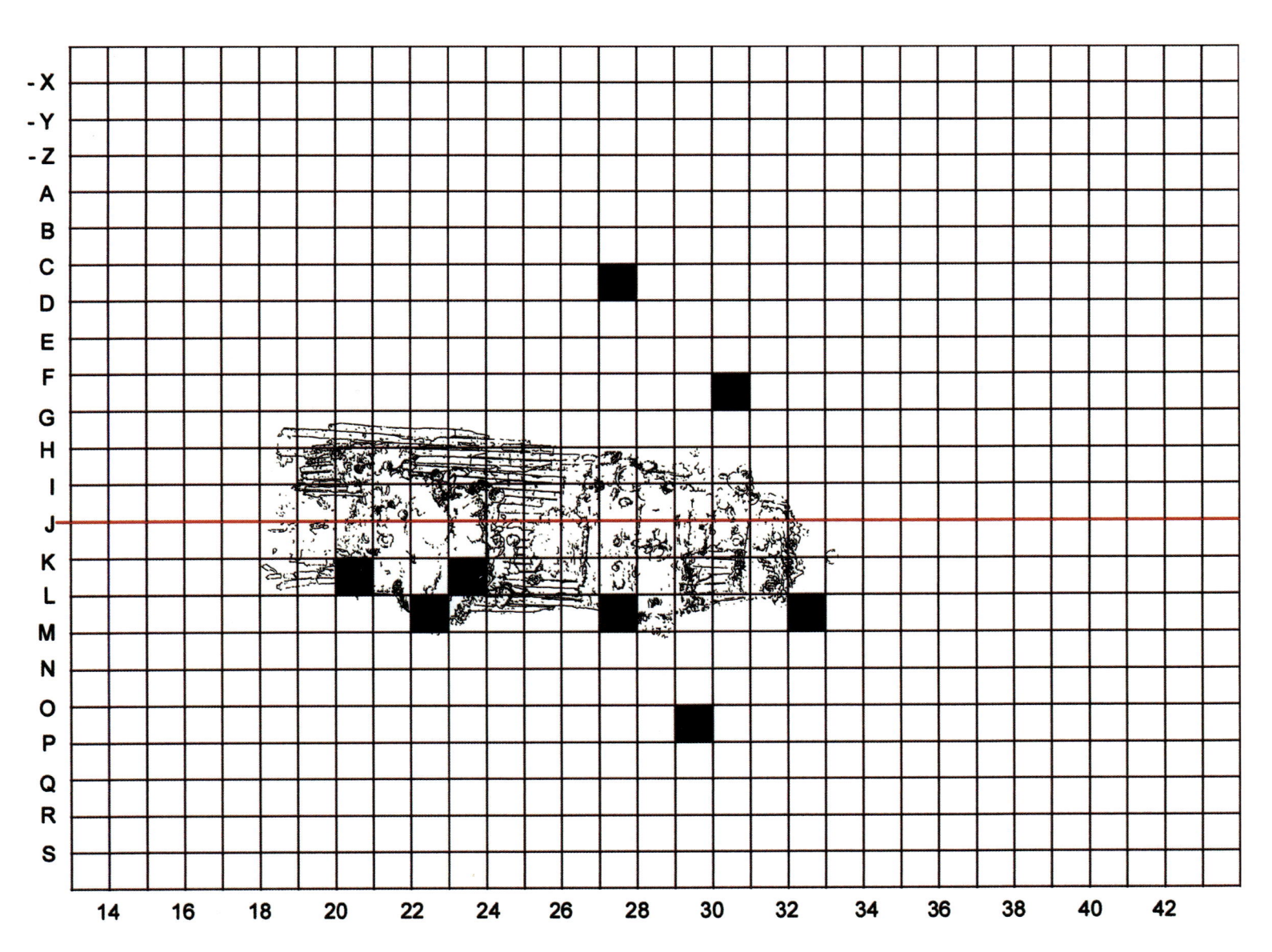

LOST AT SEA

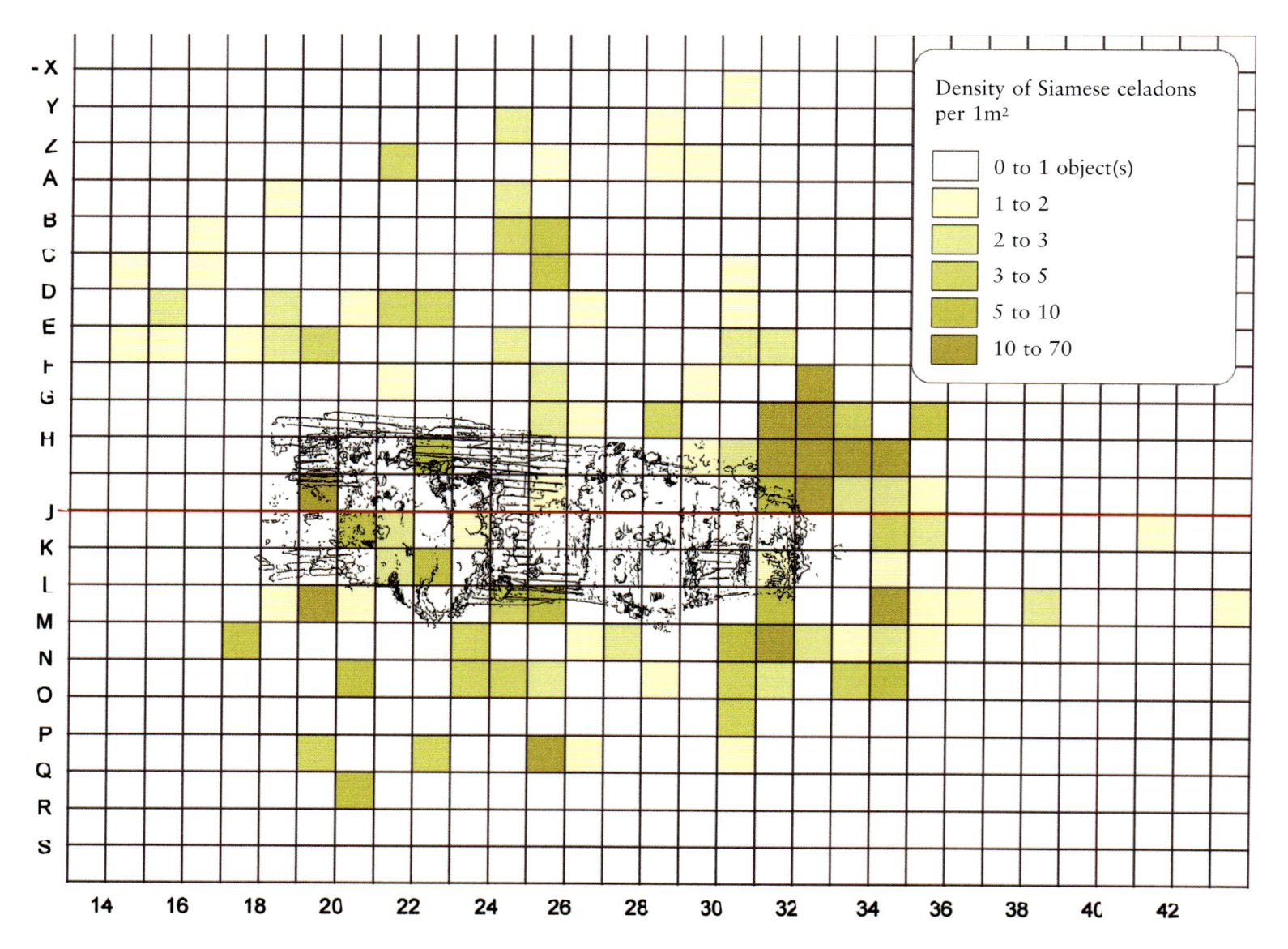

Photo 24. Examples of Siamese celadon ware.

Density of Siamese celadon

Celadon ware from Siam, mainly plates and bowls, was also stowed in various parts of the junk and there was quite a high density of them between map references 30 and 35.

36

The wreck on the Lena Shoal

Photo 25. Chinese celadon ware.

Density of Chinese celadon
Handsome Chinese celadon ware from the kilns of Longquan in the province of Zhejiang was not so widely dispersed. It was found in various positions and in different parts of the ship to the celadon ware from Siam.

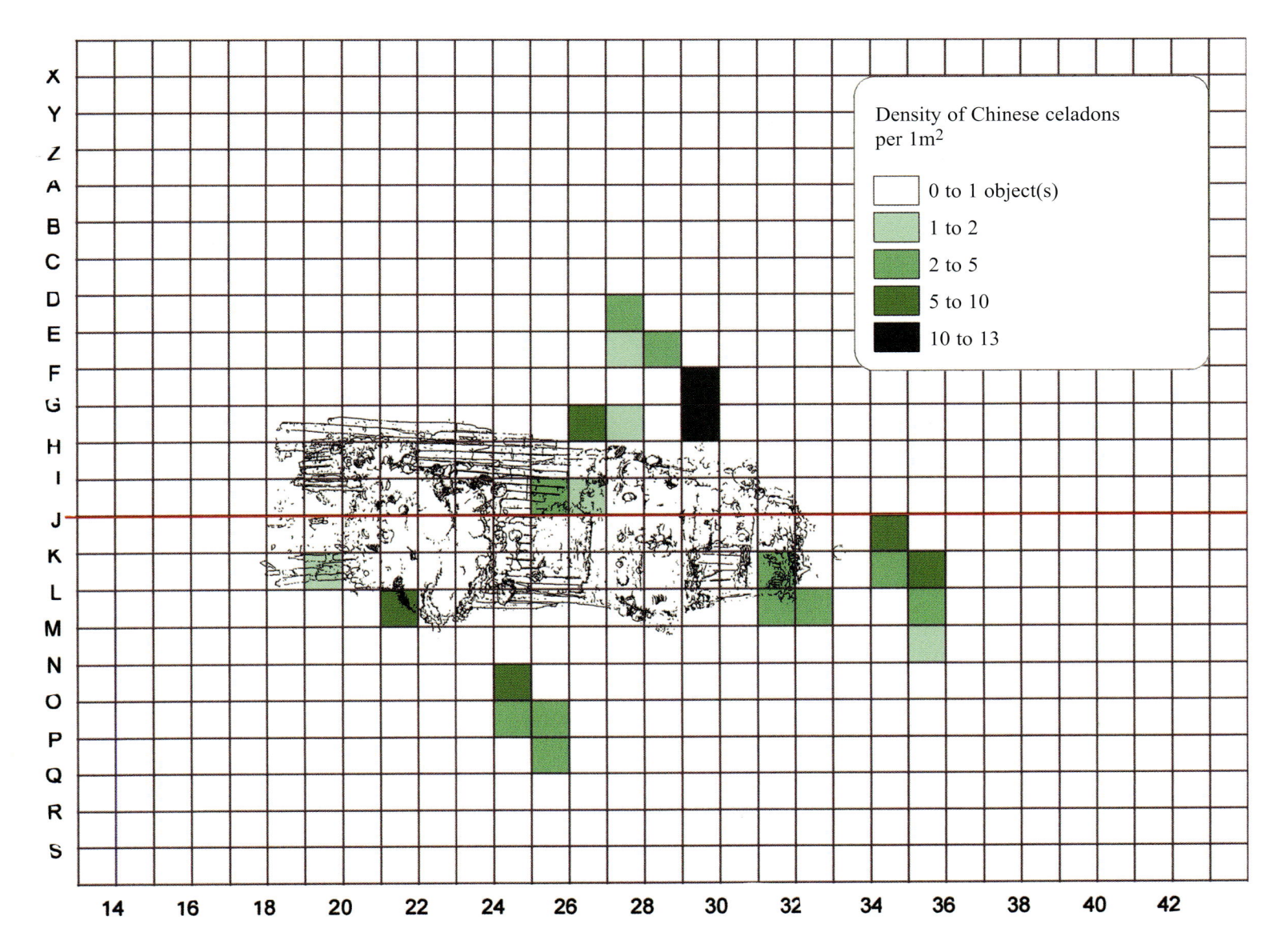

Density of Chinese celadons per 1m²

- 0 to 1 object(s)
- 1 to 2
- 2 to 5
- 5 to 10
- 10 to 13

LOST AT SEA

Photo 26. Vietnamese jars as found during the archaeological excavation.

Density of stoneware jars from Vietnam
Numerous Vietnamese jars were stored uniformly throughout the length of the ship. Their distance from the remains in the bottom of the ship could indicate that they had been stored on quite a high level, perhaps even on deck.

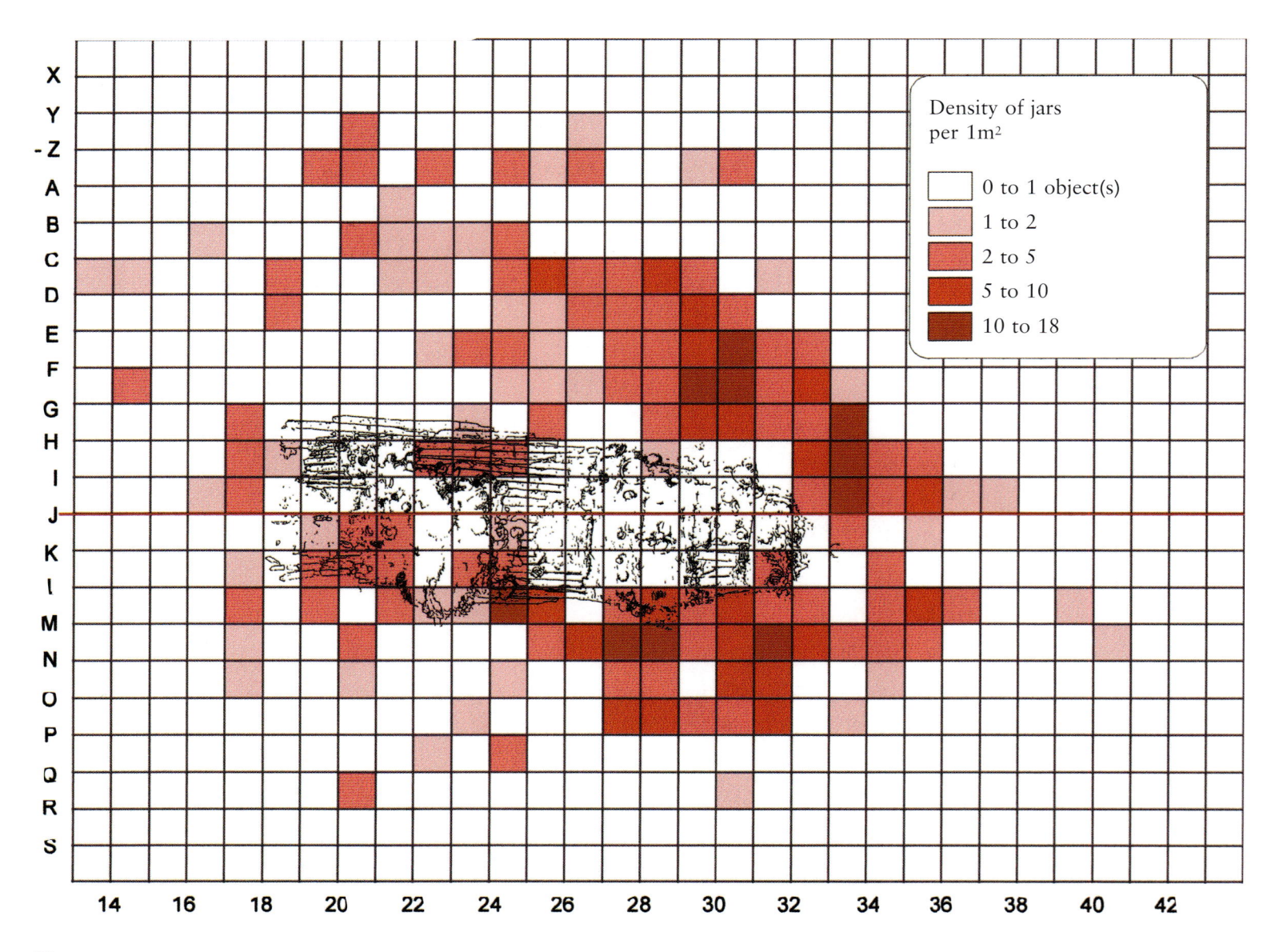

Density of jars per 1m^2

- 0 to 1 object(s)
- 1 to 2
- 2 to 5
- 5 to 10
- 10 to 18

38

Photo 27. Tin ingots and half-ingot.

Density of tin ingots and brass bracelets

The tin ingots were found at or near the bottom of the hull with concentrations along the sides at 31-J, 32-J, 31-K and 32-K. This arrangement is logical since they would have to have been stored near the bottom of the ship. The brass bracelets were clearly stored high up the ship, as indicated by the fact that many were found some distance from the bottom of the hull. The bronze gongs, of which there were few, were found around reference 17.

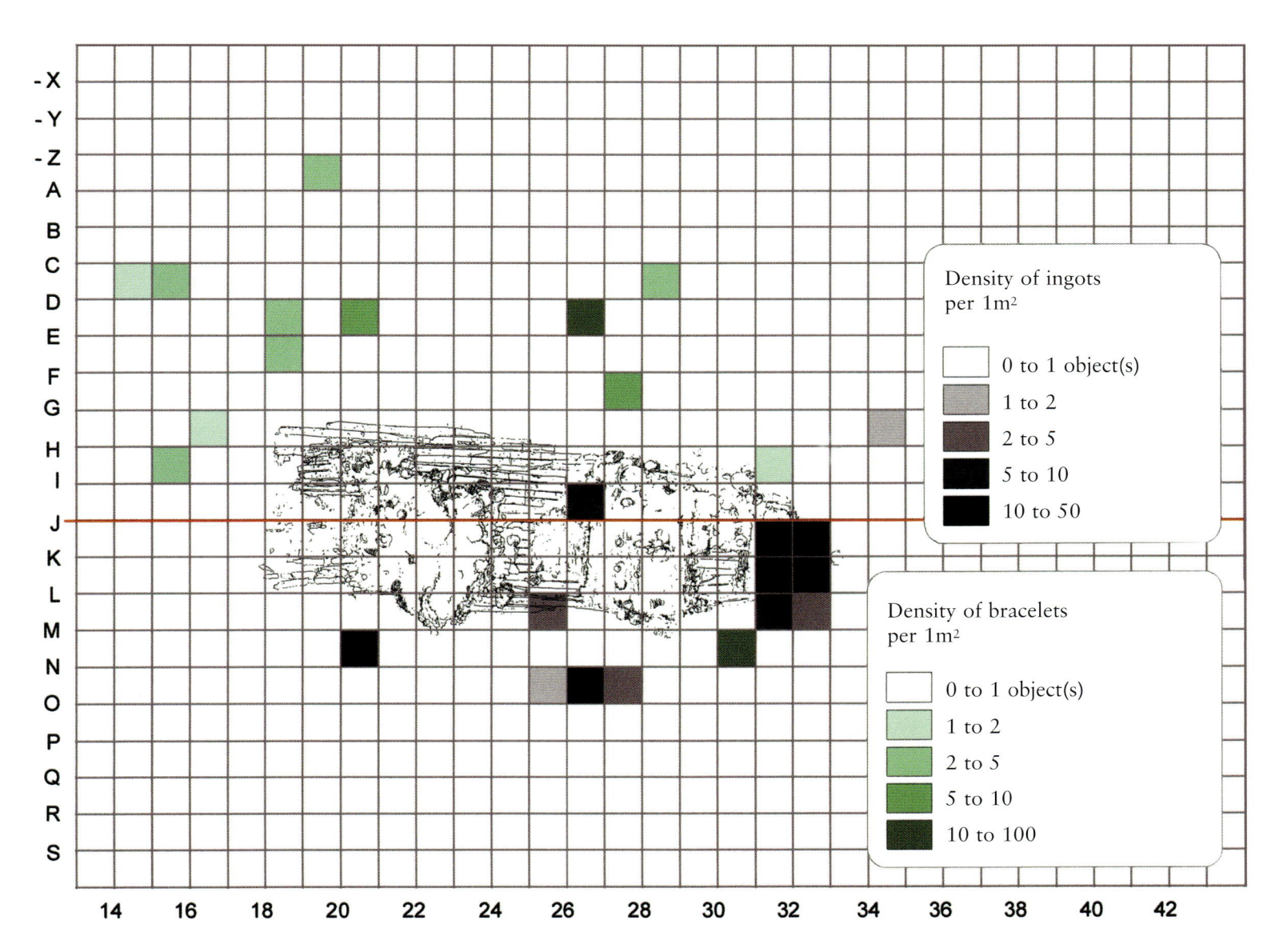

Photo 28. Spiral brass bracelet

The distribution of the iron ingots is very significant because this was used as ballast for the ship as well as merchandise and had to be stored in the bottom of the hull. It could not therefore have become displaced from its original position in the bulkheads. The layer of iron ballast extends from map reference 18.3 to reference 32.2 although there are breaks between references 24 and 25.3, and references 18.3 to 20.5, where the accretions now present are clearly debris fallen from the adjacent masses of iron. The great weight of the ballast was thus distributed along the length of the ship in the holds, with the exception of the forward and aft sections of the hull and the bulkhead situated at map reference 24 to 25.3.

The masses were distributed symmetrically along the axis of the hull which is estimated to lie along line K, with the notable exception of a half-bulkhead between map references 31 and 29.5, which contained no ingots and is filled only with the little round jars mentioned above.

The thickness of the layer of iron ingots varied from 120 cm at references 23 and 29; 100 cm at reference 27; and 70 cm at reference 26. The ingots had been tied together with bands of split bamboo in bundles of 10 and were arranged in layers separated by racks made of plaited palm leaves (since all that was left was an imprint, the species of palm could not be determined).

Five small brass cannons were discovered at 26-I with crushed copper bowls and tin ingots nearby. The trace of a small iron cannon, welded to a mass of ingots, can be seen at 27-J.

Photo 29. Imprint of braided palm leaves forming racks on which the bundles of iron pigs were stored.

Photo 30. Remains of a bamboo tie in an accretion of ingots.

Photo 31. Elephant tusks.

Density of elephant tusks
The elephant tusks were mainly stowed longitudinally on two levels of the junk, at map reference 21 and between references 27 and 35.

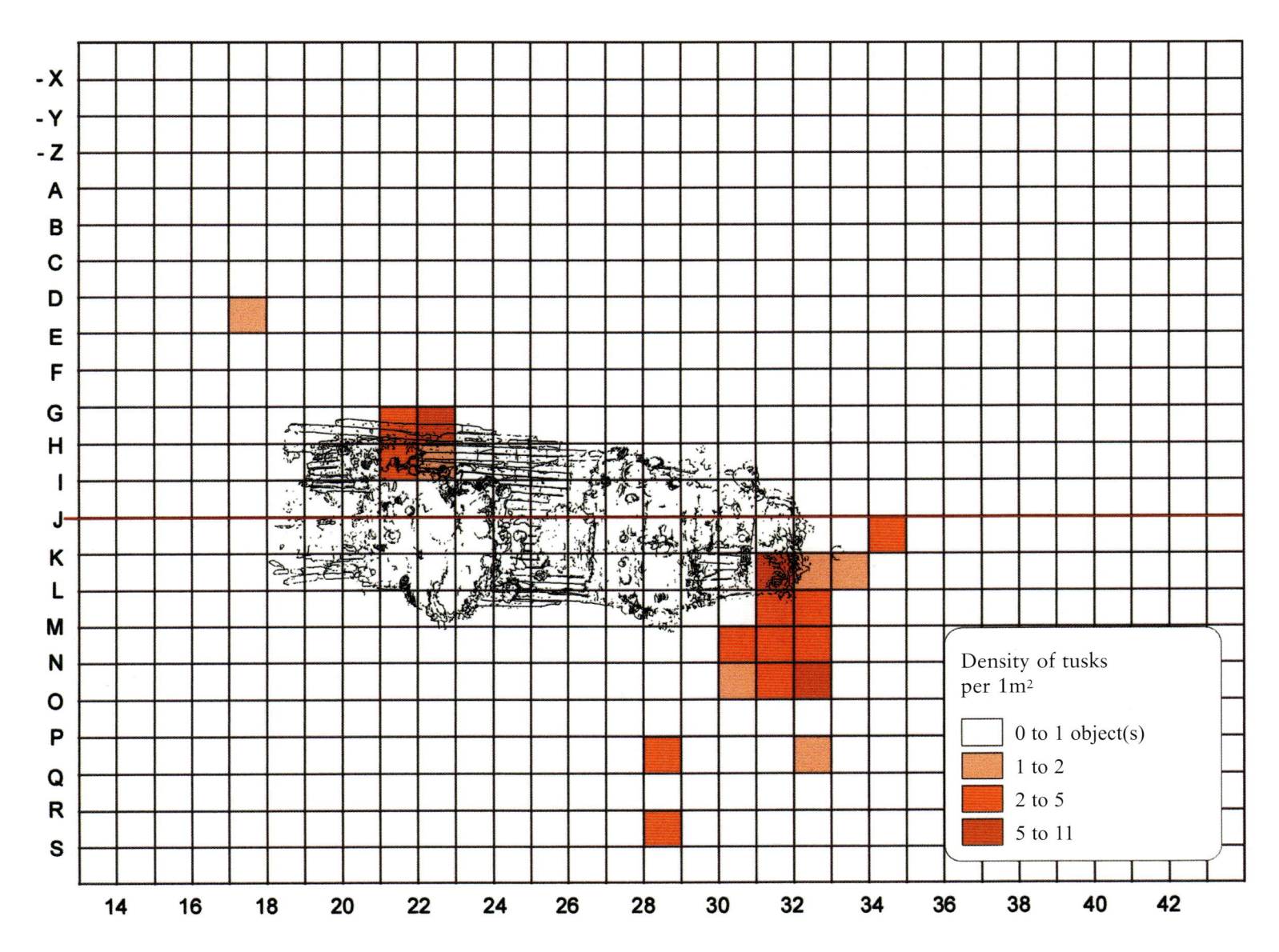

Fig. 13. Official portrait of Zhu Youtang (1470–1505), the Hongzhi emperor who reigned 1488–1505. Hanging scroll, ink and colour on silk. 209.8 x 115 cm. Collection of the National Palace Museum, Taibei.

MARITIME TRADE IN CHINA DURING THE MIDDLE MING PERIOD CIRCA 1500 AD

Peter Y. K. Lam

The year 1500 was a year of no great significance in China. The ruling emperor was Zhu Youtang (1470–1505, reigned 1488–1505), better known as Emperor Hongzhi. He was a benevolent Confucian ruler, and was probably the only monogamous emperor in the history of China.[1] He ruled wisely and his reign came to be characterised as harmonious and generally uneventful, but the whole of China was totally unaware of the happenings in the contemporaneous Europe. The late fifteenth and early sixteenth centuries had been a great age of exploration for European navigators.[2] In 1488, first year of Hongzhi, Bartolomeu Dias discovered the Cape of Good Hope, and triggered a great many expeditions by Portuguese and Spanish sailors. In 1492, fourth year of Hongzhi, Christopher Columbus set sail for the New World and in 1498, eleventh year of Hongzhi, Vasco da Gama opened the new route to India through the Cape of Good Hope.

It was only more than a decade later in the succeeding Zhengde (1506–21) and Jiajing (1522–66) reigns that the impact of the arrival of these European merchants was really felt by the Chinese. As late as 1567 (first year of Longqing), Yuegang in Fujian, was opened as the only legal seaport for overseas trade.[3] Chinese historians have long taken 1567 as a watershed in the maritime trade in Ming China.

Before that, all commercial activities were to be limited to the tributary system monopolised by the government who took a defensive attitude towards foreign trade and had, since Hongwu's reign (1368–98), imposed an exceedingly strict *haijin* or maritime prohibition policy. The Hongzhi reign falls into the heyday of this legal tributary trade system. This essay is a very preliminary and immature attempt – as my Chinese colleagues would say – to describe the trading scene during the Ming dynasty in this uneventful period of the late fifteenth to early sixteenth century.

1. Foreign trade policy of the Ming dynasty

Zhu Yuanzhang (1328–98, reigned 1368–98), the Hongwu Emperor and founder of the Ming dynasty, was known for his stern closed-door policy which had a long lasting impact throughout the whole Ming Empire. At the onset of his regime, however, he took a totally different attitude towards overseas trade and continued with the free trade policy of the earlier Song and Yuan dynasties.

In 1367, one year before Zhu was proclaimed emperor and after he had out-stripped his competitors, Zhang Shicheng and Fang Guozhen, for the mandate, he ordered the setting up of a Maritime Trade Commissioner Office at Huangdu, Taicang County (modern day Liuhe Village, Taicang County, Jiangxu Province).[4] His intention was to prolong the prosperous and lucrative overseas trade that had started in the earlier dynasties.

Custom laws on imported goods from foreign vessels were devised according to models in practice during the Yuan dynasty and written into the *Da Ming Lu* (Law Codes of the Great Ming). Special privileges were given to Chinese merchants conducting overseas trade. On one occasion it was recorded that the emperor gave an audience in the capital to a group of these merchants who came to congratulate him and brought along gifts for the new regime.

In 1369, the second year of his reign, Emperor Hongwu sent out envoys to neighbouring countries to solicit political relationships and allegiance. The Chinese, heavily influenced by the ancient *fengjian* (feudal) system, developed an attitude of superiority towards their neighbours on the Asiatic continent and overseas. The emperor felt that these neighbouring "barbarians" should show their allegiance to China in at least three ways:

a) by calling themselves vassals of the Chinese emperor,
b) by sending to China occasional envoys bringing tributary offerings of goods, and
c) by accepting the Chinese calendar and using

---

[1] L. C. Goodrich and Fang Chaoying, *Dictionary of Ming Biography 1368–1644*, Columbia University Press, New York and London, 1976, pp. 377–80.

[2] Huang Shijian, ed., *Zhongxi guangxi shi nianbiao* (A Chronological Table of Sino-Western Relations), Zhejiang renmin chubanshe, Hangzhou, 1994, pp. 338–47; see also J. A. Levenson, ed., *Circa 1492, Art in the Age of Exploration*, National Gallery, Washington, 1991.

[3] R. C. Tan, Unpublished paper delivered at Singapore Conference: *Fujian Ceramics and their Trade in South East Asia*, 1998. Quoted with permission of the author.

[4] The main reference to this paragraph is Chen Gaohua and Chen Shangsheng, *Zhongguo haiwei jiaotongshi* (History of Chinese Overseas Communications), Wenjin chubanshe, Taibei, 1997, ch. 4, section 1, p. 167ff.

Chinese year periods in memorials presented to China.[5]

Emperor Hongwu attached great importance to the implementation of the tribute system to allow foreign countries to show good faith in their positions as "the lesser serving the greater", but at the same time held no ambition for external aggression nor territorial encroachment. Foreign states which carefully and diligently observed the tribute and other obligations were assured of lasting peace with China and were treated with generosity by the Chinese.

All the above occurred in the early years of the Hongwu reign. Developments in the following years, however, forced the emperor to adopt a policy of isolationism, cutting China off from genuine intercourse with the outside world by enforcing the maritime prohibition and trade ban. There must have been many political and economic reasons for imposing these measures, but the prime concern for the Hongwu Emperor was to cut off any possible connection with the *wako*, or Japanese pirates, who were often joined by Chinese bandits from the fleeing armies of the defeated troops of Fang Guozhen and Zhang Shicheng. The Hu Weiyong incident in 1380[6] provided a further excuse for him to keep China isolated from neighbouring countries by declaring sea-faring prohibitions. Except for some brief periods, these prohibitions had been strictly carried out throughout the first half of the Ming dynasty. The great expeditions of Admiral Zheng He during the Yongle (1403–24) and Xuande (1426–1435) reigns were merely a continuation of Hongwu's policy of soliciting foreign allegiance.

After the final voyage in 1433 the expeditions became history, and in the following Chenghua reign (1465–87), files, log-books and archives of Zheng He were burnt and destroyed, leaving no trace of its impact in the succeeding reigns.[7] Indeed none of the Ming emperors had expansionist ambitions. This also justifies the measures enforced by the Hongwu Emperor for a closed-door policy.

Laws connected with maritime prohibitions had been proclaimed throughout the first half of the Ming

---

[5] Wang Gungwu, "Early Ming Relations with Southeast Asia: A Background Essay", in J. K. Fairbank, *The Chinese World Order, Traditional Chinese Foreign Relations*, Harvard University Press, Cambridge, 1968, pp. 34–62 and Wu Chi-hua, "Basic Foreign-policy Attitudes of the Early Ming Dynasty", *Ming Studies*, 12, Spring, 1981, pp. 65–80. See also Wang Yi-t'ung, *Official Relations between China and Japan, 1368–1549*, Harvard University Press, Cambridge, 1953, pp. 1–7.

[6] Wang Yi-t'ung, 1953, pp. 20–1. Hu was accused of having sought the aid of Japan to kill the emperor and overthrow the Ming Empire.

[7] Li Jinming, *Mingdai haiwai moyi shi* (History of overseas trade in the Ming period), Zhongguo shehui kexue chubanshe, Beijing, 1990, p. 46, quoting Yan Congjian, Shuyi zhouci lu, ch. 8.

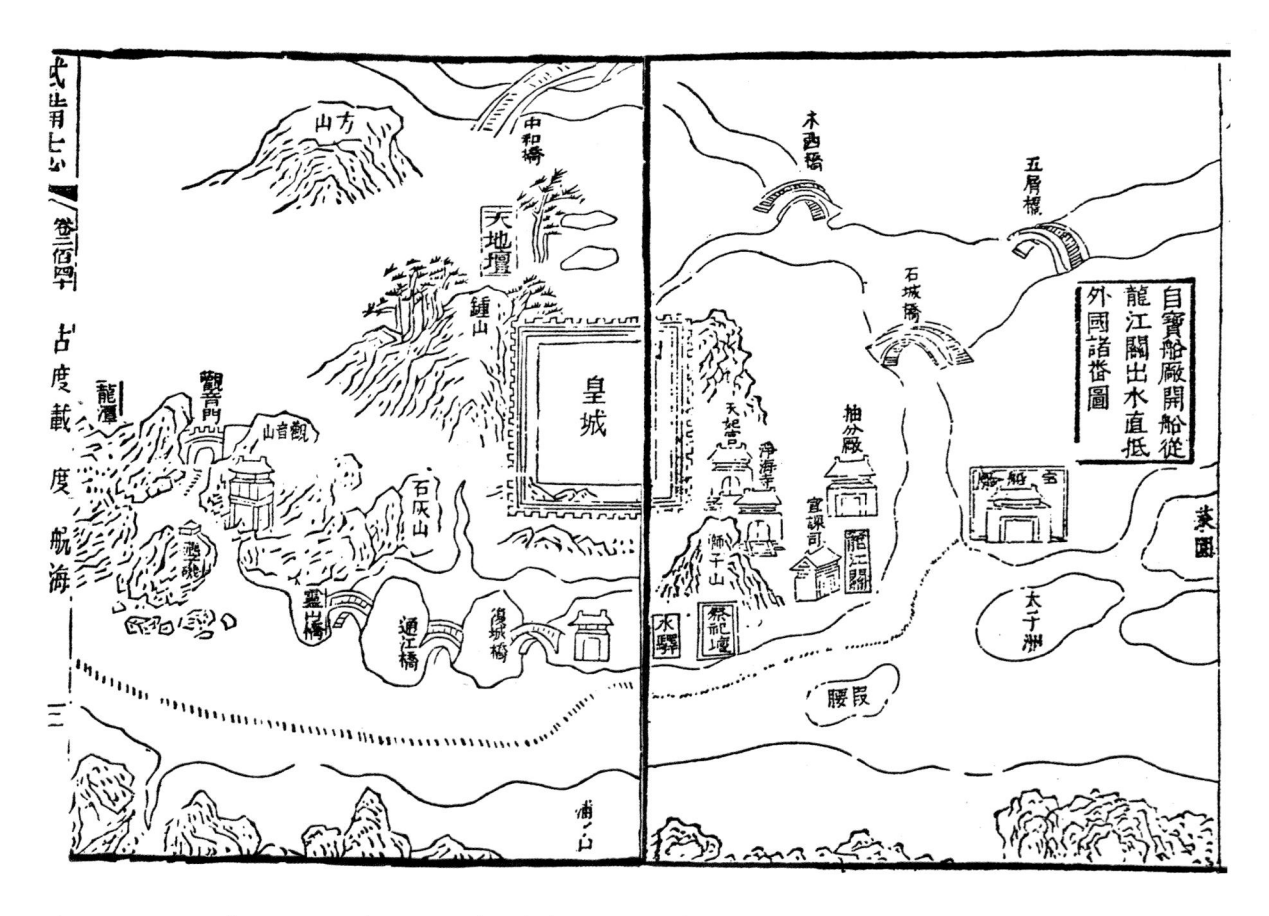

Fig. 14. Nanjing, the Ming southern capital with the Treasure Ship Yard. A page from *Zheng He hanghai tu* (Maritime Maps of Zheng He). Woodblock illustration reprint from *Wubei zhi*, 1628.

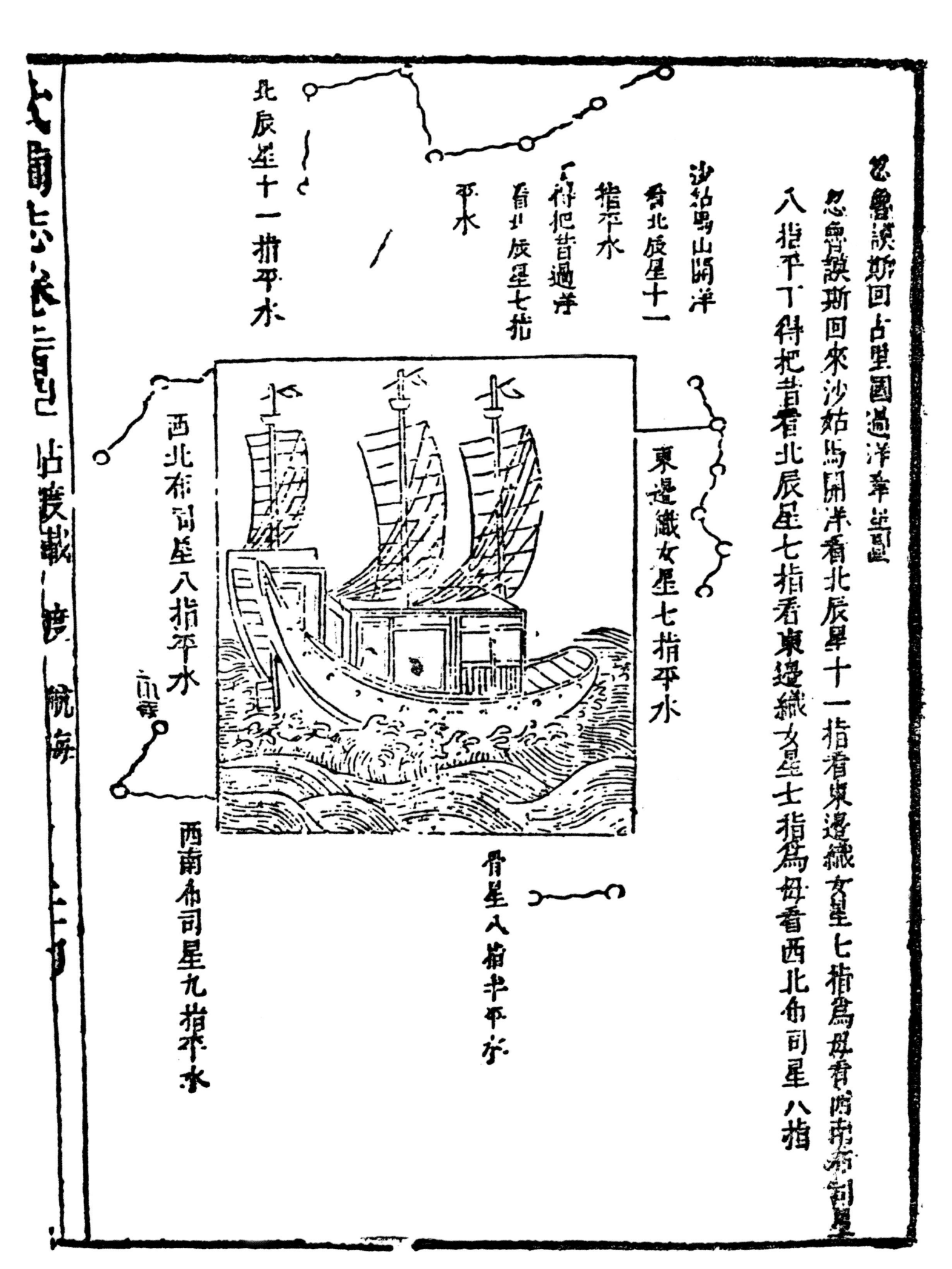

Fig. 15. A page from a fifteenth century navigation logbook supposedly used by the Zheng He team from the so-called *Zheng He hanghai tu* (Maritime Maps of Zheng He). Woodblock illustration reprint from *Wubei zhi*, 1628.

reigns and their main points were:[8]

- The prohibition of the export and sale to overseas countries of military provisions, such as horses, oxen, iron, copper, cash coins, and fabrics, silk, cotton, etc.
- Unless an official permit was acquired, no vessels with more than two masts were allowed to be built and sailed abroad.
- The prohibition of the circulation and use of imported incense and commodities.
- The prohibition of sea-faring without prior permission.
- The prohibition of private trading with overseas countries.
- Only small single-masted boats with permits were allowed to go fishing in coastal regions.
- Frontier garrisons, if found involved in private overseas trade or travelling overseas on official pretexts, were to be punished.
- Those who shipped arms and people overseas and went abroad would be strangulated.
- Overseas vessels upon arrival at the coastal port should make a declaration at the customs office.

2. The tributary trade system

These maritime prohibitions were enforced in the first half of the Ming dynasty. It was not until 1567 that the ban was lifted and Yuegang was opened for private trade. Previously, conduct of all foreign trade was restricted to the official tribute system. The ships of the tributary states were permitted to enter China's ports and were exempt from import duties. The tribute items and imported goods were purchased by the government and Chinese goods were "bestowed" on the tribute bearers. In effect, this was a form of import and export trading activity, but conducted under the guise of the tribute system.[9]

In the beginning only states or countries that had allegiance with China were allowed to send tributary ships to the designated ports of the China coast. A total of 15 such states and countries were recorded, including Siam, Japan, Champa, Java, Malacca, Cambodia, the Sulu Islands (Sulu had wider meaning in the Ming and included also Jolo, Calamian, Busuanga, which includes Lena, and Palawan),[10] Cochin, Borneo, Sri Lanka, Calicut, North Sumatra, and Mindanao. To prevent dishonest merchants from overseas coming to China under the guise of tribute bearers, as early as the sixteenth year of the Hongwu reign (1383) a *kanhe* (tally) system was devised by the Ministry of Rites. Special tickets properly stamped and in packets of 200 were issued to these tributary states. One portion of the ticket was issued to the states, while the other portion was kept in the Maritime Trade Commissioner Offices in the designated ports for verification. Every tributary ship had to bring along one of these tickets, on which names of the envoy, his crew, and an inventory of the tribute items were inscribed. A similar system and process were followed by return envoys from the Ming court to the tributary states. When a new emperor ascended to the throne, all unused tickets were returned to China and a new packet was re-issued for use during the new reign.

Tributes were to be sent to the court to coincide with either the Chinese New Year or birthdays of either the emperor or crown prince (the *Wansui jie* and the *Qianqiu jie*). Apart from this, there were rigid quotas governing the frequency of the tribute trips, number of ships and their crews, as well as the quantities of the tributary items. These limitations varied according to the different states. Friendly ones were allowed annual or five-yearly tributes. But, for example, great caution had always been given to Japan. In the second year of Yongle (1404) the emperor decreed that tributes from Japan were to be conducted once every decade and limited to two ships with a total of 200 crew members.

From historical records, most of the tributes from all overseas states and countries far exceeded these quotas. A good example was one from Japan in 1453 (fourth year Jingtai). A total of nine ships arrived with more than 1,000 crew members bringing along, among other commodities, 417 long knives and 9,483 "waist" knives.

The tribute ships could only call at three designated ports on the coast, Guangzhou in Guangdong, Quanzhou in Fujian and Ningpo in Zhejiang.[11] Each of these was equipped with *Shibo shi*, Maritime Trade Commissioner Offices, ready to receive the tribute bearers, who would then follow a prescribed route to carry the tribute items to the court in the capital in Nanjing (during the Hongwu reign) or Beijing (after the Yongle reign).

Once in the capital the tribute bearers would stay in a special hostel, the Huitong Guan managed by the Ministry of Rites. The tribute items for the court would be checked and verified against the inventory by the superintendent and staff of the hostel. The presentation ceremony of the tribute items was normally conducted at

---

[8] Chen Wenshi, *Ming Hongwu Jiajing jian de haijin zhengce* (The Sea-faring Prohibition Policy in the Early Ming Dynasty), Arts Faculty, National Taiwan University, Taibei, 1966, pp. 35–8.

[9] For a detailed technical description of the system see Li Jinming, 1990, pp. 11–34 and Chen Wenshi, 1966, pp. 41–81.

[10] See Chen Jiarong, et al., *Gudai Nanhai diming huishi* (A Dictionary of Place Names in the Nanhai Region), Zhonghua shuju, Beijing, 1986, pp. 412–13.

[11] During the Yongle reign inland Trade Commissioner Offices were set up in Yuannan, and in Vietnam at Xinping and Shunhua. See Li Jinming, 1990, p. 70 quoting *Ming Taizu shilu*, zhuan 75, 84.

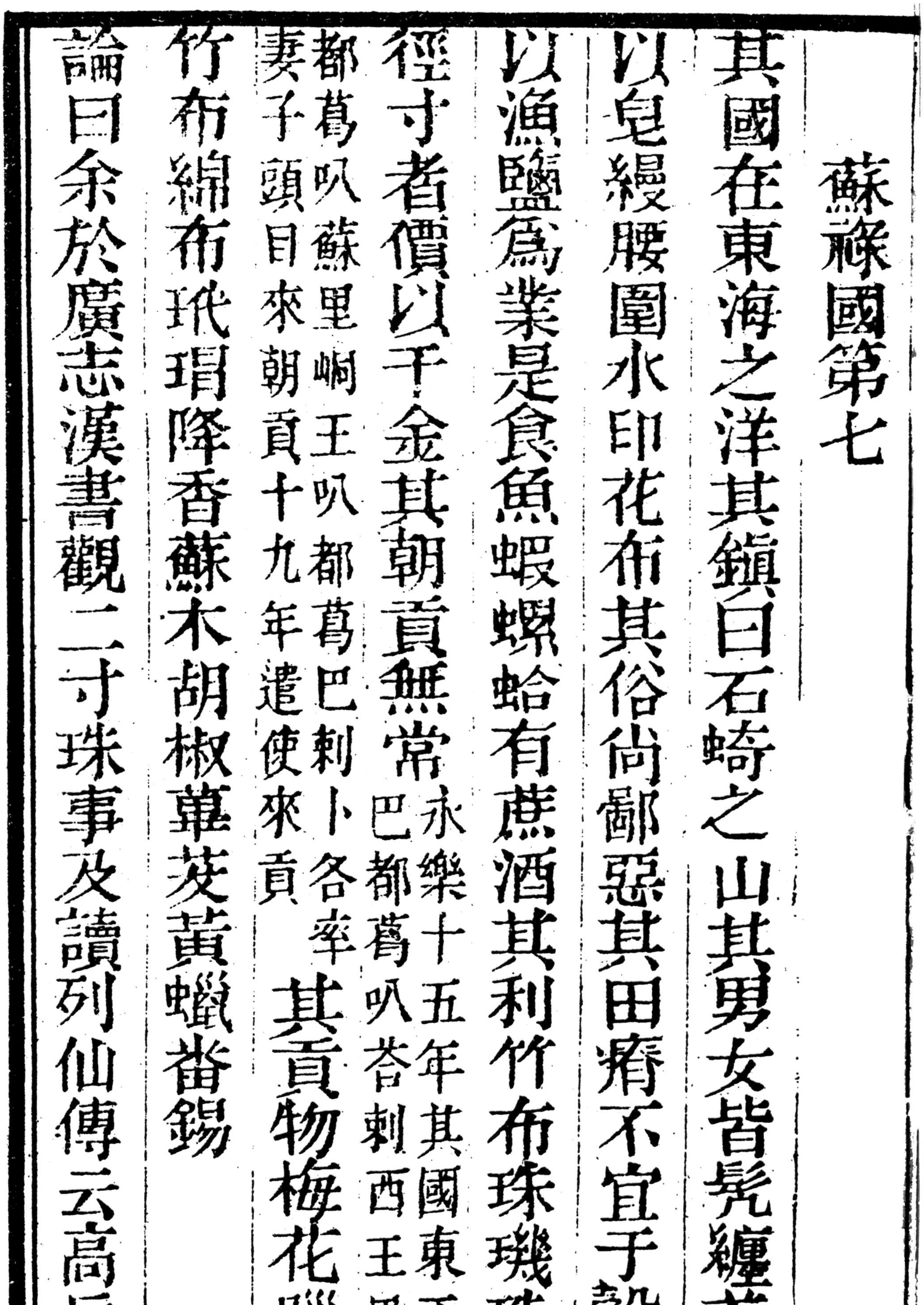

蘇祿國第七

其國在東海之洋其鎮曰石崎之山其男女皆髡纏首以皂縵腰圍水印花布其俗尚鄙惡其田瘠不宜于穀以漁鹽為業是食魚蝦螺蛤有蔗酒其利竹布珠璣珠徑寸者價以千金其朝貢無常

永樂十五年其國東王巴都葛叭荅剌西王巴都葛叭蘇里峒王叭都葛巴剌卜各率妻子頭目來朝貢十九年遣使來貢

其貢物梅花腦竹布綿布玳瑁降香蘇木胡椒薑荳黃蠟醬錫

論曰余於廣志漢書觀二十寸珠事及讀列仙傳云高后

Fig. 16. Chinese description of the Sulu Islands. A page from *Xiyang chaogong dian lu* (A Record of Tribute States from the Western Oceans) by Huang Shengzeng, preface dated 1520. Among other things the passage described that pearls were produced in Sulu. A list of tribute items was also mentioned.

one of the halls in the Forbidden City where "return gifts" were given to the bearers from the court. Apart from these tribute gifts, the kings, princes and crews would bring their own private commodities to China. These items were taxed and selectively purchased by the government. After that, the tribute bearers were allowed to dispose of their other commodities by open sale at the hostel premises. For five days Chinese merchants were permitted to visit the hostel and trade with the tribute bearers: purchasing the imported commodities and at the same time selling articles that the foreigners wanted. A further trading of any unsold items could be carried out when the tribute bearers returned to the coastal ports and prior to their setting sail to return home. Thus, these tribute visits were in actual fact inter-state/country level trading activities, the only form of overseas trading permitted by the Ming government.

According to the records in the Ming *huidian* the tribute items in the Ming dynasty were mainly native products of the tropical countries and could be classified into the following seven categories:[12]

1. Incense, aromatics, sandalwood, pepper, etc.
2. Exotic animals and birds such as elephants, rhinoceros, monkeys, bears, giraffes, peacocks, turkeys, parrots, etc.
3. Imported rarities: agate, rock crystal, elephant tusks, rhinoceros horns, peacock and kingfisher feathers, precious stones, coral, turtle shell, pearls, etc.
4. Handicrafts: gold and silver wares, furniture, boxes, fabrics and textiles, towels, mattresses, glass bottles, etc.
5. Raw materials: sulphur, ox skin, copper, tin, polishing stone, various minerals and pigments.
6. Military supplies: horses, helmets, armour, waist knives, spears, bows, saddles, etc.
7. Herbal and mineral medicine such as ginseng, aloe vera, garcinia, cardamom, myrrh, etc.

The "return gifts" bestowed on the tribute bearers by the Ming court included all types of silk and cotton products, porcelain wares, iron implements, copper cash coins, musk and books. Silk and cotton textiles constituted a major portion of these gifts, then came the cash coins, which were in wide circulation in South-East Asian countries including Java, Sirijava, South Borneo and Sri Lanka. Porcelain pieces also made up an important portion of the commodities to be taken back home by these bearers. Statistics of the return gifts to the Ryukyu Islands from the first year of Hongxi (1425) to the tenth year of Xuande (1435) show that in every tribute trip the bestowal would include twenty large blue and white dishes, 400 medium-sized blue and white dishes and 2,000 small blue and white bowls.[13]

As mentioned above, apart from these formal return gifts from the Ming court the tribute bearers were allowed to make their own private purchases in the hostel in the capital and in the coastal ports before sailing home. It is worthy of note that not all the return gifts nor the purchases made in China were brought back home by these bearers.

---

[12] Li Jinming, 1990, p. 23.

[13] Chen Wenshi, 1966, pp. 73-74.

Fig. 17. Woodblock illustrations from a 16th c. travel book. Reprinted from *Tuxiang nanbei liangjing lucheng* (Illustrated travel guide from Nanjing to Beijing). Published by Qinxian shutang, 1535. Tribute bearers/traders used such guidebooks during their journeys to the capital from the seaports and back.

Fig. 18. City scenes of Nanjing, the southern capital of the Ming dynasty by a 16th c. painter, with apocryphal signature of Qiu Ying. Section from a handscroll, ink and colour on silk. Height: 44 cm. Collection of the Chinese Museum of History, Beijing.

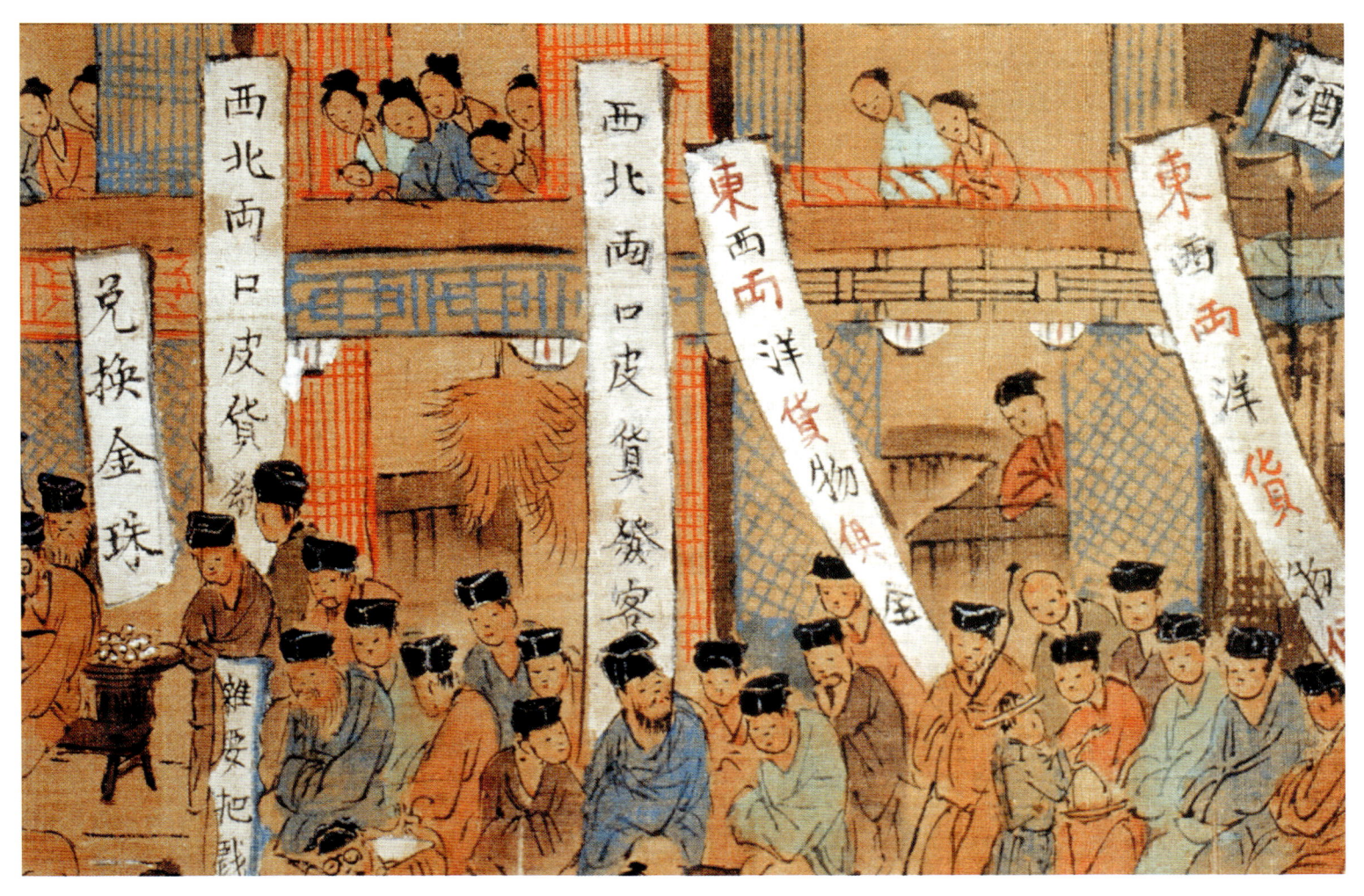

Fig. 19. Detail from Fig. 18. Characters on the banners at the right read: "Complete supplies of goods from the Eastern and Western Oceans". The Ming Chinese divided South-East Asian Countries into the "Eastern" and "Western" oceans. (The Eastern Oceans consisted of the archipelago east of Borneo and all other coastal states were called the Western Oceans.)

Very often they would sell them to nearby countries on their way home and make a profit from the sale. Thus both parties, the tribute states and the Ming government, obtained benefits from this form of tributary trade. At the court level the Ming emperor exchanged tribute items with return gifts which were in most cases much more valuable than the imported pieces, as it was the intention of the Ming empire to show generosity to the vassal states. However, in the second level of governmental purchases of private goods from the kings and crews, huge profits would be made. It was also for this reason that the Ming empire enforced the maritime prohibitions and maintained this tributary system as the only form of legal trade in the early part of the regime.

3. Private trade and smuggling

The tributary trade system had its most flourishing days during the Yongle and Xuande reigns after the Zheng He expeditions, but gradually declined in the mid fifteenth century. The system provided certain commercial benefits as an inducement to the tributary states sending envoys to pay their respects to the Chinese ruler. However, the frequency of the tribute missions was regulated by the Ming and the quantity and kind of commodities were also restricted.

Coinciding with the bad management of the tribute missions in both the seaports and during their trip to the capital and back, a great many grievances and crimes consequently surfaced. The huge expenses and great trouble involved in sending the tributes from the coastal ports to the capital and then getting them back home also aroused a lot of complaints and disorder.

According to historical records, tribute visits through Guangzhou from the first to the sixth year (1488–93) of the Hongzhi reign amounted to only two, one each from Champa and Siam respectively.[14] The middle and late fifteenth century also saw the collapse of the compulsory production system of the artisan/craftsmen. The court had not been able to obtain good quality return gifts to be bestowed on the tribute bearers. Not surprisingly, the tribute system therefore failed to satisfy the commercial desires of both the Chinese and the foreign merchants.

As a result, private trade reappeared some time in the latter half of the fifteenth century and started to flourish in the coastal cities in Zhejiang, Fujian and Guangdong provinces, especially in the neighbouring regions where the three legal Maritime Trade Commissioner Offices were situated.

All classes of people became involved in this lucrative and illegal private trade and smuggling of banned products. A commentary written in the sixteenth century describes the scene in the late fifteenth century:[15]

"During the Chenghua (1465–87) and Hongzhi (1488–1505) reigns there had been rich families and wealthy households sailing on giant vessels to carry out overseas trade. [Together with] the dishonest people they secretly obtained benefits from this, but the government officials were not able to share their profits and rights openly. In the beginning they were satisfied with the huge profits but as time went on they united to form a joint force in making trouble and disorder. When it came to the Jiajing reign (1522–66) the situation was even worse."

Another reference in the *Veritable Records of the Chenghua Reign* recorded that in 1474 (tenth year Chenghua) Chen Jin, a junior clerk of the Ministry of Works, after an unsuccessful envoy trip to Champa went back home with a large entourage of merchants and private goods. Chen made a detour and stopped at Malacca and sold his goods, making an excuse of encountering a typhoon.[16]

Corruption also caused the Maritime Trade Commissioners to turn a blind eye to the illegal private trade passing through their offices. A good example of this happened in Guangzhou during the Chenghua reign. The notorious eunuch Wei Jun and his network of agents in Guandong amassed a huge fortune by monopolising fishing and salt-making in the region and privately joined with overseas merchants in foreign trade through Canton. It was said that his warehouse of precious and exotic goods even exceeded those of the government.[17]

These historical records serve to illustrate the chaotic scene along the coastal region of China. Private trading activities were common with a high level of involvement of all types of officials, eunuchs and commoners. Some of them were even armed with soldiers and ammunition to protect themselves, their vessels and goods. The sophistication of the organisation of these private endeavours foresaw the huge armed and well equipped private trading fleets and smuggling networks that were to develop along the Chinese coast in the succeeding Jiajing reign (1522–66).[18]

---

[14] Zhang Jingyue, et al., *Shangshi tongjian* (A Chronological Record of Commerce in China), Jiuzhou tushu chubanshe, Beijing, 1996, p. 596.

[15] Chen Wenshi, 1966, p. 101, quoting *Dongxi yang kao*, zhuan 7 on custom tax.

[16] Quoted in Lin Renchuan, *Ming mo Qing chu siren haishang moyi* (Private Maritime Trade in the Late Ming and Early Qing), Huadong Shifan daxue chubanshe, Shanghai, 1987, p. 65.

[17] Chen Wenshi, 1966, p. 102, quoting *Shuanghuai suichao*, zhuan 9.

[18] See Lin Renchuan, 1987, pp. 66–72, for a discussion of these massive fleets. See also R. L. Higgins, "Privates in Gowns and Caps: Gentry Lawbreaking in the Mid-Ming", *Ming Studies*, 10, Spring 1980, pp. 30–7.

By around 1500, with the expansion of Chinese illegal maritime trade, flourishing outlaw entrepots at Canton and Yuegang emerged. In the Zhengde reign (1506–21) ships from South-East Asian tributary states were allowed to come as frequently as they wished, without verifying their tallies, nor checking whether their goods exceeded the quota or not. They merely levied a simple customs tax and as a result both ports became very prosperous.[19]

This was the eve of the arrival of the Portuguese in the early decades of the sixteenth century, which opened a new era for foreign trade in China, and led to the final opening up of Yuegang for legal foreign trade in 1567. In 1557 the Portuguese were permitted to settle in Macao, and an important trading post was soon established.[20] It was the beginning of a new page in overseas trade in China.

4. China and the Philippines

Chinese vessels had been sailing to the Philippines for several hundred years before Ferdinand Magellan arrived at the islands in 1521.[21]

Following the flourishing private trading activities between China and the Philippines, many Chinese started to settle on the islands, especially in the sixteenth century. In the *Mingshi* (Official Dynastic History of the Ming) the following entries were recorded for the Philippines:[22]

"Luzon: Situated in the middle of the South Sea, Luzon is very near to Zhangzhou (in Fujian). Being so, and because the land is fertile, tens of thousands of Fujian merchants and other people went there. Many settled down and raised their children there."

"Mindoro (in Chinese 'Hemaoli' or 'Maoliwu'): Near Luzon. A great many vessels visit Mindoro and it has been flourishing. Chinese entering this country were treated with fair trading rules and were not bullied or cheated. There was a Chinese saying therefore: 'If one wants to be rich, he should go to Maoliwu'."

Fig. 20. Portrait of Ferdinand Magellan (1480–1521). © Corbis Agency.

"Sulu: The native people trade pearls with Chinese merchants. Large pearls may sell at ten times their original value. When the trade ships are about to return home, they often leave several people behind in the hope of coming back again."

Mindanao, the Sulu Islands, Palawan, Mindoro and Luzon of the Philippines had a long history of communication with China. They were on the list of states and countries issued with the kanhe tallies by the Ming government for official tribute missions to China. According to historical records,[23] the Great Eunuch Zheng He had three times (in 1405–06, 1408–10 and 1417) dispatched side expeditions to the Philippines. Places visited included Reyayin, Manila, Mindanao and Sulu.

In the Mingshi and the Veritable Records of the Ming Reign there are entries recording sixteen visits of tributary missions to China from the Philippine states, very often led personally by the kings and princes. The most impressive of these missions was in 1417 (fifteenth year of Yongle).[24]

The mission was led by the kings of the Sulu Islands, including the East King (Sulu), the West King (Calamian) and the consort of the King of Tong (Palawan),

---

[19] D. Twitchett and F. Mote, eds, *The Cambridge History of China, Vol. 8: The Ming Dynasty, 1368-1644, Part II*. Cambridge University Press, Cambridge, 1998, ch. 7. See also Li Jinming 1990, pp. 60–2.

[20] Chuan Han-sheng, "The Overseas Trade of Macao after the Mid-Ming Period", *The Journal of the Institute of Chinese Studies of the Chinese University of Hong Kong*, vol. 5, No. 1, 1972, pp. 245–72.

[21] Chinese historical sources on the Philippines have been exhaustively documented in Zhongshan Daxue, Dongnanya Lishi, Yanjiu Suo, eds, *Zhongguo guji zhong youguan Feilubin ziliao huibian* (A Collection of Documents on the Philippines found in Ancient Chinese Texts), Zhonghua shuju, Beijing, 1980.

[22] Quoted in Chen Wenshi, 1966, pp. 103–4. The Filipino equivalents of the Ming Chinese placenames have been identified according to Chen Jiarong, et al., 1986.

[23] Wang Jienan, *Zhongguo yu Dongnan Ya wenhua jiaoliu shi* (History of the Cultural Exchange between China and South-East Asia), Shanghai renmin chubanshe, Shanghai, 1998, p. 263.

[24] Shen Lixin, ed., *Zhongwai wenhua jiaoliu shihua* (History of Cultural Exchange between China and Foreign Countries), Huadong shifan daxue chubanshe, Shanghai, 1991, pp. 103–6. This is recorded in the *Veritable Records* as well, see Wang Yude, et al., ed., *Ming Shilu neisu, shewai shiliao zhuan* (Classified Veritable Records of the Ming: Volume on Foreign Matters), Wuhan chubanshe, Wuhan, 1991, pp. 548–9.

with an entourage of 340 members. They went all the way to Beijing and were well received by the Yongle Emperor who conferred to them official titles and bestowed on them official seals, edicts, robes, hats, garments and textiles together with other gifts. These gifts included jade belts with gold mounts, 100 *liang* of gold, 2,000 *liang* of platinum, 200 bolts of brocades, 300 bolts of satin, 10,000 *ding* of paper money, 3,000 strings of cash coins, and one set of golden embroidered robes with four-clawed dragons and *qilin*.

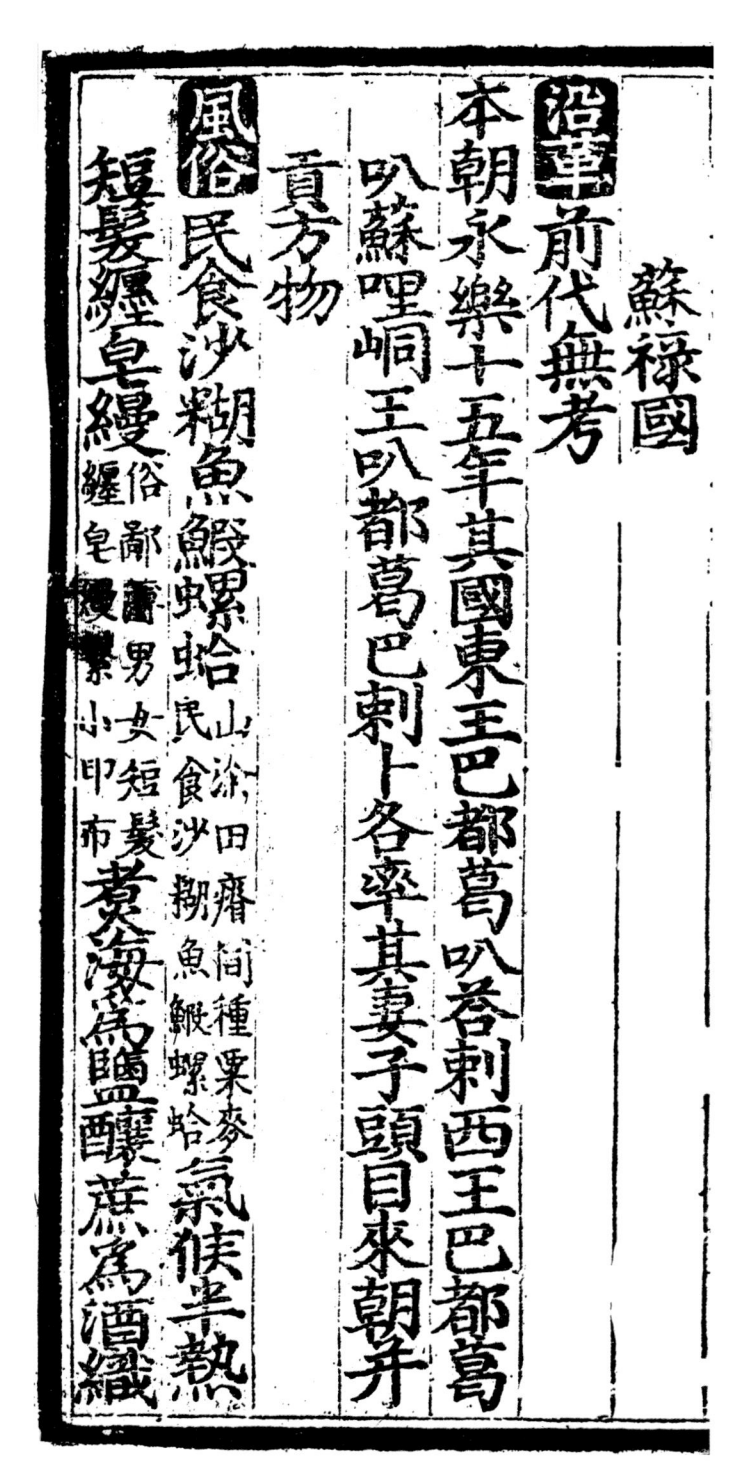

Fig. 21. Entry on Sulu from a fifteenth century Chinese publication. A page from *Da Ming yitong zhi* (Historical Geography of the Great Ming). Compiled by Li Xian in 1461. The passage mentioned the Yongle fifteenth year tribute trip of the Sulu prince.

The entourage left Beijing after eight months and went south through the Grand Canal. On the way, the East King died of illness in the Guest House in Dezhou, Shangdong. He was buried there, and the Yongle Emperor ordered the building of a grand scale tomb at the site. The king's consort, prince and attendants were asked to stay in China for three years to observe the mourning rites according to Chinese custom. After the mourning period, some of the family members of the king decided to stay in China, and the family has survived into modern times. The majestic tomb can also still be seen standing at the site. Probably because of this and other good deeds of the Sulu Island kings, the Philippines was regarded as a friendly state by the Ming, who extended special privileges to merchant ships coming from the islands, so much so that often, even when they came without a tally ticket, they were allowed to disembark and carry out trading activities in China.[25]

When summing up Chinese historical records[26] of the fifteenth and sixteenth centuries, it is possible to tabulate the native products that were produced in the Philippine Islands and sent to the Ming government as tribute items:

- Sulu Islands, Three Islands (Sulu, Jolo, Calamian, Palawan, Busuanga): *Meihua nao, minao*, various types of cotton cloth, tree cotton cloth, tortoise shell, incense, hardwood, pepper, yellow wax, tin, pearls, mother-of-pearl, round cardamom, parrots.
- Mayi, Maoliwu (Mindoro): Tree cotton, yellow wax, tortoise shell, betel nut, floral cloth, *jibei* flowers.
- Lusong (Luzon): Gold, silver coin, jibei flowers, hardwood, coconut.
- Shayao and Nabidan (Dapitan): Hardwood, *jibei* flowers.

It is interesting to see that pearl and hardwood were on the list. Pearls had been a precious export item from the Philippines for several centuries before this period and this has been thoroughly explored elsewhere.[27] It is reputed that in a tribute mission made by the Sulu kings in 1418, a huge pearl weighing 7.5 *liang* was offered to the Yongle Emperor.[28] It is also well known that gold was mined in Luzon.

---

[25] Shen Guangyao, *Zhongguo gudai duiwai moyi shi* (History of Overseas Trade in Ancient China), Guangdong renmin chubanse, Guangzhou, 1985, p. 257.

[26] The sources include *Ming huidian*, two memoirs relating to the Zheng He's expeditions, the *Xingcho shenglan* and *Yingai shengan*, and the sixteenth century *Dongxi yang kao*. After Zhang Weihua, *Mingdai haiwai moyi jianlun* (A Brief Introduction to the Overseas Trade in the Ming Dynasty), Shanghai renmin chubanshe, Shanghai, 1956, p. 72.

[27] C. Loviny, *The Pearl Road, Tales of Treasure Ships*, Asiatype, Makati City, 1996.

[28] Shen Guangyao, 1985, p. 257.

Chinese commodities imported into the Philippines would almost definitely have also included, as in all South-East Asian countries, silk and other textile products, porcelain wares, iron implements and copper cash coins. Ceramics, unlike other organic material such as silk, are always found preserved in mint condition, even after being submerged in the sea or buried in soil for hundreds of years, silently witnessing the busy overseas trade over the ages. The Lena Shoal wreck is certainly no exception.

The arrival of the Spaniards in the Philippines in the mid-sixteenth century completely changed the scene and saw a revolutionary expansion in Sino-Filipino trade. The Spaniards' eagerness to seek out the merchandise produced in China, silk in particular, in exchange for Mexican silver carried by the galleons, resulted in an unprecedented flourishing of trade. New and shorter sea routes were opened up by direct sailing from Quanzhou in Fujian, calling only at south Taiwan, instead of the earlier and longer route via Quanzhou, Champa and Borneo.

Fig. 22. Barbarian couple from Sulu. Woodblock from *Huang Qing zhigongtu* (Pictures of Tribute Bearers to the Great Qing Empire). Reprinted from *Siku chuanshu* (The Siku Encyclopedia), 1782.

Fig. 23. Spanish couple in Luzon. Woodblock illustration from *Huang Qing zhigongtu* (Pictures of Tribute Bearers to the Great Qing Empire). Reprinted from *Siku chuanshu* (The Siku Encyclopedia), 1782.

Every year some 30 to 40 ships would have sailed to the Philippines from Fujian, carrying on board not only commercial items, but also petty pedlars, bankrupted farmers and artisans, all looking forward to settling down to a new life in the Philippines. They brought with them Chinese technology, such as agriculture with the aid of oxen, metal refinery, hemp-weaving, ceramic-firing, mining, wine-brewing, sugar-making, etc. In return, the sweet potato, tobacco and peanuts were introduced into China through Fujian.[29] But these developments were in the future, well beyond the scope of this overview of the uneventful year 1500.

5. Yards and sea-faring vessels of the Ming period

The shipyards of the Ming period were located along the coastal provinces of Guangdong, Fujian and Zhejiang, but the earliest and largest one was the official yard, the *Baoquan Chang* (Treasure Ship Yards) in Nanjing,[30] set up by the Hongwu Emperor in the early part of his reign. Joseph Needham gave a very detailed description of this yard: "...This view of part of the yards is taken looking approximately south at the strip of land between the walls of the city of Nanjing on the left and the Chhin-huai Ho (river) debouching into the Yangtze at the bottom of the right... At the top of the plan is Ma-an Shan, a hill now within the city-walls, and to its left, inside them, Kua-pang Shan is labelled, the 'hill of hanging up the pass-lists of successful candidates'.

In the left-hand half of the picture from top to bottom we can make out first the main gate (*Ta Men*), then the superintendant's headquarters (*Thi-Chu Ssu*), the foremen's offices (*Tso Fang*), various administrative sections (*Fen Ssu*), the sail loft (*Pheng Chhang*), and the naval liaison command (*Chih-Hui Chu*) marked by a flag. All around are wide fields (yu ma thien) in which hemp was grown to yield oakum for caulking. In the right-hand half of the picture two shipyards are seen with their shipways and docks, the *Chhien Chhang* above and the *Hou Chhang* below; between them there is a guard post (*Hsun She*) marked by another flag. The entrances of the channels are crossed by two floating bridges, the smaller (*Hsiao Fou-Chhao*) above, and the larger (*Ta Fou-chhiao*) below; these carry the road along the bank of Chhin-huai River."

This official yard was under the Ministry of Works from which the superintendent was appointed, while the Ministry of War would send his troops to guard the premises. Craftsmen and ship-builders from all over the country – Zhejiang, Fujian, Hunan, Hubei and Guangdong, and Jiangxi in particular – were recruited to

---

[29] Zhongshan Daxue, Dongnanya Lishi, Ynjiu Suo, eds, 1980, pp. 3–4.
[30] Wang Guanzhuo, 1991, p. 41 et Needham 1971, p. 483.

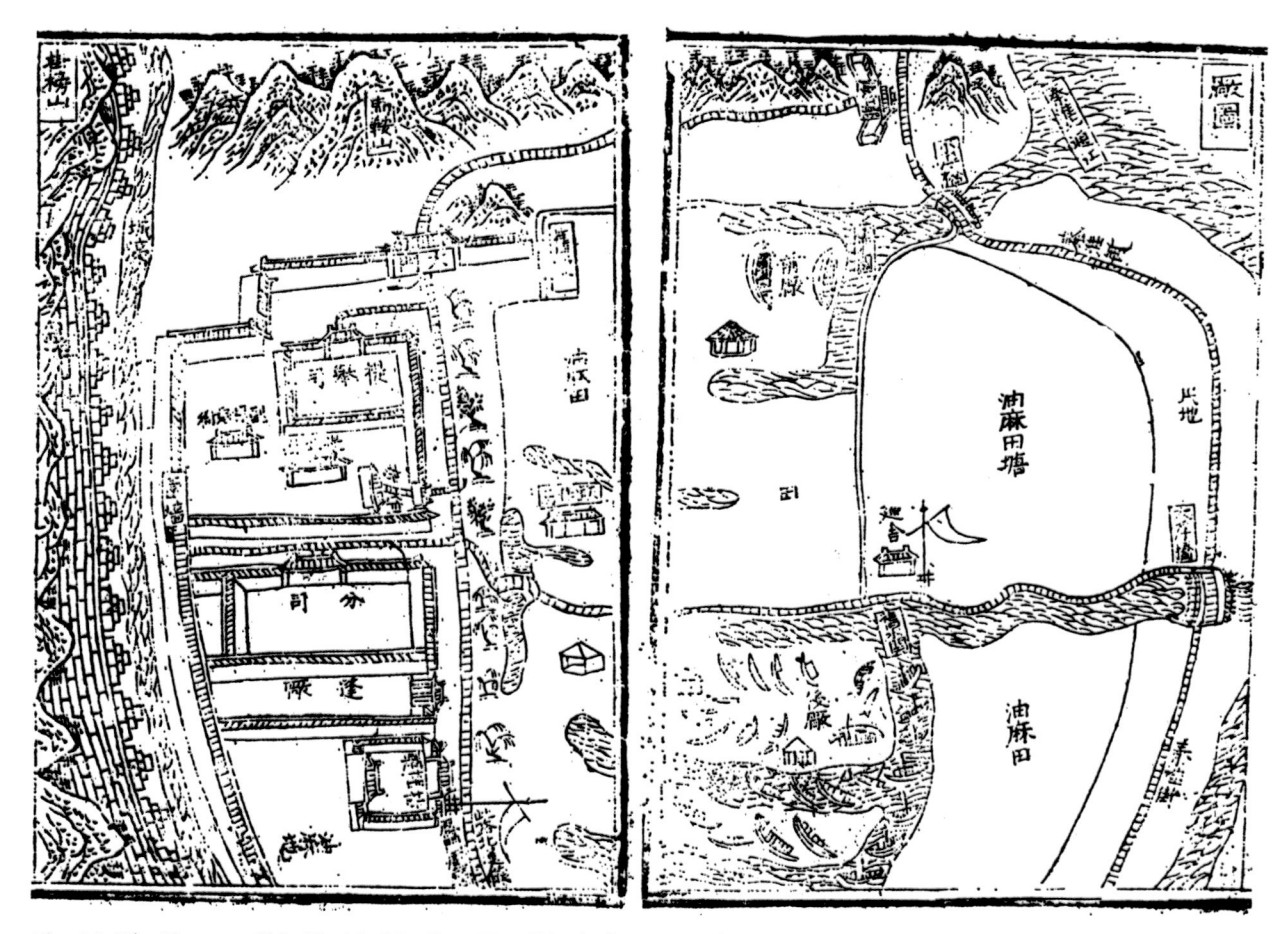

Fig. 24. The Treasure Ship Yard in Nanjing. Woodblock illustration from the 1553 edition of the *Longjiang Chuanchang zhi*. (After Needham, 1971, p. 483.)

work there. At the beginning there were 400 resident households working and divided into four *xiang*, divisions. All of the *Baoquan* treasure ships for the Zheng He voyages in the early fifteenth century were built here. A branch of this yard was in Liujiajiang, Taicang, from where all the treasure ships set sail for their expeditions.

Following the enforcement of the maritime prohibitions, a large part of the yard felt into disuse and its size shrank considerably in the second half of the fifteenth century. In 1541 (twentieth year Jiajing) the number of the workmen was reduced to 245 and later 200 households. The name of the yard was then changed to Longjiang Chuanchhang. It was still managed by the government, but the main output was now for official warships and inland passenger boats.

Apart from this yard in Nanjing, there were two more official yards devoted to the building of *Caochuan*, boats for carrying grains and provisions through the Grand Canal and coastal regions to the capital in Beijing. Both yards were located along the Grand Canal – the *Qingjiang Chuanchang* (in Qingjiang city, north Jiangsu Province) and the *Weihe Chuanchang* (in Linqing, Shangdong Province).

After the mid Ming period, following the success of the private maritime trade and smuggling, a great many private yards in Zhejiang, Fujian and Guangdong emerged. "Many large families built huge ships to go to foreign countries for overseas trade."[31] Longqi and Songyu in Zhangzhou and Hongtang in Fuzhou, all within the Fujian Province, were known to be popular sites for these illegal ship-building enterprises.

To avoid investigation from the police, it was customary for the smugglers to order these illegal ships in provinces other than their native one. For example, Fujian merchants would go to Guangdong to build their vessels and Zhejiang and Guangdong smugglers would approach Fujian yards to place their orders.[32] These private yards

---

[31] Lin Renchuan, 1987, p. 24, quoting *Fujian tongzhi*, zhuan 34.

[32] Op cit.

Fig. 25. Drawing of a five-masted freighter to give some indication of the probable type of build of the much larger treasure ships of the fleet of Zheng He in the fifteenth century. (After Needham, 1971, p. 510.)

LOST AT SEA

would then tailor ships according to their needs and specific sea routes.

Three main categories of these ships are known of, namely the *Fuchuan* (Fujian ship), the *Guangchuan* (Guangdong ship) and the *Shachuan* (Jiangsu and Zhejiang ship). The latter had a flat bottom and multiple masts adapted to the shallow waters along the Zhejiang coast. Both Fujian and Guangdong ships had a pointed hull and were more suitable for travel in deep waters and rough seas. Guangdong ships were heavier than the Fujian ones, because they were built of hardwood (*tieli mu*).

Illustrations of these three types of ships can be found in almost all treatises on military boats and ships of the Ming dynasty.[33] Fujian and Guangdong ships continued to be produced into the later Qing dynasty. To have lasted over several centuries, and as witnessed by a superb drawing in Zhou Huang, *Liuqui guo zhilue* (Gazetteer of the Ryukyu State) in 1757,[34] these ships must have been the major sea-faring vessels of the Chinese.

---

[33] Cited and illustrated in full in *Wang Guanzhuo*, 1991, these treatises include Shen Qi, *Nanchuan ji*; Li Zhaoxiang, *Longjiang chuanchang ji*; Hu Zongxian, *Chouhai tubian*; and Mao Yuanyi, *Wubei zhi*.

[34] Needham, 1971, pp. 404–406.

Fig. 26. A *Shachuan* freighter in full sails. (After Wang Guanzhuo, 1991, p. 119.)

Fig. 27. A large Fujian warship. Woodblock illustration from a Ming treatise. (After Lin Renchuan, 1987, frontispiece illustration.)

Fig. 28. A Guangdong warship. Woodblock illustration from a Ming treatise. (After Lin Renchuan, 1987, frontispiece illustration.)

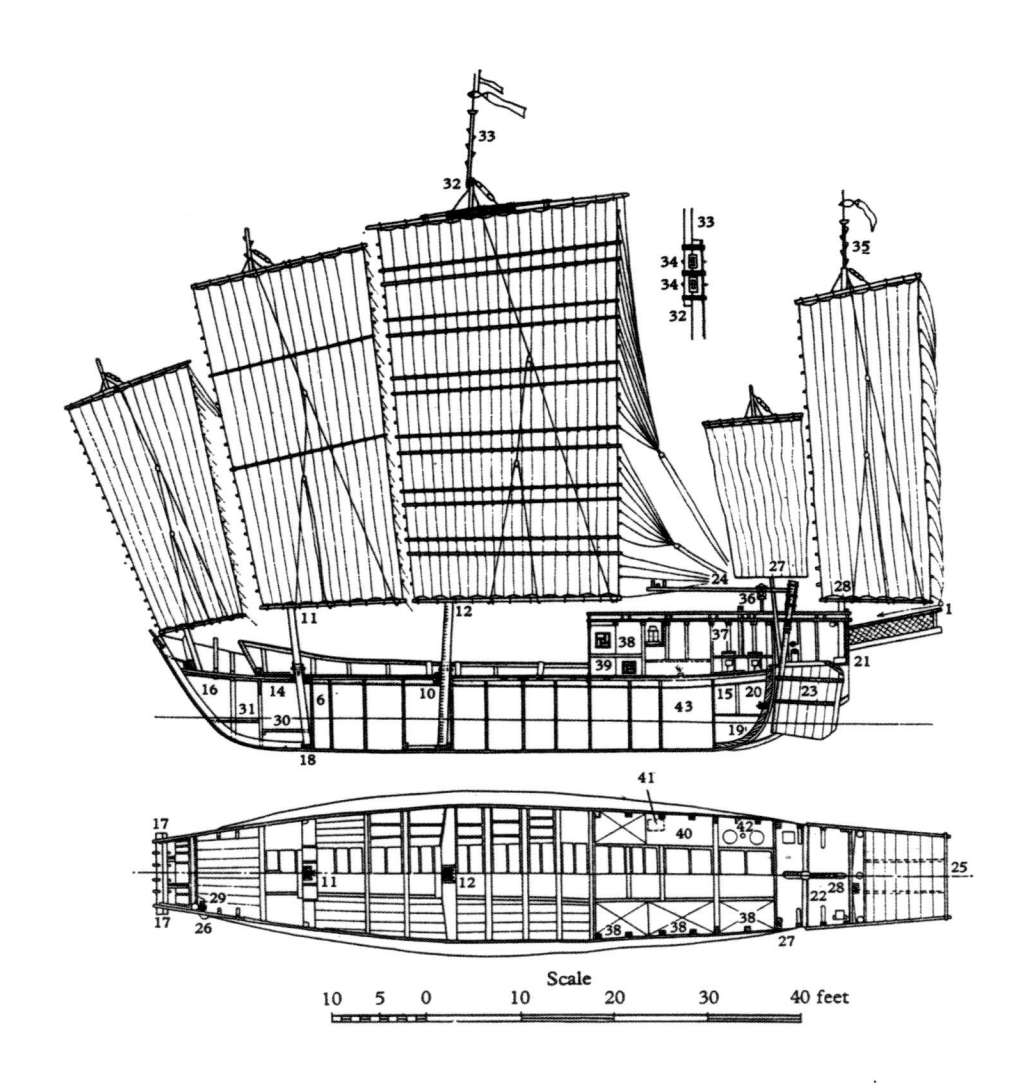

Fig. 29. Drawing of a *Shachuan* freighter. (After Needham, 1971, p. 400.)

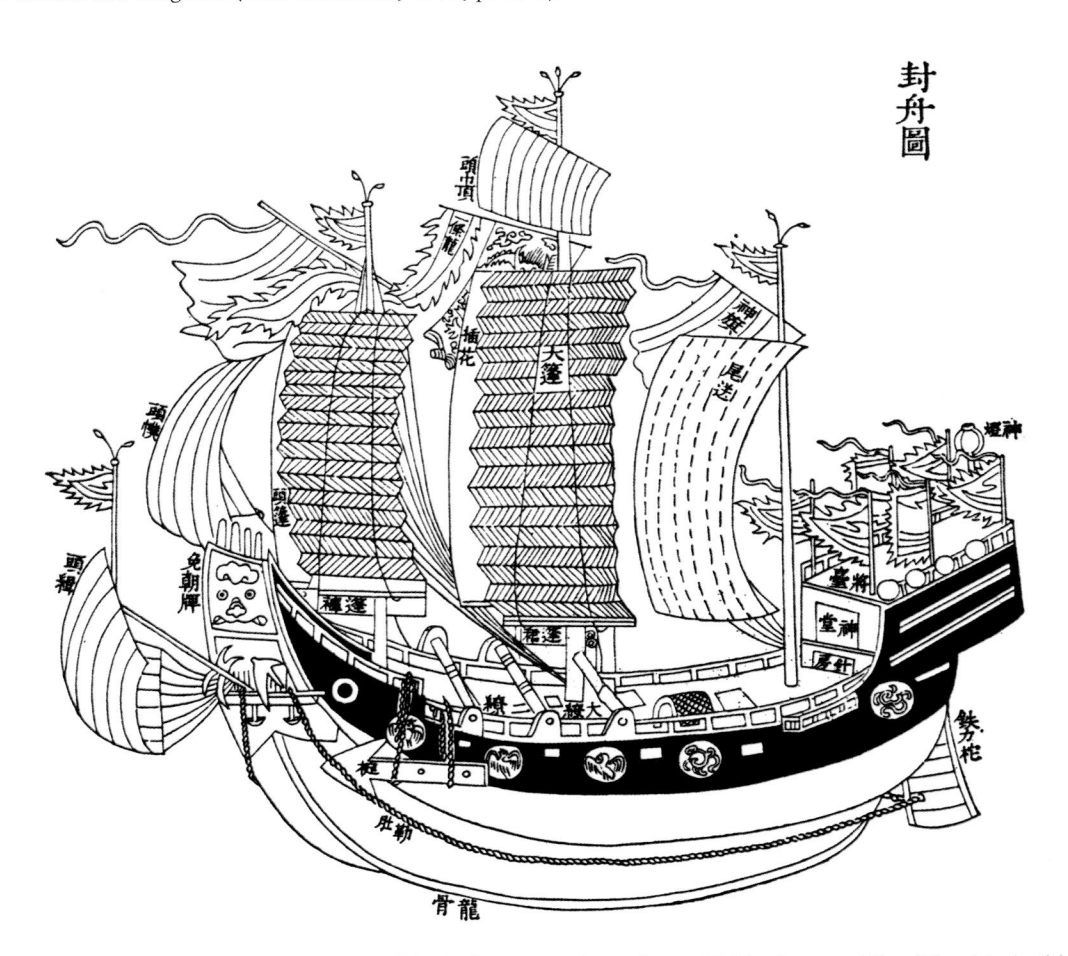

Fig. 30. A *Fengzhou*, government ocean-going junk. Woodblock illustration from the 1757 *Liuqiu guo zhilue*. The ship build matches the descriptions in two earlier memoirs of envoy trips to the Ryukyu Islands in 1532 and 1605, and must have followed earlier prototypes. (After Needham, 1971, p. 405.)

Fig. 31. Map of Chinese kiln sites.

INDUSTRIAL CERAMICS IN CHINA
ceramic production at Jingdezhen from the 10th to the 16th century

Stacey Pierson

Chinese porcelain is perhaps the most influential ceramic ever produced and the most successful type of Chinese porcelain was, and still is, "blue and white". Blue and white porcelain was invented in north China in the ninth century but the main centre for production was Jingdezhen in south-east China.

Located in Raozhou prefecture, Jiangxi province, Jingdezhen is ideally situated for the production of ceramics because the area provides abundant raw materials including china clay and porcelain stone, good transportation by river and plenty of fuel for ceramic manufacture. Jingdezhen became prominent as a ceramic production centre during the Southern Song dynasty (1125–1279 AD) after the country was divided and both the political and economic centre of China was concentrated in the south-east. Ever since then porcelains have been produced there continuously up to the present day.

Today, Jingdezhen is one of the largest ceramic factories in China and is still producing ceramics in imitation of ancient imperial wares along with modern "art" porcelain and the table wares for which they became famous. As a result of this long history of production, Jingdezhen is studied today for both its history as a ceramic factory and for the history of its wares.

1. The industrial complex

Historically, Jingdezhen cannot be described as a "factory" in the usual sense, where production is concentrated under one roof. Instead, Jingdezhen is a porcelain city where, in the past, numerous small factories and kilns were operating alongside designated imperial kilns in a vast industrial complex. The imperial history of Jingdezhen begins in the late fourteenth century but its production methods and system of organisation were established early on, in the Southern Song period, with specialisation and division of labour developing as a result of the scale of production.

This system remained relatively the same until the sixteenth century when changes in taxation introduced independent labour to the factories. Prior to this, taxation was based on land, and families were required to supply

Photo 32. Dish with underglaze cobalt blue decoration, Ming dynasty, Xuande mark and period, 1426–35 AD. PDF B679.

labour in proportion to the number of men in the household.[1] The first phase of industrial development at Jingdezhen thus ended in the mid sixteenth century.

In its second phase, the scale of production increased to vast levels in order to supply the expanding European markets. Millions of porcelains were produced at this time and production on such a scale was heavily dependent on a large and well organised labour force.[2]

The products of post-Tang period (618–906) Jingdezhen can therefore be described as "industrial ceramics". For many years these world famous ceramics have garnered more interest than the factory itself, but interest in ceramic technology has shifted attention to production methods in more recent years. There is, however, some resistance among collectors and dealers to the description of Jingdezhen wares as "industrial ceramics" because such descriptions of objects are usually pejorative.

In China however, "mass produced" does not always mean "cheap and cheerful". In fact, it can be argued that the reason there is so much "ancient" Chinese art available today is because such objects were often mass produced, but this has had little or no effect on their current value as "art objects", mainly because of their extremely high quality and their antiquity. A discussion of Jingdezhen production must therefore acknowledge the multiplicity of items produced as well as the skill involved in such large-scale production.

In a recently published study of mass production in Chinese art, Lothar Ledderose discusses the use of what he calls "modular systems", or systems of individual components, in Chinese material culture. One of the case studies he includes is the industrial complex of Jingdezhen. In view of China's long history of mass production methods, he states: "It is no accident that porcelain belongs to the range of goods for which the Chinese developed mass-production methods involving modular systems."[3] This is because Jingdezhen developed relatively late in Chinese history and mass produced ceramics had been manufactured there as early as the Neolithic period. Ledderose then compares porcelain production with that of the famous "terracotta army" manufactured in the second century BC for the mausoleum of the first emperor. "The terracotta army was another outstanding demonstration of proficiency in ceramic technology. But the crowning achievement in this field was the invention of porcelain."[4]

As an example of industrialisation and mass production methods in China, Jingdezhen is ideal, because its development as a ceramic centre parallels that of industry in China. It was in the Song and Yuan dynasties (eleventh to fourteenth centuries) that south China became the focus of a great increase in trade.[5] The trade routes included sea routes to South-East Asia, the Near East and areas between.

Trade in commodities was a major source of revenue for the government at this time and was thus carefully organised. New ships were also designed which were able to transport far more by sea than was possible previously by land. At Jingdezhen, this coincided with an increase in patronage when the court moved south to Hangzhou (Zhejiang province) in 1127. From being an area which had been used for limited local production in the Tang period, Jingdezhen soon became the primary source for table wares in the latter part of the Song dynasty.

At this time the kilns were privately owned by families who also operated them. This represented a change from casual to systematic organisation of production. The early workers at the kilns had been agricultural labourers, but in the Song dynasty they were replaced by trained craftsmen. Eventually, a highly skilled labour force was formed with the consequent development of related industries such as mining, transport and trading.[6]

From the thirteenth century, a deliberate policy of industrialisation was initiated with merchants gathering together in syndicates to provide the finance for high level production, including arranging transport and distribution over a large area and handling sales for the export trade. The consequent increase in production at Jingdezhen and the pressure exerted to maintain this increase in accordance with the specific requirements of foreign trade led to profound changes in kilns all over China, but especially at Jingdezhen where porcelain production was concentrated from the late thirteenth century onward.

The highly skilled labour force now consisted of workers who specialised in different processes and firing was controlled in kilns constructed to properly established standards in size and capacity. The firing was managed by kiln-masters with semi-skilled labourers, often on short-

---

[1] R. Scott and R. Kerr, *Ceramic Evolution in the Middle Ming Period*, Victoria & Albert Museum/Percival David Foundation, London, 1994, p. 5.

[2] Freestone and D. Gaimster, eds, *Pottery in the Making, vol 1*, British Museum Press, London, 1997, p. 19.

[3] L. Ledderose, *Ten Thousand Things: Module and Mass Production in Chinese Art*, Princeton, 2000, p. 85.

[4] Ibid.

[5] See P. Wheatley, "Geographical Notes on some Commodities Involved in Sung Maritime Trade", *Journal of the Malay Branch of the Royal Asiatic Society*, vol. 32, 1959, for discussion.

[6] See M. Medley, *The Chinese Potter*, London, 1976, pp. 169–71.

term contracts, to help with setting, stoking and unpacking the kilns. For the actual ceramics, moulding was used extensively as a means of shaping and, to an extent, decorating, and skilled throwers using the fast-wheel and templates could produce vast numbers of standardised wares.[7] This standardisation was achieved with a resultant general decline in quality, but very high quality wares could still be produced when they were required.

These standardised, industrial methods of production continued into the Ming period, but throughout that long dynasty, from the late fourteenth to the seventeenth century, the political and economic climate of the country as a whole had profound effects on ceramic production. In some periods, for example, demands from the court were such that the imperial kilns could not cope and the work was contracted out to popular, non-imperial kilns in the area. The basic production process remained the same throughout the dynasty however. According to historical records, such as the *Tian gong kai wu* (Creations of Nature and Man) of 1637, the general process was as follows:

"White clay is obtained from two [nearby] mountains and then moulded into square blocks, and transported to Jingdezhen on small boats. The clays are then mixed, decanted and then dried. The dried clay is mixed with water to form a paste which is used to make the porcelain body. Vessels are then moulded and constructed or thrown on the wheel and polished. The ware is then decorated and sprayed with water before glazing. The liquid glaze used at Jingdezhen for white porcelain is composed of water, clay and ash from the leaves of peach bamboo. The vessels are dipped in glaze vats made from large water jars. After glazing, the wares are packed into box frames or saggars using clay discs and sand for support. The kiln is then loaded with packed saggars and the fire kindled. The firing lasts for 24 hours and is stopped when a specimen removed from the kiln is deemed to be sufficiently heated."[8]

As we have seen, each of these processes was managed by a different person or group of people who were specialists, with the most difficult tasks, such as supervision of firing, managed by "masters". Throughout the period leading up to the mid-sixteenth century, advances in preparation methods and kiln technology were made. The range of techniques continued to broaden at the same time and the advent of imperial reign marks in the early fifteenth century formally designated different levels of production so that "imperial" wares could be distinguished from "popular" wares for the domestic market made by satellite kilns and from export wares. It was in the second year of the Hongwu reign period (1368–98) that the Ming imperial kilns were established. The evidence for this is both literary and archaeological, as in 1990 saggars marked *guan xia* (imperial saggar) were excavated from the early Ming stratum at Zhushan.[9] Reign marks were not applied until the early Yongle period, however, but continued to be used after that period, mainly on imperial pieces. It was also in the Ming dynasty that the famous Jingdezhen "egg-shaped" kiln design (*zhenyao*) was introduced, which is one of the most efficient kiln designs ever devised.[10]

---

[7] Medley, op. cit., 1976, p. 171.

[8] Sung Ying-Hsing, Tian gong kai wu *Chinese Technology in the Seventeenth Century*, Pennsylvania State University Press, 1966, pp. 147–54. The actual text goes into much greater detail than is summarised above.

[9] *Jingdezhen chutu taoci* (Ceramics from the Jingdezhen kilns), The Fung Pingshan Museum, University of Hong Kong, 1992, p. 50.

[10] N. Wood, *Chinese Glazes*, London, 1999, pp. 67–8.

2. The ceramics

Kilns in the Jingdezhen area began producing ceramics in the late Tang or Five Dynasties period (907–60).[11] As discussed earlier, the area is rich in raw materials as well as wood for fuel and it is these raw materials which make this site unique and which have enabled the factory to produce fine porcelains on such a wide scale. The earliest products of the kilns were simple green wares or celadons with a greyish body composed of china stone combined with a high iron clay and a yellowish green or bluish green lime glaze.[12] In 1980, a kiln that produced white wares in this period was discovered and revealed that white porcelain with a pure china stone body was also produced in conjunction with the green wares.[13]

The ceramics of this early period were therefore mainly celadons and white wares, but not of very high quality. The forms were mainly bowls and dishes, usually undecorated and not fired in saggars. However, a few very high quality white porcelains were produced with fine, translucent bodies. These were fired in saggars and were glazed on the base. The glazes for the white wares are of the lime-alkali type rather than the lime glazes used for celadons and it has been suggested that the glaze was composed of body material and crushed limestone.[14] This lime-alkali glaze was not used beyond the tenth century at Jingdezhen. Recent analyses show that this glaze was replaced by a glaze much higher in limestone that was wonderfully transparent and slightly bluish.[15] This was known as the *qingbai* or *yingqing* glaze.

These early porcelains are not in fact the earliest porcelains produced in China, as porcelain was made in north China at the Gongxian kilns in Henan province from as early as the sixth century AD.[16] It is Jingdezhen porcelains however which dominated the market from the Yuan period onwards.

In the Five Dynasties and Northern Song periods, northern porcelain was the more commercially successful product, at a time when the Chinese court was located in the north. It was in the Song dynasty that the most famous of the early Jingdezhen porcelains, *qingbai* ware, was first produced on a large scale and became the dominant Chinese porcelain with the shift in political centres. *Qingbai* can be translated as "blue white" and this ware is also known by the alternative name of *yingqing* which means "shadowy blue". In ancient texts it is referred to as "Raozhou ware" after Raozhou prefecture where Jingdezhen is located. This became the dominant product of the kilns as they began to specialise in white wares at this time.

The most important kilns producing *qingbai* ware at Jingdezhen were Hutian and Nanshan, but it was also produced at Huangnitou, Xianghu and Yangmeiding.[17]

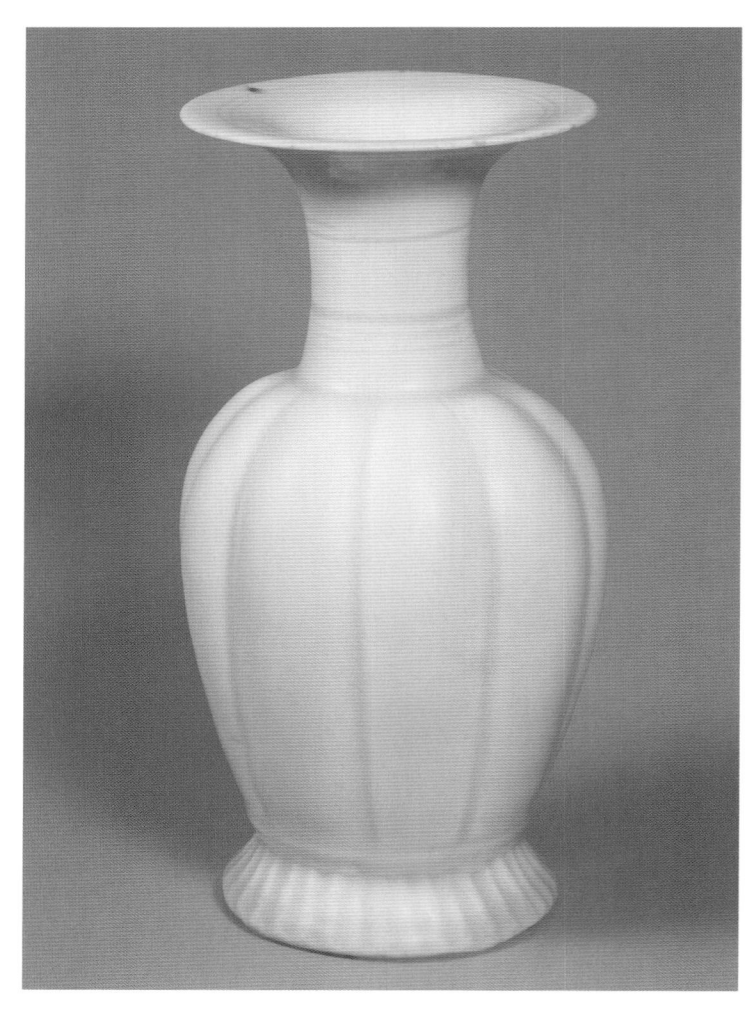

Photo 33. Lobed vase with *qingbai* glaze. Song dynasty, late 11th to early 12th c. Percival David Foundation; PDF A496.

Accordingly, the shapes of the porcelains became more varied to include bowls, dishes, vases, boxes, figures and other more complex forms. The market for *qingbai* wares and Chinese ceramics in general now included countries which were actively trading with China, including Japan and South-East Asia.

Over the course of the Song dynasty, the number of kilns at Jingdezhen increased dramatically.[18] Celadon

---

[11] The earliest excavated sherds and vessels date to this period. See The Fung Pingshan Museum, 1992, plates 1–14.

[12] The Fung Pingshan Museum, 1992, p. 69.

[13] Ibid.

[14] Wood, 1999, p. 49.

[15] See Wood, 1999, p. 51, for analyses.

[16] See J. Harrison-Hall in Freestone and Gaimster, 1997, p. 182, for discussion.

[17] The Fung Pingshan Museum, 1992, p. 36.

[18] For example, sites that produced *qingbai* ware have been found scattered over 30 villages at Jingdezhen. The Fung Pingshan Museum, 1992, p. 47.

production ceased and mainly white wares and *qingbai* wares were produced. The one exception to this is the kiln site at Hutian which also produced black wares in imitation of Jian *temmoku* ware. The quality of ceramics improved and they were now generally fired in saggars. The number of different styles produced also increased dramatically with new types of decoration not seen in the Five Dynasties, such as incising and stamping with a wide range of designs. A number of *qingbai* wares have recently been excavated from Song tombs and it appears that some *qingbai* ware was imperial or made for tribute to the emperor.[19] Traditionally, *qingbai* ware has been seen as strictly non-imperial because it does not generally appear in any official inventories or collections.

The best products of the Song kilns are mainly very high quality. In the early Yuan dynasty, quality declined somewhat overall but very fine wares continued to be made alongside coarser wares. Less *qingbai* ware was produced and instead the fine wares of the Yuan dynasty were mainly plain white glazed wares, including *shufu* and blue and white wares. The coarse wares were grey-green celadons and black-glazed wares.

Liu Xinyuan states that the "great disparity in quality of Yuan wares was a reflection of the polarisation between the rich and the poor" in that period.[20] The most important kiln sites of this period were Hutian, Luomaqiao and Zhushan, and the scale of production gradually increased in response to the export trade in blue and white wares.

In 1283, during the Yuan dynasty, the official Bureau for Imperial Manufactures was established and ceramic production was controlled by the Fuliang Porcelain Office.[21] This means, effectively, that the imperial kilns were first set up in the Yuan dynasty and that the highest quality wares were in fact among the earliest "imperial" porcelains.

Official porcelain production in the Yuan period has been confirmed by recent excavations and finds from tombs and hoards.[22] Most official porcelain was monochrome glazed but there are some that can be defined as "official" blue and white wares. The most important surviving Yuan blue and white wares are not however "official" but are a pair of vases made for a temple and dated by inscription to 1351.

The "David vases", as they are known today, show how sophisticated blue and white decoration was by the second half of the Yuan dynasty, even though very few earlier examples have been identified. As the earliest dated examples, they are very useful for identifying key features of Yuan blue and white decoration, including the style of painting, the arrangement of motifs over the surface of the vessels and the so-called "heaping and piling" of the cobalt pigment containing excess iron which precipitates on the surface and oxidises, leaving brown or blackish patches. The David vases can be compared to the large number of blue and white wares in Near Eastern collections, including Iran and Istanbul, which show different styles and forms made for export in the same period.[23]

In the second half of the fourteenth century, vast quantities of blue and white wares were produced at Jingdezhen and this scale of production was interrupted only slightly by the change of rulers from the end of the Yuan period to the beginning of the Ming. In fact, the porcelains of the early Ming period are often indistinguishable from those of the later Yuan period, with the exception of the overall emphasis on underglaze copper red decoration in the Hongwu period (1368–1402) when supplies of imported cobalt would have been relatively inaccessible.[24]

Copper red decoration has a long history at Jingdezhen and can be seen on Yuan *qingbai* wares as well as early Ming imperial wares. This style of decoration was generally held in high esteem by the Hongwu Emperor, as evidenced by the porcelain tiles decorated with copper red dragons and phoenixes found at the site of the Nanjing palace.[25]

The Hongwu Emperor's greatest influence on porcelain production was, however, his famous decree of 1369, which stated that ritual vessels for imperial altars should be made of porcelain, not metal or jade as was the practice previously. This edict is recorded in the *Da Ming hui dian*[26] and it had the effect of increasing production of official porcelains as well as introducing prescribed monochrome colours for porcelains which corresponded

---

[19] See Peng Shifan, ed., *Dated* Qingbai *Wares of the Song and Yuan Dynasties*, Ching Leng Foundation, 1998 and The Fung Pingshan Museum, 1992, p. 46.

[20] The Fung Pingshan Museum, 1992, p. 38.

[21] The Fung Pingshan Museum, 1992, p. 47.

[22] Liu Xinyuan in Scott, 1992, pp. 36–7

[23] See J.A. Pope, *Chinese Porcelains from the Ardebil Shrine*, Freer Gallery of Art, Smithsonian Institution, Washington D.C., 1956 and J. Ayers and R. Krahl, *Chinese Ceramics in the Topkapi Saray Museum, Istanbul*, vols I & II, Sotheby's Publications, London, 1986.

[24] See *Imperial Hongwu and Yongle porcelain excavated at Jingdezhen*, Chang Foundation, Taipei, 1996, for examples of both underglaze blue and underglaze red decorated porcelains of the Hongwu period.

[25] *A Legacy of the Ming: Ceramic Finds from the Site of the Ming Palace in Nanjing*, Nanjing Museum and the Art Museum of the Chinese University of Hong Kong, Hong Kong, 1996, p. 35.

[26] See C. Lau in "The porcelains of Jingdezhen", Colloquies on Art & Archaeology in Asia, No. 16, R. Scott, ed., Percival David Foundation, London, 1992, p. 86.

Photo 34. Pair of temple vases, the "David vases", with underglaze cobalt blue decoration. Yuan dynasty, dated 1351. PDF B613, B614.

Photo 35. Ewer with underglaze copper red decoration, Ming dynasty, Hongwu period, late 14th c. PDF A696.

to the four imperial altars: red for the altar of the sun, blue for the altar of Heaven, white for the moon and yellow for the earth.[27]

Photo 36. Monk's cap ewer with incised decoration and *tian bai* glaze. Ming dynasty, Yongle period, 1403–24. PDF A426.

Although the use of underglaze copper red is associated with the early Ming period, it continued to be used throughout the first half of the fifteenth century when production of imperial porcelains increased dramatically with a consequent increase in new styles of decoration and decorative techniques. At the same time, the body material and glaze recipe also changed to accommodate new forms and decorative techniques, including overglaze enamels which were used tentatively in the late Yuan period but not extensively until the fifteenth century. The enamel palette was fairly limited, being restricted to primary colours, and the lead base for the colours necessitated a lower firing temperature. The earliest Ming examples can be found on Hongwu porcelains excavated from the site of the Nanjing palace, but these were merely a single enamel colour on a white ground. It was in the Xuande period (1426–35) that multiple enamel colours were first used on a single piece and this culminated in the exquisite *doucai* decoration of the Chenghua period (1465–87).

The high-fired glaze, used on both underglaze blue and red wares and enamelled wares, was less fluid than that used on Yuan Jingdezhen porcelains as it contained less flux in the form of glaze ash and more glaze stone.[28] This ensured that the decoration was less prone to running and that monochrome colours such as copper red were more even.

The body material had also been adjusted so that it contained more clay, in the form of kaolin, which was added in ever greater proportions to the porcelain stone base material. This change occurred gradually and first began in the Yuan period when larger vessels and figures were beginning to be made. By the second quarter of the fifteenth century, the proportion of kaolin in the body clay mixture was much higher, which made for a much smoother and more workable body. At the same time, local Chinese cobalt began to be used in greater quantities and the "heaped and piled" effect seen on earlier blue and white wares gradually disappeared.

The Jingdezhen porcelains of the second half of the fifteenth century are among the most sophisticated ever produced at that factory. The Chenghua period in particular is renowned for its "perfect" porcelains and this is confirmed by the large number of wasters discovered in the Chenghua levels at Jingdezhen. Standards of quality control were very high and large numbers of "imperfect" porcelains were discarded as a result. Analysis of the body material also show that high quality raw materials were used and these were combined with extremely skilful painting and potting.

The so-called "palace bowls" are a perfect example of the high quality of Chenghua imperial porcelains. This is evident, not only in the clarity of glaze and purity of body material but also in the highly skilled painting technique which made use of two brushes of different sizes and delicate washes of blue. The "orange peel" surface of the glaze, which was common in the Xuande period, also disappeared.

After the death of the Chenghua Emperor in 1485 and the succession of his third son, the Hongzhi Emperor, the fifteenth century style of Jingdezhen porcelain began to decline, along with the general prosperity of the country after the profligacy of the earlier emperors. In ceramic terms, very little changed in the Hongzhi period with the exception of the painting style which is somewhat less skilful than in the Chenghua period. This can be seen very clearly on another dated temple vase in the Percival David

---

[27] Ibid.

[28] Wood, 1999, p. 58.

Photo 37. Jar with underglaze blue and overglaze enamel decoration in *doucai* style, Ming dynasty, Chenghua mark and period, 1465–87. PDF 797.

Photo 38. Bowl with copper red glaze, Ming dynasty, Xuande mark and period, 1426–35. PDF A529.

Foundation (see Photo 42, p. 70). This very rare piece confirms that the most common decorative motifs in this period were large-scale floral designs and dragons. It can also be seen that the porcelains of the Hongzhi period are somewhat rigid in style and that the body material had declined in purity as clay deposits began to run out and new sources were sought. The imperial wares of this period show very little change in decorative style, but the export wares exhibit interesting combinations of fifteenth century motifs which look forward to sixteenth century styles. Without the restraints of imperial taste, the export wares could appeal to popular taste as dictated by the market.

While the blue and white wares of the Hongzhi period are in general fairly conservative, new styles did emerge at Jingdezhen which became very popular in the succeeding sixteenth century, including *fahua* wares and enamel-on-biscuit decoration. Thus, the Hongzhi period closes the fifteenth century with porcelain production somewhat in transition, as reflected in the styles and techniques produced at the time.

In the sixteenth century the Jingdezhen kilns were reorganised and working practices changed to such a degree that a second phase in the history of Jingdezhen can be said to begin with the reign of Zhengde. The latter succeeded the Hongzhi Emperor while still a child, effectively giving control over imperial manufactures to corrupt palace eunuchs. This proved to be a disruptive influence on porcelain production throughout the later Ming period, as the trend for ineffectual emperors continued.

Photo 39. Jar with enamel-on-biscuit decoration in *fahua* style, Ming dynasty, Hongzhi period, 1488–1505. PDF 759.

Photo 40. Warming bowl with underglaze blue decoration, Ming dynasty, Hongzhi period, 1488–1505. PDF A623.

Photo 41. Bowl with underglaze blue decoration, Ming dynasty, Chenghua mark and period, 1465–87. PDF A650.

Photo 42. Ming temple vase from the Hongzhi period, 1496. Height: 62.1 cm. Percival David Foundation of Chinese Art; PDF 680.

TRADITIONS AND TRANSITIONS
Chinese ceramics at the end of the 15th century
Monique Crick

In August 1519, while the Portuguese were attempting to settle on the southern coast of China, the Spanish, commanded by Magellan, set sail from Seville in search of the "Spice Islands" by the western sea routes. When they made contact with the natives on arrival in the Philippines in 1521, they found signs of a well established trade with the Middle Empire. Chronicles from the expeditions frequently cited the porcelains, jars and the movement of Chinese boats in Luzon, Mindanao and Mindoro. It was reported that Magellan received "three jars made of porcelain, wrapped in leaves and filled with rice alcohol" from the chief of a small island close to Leyte.

On April 7th 1521 on the island of Cebu, at a reception given by the Rajah, the courses were served on "porcelain dishes". During the capture of a trade junk on May 8th 1570, Felipe de Salcedo noted that "the decks of the vessels are covered with earthenware jars, pottery, large porcelain vases, plates and bowls, and some fine porcelain jars that are called sinoratas".[1] It was just such a scene that Franck Goddio and his crew were to discover and that the scientific excavation restored to us, when they found the Lena Shoal junk, sunk one day in the last decade of the fifteenth century. We are thus offered a sort of time capsule, a panorama of the ceramic production of its time, and a testimony of a possible inter-Asian trade that is unique in its wealth and variety.

Only the famous collections from Topkapi Saray in Istanbul[2] and the Ardebil Shrine in Iran, kept at the National Museum of Teheran,[3] hold large quantities of pieces similar to this exceptional cargo. A few private collections put together in the Philippines also include similar pieces.[4] In the absence of written documents, the dating of a shipwrecked boat and its contents can be based on the tangible evidence of the Chinese porcelains themselves. These relics are often the only source for the dating of underwater and land excavations.

A comparative stylistic study of porcelain from the Lena Shoal junk with the porcelains from the aforementioned collections, with exhibitions, museum collections, and pieces found on the kiln sites at Jingdezhen, dates the style of the cargo to Emperor Hongzhi's reign (1488–1505) in the Ming dynasty.[5] By comparing certain designs with those on the ceramics found in dated tombs in China (such as a small bottle, 1491;[6] the bowl on stand, 1491;[7] a bowl, 1496[8]) and on pieces inscribed with a specific date (for example the vase marked the "ninth year of Hongzhi" [1496] from the Percival David Foundation of Chinese Art[9]), we may determine the date more precisely to be within the last ten years of the fifteenth century.

This precision is confirmed by the persistence of a design style depicting certain mythical animals on dishes, the fabulous *qilin* unicorn and flying phoenixes amongst lotus flowers rapidly painted in dark blue with a very wet brush which are characteristic of the period known as the "Interregnum" (1435–65).

The Chinese ware in the cargo included mostly porcelains, mainly decorated in cobalt blue under glaze, some white monochrome pieces sometimes incised with floral designs, an exceptional dish richly decorated with overglaze enamels, some *fahua* porcelain fragments and celadon-glazed stoneware.

---

[1] Blair and Robertson, *The Philippine Islands*, vol. XXXIII, p. 15, p. 119, p. 207; vol. II, p. 35, 69, 72; vol. III, p. 42, 57, 74.

[2] Regina Krahl, *Chinese Ceramics in the Topkapi Saray Museum, Istanbul, vol. II, Yuan and Ming Dynasty Porcelains*, London, 1986.

[3] John A. Pope, *Chinese Porcelains from the Ardebil Shrine*, Washington, 1956

[4] K. Aga-Oglu, *The Williams Collection of Far Eastern Ceramics*, Museum of Anthropology, University of Michigan, Ann Arbor, 1972; *The Williams Collection of Far Eastern Ceramics: Tonancour Section*, Museum of Anthropology, University of Michigan, Ann Arbor, 1975; *Shadow of the Dragon, Chinese Domestic and Trade Ceramics*, Colombus Museum of Art, 1982. U. Wiesner, *Chinesische Keramik auf den Philippinen*, Museen der Stadt Köln, Museum für Ostasiatische Kunst.

[5] Huang Yunpeng, Zhen Li, *Jingdezhen minjian qinghua ciqi* (Jingdezhen's Porcelains from Private Kilns), Renmin Meishu Chubanshe, 1988. *Ceramic Finds from the Jingdezhen Kilns, 10th–17th Century*, exhibition catalogue, The Fung Ping Shan Museum, The University of Hong Kong, 1992.

[6] J. M. Addis, *Chinese Ceramics from Datable Tombs*, London, 1978, ill. 47, p. 157, bottle decorated with "Three Friends" design.

[7] Huang Yunpeng, et al., "Provincial Blue and White Porcelain from Jingdezhen", *Zhongguo Taoci Chuanji*, vol. 19, Kyoto, 1983, pl. 65, Bowl with aquatic plants on the sides.

[8] L. Gotuaco, R. C. Tan, A. I. Diem, *Chinese and Vietnamese Blue and White Wares found in the Philippines*, Makati City, Bookmark, 1997, p. 136, fig. M7, bowl with deer design.

[9] Scrolls, rocks and waves are similar to those painted on the ceramics found in the junk.

1. Blue and white porcelains, *Qinghua*

In the second half of the fifteenth century, the kilns of Jingdezhen had fully resumed their activities after the troubled Interregnum period. The character of the pieces from the Lena Shoal junk ascribes their manufacture to the *minyao*, the private kilns of Hutian and Shibadu at Jingdezhen, in the province of Jiangxi. These are solid porcelains with thick sides. Their compact and hard bodies are in white, sometimes greyish, porcelain and usually well glazed. The glaze, still bright in spite of its time underwater, is slightly bluish and contains many suspended bubbles. The often concave bases of the dishes are generally coated with glaze, as are those of the bowls. The foot is undercut and slants inward. This is characteristic of export ceramics at the end of the fifteenth century. The designs are painted in cobalt varying from dark blue, almost black, to light blue. During this period, the imported cobalt oxide from Iran and that found locally in Pingdeng could have been intentionally mixed to produce a softer tone. The drawings are clear, except for rare porcelains where the blue ran during firing. The few pieces of the Interregnum style are painted directly with broad brush strokes, but on most of the ware the designs and details are finely outlined and filled with a wash which is occasionally shaded.

1.1 General shapes and uses

The cargo consists of domestic ware, mostly large saucer-shaped, flat-rimmed or lobed dishes, small dishes, saucers, bowls, small boxes for cosmetics, and a few jars of various sizes. The indigenous populations seem to have demanded and chosen pieces well suited to the regional living conditions and usage, objects made to be used by societies that traditionally lived squatting down on the ground where these objects were seen from above.

When Pigafetta paid a visit to the King of Cebu in 1521, it was written that he found him "sitting down on a mat..." eating "some turtle eggs placed in two porcelain dishes laid out on another mat on the ground...".[10] A Chinese document, the *Tung hsi yang k'ao*, published in 1618, describing trade in the sixteenth century, reported that the natives of Bandjermasin in Borneo used leaves from banana trees as plates, but, that after the development of trade with China, they adopted porcelain. The larger dishes do not correspond to Chinese eating habits but rather with those of societies who eat communally. These large shapes appeared during the foreign dynasty of the Yuan (1279–1368), founded by the Mongols who encouraged foreign trade. There was thus a new boom in the use of the traditional route of Nanhai. The large heavy dishes created for the Middle Eastern markets and whose export became prominent under the Ming dynasty (1368–1644) were also highly valued by the clientele in the Philippine and Indonesian archipelagos where, throughout the period, porcelains were considered imports of prestige.

Two forms specific to South-East Asia, the *kendi* and the "betel box" were also part of the cargo. The term *kendi*, a Malayan word derived from the kundika Sanskrit, indicates a ewer whose long cylindrical neck is used as a handle. Very popular in South-East Asia, it could have been used for pouring holy water during a ritual ceremony. The betel boxes are associated with an ancestral tradition in tropical areas and were part of the paraphernalia used for the preparation of betel quid; one container for areca nuts, one for the betel leaves and one for quick lime.

The small ewers in the shape of a pair of mandarin ducks, a symbol of marital fidelity, also seem to have been highly sought after. Several versions exist and they were also found modelled in enamelled stoneware. This model first appeared during the reign of Xuande (1426–35).[11] They were filled up through the opening in the backs of the birds, the spout being the open beak of the male. In China, these pieces were perhaps intended for the consumption of wine or for the scholar's table where they would be used to dispense the water used in the preparation of ink. Although the islanders must not have understood the true function and symbolism of the object, the exoticism of the shape was, on the other hand, very

---

[11] *Yuan's and Ming's Porcelains Unearthed from Jingdezhen*, Yan-Huang Art Museum, exhibition catalogue, Cultural Relics publishing House, Beijing, 1999, p. 201, ill. 165.

Photo 43. Blue and white water-dropper modelled as a mandarin duck. Inv. No. 165, from *Yuan's and Ming's Imperial Porcelains Unearthed from Jingdezhen*, Yan-Huang Art Museum, Beijing, Cultural Relics Publishing House, Beijing, 1999.

---

[10] Blair and Robertson, *The Philippine Islands*, Vol. XXXIII, p. 149.

attractive. Were these ewers not sometimes given as precious gifts, as their placing in the Lena cargo would prove? They were, we should remember, found set aside with other porcelains in a special box.

The technical superiority of Chinese ceramics made them different from local terracotta productions. They were solid, non-porous and their clear and brilliant surface, in a way, seemed magical. Their resonance and decorative designs seemed to reinforce their supernatural power. The arrangement of decorations on the inside of the dishes and bowls and on the neck and shoulders of the vases forced attention and, by their exoticism, struck people's imagination. These ceramics were regarded as treasures and their use was sometimes quite different from their original intention. The small jars were normally used to hold fish brine, make-up and oily perfumes based on a mixture of wax, grease and jasmine, or camphor and musk oil. A narrow opening allowed the slow and measured flow of these precious liquids.

Very soon, these miniature containers, as well as the small cosmetic boxes, were used by sorcerers for holy oils, drugs and magic ointments that cured illness and chased away evil spirits from the body. Often believed to have a supernatural origin, these ceramics were thought to absorb the magical power or healing virtue of their content.

Chipped jars and boxes are often found and it is believed that the minuscule fragment was reduced to a powder before being mixed with food or drink. Small slivers may even have been used as magical bait with a view to having a miraculous catch. In the same way, the large porcelain dishes were highly valued by sorcerers for their clear, musical resonance, which was easily detected by the divinities or those family spirits called upon.

Porcelains from the end of the fifteenth century, similar to those from the Lena Shoal junk, have been found in tombs, particularly those from the three cemeteries of Hacienda of Calatagan in the province of Batangas, in the centre of Luzon.[12] Intentionally buried with the deceased, they accompanied him in his voyage towards the "beyond". They were placed at the foot, at the head or upside down on the body. This practice was common in many animist societies in South-East Asia before the arrival of Islam and Christianity. Spanish writings mention that, at the time, it was a custom to bury "the most beautiful clothing, porcelains and gold jewellery" with the body.[13]

Chinese ceramics have also been discovered on settlements sites, showing that they were used by affluent classes.[14] Regarded as family treasures, they were preserved in families for centuries, transmitted from generation to generation. Part of everyday life, linked to marriage ceremonies, births and family festivals, they played an important role as a symbol of wealth, prestige and social status.

Photo 44. Underwater photograph showing blue and white porcelain duck ewer with oval boxes.

1.2 Special shapes

The large ewers with lids, small pear-shaped ewers with a central medallion in relief, bottles with filters, writing boxes with their inkstands, and oval boxes with small interior trays are quite exceptional and unusual pieces.

Ewers were among the first shapes, originating from the Middle East, which were copied and adapted by Chinese gold and silversmiths as well as potters, to the point where it becomes difficult to determine the ceramic's original prototype.

The ewers with a flat, bare base have a squat body that was uncommon. Similar pieces are preserved at the Museum of Topkapi Saray in Istanbul, in Tehran, and another, from the Philippines, in the Detroit Institute of Art.[15] The small pear-shaped ewers in monochrome blue

---

[12] R. B. Fox, "The Calatagan Excavations", *Philippine Studies*, Manila. vol. 7, 1968, S.321 ff.

[13] Blair and Robertson, vol. II, p. 139.

[14] Junker, Laura Lee, "Archaeological Excavations at the Late First Millenium and Early Second Millenium AD Settlement of Tanjay, Negros Oriental: Household Organization, Chiefly Production and Social Ranking", *Philippine Quarterly of Culture and Society*, 21, 1993.

[15] D. Lion-Goldschmidt, *La Porcelaine Ming*, Office du Livre, Fribourg, 1978, p. 140, ill. 131.

or with the blue and white decoration with a curved spout are embossed with a tear-shaped medallion. This shape comes from contemporary Chinese silverware[16] inspired from Middle Eastern prototypes. These various ewers were perhaps ordered for use during meals for ablutions, as was habitual in the Muslim courts.

The bottle with a filter, a globular body, and an hourglass-shaped neck is very rare and has an equivalent in the Topkapi Saray Museum. It copies the shape of a metal model that remains unknown to this day. The neck is sealed with a porcelain disk pierced with four or five oval openings, which was used as protection against dust and insects. It was most certainly a water bottle. The disk, with its open-work design follows the principle of the Eastern goglets where the filter is a practical measure for protection, but also allows ventilation of the liquid, keeping it cool in vessels made of porous pottery.

The porcelain writing box appeared in China at the beginning of the fifteenth century during the reigns of Yongle[17] and Xuande. It is not surprising that this shape, foreign to Chinese traditions and inspired by an Islamic metal prototype, was copied during a period of prosperity and expansion when links with the Middle East were re-established and when Muslim communities were developing in China. This shape, as well as other forms originating from the Islamic world, was revived at the end of the fifteenth century, also a time of flourishing foreign trade and of the spread of Islam in South-East Asia.

The pen boxes from the Lena Shoal junk are unique in that they are complete with their inkstand and the small containers for powder and silk thread, made from porcelain. Even the hole to attach the metal fittings was left in the porcelain by the potter! They were certainly intended for Muslim customers, the only ones to make use of these.

The oval boxes with small trays inside were also rare. Their unusual shape was probably inspired by metal boxes from the Middle East which take the shape of a lunch box but which would have been used for precious objects at the time.[18] Indeed, the porcelain boxes from the Lena Shoal junk did contain precious objects, such as red lacquer combs, a red lacquer box, glass beads or spices, pepper and areca nuts. They were also arranged separately in a special box with the duck-shaped pots.

---

[16] J. M. Addis, *Chinese Ceramics from Datables Tombs*, London, 1978, p.139, ill. 45 ; "Graves from the Xu Da family, Prince of Zhongshan of the Ming dynasty", *Wenwu*, 1993, No. 2, p. 69.

[17] Liu Xinyuan, et al., *Imperial Hongwu and Yongle Porcelain Excavated at Jingdezhen*, exhibition catalogue, Chang Foundation, Taibei, 1996, p. 296, Cat. 118.

[18] J. W. Allan, "Later Mamluk Metalwork, II: A Series of Lunch-Boxes", *Oriental Art*, Vol. XVII, Summer 1971. J. Carswell, *Blue and White, Chinese Porcelain and Its Impact on the Western World*, The University of Chicago, The David and Alfred Smart Gallery, 1985, pp. 90–1, cat. 34.

Photo 45. Porcelain writing box. Ming, Xuande period, 1426-1435. Length: 31.2 cm. Percival David Foundation of Chinese Art. PDF A629.

Traditions and transitions

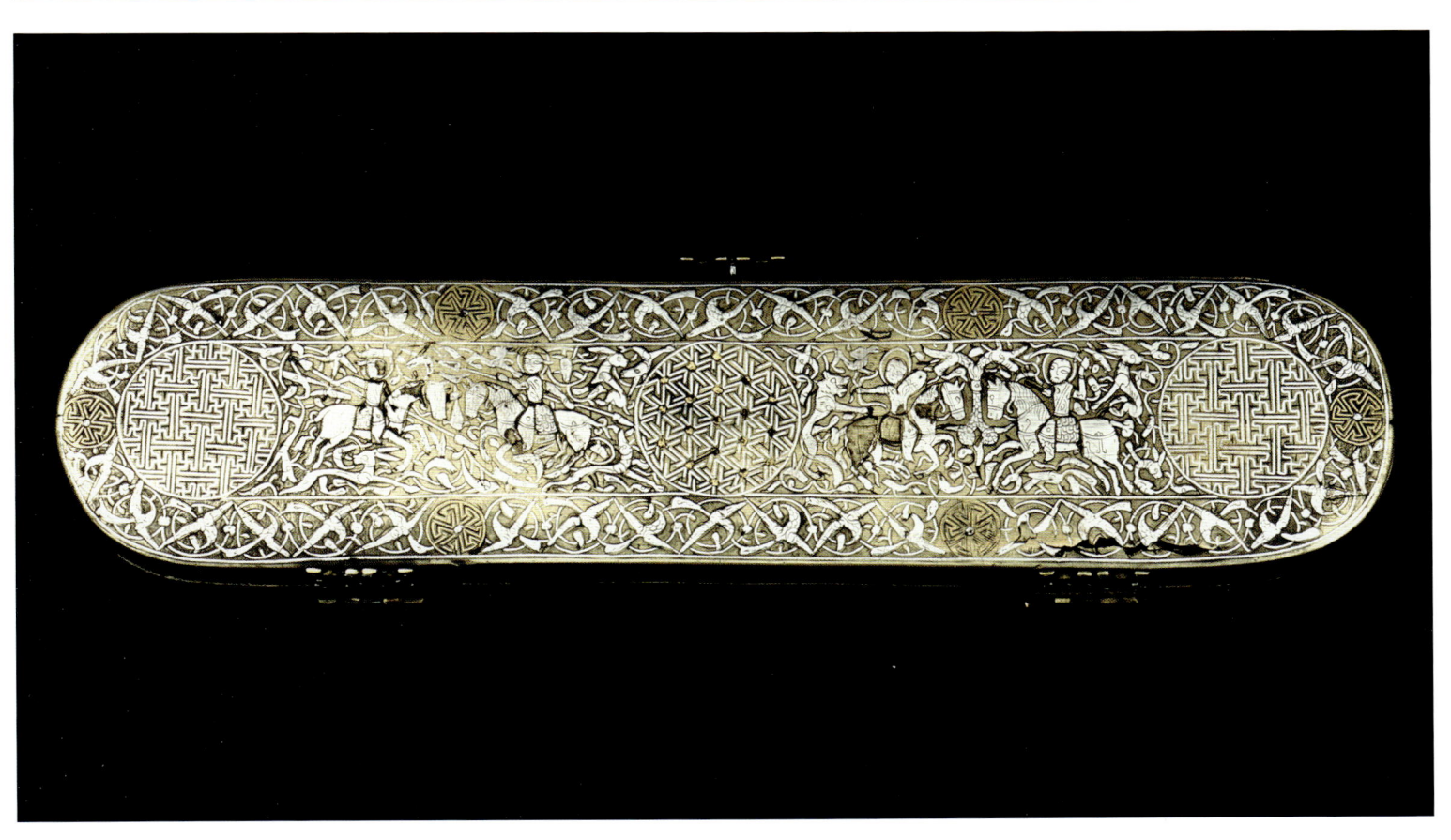

Photo 46. Brass pen box, 1281. Designed by Mahmud ibn Sunqur. The British Museum (Inv. 91 6-23 5).

Photo 47. Brass pen box, as above.

LOST AT SEA

Photo 48. Brass casket, engraved and inlaid with silver. Syrian, 15th c. The Metropolitan Museum of Art, The Edward C. Moore Collection, bequest of Edward C. Moore, 1891 (91.1.538).

1.3 Origin and characteristics of the decorative themes

The imperial porcelains inscribed with *nianhao* from the Emperor Hongzhi generally remain faithful to the traditional decoration of dragons. They are of very high quality with careful crafting and harmonious shapes. The development of enamelled polychrome and the prominence of *fahua*-glazed pieces remain the main characteristic of this reign. The imperial blue and white pieces present few innovations whereas porcelains manufactured by the private *minyao* kilns are very varied. The painter's repertory delves into the inexhaustible resources of Chinese cultural heritage. Allegiance to the most classic traditions of the reigns of Yongle and Xuande is expressed in the diversity of the designs, drawings of birds, flowers and fruits, fabulous animal representations, and emblems of good omen, however, foreign influences are also noticeable.

1.3.1 Composition of the decoration

Two different styles characterise the layout of the decoration, a radial geometrical arrangement and a decorative design centred on a painting.

The first style presents a very dense ornamental decoration that covers the entire surface, almost as if in horror of emptiness, contrary to Chinese culture. Under the Yuan dynasty, a geometrical pattern developed from the rhythmic movement of Islamic aesthetics had already emerged with its rigorous composition defined by concentric circles. Certain dishes from the cargo have small lobed panels, on an overall Y-trellis ground, arranged in concentric rings around a central medallion. This arrangement was new and may have been derived from metal dishes of the Middle East.

Another group combines a decoration of cloud-collar panels radiating outwards around the central medallion and inwards from the edge, which appeared in the fourteenth century and which is reminiscent of the star-shaped design found in the centre of Eastern carpets.

The Y-shaped motifs, which were used as backgrounds would have come from the same origin. They were firmly established in the repertory of the Middle East in the thirteenth century and were notably used on the Syrian ewer dated 1232, known as the "Blacas ewer" preserved in the British Museum.

Photo 49. Brass tray, inlaid with silver, c. 1290. Made for Yusuf, Rasulid sultan of Yemen. Inv. No. 15153. Museum of Islamic Art, Cairo.

Photo 50. Detail of brass tray (as above).

Occasionally the decoration is arranged in concentric friezes with alternating colour schemes, inherited from the compositions of craftsmen under the Yuan dynasty. But within this foreign arrangement the Chinese essence with its flora, fauna and religious beliefs

Photo 51. Brass candle holder for Ahmad Shah *al naqqash*, Shiraz (?), third quarter of the 14th c. Pierre et Maurice Chuzeville/Musée du Louvre. Département des Antiquités Orientales, section Islam. No. OA7530.

is visible. The medallions are decorated with branches of flowers or fruits, lions with a brocade ball, phoenix, and other symbols.

Curiously, the base of some of these dishes is painted, using quick strokes, with a lion, a phoenix with wings spread out, a floral branch or even the character *Shou* for longevity.[19]

The same layout of concentric friezes can be found on dishes with more traditional designs. Rings of waves encircle a central medallion decorated with various illustrations. A deliberate intent of the artist to create

[19] For similar pieces see Regina Krahl, 1986, vol.II.

Photo 52. Detail of the central medallion of a blue and white porcelain dish from the Lena Shoal junk's cargo. Inv. No. 2924.

convergent motifs is evident whether they are of mountains, ducks or waders in the middle of aquatic plants.

The artist did not wish to express a realistic image but simply to reproduce the designs of an engraving laid out in front of him, which he looked at from above and copied several times while gradually turning the dish.

He sometimes seems to have enjoyed varying the designs by making small changes to details on the waders among the aquatic plants, or on those that are hard to see inside a small medallion on a field of lotus emerging from the waves. The result is these strange drawings characteristic of the porcelain produced by private kilns of this period where a certain humour and an imaginative freedom of the craftsman are apparent, far from the constraints of an approved production. The traditional floral scrolls were themselves also transformed and became fine lianas with a multitude of flowers and leaves that cover the ceramics with a very dense network almost resembling calligraphic friezes.

The Chinese concept of decoration has a different inspiration and requires more openness. The work is no longer based on a geometrical rhythm but is orchestrated in a space. Large decorations are generally centred on a painting. The essential themes that form the main part of the decoration are accompanied by secondary designs, which frame them and decorate the rims. Their layout gives rise to infinite combinations that reflect the style of the period.

The arrangement and choice of traditional designs for the Lena Shoal junk porcelains were inspired by the creations of earlier reigns. Large dishes and bowls are entirely decorated with abundant scrolls or a spray of flowering peonies. These wide interrupted floral scrolls can be compared to the two porcelains bowls reproduced in the painting entitled, *The Feast of the Gods,* by

LOST AT SEA

Giovanni Bellini dated 1514.[20] Branches spread their leaves and fruit over the plates like a page from an album but are curved to adapt to the circular space of the central medallion with its *ruyi*-type border.

A dense decoration covers the surface of the ewers with a squat body: flowers are arranged around the sides in isolated scrolls or grouped in twos like those during the reign of Chenghua (1465–87), in lotus panels, cloud collar panels and upright leaves. The same taste in floral ornamentation governs the decoration on boxes, writing boxes and jars. Light scrolls cover the interior of the medallion of small ewers, flanked by two floral twigs, whilst panels and upright leaves outline the base and the neck. A classic lotus scroll is quickly painted on the squat body of the *kendi*, and cloud collar panels wrap around its shoulder.

---

[20] J. Carswell, p. 89.

Fig. 32. *Suihan sanyou tu* (The Three Friends of Winter) by Zhao Mengtian (1199–1264), Southern Song dynasty, painted on paper, *Molin bacui ce*, No. 6. National Palace Museum, Taibei, Taiwan.

Fig. 33. *The Feast of the Gods* by Giovanni Bellini, oil on canvas, 1.7 x 1.9 m, National Gallery of Art, Washington. Widener Collection.

Photo 53. Large dish with peony decoration in the central medallion.

1.3.2 Flora and fauna

The painter never chooses the designs randomly. They represent a language full of symbolism and express a wish for longevity, happiness, prosperity and success. The wish of longevity, one of the paramount wishes in the country that founded Taoism, is expressed by some well codified drawings. The sacred *lingzhi* fungus, which is an ingredient of the elixir of immortality, is usually present as a scroll, on vessels and the inside of the small dishes, or depicted growing in an undergrowth populated with deer. The chrysanthemum, the flower of autumn which resists the first frosts, is also a component of the liquor of immortality. Its timid representation in the Tang dynasty (618–907) became more naturalistic under the Song. It is painted on the dishes, ewers and bowls found in the junk as scrolls grouped in pairs or in bushes on each side of a decorative rock. This image derives from a favourite theme of Chinese paintings where the symbolism of the stones is integrated into the vision of the world. The peach, fruit of a fabled tree which grows in the orchard of the Queen Mother of the West, Xi Wangmu, most often takes its place in the central medallion of the dishes. This fruit became the most famous symbol of immortality probably due to its pre-eminence in various popular legends.

The theme of "Three Friends of Winter", pine, prunus and bamboo, which are so often represented on the porcelains from the junk, expresses longevity, beauty and endurance. The evergreen pine is also an emblem of friendship resisting adversity. The bamboo represents perseverance, and the prunus, a tree that flowers in the winter, renewal and eternal youth. This design on traditional paintings already appeared on *ding*-type porcelains under the Song dynasty and was to be very popular under the Yuan dynasty. Among the significant allegories are those that symbolise numerous offspring like the pomegranate or the melon whose abundant seeds convey a wish of fertility. The peony, a symbol of spring, wealth and social success, is frequently used as a decorative design in the centre of the dishes. Firmly established in the decorative repertory of ceramics since the Song dynasty, it often appears in the scrolls in symbolic association with the lotus.

Among the fauna, some animals are also chosen for their allegorical connotation. The fish, in its most common meaning, is used as a symbol of wealth and abundance. It is a common subject in various forms of art

Fig. 34. *Sui zhao tu* (Flowers of the New Year) by Zhao Chang (active 960–1016), Northern Song dynasty, painted on silk scroll. National Palace Museum, Taibei, Tawan.

LOST AT SEA

Fig. 35. *Two Carps Leaping Among Waves,* anonymous, Yuan dynasty, 14th c., hanging scroll, ink, light colour and gold on silk. Reproduced courtesy of the Museum of Fine Arts, Boston. ©2000 Museum of Fine Arts, Boston, all rights reserved.

that finds its most beautiful expression in painting. Present on ceramics from as early as the Neolithic age, they became very popular from the Song onwards. The carp leaping from the waves remains an illustration of the wish for success in imperial examinations and an official career.

1.3.3 Pictorial themes

One of the most delicate decorations revived a design widely used in paintings since the Tang period and whose poetic expression was found on ceramics from the Song dynasty onwards. It depicts the aquatic world of the lotus and other plants among which ducks, egrets and fish move around.

The supple stems, with their smooth curve, enhance the shape of the bowls and dishes. The contours and details are meticulously drawn before exposure to a very nuanced wash which highlights the designs. A peaceful charm emanates from the refinement of the drawing and the softness of the shades of blue. In the same way, the bird perched on a branch evokes the painting of "birds and flowers" and illustrates the importance of this theme in Chinese painting. The scenes with figures also belong to the literati painting. The simplified interpretation of the solitary scholar standing or sitting under a tree maintains the feeling of rhythm in the lines and the brushwork on the only two examples found. The landscape art with its cosmic symbolism of mountains and rocks is simplified, to the extreme, on the edges and the centres of a series of plates where, the "mountain rocks" emerge from the waves.

Fig. 36. *Qiupu shuangyuan* (Two Birds in the Autumn) attributed to Huichong (965–1017), Northern Song dynasty, painted on paper, *Lichao hua fuce*, No. 2. National Palace Museum, Taibei, Taiwan.

Photo 54. *Ding* plate, 13th c. Diameter: 22.1 cm. Percival David Foundation of Chinese Art; PDF 171.

Fig. 37. *Kumu zhu shi* (Old Tree with a Bird, Bamboo and Rock), attributed to Zhao Mengfu (1254–1322), Yuan dynasty, painted on a silk scroll. National Palace Museum, Taibei, Taiwan.

Fig. 38. *Scholar Seated under a Tree*, by Wu Wei, Ming dynasty, hanging scroll, ink and traces of colour on silk. Reproduced courtesy of the Museum of Fine Arts, Boston. ©2000 Museum of Fine Arts, Boston, all rights reserved.

Photo 55. Large blue and white dish painted with a sea creature, Ming dynasty, Xuande mark and period, Jingdezhen Institute of Ceramic Archaeology, Jingdezhen, Jiangxi province, China.

1.3.4 Fantastic themes

Symbols abound in Chinese art but the ones most emblematic of China remain the dragon and the phoenix. One group of dishes takes its designs from these two traditional themes combined with clouds or floral scrolls.

The dragon, symbol of rain, dispenser of fertility, and the phoenix, a red bird from the south that brings the sun and the heat of the summer, both necessary for the harvests, have, since antiquity, been associated with imperial power. These themes present on Song ceramics are developed on the *cizhou* and the blue and white of the Yuan dynasty and lasted in various forms.

The traditional long dragon with four claws could be represented front on, in profile, in an ascending or descending position. Only one dish with a descending dragon surrounded by clouds was found among the cargo. On the other hand, another style of dragon also frequently appears on dishes and bowls from the Lena Shoal junk. With only two front legs it has a sort of elephant trunk, round horns, small curved wings and its body is elongated into a foliate tail. A lotus stem issues from its mouth.

Its morphology may derive from the marine monster, *makara*, revered in India and its reappearance as a popular design on porcelain in the fifteenth century could be related to the development of Buddhism at that time. There is another aspect, the sea dragon *feiyu*, with wings and no legs, with fins and a fish tail, illustrated on a dish in a vigorous and spontaneous style.

The phoenix corresponds in a way to the dragon and symbolises the Empress. It is a mythical bird represented in profile with its wings spread, either alone or in continuous circle with another phoenix, in the middle of clouds or scrolls. Among the other fabulous creatures found on the porcelains, the *qilin* represents a kind of horned deer with the head of a dragon, cloven hooves and a bushy tail. This Chinese unicorn that could live for 1000 years symbolises longevity, perfect goodness and predicts an era of peace and prosperity.

1.3.5 Religious themes, Buddhism and Taoism

Religious themes were also very apparent on the porcelains from the junk as both the main and secondary designs. The theme of the *hai shou*, mythical sea animals galloping over the waves, was approached with vigour and a boldness of strokes, which has retained the force of the Xuande model.

The piece most remarkable for its dynamism is the large dish decorated with a flying elephant set against a field of turbulent waves. The movement of the animal swept forward by its momentum is striking, as well as the contrast between the deep blue of the animal and the light blue of the foam whose bubbling waves evoke the sea. A lotus scroll evenly painted in an intense tone is unfolded on the inside and surrounds the composition.

The elephant is seldom represented alone in the central decoration. A dish from the Xuande period, with the same design, was found at Zhushan, the site of the imperial manufactory of the Ming period in Jingdezhen.[21] The representation is obviously religious since the elephant is considered to be the symbolic mount of Samantabhadra, the "Bodhisattva of universal benevolence". It is usually painted in the company of other flying animals around a bowl. Galloping flying horses, the *tianma*, deer, goats, various snakes, foxes, winged dragons, fish leap through clouds and over waves, in a circle around the sides of the bowls or in the central medallion of the Lena Shoal junk plates.

These themes, often associated with the design of a sea conch from which emerges a small creature (that could be the *ershu*, a long-eared mouse, that immunises against poisons) has a strong connotation of Tibetan Buddhism.[22] Emperors Chenghua and Hongzhi were both keen Buddhists. The less tolerant, Hongzhi, was to burn Taoist books and order the expulsion of foreign monks from China. It was normal in such a context to find religious symbols in the repertory of imperial manufactories and private kilns.

The deer surrounded by a scroll of leaves, with a lotus flower at its mouth, also has a Buddhist connotation

---

[21] *Yuan's and Ming's Porcelains Unearthed from Jingdezhen*, op. cit., p.189, ill. 148.

[22] Chen Ching-kuang, *Sea-Creatures on Ming Imperial Porcelains*, Colloquies on Art & Archeology in Asia, No. 16, SOAS, Percival David Foundation, 1993.

Photo 56. Central detail of a blue and white dish with an elephant from the Lena Shoal junk.

LOST AT SEA

of an animal of good omen. The lions, guardians of the throne of Buddha, are transformed by the decorative art into tame felines playing with a brocade ball, the origin of which is the sacred jewel of Buddhist law. We find them painted on porcelain from the beginning of the fifteenth century, but their appearance in the decorative arts is much older.

Amongst the religious images are the beribboned double *vajra*, crossed thunderbolts, emblem of the divine force of Buddha's doctrine; the lotus bouquets and scrolls where, each flower, a symbol of purity, supports one of eight symbols of Buddhism; and the invocations in Sanskrit.

Taoism is not however omitted from the repertory. The dishes decorated with three mountainous islands emerging from the foaming waves illustrate the old Taoist theme of heavenly islands where the immortals reside.

This image has existed in Chinese art since early times as under the Han dynasty (140 BC–220 AD), in the second century BC, incense burners with bronze lids or ceramic boxes were moulded in the shape of a mountain. According to Taoist tradition it is in the "Three Islands of Immortals", Penglai, located in the Eastern Ocean beyond the coasts of Jiangsu province, that the herb of immortality grows. Immortals with wings and feathers live there, take nourishment from precious stones and drink water from the fountain of life. The immense knotty pine drawn on the central peak reinforces, through its symbolism of longevity, this idea of the quest for immortality.

We know of only one piece with such an evocative power, that of a perfume-burner discovered at Jingdezhen dating from the period of Yongle (1403–24).[23]

---

[23] Liu Xinyuan, 1996, op. cit., p. 204, cat. 71.

Photo 57. Porcelain stem cup, 15th c., Ming dynasty, Xuande period, 1426–35. diameter: 10 cm. Percival David Foundation of Chinese Art; PDF B638.

Photo 58. Tripod perfume-burner with mountains and waves decoration, Ming porcelain, Yongle period. Jingdezhen Institute of Ceramic Archaeology, Jianxi, China.

1.3.6 Innovative trends

Although there is no break with the past, new trends are manifest in the reappearance of the deer decoration, which already existed on *cizhou* ware and the moulded *ding* ware of the Song period and was present in contemporary painting.

The deer *lu* may be represented strolling joyfully alone or with company within a pastoral framework in the shade of a pine, and would be seen as a symbol of prosperity and longevity. This design was to be developed further, becoming a characteristic theme of the second half of the sixteenth century.

Another revival of moulded decoration on *ding* ware is the evocation of a garden with a tree growing out of a vase, in front of a balustrade. It illustrates an understanding of nature and gardens typical of the elegant life of the scholars. This theme, seldom adopted during the reign of Hongwu (1368–98), presages the *kraak* porcelain of the following century.[24]

---

[24] For an illustration of one of the two existing Hongwu plates with this design see Liu Xinyuan, 1996, op. cit., p. 356–7.

Photo 59. Plate, *ding* ware, 11th to 12th c. diameter: 28.7 cm. Percival David Foundation of Chinese Art; PDF 117.

Fig. 39. *Deer in an Autumnal Wood*, anonymous, Five Dynasties, 10th to 11th c., ink and paint on a silk scroll. National Palace Museum, Taibei, Taiwan.

Fig. 40. *Renwu* (Portrait of a Scholar), anonymous, 11th c., Northern Song dynasty, painted on silk, *Lidai huafujice*, No. 1, National Palace Museum, Taibei, Taiwan.

2. Monochrome porcelains

There were some monochrome porcelains in the cargo: white dishes, white bowls, a small white bell-shaped cup, and two blue ewers. White monochrome porcelain had renewed importance at the beginning of the fifteenth century. Great care was taken in the smoothness of the pastes, glazes and decorations, so affirming the virtuosity of the Chinese potters. But such success did not last long during the following reigns.

The Hongzhi period in particular was known for these imperial monochrome pieces glazed in a yellow enamel. The white and enamelled monochromes do not seem to have been produced in great quantities for export as testified by the rarity of known examples and the small load in the Lena Shoal junk compared to other ceramic categories. The saucer-shaped dishes are made from thick porcelain covered with an opaque glaze for the plain monochromes, or a transparent one for those with incised drawings. The bowls and cups are of a finer quality. The large plain dishes, unlike the blue and white have an unglazed base and a straight foot. The medium-sized incised dishes employ the common designs of a floral branch in the central medallion and a lotus scroll on the side. The dish with traces of red and green polychrome enamels has a denser floral scroll decoration that occupies the central medallion and the sides. Exportation of these enamelled pieces began at this time but remained rare. There are only a few examples in the Chinese porcelain collection of the sultans in Istanbul.

The ewers evenly painted in blue do not have any equivalents and were certainly not produced in great quantities. Similar pieces dating from the sixteenth century with a more elongated shape, a less curved spout and without a loop on top of the handle are preserved at the Topkapi Saray Museum.

3. *Fahua* porcelains

The production of glazed porcelains known as *fahua* appeared at the end of the fifteenth century. The decoration of these pieces was delineated by means of raised slip outlines that separate the various coloured glazes. The dominant colours are a very even cobalt blue and a vivid turquoise used in the backgrounds combined with yellow and green. Certain "reticulated" pieces have an open-work decoration overlayed on the body. The designs again use the dominant themes of blue and white except for the fantastic animals.

Fragments with turquoise, blue and yellow enamel traces were found in the cargo. Turquoise and yellow flowers and leaves moulded and incised are separated by a dark blue painted line. These fragments undoubtedly belonged to a small jar with a reticulated decoration on the outside. Their presence confirms their dating at around 1500, the date generally given to the *fahua*.

4. Celadon-glazed stoneware

In lesser quantities, green-glazed stoneware formed part of the cargo of Chinese ceramics from the Lena Shoal junk. They were produced in the provinces of Zhejiang and Guangdong. However, only a few bowls came from Guangdong, from the kilns of Huiyang or Sancun in Xin'an village, which imitated the stoneware of Longquan and Zhejiang. Most of the pieces were from the region of Longquan.

4.1 Green-glazed stoneware from Longquan

The kilns were mostly distributed around the town of Longquan whose name became the generic term for a particular type of production. More than 360 sites have been discovered there, the most famous being Dayao, in the hills of Gaojitou. A civil servant from Zhejiang province, Lu Rong, wrote in 1466, that the most beautiful celadons came from Dayao.[25]

It was only natural for potters to settle here as they could easily get hold of the clay, water and wood they needed, and the proximity of the river facilitated the transport of the goods. Green-glazed stoneware production seemed to have started around the time of the Six Dynasties (220–580). It experienced its golden age during the Southern Song dynasty (1128–1279) when a dense, smooth glaze, particularly soft to touch, with a cloudy opaqueness resembling jade appeared. The shapes from this period were quite varied, but bowls, small dishes and cups remained dominant.

The ceramics were fired in saggars laid out in the "dragon" kilns, a kind of long tunnel built on the side of a hill. Several thousands pieces could be fired at once, producing, economically, the enormous quantities intended for export.

Under the Yuan dynasty, there was a veritable "cultural revolution" with the appearance of porcelains decorated with cobalt blue underglaze. The Song potters aimed primarily to attain purity of shape and the mastery of monochrome glazes. Under Mongolian domination, new ideas and fashions were introduced and the bulk of production was geared towards the tastes of foreign clients. The potters were to remain faithful to the technique of the Song, but the celadons would gradually lose the sobriety and delicacy of their shapes and glazes. To meet an increasing demand, the ceramics were produced using moulds and the quality of the finish was variable.

---

[25] Zhu Boqian, *Celadons from Longquan Kilns*, 1998, p. 30.

Photo 60. Dayao village at the foot of the kiln sites.

The decoration may even have been moulded and then applied to the surface using slip. This process took the craftsmen less time than an incised decoration that required a deft and precise movement. These stoneware pieces differed from those of the previous dynasty by their colour, glaze and more accentuated relief of the decoration, and their more voluminous shapes which were highly sought after by the merchants, mostly Arabs and Persians, who dominated the export trade.

They were more solid and so well suited for the long ocean voyage towards South-East Asia, India and the Near East where magic powers were attributed to the celadons. They were actually thought to change colour when in contact with poison. Shaken as they were by palace intrigues, we can understand the infatuation of the eastern courts with these ceramics. The Topkapi Saray Museum, alone, harbours 1350 Yuan and Ming celadons. In his Istanbul Diary in 1673, Antoine Galland wrote: "I saw a vase of a certain green earth that comes from the Indies which the Turks... hold in great esteem and pay dearly to buy because of its property to break in the presence of poison...".

It was undoubtedly this increased demand that encouraged the potter to create and invent new shapes and decorations. The artist was to design a decoration on a large scale, laid out in superimposed zones, following the example of the compositions of Jingdezhen porcelains. The temple vase dated 1327 and preserved at the Percival David Foundation is representative of this taste. The size of the pieces and the vigour in their interpretation of traditional forms and designs were characteristic of the Yuan ceramics.

After turning small bowls of about 20 cm, which correspond to Chinese social and culinary practices, the potters created wider bowls for export. Their lines however remained graceful and well proportioned. The shape and the size of the dishes also changed in response to the tastes of the Middle East and South-East Asian markets.

From bowls and individual dishes, they changed to large dishes of more than 40 cm in diameter, with curved sides and a rim. The central decoration that was often a design of a dragon among clouds was either incised or applied. There were also lotuses, peonies, fishes, and abstract designs like the cash-trellis pattern which evokes basketry work. As the fourteenth century progressed, contacts with the neighbouring province of Jiangxi and the centre of Jingdezhen become more apparent. The kilns of Longquan had preserved the originality of their style until the end of the fourteenth century but were now to produce celadons with designs similar to those of blue and white porcelains. The artists attempted to make their work closer to painting. It was difficult, however, to match the engraving technique and celadon glaze with the complexity and fineness of the painted models and the effect was often too busy and confused.

Nevertheless, pieces from the beginning of the fifteenth century were still beautifully executed but sometimes lacked the boldness and originality of the Yuan celadons, undoubtedly because these were copies of ceramics, which were themselves copies of paintings. The designs on both the outside and inside began to cover the entire surface of the object. This style, although suited to porcelain, would often seem a little cluttered on the celadons from the Ming period.

Throughout the fifteenth century incision remained the most common method of decoration. The temple vase dated the "fifth year of the Jingtai era" (1454) at the Percival David Foundation is representative. The Longquan potters seemed unable to match the competition of the blue and white from Jingdezhen with new ideas and the quality gradually deteriorated from the end of the fifteenth century. The decorations became more schematic and simplified. The body became thicker, the glaze thinner and transparent, and the designs hurriedly executed. Under the Qing dynasty, few kilns were still active and they made only utility ware, although gradually production continued until the end of the dynasty.

Photo 61. This river, running by Longquan, was used for transportation and had higher water levels at the time of production.

4.2 General characteristics of the celadons from the Lena Shoal junk

The celadons from the Lena Shoal junk show the particular characteristics of this period. The pieces were made of greyish-white stoneware, with a fine grain and a very dense structure. The sides and the bases of the dishes are thick and the pieces are very heavy. On the glazed base is an uneven circle without glaze, generally of a grey colour due to the circular support on which the piece stood during firing. The foot was rounded on the outside, straight on the inside and glazed.

The glaze was applied in a thin film, as was typical on Ming celadons, in contrast with those from earlier periods, and varied from light to dark green. It was occasionally hurriedly applied, as we may deduce from those pieces with an irregular glaze. The components of the lime-alkaline glaze enabled a substantial vitrification while firing resulting in a glossy appearance and a translucidity which allowed the incised decoration to show through. It would seem that this composition is not stable during a long stay in a marine environment. Some of the junk's celadons indeed lost their brilliant surface by a process of devitrification. However, those that were hidden in the sand maintained a certain gloss that those on the tumulus and exposed to the currents lost.

The cargo consists of saucer-shaped or rimmed dishes that vary in size from 21 to 50 cm, as well as small dishes, bowls and cups. The pieces display elegant lines and a harmony of proportions in the spirit of earlier dynasties. The potter seems to have adopted the shapes of the porcelains. The appearance of the bowls with thick sides is similar to a shape known as *lianzi* (lotus pod), which was widespread at the beginning of the fifteenth century.

Broad incisions and imprinted designs remain the main decorative techniques. The designs were simpler and less varied than at the beginning of the century and have no direct correlation with the blue and white cargo except for the organisation of space where the floral foliage frames the central medallion and outlines the morphology of the pieces. Some are very well made, others more negligently.

However, influences from the neighbouring province of Jiangxi and Jingdezhen remain noticeable in the decoration. The relief work, which was marked under the Yuans, is softened and is simply suggested by a cash-trellis pattern print or incised floral design. The incision of leaf or flower scrolls in double or triple lines maintains the fluidity of the creations from Jingdezhen but the engraver was not able to reproduce the complexity of painted models. The artisan was, however, happy to reproduce the natural blue and white motifs by incising a peony or lotus flower whose supple radiating leaves covered the space of the central medallion. The transparent glaze accumulated in the incisions creating shaded areas which nicely accentuate the contours of the designs. Sometimes thicker, it would give a slightly misty appearance to the decoration. The refined details such as the fine, supple frames of the lobed panels and the lobed rims remain, although at times they were poorly executed.

Simplified "classical scrolls" emphasise the rims of the dishes and lotus or peony scrolls cover the sides on the inside, and also the back of the more beautiful pieces. The lotus petals in relief on the sides of the bowls are simplified into fine incised petals resembling those of chrysanthemums. The cups with everted and discreetly grooved sides and small lobed dishes with a slight, incised wave design remain loyal to the tradition of such subtle decoration being subordinate to the shape. The wave design on the small dishes and the seal mark printed in their centre, read as *Gushi*, both seem to have been a creation of the end of the fifteenth century. Identical marks were found on the sites of the kilns of Dayao and Fengtang. The archaeologist Zhu Boqian attributed their origin to the legendary potter Gu Shicheng from the Zhentong period (1436–1499).[26]

Except for these particular designs, the decorative repertory of celadons from the junk is common to the fifteenth century. Some were very well made, others poorly, therefore we cannot base the dating on criteria of artistic quality alone. The inspiration of the Longquan potter no longer seems to depend on the creativity of the artist from Jingdezhen. The craftsmen continued to produce pieces with well known designs that had proved successful with their foreign customers.

This set of celadons, however, shows that a broad and simplified style characterised the end of the fifteenth century. Until now we have had no comparison point to give an exact dating within this century. The discovery of the Lena Shoal junk offers us a new chronology of celadons which will make it possible to correct erroneous datings, to date a certain style from the second half of the fifteenth century and to attribute some specific types to the end of the fifteenth century.

Celadons also formed part of the offerings that accompanied the deceased beyond the grave. The funeral sites in the Philippines that are contemporary with the Ming period contained far fewer than those of previous periods, an observation which would appear to confirm that the export of Longquan stoneware decreased in this period. The exceptional cargo of export ceramics from the

---

[26] P. Lam, "Ceramic Finds of the Ming Period from Penny's Bay. An Addendum", *Journal of the Hong Kong Archaeological Society*, XIII 1989–1992, p. 88.

Lena Shoal junk with an abundance of blue and white porcelains reinforces this interpretation. The private kilns of Jingdezhen had developed a very diverse production of porcelains as the cargo of the junk testifies.

It is often said that the decline of the kilns of Longquan was linked to the success of Jingdezhen and that the green-glazed stoneware had lost their attraction for foreign customers. Nevertheless the cargo included many celadons such as large dishes, bowls and jars, other than those from China. The majority of the celadons came from Thailand, from the kilns of Kalong, Phan and Si Satchanalai. Therefore, it seems that celadons were still much appreciated and exported at the end of the fifteenth century.

The blue and white porcelains most certainly had to compete with the stoneware, in the choice of the populations, but should we not also consider the Thai celadons to have been serious competitors? The Thai production was indeed less sophisticated but was it also not cheaper? In any event, it was sufficiently valued to be exported in mass quantities to South-East Asia.

5. Conclusion

In view of the exceptional cargo of the Lena Shoal junk, one question arises: was the final destination of the boat a port in the Philippines?

We are used to regarding certain large blue and white dishes and celadon plates as productions of Jingdezhen and Longquan for the markets of the Middle East. The ewers, bottles, large boxes and writing boxes reinforce the idea of a remote destination. However, the cargo of celadons from Thailand, including more than 300 small jars, the large brown-glazed jars, a large part of the porcelain ware of which no trace has been found in the Middle East, metal objects, woks, basins and bronze bracelets, imply a more Asian destination.

Careful examination of publications on excavations carried out in the Philippines, on collections gathered in the Philippines, and on exhibitions which have taken place in South-East Asia, has shown that porcelains identical to those on the junk formed part of trade in this region, although little seems to have survived through the centuries. Is it not also surprising that similar dishes were found in a Chinese tomb in the province of Jilin in the north of China?[27]

At the end of the fifteenth century, Islam had already been established in the Indonesian archipelago and had penetrated into the Philippine islands. Could it not be that the Lena Shoal junk was heading towards a sultanate and was transporting princely gifts? Could the porcelains of special shape and design, such as the ewers, bottles, pen boxes, certain blue and white dishes, white dishes, and the celadons from Longquan have been a special order for a local nobility? We cannot overlook the fact that the porcelain boxes contained rare and precious combs and lacquer boxes, pearls and spices, and that the miniature jars were filled with iron needles, which were of great value on islands with a shortage of metal. Were not the other porcelains, the green-glazed stoneware, the jars, which better reflected the taste of the islanders, intended to be sold locally?

The Lena Shoal junk reflects the commercial trade and production of a specific period and the huge quantity and quality of its cargo ensure that it will serve from now on as a unique source for comparison and dating.

---

[27] *Wenwu*, 1994, 9 ; 1995, 4 ; 1996, 11.

Photo 62. Blue and white porcelain bottle decorated with the symbols of the Passion. Height: 38.5 cm. British Museum (Brook Sewell Bequest 1963.5-20.7).

CONNOISSEURSHIP AND COMMERCE

Rosemary E. Scott

When a Han Chinese dynasty was once again established by General Zhu Yuanzhang in 1368, the name chosen for the new dynasty was Ming (brilliant). Such nomenclature was inevitably selected to convey an auspicious message, but certainly the arts of this dynasty fulfilled the promise of the name. The arts of the Ming – fine, decorative, literary or performing – attained new heights of perfection and diversity and also found new patrons. In an era that saw vast swings in political and economic fortunes, the arts generally flourished. The reinstatement of Chinese rule restored traditional patrons to positions of wealth and power, while social change provided new classes of patrons with distinct preferences. In addition, exploration and expansion of trade brought new and extended foreign markets.

This is not to belittle the role of the court in the development of taste, usage and technology especially in the early Ming period. This imperial impetus is particularly clear in the field of ceramics, which will be the main focus of this essay. Even in the imperial arena, however, some significant changes were driven by economic imperatives. One such change related to the ritual vessels for use on imperial altars. In the first year of his reign Zhu Yuanzhang, the Hongwu Emperor (1368–98), issued an edict in which it was decreed that thenceforth ritual vessels on the imperial altars should be made of porcelain rather than metal.[1] The reason for this change was undoubtedly the shortage of copper, but its corollary was increased concentration on the production of fine monochrome porcelains at the imperial kilns.

Yellow-glazed vessels were required for sacrifices at the *Diqitan* (Altar of Earth); blue-glazed vessels for the *Tiantan* (Altar of Heaven); red for the *Chaoritan* (Altar of the Sun); and white for the *Xiyuetan* (Altar of the Moon), as well as for sacrifices to the imperial ancestors. While versions of these monochrome porcelains had been produced at Jingdezhen in the Yuan dynasty (1279–1368), it was in the late fourteenth century and the first half of the fifteenth century that experimentation at the imperial kilns produced glazes of hitherto unseen clarity and beauty. These fine early Ming monochrome porcelains set the standards to which succeeding generations aspired.

Most connoisseurs would agree that these monochromes reached perfection during the reigns of the Yongle (1403–24) and Xuande (1425–36) emperors. Excavations at the site of the imperial kilns at Jingdezhen have shown that in the Yongle Emperor's reign a fine new white porcelain with an unctuously textured colourless glaze, known as "sweet-white", predominated. This can be directly linked to imperial requirements. On the one hand the emperor is known to have had a personal aesthetic preference for plain white objects,[2] on the other hand he was an ardent follower of Lamaist Buddhism, who regularly invited Tibetan hierarchs to perform rituals at the Chinese capital, and who also conducted extensive Buddhist ceremonies in honour of his deceased parents. Such activities required large quantities of white porcelain – either plain or decorated with finely incised Buddhist designs or prayers.

In relation to underglaze decorated ceramics, the early Ming reigns were important on a number of levels. Recent archaeological exploration has revealed that the Hongwu reign was a significant period for blue and white porcelains. The material excavated from the Hongwu stratum of the imperial kilns at Jingdezhen illustrates the transitional stages between the style of the late Yuan and that of the Yongle reign.[3] The Hongwu reign is also significant for the quantity of underglaze copper red porcelains produced. Once again the majority of these can be seen as a development of techniques produced in the late Yuan, but excavations at the site of the early Ming palace in Nanjing also revealed eave tiles of both *goutou* and *dishui* type, decorated with dragons and phoenixes moulded and then painted in underglaze copper red.[4]

The use of porcelain, albeit of relatively low quality, and the employment of such a difficult technique as underglaze copper red on tiles, provides an indication of considerable extravagance, and no doubt a desire to reinforce the emperor's supremacy. This use of porcelain as a royal building material was continued, of course, by the Yongle Emperor in projects such as the famous *Bao'ensi* "porcelain pagoda" built outside Nanjing, and by the Xuande Emperor in the employment of very fine blue and white decorated porcelain tiles such as those excavated at Jingdezhen.[5]

---

[1] C. Lau, "Ceremonial Monochrome Wares of the Ming Dynasty", *The Porcelains of Jingdezhen*, Colloquies on Art & Archaeology in Asia, No. 16, R. Scott, ed., Percival David Foundation, London, 1993, p. 86.

[2] For further discussion see R. Scott, "The Imperial Collections", *Collecting Chinese Art: Interpretation and Display*, Colloquies on Art & Archaeology in Asia, No. 20, S. Pierson, ed., Percival David Foundation, London, 2000, pp. 23–4.

[3] *Imperial Hongwu and Yongle Porcelain Excavated at Jingdezhen*, Chang Foundation, Taipei, 1996.

[4] *A Legacy of the Ming*, Nanjing Museum and the Art Museum, The Chinese University of Hong Kong, 1996, p. 35.

[5] *Xuande Imperial Porcelain Excavated at Jingdezhen*, Chang Foundation, Taibei, 1998, Nos. F18–21.

Imperial building projects were one of the ways in which the Ming emperors emphasised their legitimacy and their power. It is interesting to note not only that the Hongwu Emperor virtually razed the Yuan capital, Dadu, to the ground, but that he began construction of his new capital and new palace at Nanjing in 1366, some two years before the Ming dynasty was formally established. The Nanjing palace was used by the first three Ming emperors, until the third emperor, Yongle, decided that the capital should once again be transferred to the north and began the mammoth project of constructing what is known today as the Forbidden City in Beijing.

The enthusiasm of the Ming emperors for building projects, while providing stimulation for the arts, was a great drain on the treasury. The Chenghua Emperor (1465–87) not only failed to curb the extravagance of the members of his court, but expended a great quantity of funds himself on luxuries, including porcelains, and on the building of numerous Buddhist and Daoist temples in Beijing and elsewhere. He depleted the treasury to such an extent that his successor, the Hongzhi Emperor (1488–1505) was forced to stop all unnecessary expenditure as soon as he ascended the throne.[6]

In porcelain production, the Xuande and Chenghua reigns are seen as two pinnacles of achievement. Both are characterised by superb technical skill and remarkable artistic flair. The underglaze blue decorated porcelains of the Xuande reign, for example, are particularly prized for the intensity of their colour and the vitality of the painting style. The Chenghua porcelains incorporating overglaze enamels in their decoration are particularly prized for their delicacy and refinement.

The scale of production was also immense in these reigns. At one time during the Xuande reign, for instance, there were 58 kilns at Jingdezhen working to fill court orders. In both periods, however, the quality control at the imperial kilns was extremely tight, as is evidenced by the huge quantities of deliberately broken vessels found on the waste heaps at the kiln site.

From the time of their production, the porcelains of these two periods have been sought after by connoisseurs and have provided models for the porcelains of succeeding reigns. It is not surprising to find that a number of the porcelains found on the *Lena* junk, which has been dated to the Hongzhi reign, have close links with imperial porcelains of the Xuande and Chenghua periods. Although oval writing boxes have their origins in Near Eastern metalwork, the blue and white porcelain version found in the Lena Shoal junk cargo can be directly related to Xuande porcelain examples like that in the collection of the Percival David Foundation.[7]

The sea-creature motif, which probably developed from creatures described in the Chinese classic text *Shan Hai Jing*, and which can be seen on a large dish in the Lena Shoal junk cargo, rose to popularity on the imperial wares of the Xuande reign, and continued to be favoured on wares of Chenghua and Hongzhi before declining in popularity and re-emerging in the Wanli reign (1573–1620).[8]

The double *vajra*, associated with Tibetan Buddhism, first appeared on blue and white porcelains of the Yuan dynasty, but became a frequent motif inside vessels with Buddhist associations made in the Chenghua reign. Its use on porcelains, like those of the Lena Shoal junk, made in the reign of the Hongzhi Emperor, who was himself an ardent Buddhist, is therefore not surprising.

The influence of Xuande and Chenghua ceramics, however, extended much further than the Hongzhi reign and can be seen through the later Ming dynasty, the Qing and into the present day. By the sixteenth century collectors were prepared to pay extraordinarily high prices for Xuande and Chenghua porcelains, and they have been revered by connoisseurs and collectors ever since. They have also been the most frequently copied by those producing fakes.

While court taste dominated the early Ming period, this was not so later in the Ming dynasty. Increasingly the tastes of the educated élite were not tied to those of the court and the cultural centre of the country was not so much Beijing, but the Jiangnan region, where the literati devised their own particular, well documented tenets.[9] Their tastes were more scholarly, tending towards a painterly style in the decorative arts, and historical, philosophical and literary allusion in the motifs chosen as decoration. In addition to, but sometimes overlapping this literati market for decorative arts, was another. The rise of the merchant class in the Ming period provided a group of patrons with considerable disposable income and an inclination to buy works of art – both fine and decorative. The market for antiques, imitation antiques and contemporary art blossomed in the second half of the

---

[6] R. Scott and S. Pierson, *Flawless Porcelains: Imperial Ceramics from the Reign of the Chenghua Emperor*, Percival David Foundation, London, 1995, pp. 5–6.

[7] R. Scott, *Elegant Form and Harmonious Decoration: Four Dynasties of Jingdezhen Porcelain*, Percival David Foundation and Sun Tree Publishing, London/Singapore, 1992, p. 50, No. 40.

[8] Chen Ching-kuang, "Sea Creatures on Ming Imperial Porcelains", *The Porcelains of Jingdezhen*, Colloquies on Art & Archaeology in Asia, No. 16, R. Scott, ed., Percival David Foundation, London, 1993, pp. 101–22.

[9] See C. Clunas, *Superfluous Things*, Polity Press, Cambridge, 1991.

Ming dynasty, with trade in art objects being carried out with varying degrees of openness on various social levels.

It is worth noting that even in the sixteenth century the porcelains made for the court were to some extent influenced by those being made for other groups. Part of the reason for this was practical. The imperial kilns at Jingdezhen could not keep pace with the huge orders sent from Beijing. Despite considerable reorganisation of working practices at the imperial kilns, the orders were just too vast and some of the work had to be contracted out to private kilns. Part of the reorganisation was linked to the institution of the "single whip" system of taxation, which replaced inflexible corvée labour with the possibility of offering a monetary substitute.[10] One result of this was that craftsmen were able to hire themselves out to different kilns.

Painting styles on both imperial and non-imperial porcelains became more varied, and although the court orders were sometimes quite specific as regards decoration, some of the greater variety seen on non-imperial wares began to creep in. As a result it is much harder to distinguish between imperial and non-imperial wares of the later Ming period. As an economic necessity, imperial production ceased in the thirty-sixth year of the Wanli reign (1608) and the eunuch in charge was recalled to the capital. Thus, no Ming porcelain after that date can properly be regarded as "imperial production". The potters and other kiln workers in the Jingdezhen area would therefore have needed to concentrate on the other domestic markets and overseas trade in order to prosper.

The Hongwu reign was a crucial one, not only in re-establishing Han Chinese rule but in its reaffirmation of traditional Chinese culture. Although artistic influences continued to filter into China from outside her borders, the return to positions of power by Han Chinese and the economic resurgence of Han Chinese families, and thus their influence as patrons, inevitably affected the arts.

Nevertheless, the role of overseas trade was also of increasing importance. Relations with East Asia, South-East Asia, South Asia, the Near East and Europe were the subject of much official activity and concern. Early in 1369, for example, the Hongwu Emperor sent an announcement of his defeat of the Mongols and the establishment of the Ming dynasty to Korea and to Vietnam, and shortly afterwards to South India, Japan, Java and Champa.[11] He resumed relations with the states in the form of established rhetoric, specific rituals and tribute.[12]

This latter involved the presentation of gifts by the foreign rulers and the emperor's sending gifts in return. The Hongwu Emperor was also concerned to avoid the potential disruption that could be caused by unregulated trade with these foreign countries and he therefore banned private trade. This was a ban doomed to failure, and the illegal trade that inevitably took place was even less susceptible to regulation than normal private trade would have been. Official efforts to control private trade were an ongoing feature of the Ming period.

On the other hand the Ming period was also one of exploration. Among the most famous expeditions were the seven voyages into the South China Sea and the Indian Ocean undertaken between 1405 and 1433 by the eunuch admiral, Zheng He (1371–1433) on the orders of the Yongle Emperor. These voyages, undertaken in the largest ships of their day, demonstrated Chinese power and extended its influence. They also introduced Chinese goods to the peoples of these regions and brought back exotic goods, animals and people, as well as information, to the Chinese court.

Chinese goods were traded world wide during the Ming period, and it is worth noting that in "the late fifteenth century China was still the greatest economic power on earth. It had a population probably in excess of 100 million... a vast and sophisticated domestic trading network, and handicraft industries superior in just about every way to anything known in other parts of Eurasia".[13]

The most prized of China's products were silk and porcelain, both of which had been traded along the Silk Road for centuries. The trade across Central Asia had been greatly facilitated by the Mongols' preoccupation with improving and securing the roads, and despite the need to protect borders, Ming traders continued to benefit from these trade routes.

The appreciation of fine Chinese ceramics in the Near East can be seen in the magnificent collections surviving today from the Topkapi Saray, Istanbul and from the Ardebil Shrine, which is now in the Iran Bastan, Tehran. Chinese porcelains have been found in modern day Syria, Iraq and Egypt, and indeed at numerous sites on the Persian Gulf. The east coast of Africa, especially Kenya, has also yielded ample evidence of the trans-shipment of Chinese ceramics.

---

[10] M. Medley, "Organization and Production at Jingdezhen in the Sixteenth Century", *The Porcelains of Jingdezhen*, 1993, p. 73.

[11] Wang Gungwu, "Ming Foreign relations: Southeast Asia", *The Cambridge History of China: Vol. 8*, D. Twitchett and F. Mote, eds., Cambridge University Press, Cambridge, 1998, pp. 304–5.

[12] Ibid.

[13] W. Atwell, "Ming China and the Emerging World Economy, c. 1470–1650", *The Cambridge History of China: Vol. 8*, 1998, p. 378.

Chinese porcelain had been appreciated in India from at least Yuan times, as evidenced by the fine blue and white sherds found at the site of a fourteenth century Tughlaq palace in Delhi.[14] Chinese ceramics continued to find their way to India during the Ming dynasty, and considerable quantities of sherds have been found at ports along the west coast as well as at other sites. It was in India, of course, that Vasco da Gama acquired the Chinese porcelains which he presented to King Manuel I on his return to Portugal after his famous voyage of 1498–99.

Although a small number of Chinese ceramics had reached Europe prior to the Ming dynasty, it may fairly be said that the voyages of Vasco da Gama and Pedro Alvares Cabral spurred an increased desire for Chinese porcelains in Portugal, and between 1511 and 1514, for instance, João de Sá, the treasurer of spices at the Casa da Índia de Lisboa, noted that some 692 items of porcelain were received into the royal warehouse.[15] By the 1580s there were at least six emporia in just one street in Lisbon that specialised in Chinese porcelain.[16]

This desire for Chinese ceramics was not limited to Portugal. King Manuel made presents of porcelain to a number of royal households elsewhere in Europe, and cargoes arriving in Lisbon were soon spread through other countries. When the Dutch were no longer allowed access to these cargoes, they began expeditions of their own to Asia and were soon aggressive participants in the Chinese porcelain trade. Vast quantities of porcelain ware sold in Amsterdam in the latter part of the Ming period and disseminated to the rest of northern Europe.

Japan had been a recipient of Chinese ceramics since Tang times (618–907), but the Ming dynasty brought two new and significant features of the Sino-Japanese trade. Firstly, Chinese potters had rarely taken into account the tastes of their overseas buyers. Some special commissions were completed for Europeans in the Ming, such as the ewer decorated with an armillary sphere made for King Manuel in about 1519, now in the Fundação Medeiros e Almeida, Lisbon, and pieces bearing Christian iconography.

Generally, however, traders were expected to accept the designs commonly in use for the domestic market, or used on porcelains, like the so-called *kraak* ware, which were widely traded in Asia and Europe. At the end of the Ming period, however, certain special types of porcelain were made, particularly for the Japanese. These are commonly known as *Ko-sometsuke* and *Shonzui*, and although quite different from each other, these two wares

---

[14] E. Smart, "Fourteenth Century Chinese Porcelain from a Tughlaq Palace in Delhi", *Transactions of the Oriental Ceramic Society*, vol. 41, 1975–77, pp. 199–230.

[15] P. Dias, "Symbols and Images of Christianity on Chinese Porcelain", *Reflections: Symbols and Images of Christianity on Chinese Porcelain*, Museu de São Roque, Lisbon, 1996, p. 24.

[16] Atwell in *The Cambridge History of China: Vol. 8*, 1998, p. 395.

Fig. 41. Still-life oil painting depicting *kraak* porcelain bowls holding fruit, attributed to Osias Beert. Height: 46.5 cm, length: 79 cm. Rijkmuseum, Amsterdam; Inv. A2549.

reflected specific Japanese aesthetics and were generally made for use in the Japanese tea ceremony.

The second influence of the Japanese trade related to silver. Throughout the Ming dynasty there was a shortage of both copper and silver. Spanish-American silver came to China by way of Spanish and Portuguese trade, but in the late sixteenth and early seventeenth centuries silver production in Japan increased dramatically. The Ming government tried, without much success, to prevent direct trade between China and Japan, but in the sixteenth century the Portuguese acted as middlemen and were joined by the Dutch in the early seventeenth century.

Large quantities of Japanese silver thus came into China in exchange for the Chinese luxury goods, such as silk and porcelain, sought after by Japanese enjoying a period of relative peace and economic prosperity.[17] The impact of this influx of foreign silver on the economy of the late Ming period was quite dramatic. Some of the Japanese silver entered the Chinese economy via the countries of South-East Asia. It was used to purchase Chinese goods such as silk and porcelain, which could then be re-sold for very high prices in South-East Asia and the Philippines. South-East Asia had long been an important area for Chinese trade, either directly or as part of the Sino-Indian trade. The Philippines took on a new importance in the Ming dynasty in the Sino-Spanish trade, but while this trade was very profitable for both sides in its early years, it was precarious. Problems between Manila and Acapulco, or Manila and Macao, not to mention restrictions imposed by Spain or China, held the potential for financial disaster.

Shipwrecks off the Philippine coast, like that of the Lena Shoal junk, provide invaluable information regarding the trade in Chinese (and other) ceramics in the Ming period. The Lena Shoal junk cargo clearly reflects the dominance of Jingdezhen porcelains in this trade in the period c. 1500. While some Longquan-type celadons were included, there appears to have been relatively few ceramics from the popular kilns of the south-east. While Longquan celadons had a significant share of trade in the early Yuan dynasty, the kilns at Jingdezhen received considerable support from the Yuan government, and expanded.

By the beginning of the Ming period Jingdezhen had overtaken Longquan as the major ceramic production centre in China. While in the fifteenth century Chinese celadon wares were still sought after by Near Eastern and South-East Asian buyers, blue and white porcelains and enamelled wares gained increasing popularity.

The porcelains of the Ming period provide an endlessly fascinating subject for study. As more archaeological excavations are undertaken at the site of the imperial kilns at Jingdezhen we gain greater insight into imperial porcelains. As more textual research is done, we learn more of the domestic tastes and markets. As more maritime archaeology is carried out, the intricacies of international trade are revealed.

---

[17] Atwell dans *The Cambridge History of China*, vol. 8, 1998, p. 399.

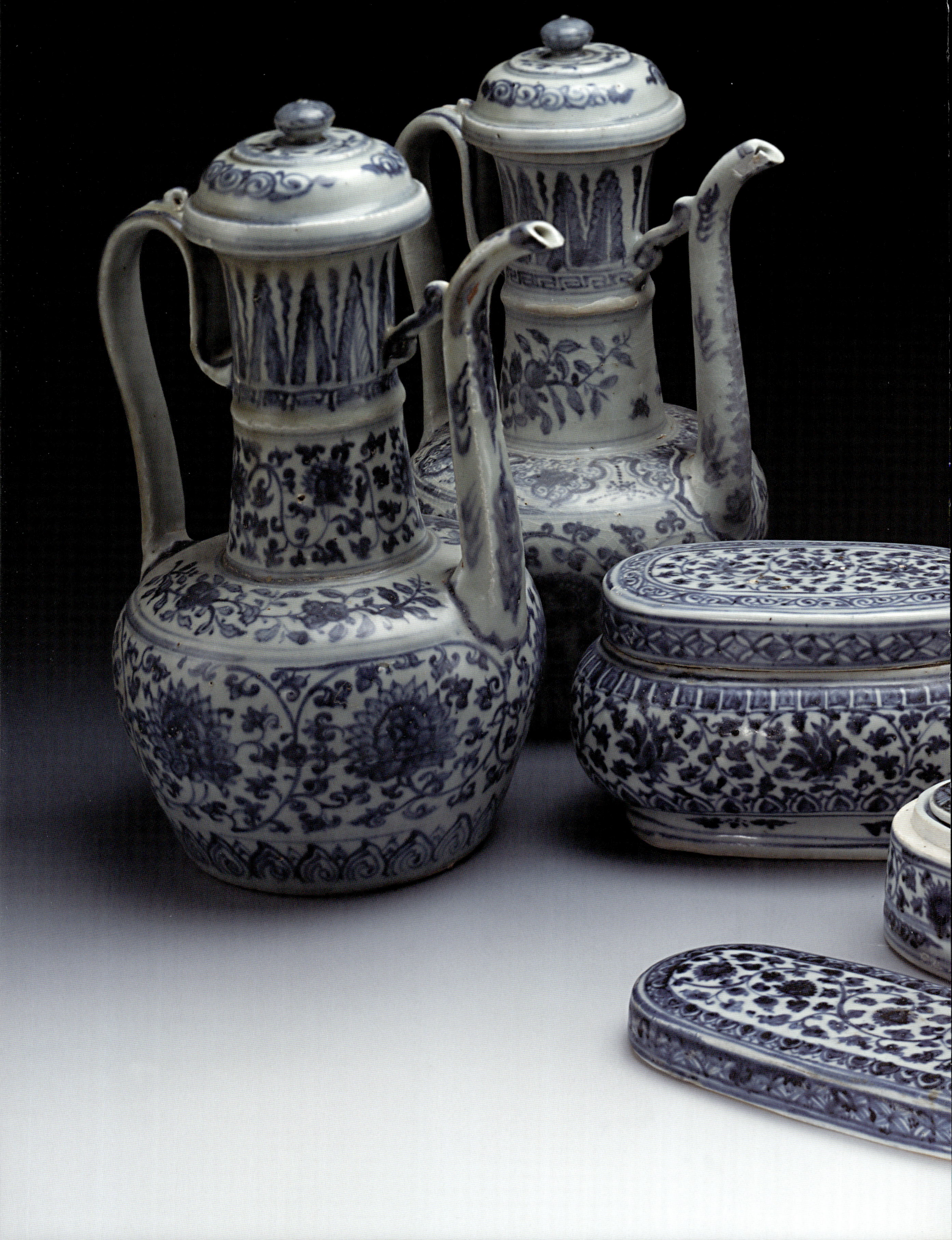

TYPOLOGY
the cargo of the wreck on the Lena Shoal

1. Ewers, bottles and *kendi*

Monique Crick

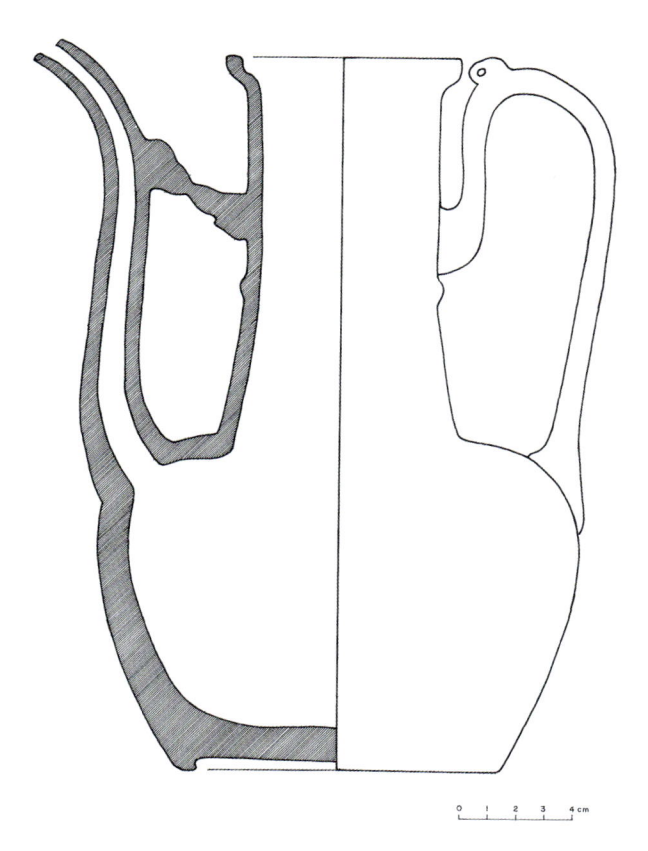

1.1 The large ewers

These ewers have a squat round body recessed towards the base and a long cylindrical neck, with a raised rib, ending in a flat raised rim. The curved handle is flat and has a loop on the top with which to attach the lid. The straight spout is curved at the tip and is attached to the neck by an S-shaped strut. The handle and spout end in a *ruyi*-head pattern. The ewers are made of thick white porcelain and stand on a wide, barely perceptible foot-rim. They are covered with a thick bluish glaze with the exception of the foot and the base.

Several ewers have been found which are identical in shape but each is decorated differently. The patterns are generally floral with the exception of one piece (Inv. 2192) whose neck is surrounded by animals galloping over waves. Ewers of this size constituted an exceptional cargo, although similar items can be found in the collections in the Topkapi Saray Museum in Istanbul and in the Teheran National Museum. A ewer in the same style, originating from the Philippines, is preserved in the Detroit Institute of Arts and another was exhibited in Hong Kong. Such ewers are unusual in the Philippines, and they may well have been destined for some Moslem sultanate, to be used during meals and thus for the ritual hand-washing customary in the Moslem world.

Pieces for comparison: Krahl, 1986, pp. 544–5; Pope, 1956, cat. 70; D. Lion-Goldschmidt, 1978, p. 140, ill. 131; *South-East Asian and Chinese Trade Potteries*, 1979, cat. 103.

1

Around the sides, a scroll of double-flowered chrysanthemums above lotus panels. Large frieze of lotus panels separated by narrow spaces around the shoulder. Branch with a bird perched on it on each side of the neck, above which there are friezes of *leiwen* and upright leaves. Handle and spout decorated respectively with scrolls, stylised flames and a branch of blossom.

H: 26.8 cm
Inv. 2042

2

Around the sides, a scroll of double-flowered chrysanthemums above lotus panels. Cloud collar panels alternating with pendant pearl strings around the shoulder. On each side of the neck, a branch with a bird perched on it, above which there is a frieze of *leiwen* and upright leaves. Handle and spout decorated respectively with scrolls, stylised flames and a branch of blossom.

H: 26.7 cm.
Inv. 2041

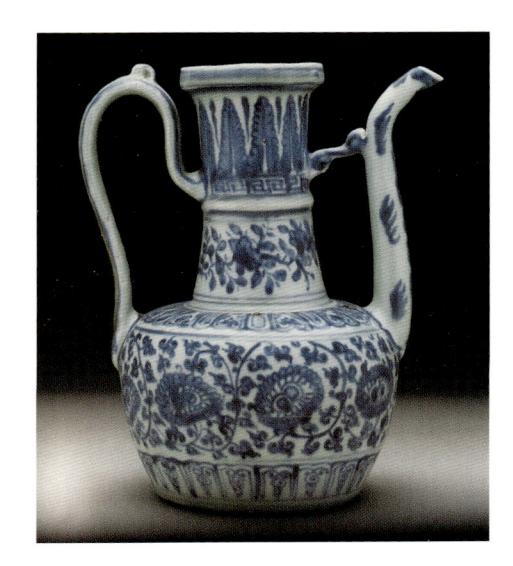

3

Around the body, a lotus scroll above a frieze of pointed petals. Two floral branches around the shoulder. Lotus scroll on the neck beneath a frieze of *leiwen* and upright leaves. Handle and spout decorated respectively with classical scrolls, stylised flames and a branch of blossom.

H: 26.8 cm.
Inv. 2140

4

Ewer decorated with a lotus scroll above pointed petals. Around the shoulder, cloud collar panels with lotuses alternating with pendant pearl strings. On each side of the neck, a branch on which a bird perches and above this a frieze of *leiwen* and upright leaves. Handle and spout decorated respectively with classical scrolls, stylised flames and a branch of blossom.

H: 26.6 cm
Inv. 2428

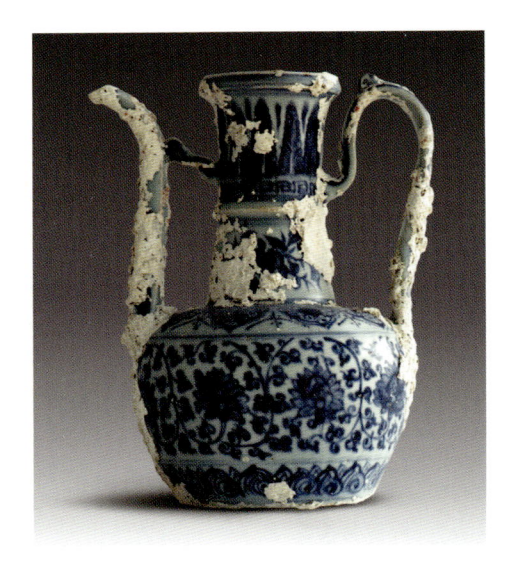

LOST AT SEA

1.2 Blue and white pear-shaped ewers
These pear-shaped ewers have a flattened body decorated on each side with a teardrop-shaped medallion in relief. The neck flares at the top, and the straight spout is curved at the tip. It is attached to the neck by an S-shaped strut. The handle is curved. They stand on a low straight foot. The pieces are made of thick white porcelain covered with a bluish glaze except on the foot-rim. The shape is based on that of contemporary silverware. Such ewers are rare, only four identical ones were found in the cargo.

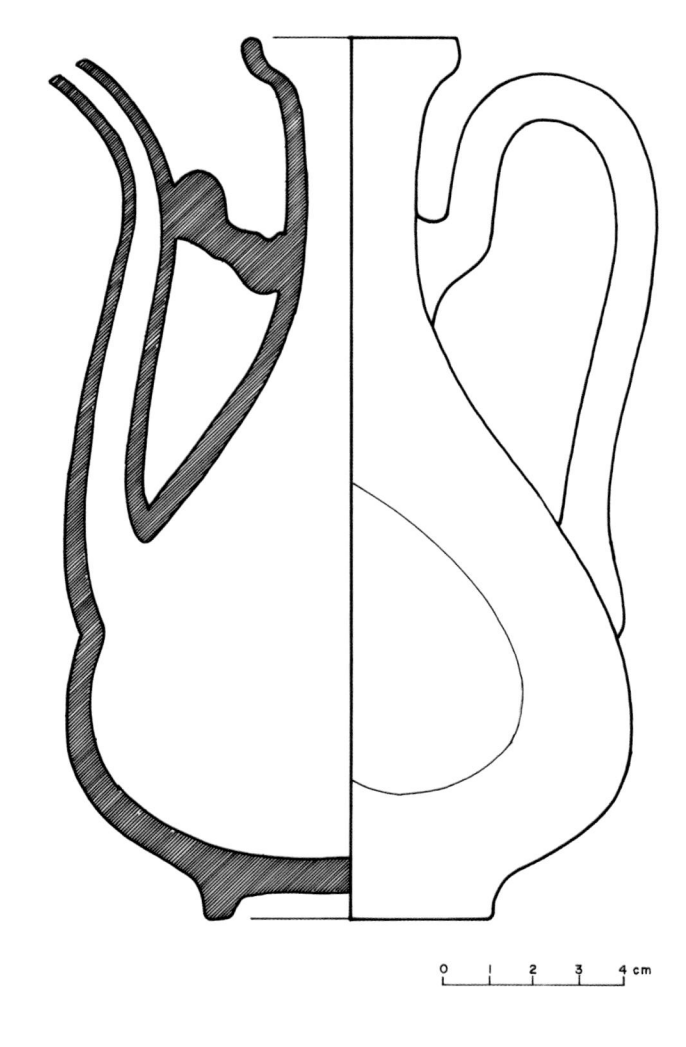

5

A decoration of lotus scrolls in the teardrop-shaped panels in relief, flanked by branches of blossom, and little clouds below the handle and spout. A frieze of pointed petals above the foot and superimposed bands in registers around the neck, consisting of small rectangular panels, *leiwen* and stiff leaves. Scrolls amongst flames on the spout and a series of emblems above a *ruyi*-shaped motif on the handle.

H: 21.1 cm
Inv. 2118

1.3 Blue monochrome pear-shaped ewers

These pear-shaped ewers have a flattened body decorated on each side with a teardrop-shaped medallion in relief. The neck flares at the top. The spout is very curved at the tip and emerges from the moulded head of a dragon. The curved handle has a loop by which the lid is attached at the top. The low foot is straight. These pieces are covered in a monochrome blue glaze, with the exception of the interior and the base whose glaze is colourless. The foot-rim is unglazed. No trace of decoration has been detected. The shape is based on that of a metal prototype. Such monochrome ewers are unique for the period and the cargo only contained two identical ones.

6

H: 20.8 cm
Inv. 2040 (or 2119)

1.4 Ewers with an ovoid body

These two incomplete ewers have a squat ovoid body and a long, flared neck. They are made of thick, greyish porcelain and are covered with a dull glaze with the exception of the slightly recessed base. The decoration, in bluish-black, is perfunctory and carelessly painted. A similar ewer of better quality is preserved in the Topkapi Saray Museum in Istanbul. In the sixteenth century, this type of ewer would have had a small flared foot.

Pieces for comparison: Krahl, 1986, Vol. II, cat. 670, 815; Yeo, Martin, 1978, pl. 26.

7

Lotus scrolls around the body above a band of lotus petal panels. A branch of blossom on each side of the neck surmounted by friezes of small scrolls and upright leaves.

H: 19 cm
Inv. 2404

LOST AT SEA

1.5 Duck-shaped ewers

These little ewers are moulded into the shape of a pair of mandarin ducks swimming side by side. With the exception of the base, they are covered in a bluish glaze. They exist in several versions of which two are represented in the cargo. They are filled through the opening in the back of the birds and the liquid is poured out through the beak if it is pierced. This shape of receptacle first appears in the early fifteenth century and was part of a set of small porcelain objects, including cricket cages and bird-feeders, which were made for the wealthier classes. Such pieces were originally used for pouring the water needed for the preparation of ink. They are often found in collections formed in South-East Asia. The cover may be domed with a knob on the top, or shaped like a lotus leaf. Both models have been found in the cargo.

Pieces for comparison: Aga-Oglu, 1975, cat. 129; 1982, cat. 184; Jörg, 1997, cat. 9; Li Zhen, 1996, No. 409; *South-East Asian and Chinese Trade Potteries*, 1979, cat. 91; Wiesner, cat. 179; Wiesner, 1983, cat. 62; Yeo, Martin, 1978, pl. 28; *Yuan's and Ming's Porcelains*, 1999, ill. 165.

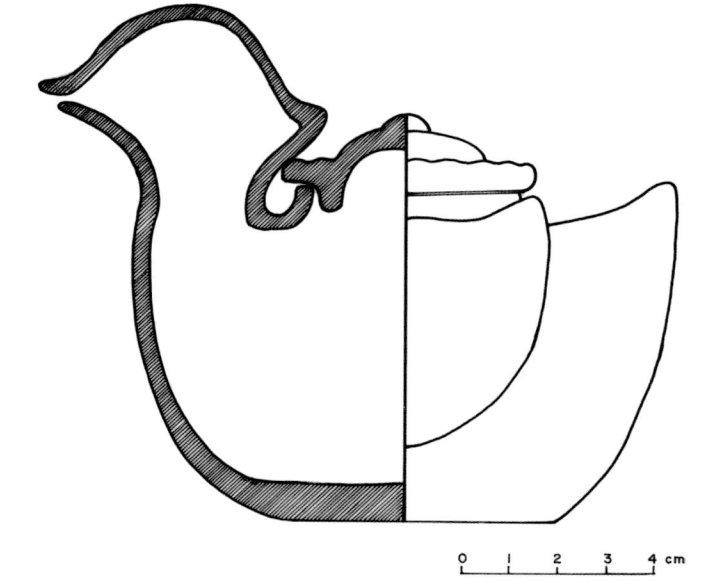

8

Moulded ewer in two parts, joined in the middle of the ducks' bodies. Details of the anatomy and plumage carefully painted in blue-grey cobalt.

H: 11 cm; max. length: 13 cm
Inv. 2090

9

Moulded ewer joined in the middle of the ducks' bodies. Details of the anatomy and plumage carefully painted in light blue cobalt.

H: 10.9 cm; max. length: 13 cm
Inv. 2091

10

Moulded ewer in the form of two ducks whose beaks are touching. Details of the anatomy and plumage hastily painted in blue-black cobalt under a whitish glaze.

H: 7 cm
Inv. 2092

11

Moulded ewer in the form of two ducks whose beaks are touching. Details of the anatomy and plumage carefully painted in grey-blue cobalt bleu under a bluish glaze.

H: 7 cm
Inv. 2120

LOST AT SEA

1.6 Bottles with globular body

These bottles with globular bodies have a neck narrowed in the centre, somewhat resembling an hour-glass in shape, and end in an everted rim. Three horizontal raised ribs around the body delimit the decorated areas. The pieces are fashioned from thick, white porcelain and stand on a low, straight, wide foot. They are covered in a thick, bluish glaze with the exception of the foot-rim. The opening is sealed with a porcelain disk pierced with oval holes. The bottles are copies of a metal shape, although the original model was still unknown at the time of writing. These were almost certainly water-bottles and the pierced opening borrows the principle of oriental water jugs in which the filter acts as protection against dust and insects. It also permits the aeration of the liquid and keeps it cool when the ewer is made of porous pottery. These pieces are represented by only a few examples in the cargo and are very rare. Similar examples are found only in the Topkapi Saray Museum in Istanbul. The decoration is arranged in successive registers according to the shape of the items.

Pieces for comparison: Krahl, 1986, Vol. II, cat. 665.

12

Designs painted without an outline in blue-black cobalt which has dripped due to the brush being saturated in paint. A frieze of waves and rocks around the base, and a scroll of *lingzhi* fungi alternating with lotus scrolls on the body and neck. A light scroll of leaves on the upper part of the neck. Opening sealed by a pierced porcelain disk with oval holes.

H: 20.1 cm; max. width: 12.1 cm
Inv. 2143

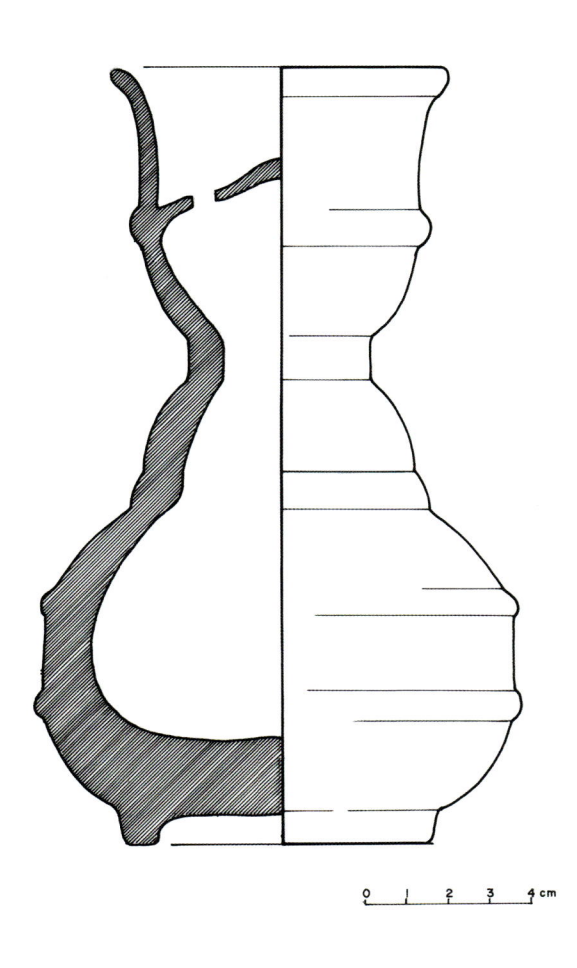

Typology

13

Designs painted without an outline in blue-grey cobalt. Large border of lotus panels separated by narrow spaces around the base. A scroll of *lingzhi* fungi and star-shaped flowers, and a lotus scroll on the body. Four cloud collar panels decorated with lotuses on the base of the neck, zigzag motifs on the narrowed part and superimposed registers of lotus scrolls and small leaves at the top of the neck. Opening sealed by a pierced porcelain disk with four oval holes.

H: 19.2 cm; max. width: 11.4 cm
Inv. 2144

14

Designs painted without an outline in dark cobalt blue. Petals moulded around the base of the neck. Three successive registers on the body consisting of *lingzhi* fungi, small lotuses and lotuses with larger flowers and carefully drawn petals. Foliate scroll motifs arranged around the base of the neck and scrolls of small lotus and leaves on the upper part. Opening sealed by a pierced porcelain disk with five oval holes.

H: 20.9 cm; max. width: 12.5 cm
Inv. 3110

LOST AT SEA

1.7 *Kendi* ewer

The *kendi* ewer is made of thick white porcelain and is covered with a bluish glaze with the exception of the base. It has a bulbous shape ending in a straight cylindrical neck which terminates in a rounded lip, and a tapering spout. The decoration is painted directly without outlines in dark blue and is arranged in successive registers. A frieze of pointed petals emphasises the base while a scroll of small-leaved lotuses surrounds the body and the spout. The shoulder is decorated with four cloud collar panels, inside which there is a lotus scroll. A classic scroll above which there is a branch of prunus blossom surrounds the base of the neck. A single example was found in the cargo. This type of ewer, whose neck also serves as a handle, may take a variety of forms. It is specific to South-East Asia where it is still very popular and continues to be made there in terracotta.

Pieces for comparison: Adhyatman, 1990, ill. 149; Krahl, 1986, Vol. II, cat. 668; Pope, 1956, pl. 69; *South-East Asian and Chinese Trade Potteries*, 1979, cat. 102; Wiesner, cat. 184; Yeo, Martin, 1978, pl. 27, 30.

15

15 cm
Inv. 2129

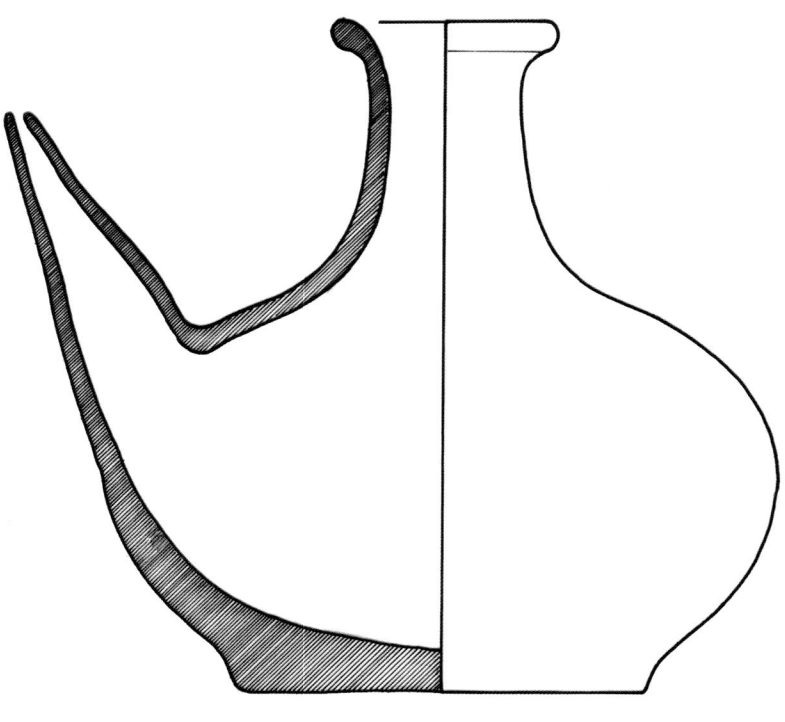

2. Jars and lids

2.1 *Guan* jar

In China, the *guan* jar was a utilitarian container that was used for holding water or food and it was imported for the same purpose into South-East Asia. When transported on junks, the jars were used for holding other goods, such as cups, little jars, glass beads or spices. They were introduced into Europe through the Portuguese, for whom they may have had a different use. They became rare, decorative items and often served as vases in private homes and as altar vases in churches.

This *guan* jar is of fine white porcelain with an ovoid body, rounded shoulder and straight neck. It is covered with a slightly bluish glaze with the exception of the flat base. The decoration, which is painted in grey-blue, is placed between two parallel lines. The foot is outlined with a frieze of upright lotus panels. *Ruyi*-shaped motifs appear on the curve of the shoulder interspersed with a design of leaves, the whole pattern being underlined with a series of dots. An ample lotus scroll, showing the lotuses alternately facing and in profile, with small spearhead leaves, is coiled around the bulb. Only two *guan* porcelain jars were found in the cargo, one of them a fragment. Their relative fragility made them unsuitable for mass export. Similar pieces were included in the funeral furniture of tombs in China. Pieces of similar shape are, however, well represented in collections in Portugal, the Middle East and Asia, but they are usually much larger and thicker.

Pieces for comparison: J. Addis, 1978, pp. 134–135; Aga-Oglu, 1982, cat. 86; Pinto de Matos, 1996, p. 18–19; Wenwu, 1973, no. 12; Yeo, Martin, 1978, pl. 18, 31; Yunpeng Huang, Li Zhen, 1988, ill. 15, 86.

16

16: H: 16.3 cm
Inv. 2611

2.2 Jarlets

The cargo also contained 28 intact jarlets of different shapes and sizes, of which some had lids that fitted them perfectly. Jarlets were very popular and much prized by the inhabitants of the archipelagos, who often used them to hold fish sauce, cosmetics, perfumes made of wax, grease and jasmine, or camphor oil and musk. These miniature receptacles were soon adopted by witch-doctors for preserving holy oils, medicines and magic unguents to cure ills and chase away the evil spirits of the body. If a person stopped being a faith healer, it was advisable to throw away such a receptacle. If it had been used for evil purposes, its powers might turn against members of the owner's family. It was thus wise to perform a ceremony at the base of a tree and leave the container there. It would then become safe because the evil spirit inside it would rise into the leaves of the tree and render the jar harmless. These ceramics were often supposed to be of supernatural origin and were believed to absorb the magic or curative powers of their contents. Such little jars are often found with damaged rims. A minuscule fragment would be reduced to powder before being mixed in food or drink. Tiny shards could even serve as magic bait for making a miraculous catch of fish. These useful containers are often represented in collections in Asia.

17

Small jar with a straight, narrow neck and rounded sides. Flat unglazed base. Design painted in dark blue under a bluish glaze. Lotus blossoms amidst scrolls on the body, above a frieze of lotus panels around the base. Medallions in the form of cloud collar panels on the shoulder, decorated with lotuses and alternating with a half flower head. Cloud motifs on the neck.

Inv. 2608
H: 10.8 cm

Piece for comparison: Jörg, 1997, cat. 8.

18

Small jar with an ovoid body, rounded shoulder and splayed neck with round rim. Base slightly concave and unglazed. Design painted in grey under a bluish glaze. Around the body, branches of blossom between two blue concentric circles. Lotus panel frieze around the base. A border of *ruyi* heads runs around the shoulder and there are two blue lines on the neck.

No Inv.
H: 10.2 cm

Pieces for comparison: Yunpeng Huang, Li Zhen, 1988, ill. 78; for the central motif: Sorsby, 1974, cat. 103.

19

Small jar with an ovoid body, rounded shoulder and straight neck. Flat unglazed base. Design painted in grey-blue under a bluish glaze. Discontinuous scroll of stylised lotuses with spearhead leaves on the body above a frieze of lotus panels. Ring of small, simplified leaves on the shoulder and two blue lines on the neck.

Inv. 2126
H: 9.8 cm

Pieces for comparison: Aga-Oglu, 1982, cat. 152; Yeo, Martin, 1978, pl. 79; Yunpeng Huang, Li Zhen, 1988, ill. 85.

20

Small ovoid jar with rounded shoulder and narrow straight neck. Decoration painted in blue-grey under a bluish glaze. Spiral lotus scroll with small spearhead leaves on the body, between two blue lines. One blue line on the neck.

Inv. 2023
H: 5.4 cm

Piece for comparison: Aga-Oglu, 1975, cat. 141.

21

Small ovoid jar, with rounded shoulder and narrow straight neck. Unglazed base. Design painted in blue-grey under a bluish glaze. Motifs of cloud collar panels with pendant pearl strings on the body. A blue line on the neck.

Inv. 2016
H: 5.4 cm

Pieces for comparison: Aga-Oglu, 1972, cat. 22; 1982, cat. 145.

22

Small ovoid jar with rounded shoulder and short neck with wide opening. Unglazed base. Design painted in dark blue under a bluish glaze. Cloud collar panels with pendant pearl strings on the body. A blue line on the neck.

Inv. 2150
H: 9.4 cm

Pieces for comparison: Wiesner, 1983, cat. 60; Yeo, Martin, 1978, pl. 79.

23

Small jar with globular body and straight narrow neck. Shallow inclined foot and slightly recessed unglazed base. Design painted in grey-blue under a bluish glaze. Stylised lotus scrolls with small spearhead leaves on the body between two blue lines. A blue line on the neck.

Inv. 592
H: 6.2 cm

Pieces for comparison: Aga-Oglu, 1982, cat. 143; Yeo, Martin, 1978, pl. 79.

24

Miniature jarlet with globular body and straight narrow neck. Flat unglazed base. Design painted in dark blue under a bluish glaze. Stylised lotus scrolls with small spearhead leaves on the body between two blue lines. A blue line on the neck.

No Inv.
H: 4.1 cm

Pieces for comparison: Aga-Oglu, 1982, cat. 143; Yeo, Martin, 1978, pl. 79.

25

Small rectangular jar with narrow neck. Small inclined foot and slightly recessed unglazed base. Design painted in grey-blue under a bluish glaze. Flower sprays on each side between two *ruyi*-like motif borders.

Inv. 3794
H: 8.6 cm

Pieces for comparison: Aga-Oglu, 1975, cat. 114; Wiesner, cat. 175.

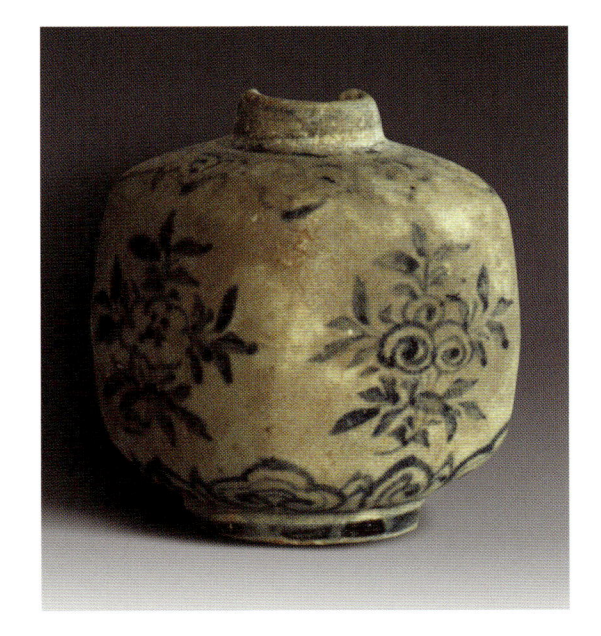

26

Small spherical jar. Low sloping foot and slightly recessed unglazed base. Design painted in dark blue under a bluish glaze. Scroll of stylised lotuses with small spearhead leaves on the body. Border of small petals along the rim and stylised lotus panels around the base. This little jar contained a batch of iron needles.

No Inv.
H: 8 cm

Pieces for comparison: Aga-Oglu, 1982, cat. 135, 140, 147; Sorsby, 1974, cat. 101.

27

Small spherical jar. Low sloping foot and slightly recessed unglazed base. Design painted in dark blue under a bluish glaze. Stylised floral sprays alternating with foliate scroll motifs. Small petals border on the rim. Rounded lid with pointed knob decorated with twigs.

No Inv.
H: 8 cm

LOST AT SEA

2.3 Lids

Thirty-nine lids were found, in six different shapes and potted in thick porcelain. They were destined for large ewers, duck-shaped ewers and jars. The lids of the large ewers, of which there are 19 in all, have a straight, clearly defined rim and are very domed in shape. A special feature of these lids is an interior cone-shaped partition which was used to keep the lid in place. The second type of lid, of which six have been found, has the more usual rounded shape, with a pointed knob of various sizes and a thin, rounded rim. (Yunpeng Huang, Li Zhen, 1988, ill. 15, 78, 86). The decoration consists of small scrolls. There are also 11 small lids of the same shape, all decorated with sprigs. One single small lid was found with a rounded shape and pointed knob (Inv. 3605) but in monochrome blue. It is assumed to have been destined for one of the blue ewers found in the cargo. Two lids in the form of lotus leaves are also in monochrome blue and fit the duck-shaped ewers perfectly.

28

Domed lid for large ewer with straight edge and onion-shaped knob. Thick bluish glaze on the outside, unglazed interior surface with a central partition in the form of an open cone. Designs of classic scrolls and branches painted in dark blue. Tip of the knob painted blue.

Inv. 4119
D: 9.4 cm; H: 5.8 cm

29

Domed lid for large ewer with straight edge and onion-shaped knob. Thick bluish glaze on the outside, unglazed interior surface with a central partition in the form of an open cone. Design of *ruyi*-like motifs and small petals painted dark blue. Tip of the knob painted blue.

Inv. 2147
D: 9.4 cm; H: 5.4 cm

30

Domed lid for large ewer with straight edge and onion-shaped knob. Thick bluish glaze on the outside, unglazed interior surface with a central partition in the form of an open cone. Design painted in dark blue; floral scrolls and border of trilobed designs around the knob. Tip of the knob painted blue.

Inv. 8
D: 9.5 cm; H: 5.7 cm

31

Small rounded lid with thin, rounded edge and pointed knob. Bluish glaze on the outside, unglazed interior. Designs of twigs painted in blue-grey. Tip of the knob painted blue.

Inv. 2102
D: 4.5 cm; H: 2.5 cm

Piece for comparison: Sorsby, 1974, cat. 101

32

Small moulded lid shaped like a lotus leaf in blue monochrome.

Inv. 4121
D: 5.4 cm; H: 2.2 cm

Pieces for comparison: Jörg, 1997, cat. 9; Wiesner, 1983, cat. 62.

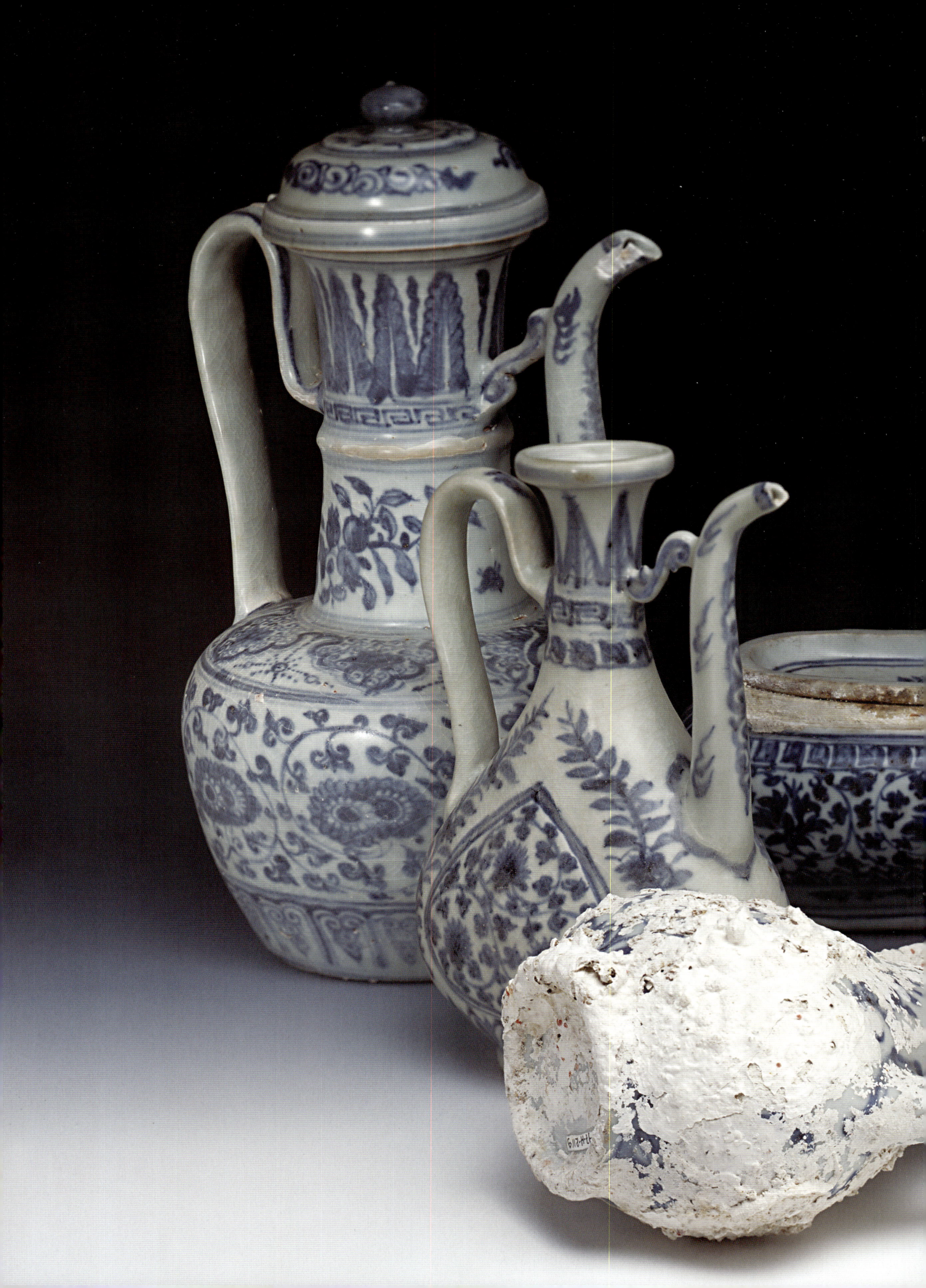

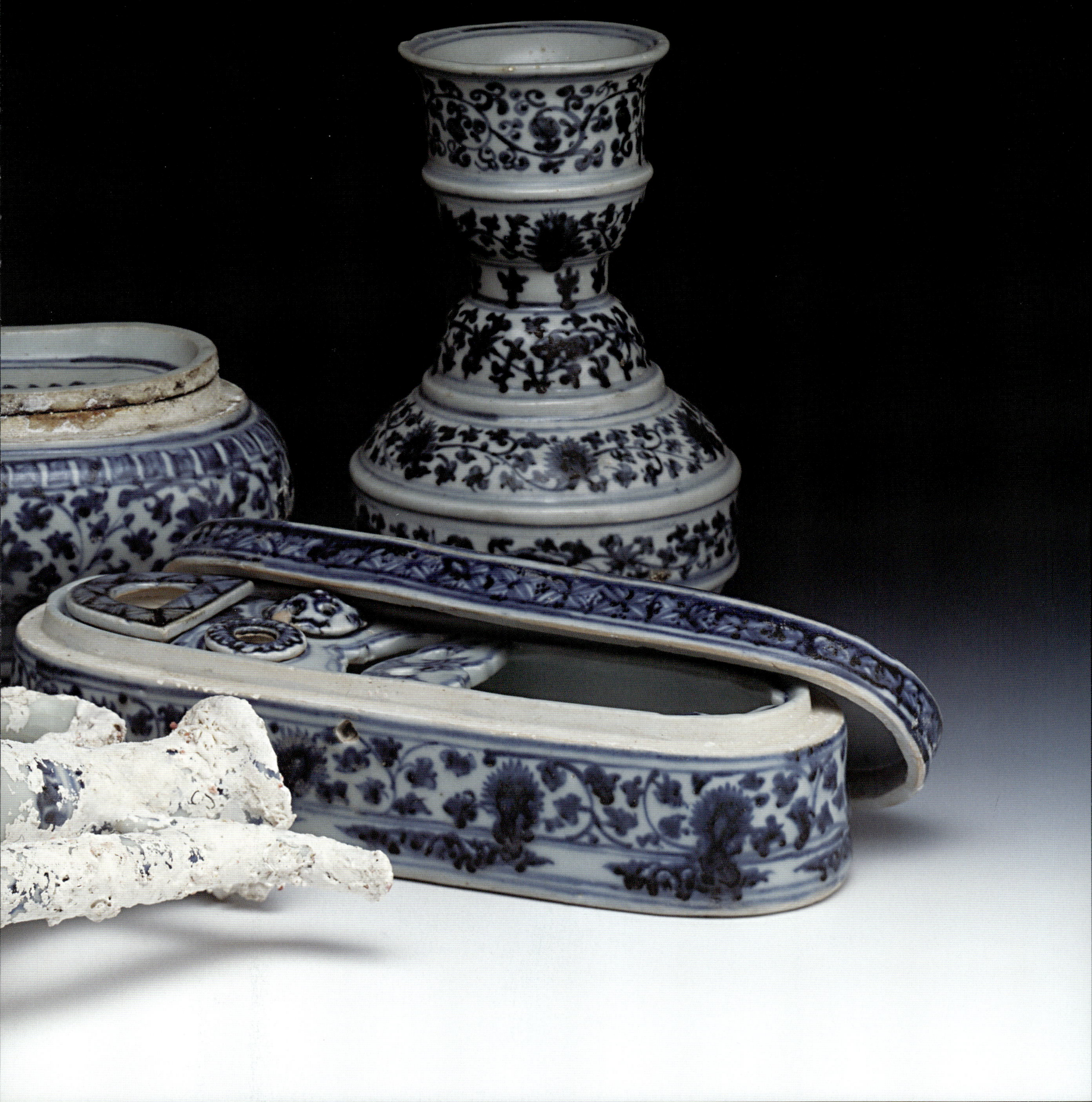

3. The boxes

3.1 Pen boxes

The thick porcelain pen boxes have an elongated oval shape with vertical sides and a slightly domed lid. They are painted in dark cobalt blue and covered with a bluish glaze with the exception of the rim and the slightly recessed base. The interior is divided into compartments. On one side there is a long, oval, lobed compartment ending in pierced decoration in the form of the head of a *ruyi* sceptre and on the other side there are three openings. The D-shaped opening was destined to hold the ink-well and the circular openings were for the sand porcelain container pierced with little holes and the silk or linen thread porcelain container. The thread was inserted into the ink-well to stop the tip of the quill touching the bottom and thus wearing out. The ancient calligraphers were highly concerned with their art and put great store by the quality and preservation of their quills. The inkstands found in the Lena Shoal junk are unique because they are complete with their porcelain accessories. Even the hole to which metal fittings would be attached was left in the porcelain by the potter. These pen boxes were certainly destined for Moslem clients who were the only ones who used them. The shape of the pen boxes is foreign to Chinese tradition and first appears in the early fifteenth century, inspired by an Islamic metal prototype. The Emperor Yongle had set up a language academy at this time, first in Nanking then in Peking, so as to maintain a secretariat capable of keeping up a correspondence with foreign countries. These pen boxes may have been produced for the foreign clientele as well as for imperial civil servants. The late fifteenth century was a period of prosperity and expansion and it is not surprising that this shape was copied once again at a time when links with the Near East had been renewed and Moslem communities were developing in China and South-East Asia. Three pen boxes were found in the cargo, two of which are complete.

Pieces for comparison: Liu Xinyuan, et al., 1996, p. 296, cat. 118; Gotuaco, Tan, Diem, 1997, cat. M34; Krahl, 1986, Vol. II, cat. 666; Yeo, Martin, 1978, pl. 12.

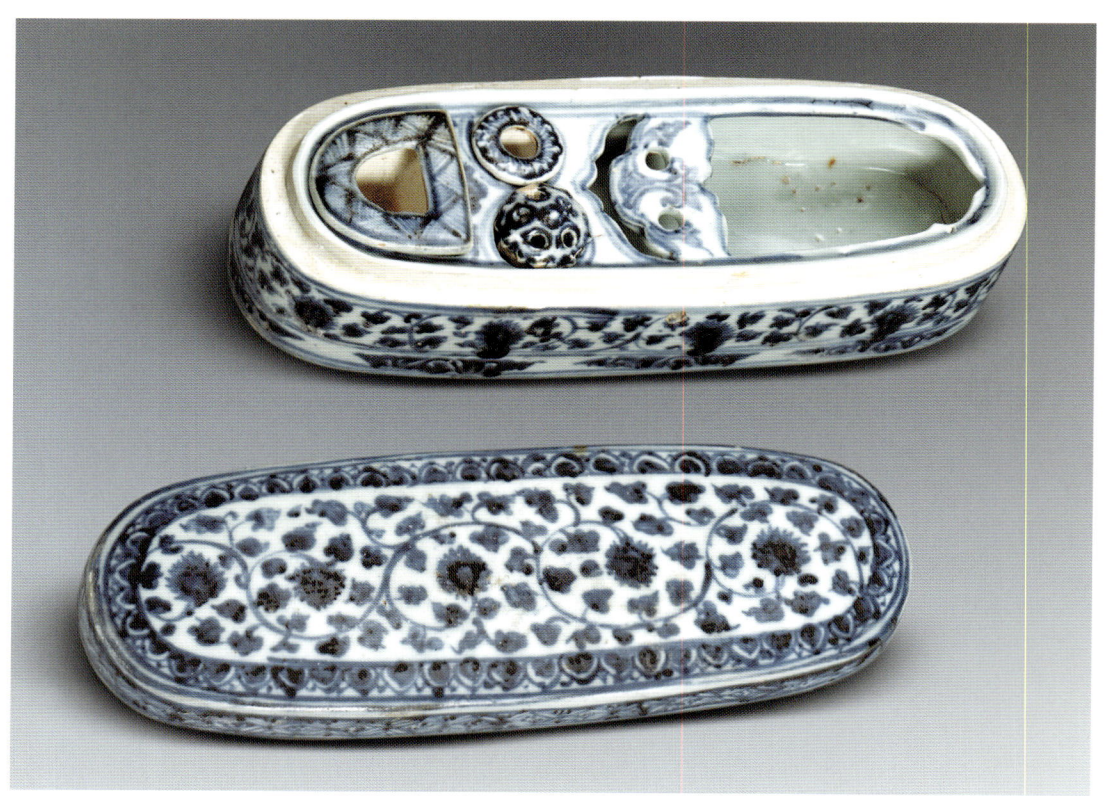

33

Design painted without a contour. A border of small scrolls around the base. On the sides, stylised interrupted lotus scrolls with pointed petals between two parallel blue lines. Inside, there is a blue line around the edge and the openings, and foliate scroll motifs on the *ruyi*-shaped opening. Trellis designs on the straight side of the lid. A lotus scroll surrounded by a frieze of pointed petals inside a double fillet on top of the lid. The flat top of the inkstand is decorated with a border of chevrons, and the top of the thread-holder has a frieze of little petals. The holes in the sander are outlined with a blue line, as is the edge.

Inv. 2610/2025/2026/2027
L: 23.4 cm; H: 7.4 cm

3.2 The oval boxes

Various shapes of porcelain box existed at this period. They were usually round but were also shaped like a metal ingot, a crescent or a peach. Large oval boxes are unusual. These oval boxes with convex sides mounted on a small splayed foot have a flat lid with straight sides and contain a curved fitted tray. They are usually painted in dark cobalt blue without an outline being traced first and covered in a bluish glaze with the exception of the rounded foot which is unglazed. The slightly recessed base is generally glazed. Some pieces have distorted slightly during firing.

These oval boxes with their small interior trays are fairly rare but are represented in a few collections. This model also exists in blue monochrome but only one example is known. Other oval boxes, which are not represented in the cargo, are slightly different in appearance, having a lid whose sides are rounded and being without a differentiated base. The unusual shape of the cargo boxes is inspired by the metal boxes of the Near East which are shaped like a Chinese style lunch box but which were used for holding precious objects. Indeed, the porcelain boxes on the Lena Shoal junk contained precious objects such as combs, a red lacquer box, glass beads, or spices, pepper and areca nuts. Some were stored separately in special packaging and were no doubt to be used as gifts for an important person.

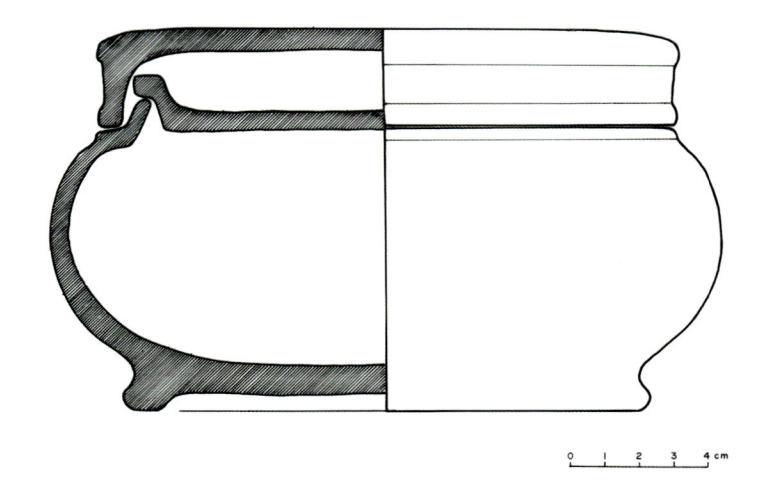

Pieces for comparison: J.W. Allan, *Oriental Art*, 1971; J. Carswell, 1985, cat. 34; Harrisson, 1986, cat. 50; Gotuaco, Tan, Diem, 1997, cat. M35; *South-East Asian and Chinese Trade Potteries*, 1979, p. 109, ill. 96; p. 139, ill. 148; Wiesner, cat. 181; Yeo, Martin, pl. 29.

34

Design arranged in successive registers. Border of little flowers edged with leaves around the base. Branches of blossom on the sides (camellias or pomegranate flowers) between two friezes of small rectangular panels. Border of little petals around the edge. Classic scrolls on the straight edge and around the lid and a branch of blossom on the top.

Inv. 2609
L: 20.5 cm; H: 11.4 cm

35

Design arranged in successive registers. Lotus scroll with large petals on the side between a frieze of vertical leaves and a band of small rectangular panels. Flowers flanked with elongated leaves around the foot. Identical lotuses on the top of the lid, edged with classic scrolls. Trellis designs on the straight sides. Unglazed base. Branch of blossom on the interior tray.

Inv. 2616
L: 20 cm; H: 10.9 cm

36

Design arranged in successive registers. Scroll of small lotuses with pointed petals on the sides between a frieze of vertical leaves and a band of small rectangular panels. Flowers flanked with elongated leaves around the foot. Looped lotus scrolls on the top of the lid, surrounded by two blue lines. Border of classic scrolls on straight sides. Prunus branch on the interior tray.

Inv. 2617
L: 20.1 cm; H: 10.3 cm

37

Design arranged in successive registers. Scroll of small lotuses with pointed petals on the sides between a frieze of vertical leaves and a band of small rectangular panels. Border of small petals around the edge. Flowers flanked with elongated leaves around the foot. Lotus scroll on the top of the lid surrounded by a trellis border. Classic scroll pattern on the straight sides.

Inv. 2618
L: 19.5 cm; H: 10.4 cm

38

Vertical lotus flowers alternating with foliate scroll motifs on the sides between a frieze of petals and a band of small rectangular panels. Border of little petals around the edge. Flowers flanked with elongated leaves around the foot.

Inv. 2753
L: 19 cm; H: 11.3 cm

39

Design arranged in successive registers. Border of small flowers flanked by leaves around the base. On the sides, branches of blossom (camellias or pomegranate flowers) between two friezes of small rectangular panels. Border of little petals around the edge. Inside objects covered in concretions.

Inv. 2756
L: 20 cm; H: 7.5 cm

40

Scroll of lotus flowers, each bearing one of the Eight Emblems of Buddhism, on the sides between a frieze of lotus panels and a band of small rectangular panels. Border of little petals around the edge. Flowers flanked with elongated leaves around the foot.

Inv. 3759
L: 18.9 cm; H: 8.9 cm

41

Small interior tray with a prunus branch design surrounded by two parallel blue lines.

No Inv.

42

Small interior tray with a branch of blossom design on the bottom surrounded by two parallel blue lines. Small scrolls on the side and two blue lines under the edge.

No Inv.

LOST AT SEA

43

Small interior tray with a bouquet of lotuses tied with a ribbon on the bottom, surrounded by two parallel blue lines. Two blue lines under the edge.

No Inv.

3.3 Ingot-shaped boxes

Only the metal ingot-shaped lid of this box was found. It is made of thick porcelain and decorated on top with two phoenixes flying amidst lotus scrolls. The pattern is inspired by the designs seen on embroidered or woven textiles. It is painted in blue-grey cobalt under a bluish glaze.

Pieces for comparison: Aga-Oglu, 1975, cat. 127; 1982, cat. 128; Wiesner, cat. 189; Yeo, Martin, 1978, pl. 29, ill. 51.

44

Inv. 2547
W: 11.1 cm; H: 2.2 cm

3.4 Betel-nut boxes

These thick white porcelain boxes stand on a small foot. They are covered in bluish glaze, with the exception of the base and the funnel-shaped neck. Only two lidless boxes were found. They were part of the paraphernalia needed to prepare betel nuts for chewing – receptacles for areca nuts, betel leaves, and quicklime. This particular type of long-necked container was for the quicklime. Betel-nut boxes are associated with an ancestral tradition in the tropics. They are often produced locally in metal, silver, or brass and occasionally they consist of a combination of Chinese or Vietnamese porcelain mounted in a metal frame.

Piece for comparison: Adhyatman, 1990, ill. 103, 107; McElney, 1995, cat. 17.

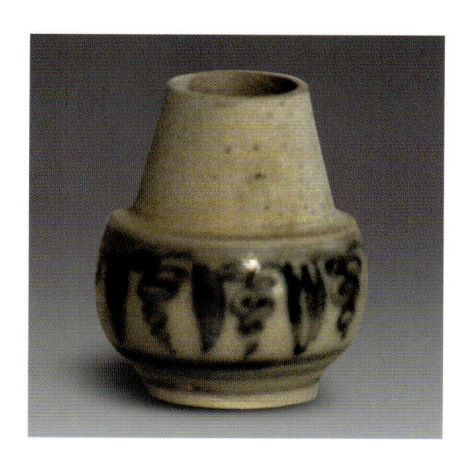

45

Designs of leaves hanging between blue lines.

Inv. 2457
H: 5.8 cm

46

Lotus flower scroll with pointed petals and a spiral-like centre between blue lines.

Inv. 3089
H: 7 cm

3.5 Small round boxes

Only three small boxes were found in the cargo. They are circular in shape with rounded sides and a flattened lid. They stand on a flat base. They are covered in a bluish glaze, with the exception of the rims and the base. These receptacles, which were originally cosmetics boxes, were very popular with the inhabitants of the archipelagos who used them for storing betel-nuts, medicines or magic unguents.

Pieces for comparison: Aga-Oglu, 1982, cat. 129.

47

Pattern painted in dark cobalt blue. Branches of blossom on the base and floral motif consisting of petals in the form of *ruyi* surrounded by a border of small scrolls on the lid.

Inv. 2039/2089
Base: H: 3.6 cm; 5.7 cm

48

Pattern painted in blue-grey cobalt. Branches of blossom on the base and floral design consisting of petals in the form of *ruyi* surrounded by a border of small scrolls on the lid.

Inv. 3602/4457
Base: H: 3.9 cm; D: 6 cm

49

Design of lotus petal panels covering both the base and lid painted in dark cobalt blue.

Inv. 2033/2034
Base: H: 2.3 cm; D: 3.5 cm

4. Rimmed dishes

4.1 Large dishes with bracket-lobed rims

These large deep dishes, with a bracket-lobed rim, are made from thick white porcelain. The rounded sides are prolonged into a barely perceptible foot whose size varies. The base is recessed. These dishes, which have very thick, clearly-defined rims, seem to have been made using two moulds. They are covered with a thick bluish glaze with the exception of the foot-rim. The patterns are drawn then filled in with a wash or traced in reserve on a coloured background. The cargo contained only 16 dishes of this type.

The design is divided into concentric zones arranged around the central medallion and edged with blue lines. The designs are either pictorial with familiar scenes from Chinese paintings depicting a lotus pond with mandarin ducks or egrets, or religious, showing a deer with a lotus flower and *hai shou* sea creatures. The theme of sea creatures appears in the reign of Xuande and experienced a revival of interest in the last quarter of the fifteenth century. The iconography of this fantastic bestiary may have been influenced by the popularity of *Shan Hai Jing*, the "Classic of Mountains and Seas". Dishes with such religious designs are unique to this cargo at the time of writing.

Reference: Chen Ching-kuang, 1992, pp. 101–22.

Inv. 2991

50

Design painted in pale grey blue cobalt. There are two mandarin ducks in the centre, one on the shore and the other swimming amongst lotus bushes. Lotuses and aquatic plants emerge from stylised waves on the well and there is a trellis pattern on the border. The reverse is decorated with a lotus scroll showing the Eight Emblems of Buddhism – the wheel, the conch, the parasol, the dais, the lotus, the vase, the fish and the endless knot. There are small stylised clouds under the rim.

D: 32.4 cm; H: 6.4 cm
Inv. 1128

Pieces for comparison: pieces with a similar design have been found at Hutian, in strata of the Zhengtong period (Bai Kun, assistant director at the Jingdezhen Ceramic History Museum; verbal communication). The theme of mandarin ducks, which has been used extensively since the Tang dynasty, symbolises conjugal happiness and found its poetic expression in ceramics from the Song dynasty onwards. For an enamelled plate of the Chenghua period, see Scott, Pierson, 1995, cat. 26.

51

Four mandarin ducks swim between lotus bushes. Insects fly around the plant in the centre. The medallion is surrounded by a frieze of waves. Lotus and aquatic plants emerge from stylised waves on the cavetto, and there is a diaper trellis design around the edge. The reverse is decorated with a lotus scroll and the Eight Emblems of Buddhism. A frieze of small stylised clouds runs around below the rim. The designs are painted in cobalt blue.

D: 32.7 cm; H: 6.3 cm
Inv. 905
Pieces for comparison: Krahl, 1986, Vol. II, cat. 721.

52

The designs are painted in cobalt blue. There are four egrets in various attitudes, standing between sprays of lotus, and a border of stylised waves. An egret in flight is in the centre of the composition. Lotus and aquatic plants emerge from stylised waves on the cavetto, and there is a trellis design on the rim. The back is decorated with a discontinuous peony scroll with a stem drawn with a double line. A frieze of small stylised clouds runs below the rim.

D: 32.5 cm; H: 6.5 cm
Inv. 1235

53

Four egrets in various attitudes adorn the medallion, between flowers and lotus leaves. There is a border of stylised waves. An egret in flight is in the centre. A frieze of waves surrounds the medallion. Lotus and aquatic plants emerge from stylised waves on the cavetto, and there is a trellis design on the border. The reverse is decorated with a lotus scroll with the Eight Emblems of Buddhism. A frieze of small stylised clouds runs below the rim. The designs are painted in dark cobalt blue.

D: 33.2 cm; H: 6.1 cm
Inv. 4056

54

Designs painted in blue grey cobalt. Four egrets in various attitudes, standing between sprays of lotus, and an egret in flight in the centre. A trilobed pattern borders the medallion. A light lotus scroll with a mass of little leaves decorates the cavetto, and there is a diaper trellis pattern on the rim. On the reverse, a lotus scroll with the Eight Emblems of Buddhism. A frieze of stylised clouds runs below the rim.

D: 37.7 cm; H: 6.5 cm
Inv. 911
Pieces for comparison: Yeo, Martin, pl. 54, cat. 91.

55

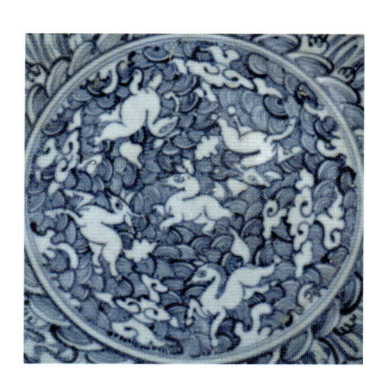

The central medallion shows a deer with a lotus flower in his mouth, surrounded by a scroll of leaves. The cavetto is covered with lotuses and aquatic plants emerging above a line of blue waves, a trellis band on the rim. The exterior cavetto has a lotus scroll containing the Eight Buddhist Emblems. Small, curly stylised clouds decorate the area below the rim. The designs are painted in dark cobalt blue.

D: 33.4 cm; H: 5.9 cm
Inv. 2991

The theme of a deer has figured in the decorative vocabulary since antiquity, where it appears on archaic bronzes. During the Tang dynasty, it was used on gold and silver ware and *Changsha* ceramics. Its evocation varied on Song ceramics where it was represented alone or in pairs. On this dish, the lotus flower in the animal's mouth has a symbolic meaning in Buddhism, harmonising with the emblems on the back.

56

On the reverse, the Eight Emblems of Buddhism are supported by a lotus flower scroll. A frieze of little flowers surrounds the edge. Inside, a trellis border, and lotuses and stiff aquatic plants above stylised waves on the cavetto. In the medallion, animals frolic between the clouds, standing out in white against the blue waves. They include an elephant, a horse, a deer and a goat. In the centre of the composition there is a shell and an animal which may be an *ershu*, a long-eared mouse.

D: 32.2 cm; H: 6.4 cm
Inv. 639

Pieces for comparison: for a bowl with similar designs, Aga-Oglu, 1982, cat. 166.

57

Inside, a trellis border on the rim, and lotuses and aquatic plants rising above stylised waves on the cavetto. In the medallion there are animals frolicking between the clouds which are silhouetted in white against the blue waves. The animals consist of an elephant, a horse, a buck, a goat and in the centre of the composition, a fox (?). On the reverse, a lotus scroll containing the Eight Buddhist Emblems. A frieze of small clouds surrounds the rim.

D: 32.8 cm; H: 6.2 cm
Inv. 717

58

On the reverse, a lotus scroll with the Eight Emblems of Buddhism. A frieze of little clouds surrounds the edge. Inside, a trellis border on the rim, lotuses and stiff aquatic plants above the stylised waves in the cavetto. In the centre, animals frolic between the clouds, standing out in white against the blue waves. They include an elephant, a horse and two serpent-like winged dragons.

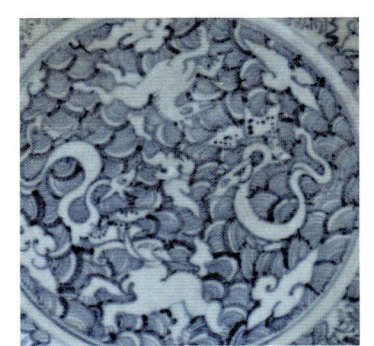

D: 32 cm; H: 6 cm
Inv. 2248

4.2 Flat-rimmed dishes

These large flat-rimmed dishes are made of white porcelain. With the exception of the "elephant" dish, the cavetto extends into a barely differentiated foot which varies in size. The base is recessed. These dishes are covered in a bluish glaze with the exception of the foot-rim. The motifs are drawn then coloured with a wash. The cargo included only thirteen of these dishes, fewer than those of the previous type. The decoration, of varying designs, is divided into concentric areas arranged around the central medallion and edged with two parallel blue lines.

Small flat-rimmed dishes are included in this section due to their having a similar central feature in their design, they are however made of thinner porcelain. They stand on a small, unglazed foot which slopes towards the centre and is retracted on the inside. The bases are glazed and covered in radial lines.

59

In the central medallion, a flying elephant painted in dark blue against a background of stormy, foaming waves. A lotus scroll with stiff pointed leaves in the cavetto and a classical scroll on the rim. Reverse decorated with an identical lotus scroll between two blue lines and little clouds under the rim. The foot is surrounded by two blue lines. The designs are painted in dark cobalt blue. The dish is made of a porcelain that contains impurities, as indicated by black and brown specks visible in the paste. The foot slopes towards the centre and is recessed on its inner surface. Flat unglazed base, marked with radial and circular lines.

D: 38.7 cm; H: 9.6 cm
Inv. 805

Pieces for comparison: The elephant is rarely represented alone in a central decoration. A dish of the Xuande period using the same design was found at Zhushan, site of the imperial manufactory of the Ming dynasty at Jingdezhen; *Yuan's and Ming's Porcelains unearthed from Jingdezhen*, p. 189, ill. 148. Another dish, probably of the Chenghua period is illustrated in Soame Jenyns' *Ming Pottery and Porcelain*, ill. 67.

60

In the central medallion, two spotted deer on either side of a flowery stem beneath a large pine with drooping branches. A rock in the foreground and a rock at the side with *lingzhi* fungi. An insect flies over one of the deer. On the cavetto, interrupted lotus scrolls with a stem indicated by two lines and a classic scroll on the edge. Reverse decorated with a lotus scroll and small clouds under the rim. The designs are painted in blue-grey cobalt. Concave unglazed base.

D: 31.3 cm; H: 6.1 cm
Inv. 336

Pieces for comparison: For plates with a straight edge, Addis, 1968, pl. 47; Aga-Oglu, 1962, fig. 5, 1982, cat. 118; Pope, 1956, pl. 71; *Wenwu*, 9, 1994.

This theme of deer represented as a couple gambolling playfully in a rustic setting appears on moulded *ding* and ceramics of the *cizhou* type of the Song dynasty. The image of the deer, *lu*, is used as the word sounds similar to that for "salary" and became the symbol of administrative promotion, a synonym for wealth and prosperity. The deer is also linked to Daoist superstitions. Bucks could live to a ripe old age and were believed to be the only creatures able to find the *lingzhi* fungus which conferred longevity. This is why on some pieces, they are shown grazing or near a clump of *lingzhi*. Several species of deer are native to China, but the most frequently represented is the deer with a spotted coat known as *sika*, whose velvety, young antlers are also used in Chinese medicines to promote long life.

The series of 24 little plates found in the cargo illustrates the introduction to the decorative vocabulary of the theme of "bucks in the undergrowth" which would predominate throughout the second half of the sixteenth century. The image had not yet become stereotyped and varies from one dish to another. The artist's imagination is allowed licence in the position of the pine tree, which may be central or on either side of the medallion, and in the secondary designs, such as flying insects used to fill the space, and flowering shrubs, *lingzhi*, and rocks. The deer may be represented alone but are more frequently shown in pairs, one animal facing, the other shown in profile, its heard turned towards its companion.

61

In the central medallion, a single deer next to a large pine tree. There are rocks in the foreground and to one side. Medallion delimited by a band of criss-crossed lines and a scroll of *lingzhi* fungi on the cavetto. A trellis frieze on the rim. On the reverse, a peony scroll and a design of little leaves around the edge. The designs are painted in blue grey cobalt.

D: 25.1 cm; H: 4.4 cm
Inv. 1746

62

A white buck stands on either side of a large pine tree with drooping branches in the central medallion surrounded by a band of criss-crossed lines. Rocks in the foreground and at the sides. Cavetto decorated with scroll of *lingzhi* fungi and a trellis frieze on the rim. Reverse decorated with a scroll of peonies and little leaves beneath the rim. The designs are painted in dark cobalt blue.

D: 25.4 cm; H: 4.5 cm
Inv. 1592

63

Central medallion surrounded by a border of criss-crossed lines, decorated with two spotted deer on either side of central rock. Large pine at one side with insects flying beneath its branches. A scroll of *lingzhi* around the cavetto and a trellis frieze around the rim. Reverse decorated with a peony scroll and small leaf designs below the rim. The designs are painted in light cobalt blue.

D: 25.5 cm; H: 4.3 cm
Inv. 1745

Piece for comparison: Gotuaco, Tan, Diem, cat. M25.

64

Central medallion encircled by a trefoil patterned frieze, with a branch of peonies in a vase in front of a balustrade and five butterflies around the flowers. Discontinuous peony scroll around the well and a row of cash diaper designs along the rim. On the reverse, a discontinuous lotus scroll and small stylised clouds under the rim. Unglazed recessed base. The design is painted in grey-blue cobalt.

D: 31.7 cm; H: 5.7 cm
Inv. 1131

This evocation of a garden and terrace with a balustrade has existed since the Song dynasty in the decoration of moulded *ding*. The theme reappears in the Yuan dynasty and under the reign of Hongwu (1368–98). The design had become very rare by the late fifteenth century and it is only found on three dishes in the cargo. It is a forerunner of the *kraak* ware of the following century, when it would very frequently be used for the central medallion.

Pieces for comparison: Wirgin, 1970, pl. 99, 102a; Krahl, 1986, Vol. II, cat. 562, 571; Liu Xinyuan, 1996, p. 356–7.

65

In the central medallion, a fish leaping over foaming waves. Around the cavetto, phoenixes with spread wings alternating with clouds. Classic scroll around the rim. On the reverse, a lotus scroll and small stylised clouds beneath the rim. The designs are painted in dark cobalt blue.

D: 30.9 cm; H: 6.2 cm
Inv. 1700

The theme of a fish has figured in the decorative vocabulary since antiquity when it appears on neolithic pottery and ceramics and bronzes of the Han dynasty. Under the Tang dynasty, it is used on gold and silverware. It became very popular after the Song dynasty on porcelain and stoneware where it is represented alone or in pairs. The fish, *yu*, was most commonly used as a symbol of wealth and abundance on account of a pun on the "yu" sound. According to legend, sturgeons swimming up the Yellow River turned into dragon-fish if they managed to pass through the Longmen gorge, the so-called "Dragon Gate". The fish leaping from the waves, a symbol of strength, courage and perseverance, remains the illustration of the wish to succeed in the competitive administrative examinations taken by those wishing to become a government official. This very decorative design features frequently on export porcelain.

Pieces for comparison: Krahl, 1986, Vol. II, cat. 718; Wiesner, 1983, cat. 70; Yeo, Martin, 1978, pl. 20, cat. 41.

66

In the central medallion, a winged dragon, *feiyu*, leaping over the foaming waves and surrounded by small clouds. Around the cavetto, phoenixes with outstretched wings alternating with clouds. Small spiralling scrolls around the edge. On the reverse, a lotus scroll and small spiral patterns below the rim. The designs are painted in dark cobalt blue. The base is glazed.

D: 31 cm; H: 6.1 cm
Inv. 4724

Pieces for comparison: for a similar central theme, see Gotuaco, Tan, Diem, 1997, cat. M41, M48; Pope, 1956, pl. 70; *South-East Asian and Chinese Trade Pottery*, cat. 95. For enamelled dishes, Addis, 1968, pl. 48; Scott, Pierson, 1995, cat. 27.

67

Small central medallion decorated with a *kui* dragon with a foliated body, surrounded by a border of small trefoil designs. On the bottom and cavetto, there is a chrysanthemum scroll and a classic scroll on the rim. A floral scroll on the reverse. The designs are painted in dark cobalt blue. The base is glazed.

D: 31.5 cm; H: 5.6 cm
Inv. 335

The *kui* dragon has two front legs without claws, a nose like the trunk of an elephant, rounded horns and small curved wings. The shape derives from a sea monster, the makara, which was worshipped in India. The dragon was considered to be the water-sprite of the river where it represented the origin of life. Its appearance in China towards the end of the fourth century is linked to the development of Buddhism. The dragon is carved on the walls of Buddhist caves in northern China and represented in gold, silver and ceramic pieces under the Tang dynasty and in the early Song dynasty. Its ferocious appearance was gradually transmuted into that of a more benign-looking dragon. Its reappearance in the late fifteenth century is certainly associated with the influence of Buddhism on the emperors Chenghua and Hongzhi. It is frequently found on porcelain of the Chenghua period in underglaze blue or *doucai* enamels.

Piece for comparison: for a similar central design see *A Legacy of the Ming*, 1996, ill. 113, 118.

68

Small central medallion decorated with a vajra and lanceolate leaves pointing towards the centre. Trellis pattern border. The bottom and cavetto feature a peony scroll. Classic scroll around the edge. On the back, discontinuous peony scroll with a stem represented as a double line, and small spiral patterns under the rim. The designs are painted in dark blue-grey cobalt.

D: 30.8 cm; H: 6.1 cm
Inv. 1601

69

Inside, border of chevrons on the rim, and on the cavetto, four groups of plants on either side of rocks, alternating with sprays of herbs. In the central medallion, two phoenixes in flight facing each other between two lotus sprays. On the reverse, a peony scroll traced in outline and coloured with a pale wash. The low foot is unglazed and the base is recessed. The designs on the inside of the dish are painted directly with large brushstrokes in dark cobalt blue in the style of the so-called "Interregnum" period.

D: 30.7 cm; H: 5.8 cm
Inv. 291

Pieces for comparison: Gotuaco, Tan, Diem, 1997, cat. M7, M17, M18; Krahl, 1986, Vol. II, cat. 646; Pope, 1956, pl. 73–4; *South-East Asian and Chinese Trade Pottery*, cat. 88; *Wenwu*, 2, 1981, pl. 5.

4.3 Small dishes with straight or everted rims

These saucer-shaped dishes are made of thin white porcelain and they stand on a small, unglazed, sloping foot, which is recessed at the point where it joins the base. These dishes are covered in a bluish glaze and the bases are often marked with radial lines. Fifty-nine little dishes of this type were found in the cargo.

The design is divided into concentric circles starting from the central medallion with the exception of a group of dishes whose scrolls cover the whole surface. The designs are drawn then coloured in with a wash, except on pieces painted in the Interregnum style.

A group of 35 little dishes are stylistically linked to the large dish Inv. 291.

70

Inside, a chevron border and a stylised lotus scroll on the cavetto. In the central medallion, a phoenix in flight surrounded by a lotus scroll. On the back, a scroll of lotuses with a white centre and petals with a white edge. The designs are painted directly with large brush strokes in dark cobalt blue in the style of the Interregnum period.

D: 25.6 cm; H: 4.5 cm; Inv. 1155

71

Small dish with straight rim. Inside, a lotus scroll with pointed petals around the cavetto. In the central medallion, a phoenix in flight between two lotus flowers and stylised clouds. On the back, a scroll of lotuses with a white centre and petals with a white edge. The designs are directly painted with broad brushstrokes in dark grey cobalt blue in the style of the Interregnum period.

D: 24.9 cm; H: 4.5 cm
Inv. 779

Piece for comparison: Aga-Oglu, 1982, cat. 120.

71a

Small dish with a rim. Inside, border of chevrons on the rim and a scroll of *lingzhi* fungi and long dentate leaves. In the central medallion, two phoenixes in flight in the centre of a lotus scroll. On the back, a scroll of leaves. Designs directly painted with broad brushstrokes in dark grey cobalt blue in the style of the Interregnum period.

D: 25.2 cm; H: 4.7 cm
Inv. 632

The scroll of *lingzhi* and long dentate leaves design has been found on porcelain of the Chenghua period (Liu Xinyuan, et al., 1993, p. 221). It was copied on Islamic ceramics in the second half of the sixteenth century.

Pieces for comparison: Aga-Oglu, 1962, fig. 3a.

72

Small dish with a rim. Inside, border of chevrons on the rim, *lingzhi* fungi and long dentate leaves. In the central medallion, two phoenixes in flight between two lotus flowers and stylised clouds. The reverse features two *kui* dragons with foliated bodies. The designs are directly painted with broad brushstrokes in dark grey cobalt blue in the style of the Interregnum period.

D: 25 cm; H: 4.5 cm
Inv. 3460

Pieces for comparison: Krahl, 1986, Vol. II, cat. 648; A Legacy of the Ming, 1996, p. 57, ill. 99.

73

Small dish with flat rim. Inside, border of chevrons on the rim and lotus scrolls on the cavetto. The central medallion features a *qilin*, the mythical unicorn surrounded by stylised vegetation including a *lingzhi* fungus. Lotus scroll on the back. The designs are painted in dark cobalt blue, without outlines, with thick brushstrokes in the style of the Interregnum period.

D: 25.2 cm; H: 4 cm; Inv. 3156

Pieces for comparison: Krahl, 1986, Vol. II, cat. 646; Lam, 1989–92, ill. 9; Pope, 1956, pl. 73.

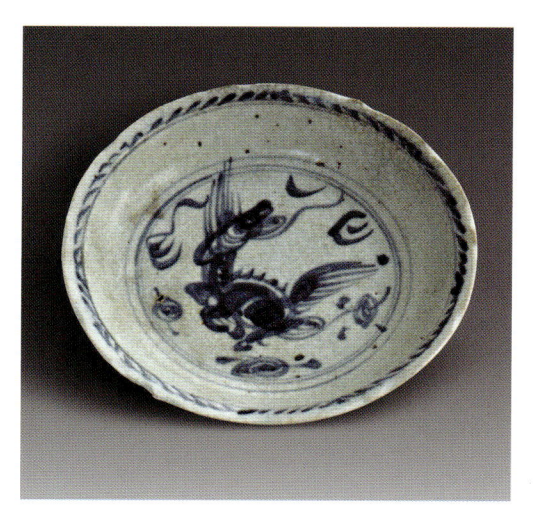

74

Small dish with lobed everted rim. Chevron border on the rim. In the central medallion, a *qilin*, its head facing the moon, with three stylised emblems and clouds. Light lotus scroll on the reverse. The designs are painted in dark cobalt blue, without outlines, in the Interregnum style.

D: 18.7 cm; H: 3.5 cm; Inv. 3050

Pieces for comparison: Aga-Oglu, 1972, cat. 34, 1975, cat. 136; Gotuaco, Tan, Diem, 1997, cat. M6c; *A Legacy of the Ming*, 1996, p. 57, ill. 97, 98.

75

Small dish with everted rim. In the central medallion, a *qilin*, its head facing the moon, with three stylised emblems and clouds. Undecorated reverse. The rim of the dish is unglazed. The designs are painted in dark cobalt blue, without outlines in the Interregnum style.

D: 18.2 cm; H: 3.5 cm
Inv. 4401

Pieces for comparison: Aga-Oglu, 1982, cat. 122; Gotuaco, Tan, Diem, 1997, cat. M6a; Locsin, 1962, ill. 197.

76

Small dish with everted rim. In the central medallion, a *qilin*, its head facing the moon, with two stylised emblems and clouds. The reverse is undecorated. The rim of the dish is unglazed. The designs are painted in dark cobalt blue, without outlines in the Interregnum style.

D: 12 cm; H: 2 cm
Inv. 1380

Pieces for comparison: Lam, 1989–92, fig. 5; *Wenwu*, 9, 1994; Wiesner, cat. 177.

77

Small dish with everted rim. Inside, a scroll of peonies with small leaves covers the whole surface. On the back, a peony scroll and a pattern of small leaves under the rim. The designs are painted in blue-grey cobalt.

D: 26 cm; H: 3.8 cm
Inv. 4043

78

Small dish with everted rim. Inside, a scroll of peonies with small leaves covers the whole surface. On the back, a peony scroll and blue lines beneath the rim. The designs are painted in blue-grey cobalt.

D: 24.3 cm; H: 5.1 cm
Inv. 2872

79

Small fragmented plate with flat rim. In the central medallion, flowering shrubs each side of an ornamental rock. Around the cavetto, lotuses and aquatic plants raised above a line of simplified waves. A classic scroll decorates the rim. On the back, a lotus scroll and a frieze of little leaves beneath the rim. The designs are painted in cobalt blue.

Inv. 463

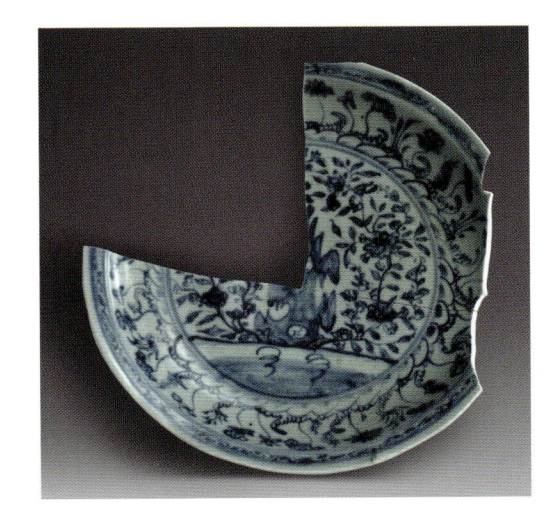

80

Small dish with everted rim, made of very fine porcelain with designs carefully painted in light blue cobalt. Central medallion surrounded by white cloud collars pointing to the centre against a background of blue waves, with small white clouds in the middle. On the outside and inside of the cavetto, lotuses and aquatic plants rising above a line of simplified waves.

D: 20.1 cm; H: 4.1 cm
Inv. 663

81

Small dish with slightly everted rim, very carefully painted in grey-blue cobalt. A small medallion decorated with a conch shell with a long-eared animal, an *ershu* (?), in reserve against a background of blue waves. The bottom and sides feature lotuses and aquatic plants above a line of simplified waves surrounding the medallion. On the back, a scroll of small lotuses and a classic scroll on the foot.

D: 16.2 cm; H: 3.4 cm
Inv. 6621

82

Small dish with slightly everted rim, very carefully painted in grey-blue cobalt. A small medallion decorated with a flying fish in reserve against a background of blue waves. The cavetto is undecorated. The back features four leaping animals (a horse, a goat, an elephant and a deer) in reserve against a background of foaming waves.

D: 14.2 cm; H: 2.2 cm
Inv. 3850

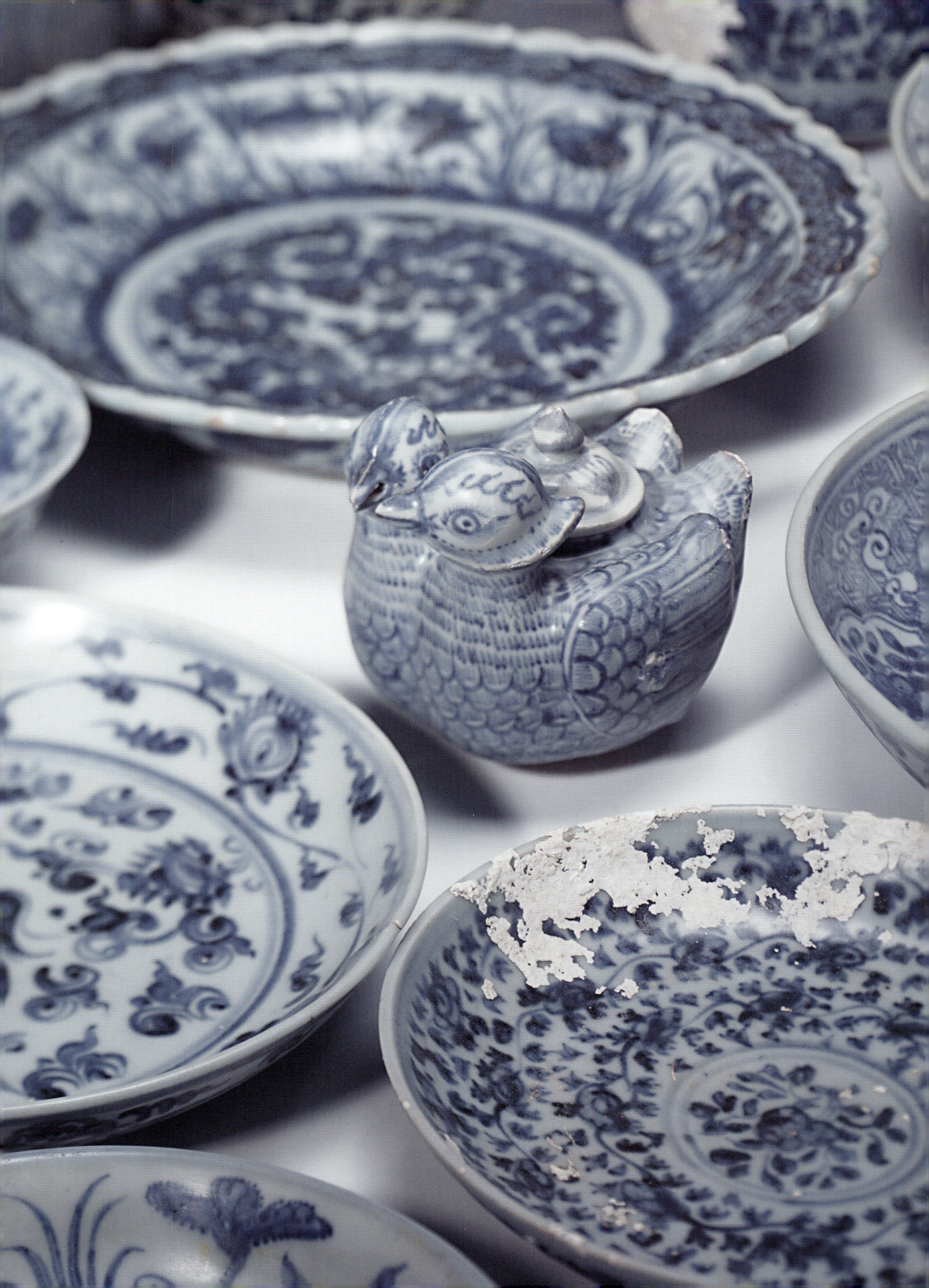

5. Large saucer-shaped dishes

These dishes are the largest group in the cargo. They are potted from thick white porcelain but not all have been fired completely. The rounded sides extend into an inward slanting, slightly undercut foot and they are coated in a shiny, bluish glaze, with the exception of the foot-rim. The designs are usually drawn in, then brushed in with a wash. The decoration either covers the whole surface or is arranged in concentric circles. The designs on the back are varied and generally unrelated to the decoration of the interior surface. Patterns include floral scrolls, lotus scrolls with phoenixes in flight, lotus scrolls with Buddhist emblems, thin scrolls of little leaves, thin scrolls of tiny leaves, mountains surrounded by light lotus scrolls or white lotuses set in reserve against a background of blue waves.

5.1 Large dishes with scroll decoration on the cavetto

The decoration is arranged in concentric circles around a central medallion which is outlined by parallel blue lines. The patterns are generally floral, occasionally pictorial. There are only 19 such dishes in the cargo.

83

Designs painted in blue-grey cobalt. Central medallion, ringed with a frieze of trefoils, with a three-flowered peony branch with a multitude of leaves and two small lotus flowers. A discontinuous lotus scroll with small lanceolate leaves and a stem consisting of a double line, with a trellis around the edge adorns the cavetto. Reverse decorated with a lotus scroll between a zigzag diaper interspersed with trefoils below the rim and a frieze of classic scrolls. The base is unglazed.

D: 46 cm; H: 9.2 cm
Inv. 1639

This exceptionally large dish was unique in the cargo.

84

Inside the medallion, a melon vine with three fruits, surrounded by a border of trefoil and foliate patterns. Cavetto decorated with a scroll of peonies and camellias. On the reverse, a lotus and camellia scroll above a frieze of waves. The designs are carefully drawn and painted in cobalt blue, with care being taken over the shading.

D: 32.3 cm; H: 6.7 cm
Inv. 519

Pieces for comparison: Dishes of this type are decorated in a style inspired by the reigns of Yongle and Xuande. (Liu Xinyuan, 1996, cat. 46; Gotuaco, Tan, Diem, 1997, cat. M22, M37; Locsin, 1967, ill. 201). A fragment of a dish with an identical scroll has a large medallion showing a scene with ducks by the water surrounded by a border of waves.

85

Dish identical to No. 84, design of a branch bearing three peaches in the centre.

D: 31.4 cm; H: 6.3 cm.
Inv. 701

Pieces for comparison: *Yuan's and Ming's Imperial Porcelains*, cat. 68.

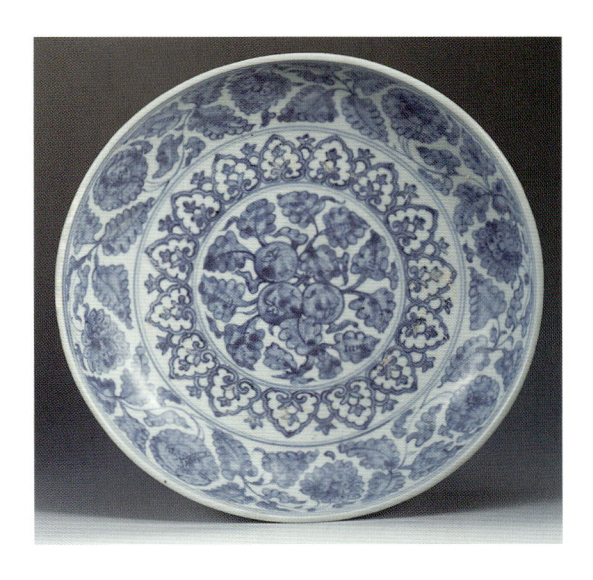

86

Peony branch in the centre, surrounded by a border with a small lotus scroll. There is a chrysanthemum scroll on the cavetto and a frieze of *leiwen* on the rim. The back is decorated with a carefully painted lotus scroll between two borders of classic scrolls. The designs are painted in blue-grey cobalt.

D: 31.9 cm; H: 6.4 cm
Inv. 703

Pieces for comparison: The decoration of this high quality plate is unusual for the period and imitates compositions of previous reigns. Liu Xinyuan, 1999, cat. 24.

87

Wide central medallion surrounded by trefoil motifs with four lions with beribboned balls between four rocks and flower scrolls. Cavetto decorated with scrolls of single-flowered and double-flower chrysanthemums. The back is decorated with a chrysanthemum scroll.

D: 31.9 cm; H: 6.4 cm
Inv. 17

88

Large central medallion with a fish surrounded by white lotus flowers against a background of blue waves. Lotus scrolls with a Tibetan character inside each flower around the well. Painted in dark blue.

D: 31.5 cm; H: 6 cm
Inv. 4508

5.2 Large dishes with lotus bushes around the cavetto

One hundred and sixty-five dishes with this type of border, whole or slightly damaged, were found in the cargo. The cavetto is decorated with lotus bushes, interspersed either with symbols and clouds, with two ducks, or with aquatic plants. The outer surfaces are usually decorated with rocks surrounded by lotus scrolls emerging from a row of waves above a ring of classic scrolls or, more rarely, with a floral scroll running right around the cavetto. A large medallion decorated with a variety of motifs covers the bottom of the dish. These may consist of mountains, lotus flowers, aquatic scenes, fruit or dragons. The decoration, which generally converges towards the centre of the dish, does not seem to have had any immediate predecessor or successor. It is a typical product of the privately-owned kilns of the late fifteenth century, whose area of distribution was generally South-East Asia, to judge by collections containing similar pieces.

Pieces for comparison: Aga-Oglu, 1982; Wiesner; Yeo, Martin, 1978.

89

Lotus bushes interspersed with symbols and clouds on the cavetto. The wide medallion, surrounded by trefoils, depicts three islands with steep peaks, painted in blue above the waves; a large knotty pine rises from the central peak.

D: 30.9 cm; H: 6.2 cm
Inv. SN/369

This surprising design illustrates the ancient Taoist theme of *Penglai*, the "Three Islands of the Immortals", which are located in the Eastern Ocean beyond the shores of the province of Jiangsu.

Pieces for comparison: Liu Xinyuan, 1996, p. 204, cat. 71.

90

Three islands with steep peaks rising above the waves and surrounded by lotus scrolls.

D: 31 cm; H: 6 cm
Inv. 321

91

Three islands with steep peaks, reserved in white against a background of blue waves from which lotus flowers emerge; there is a large knotty pine on the central peak.

D: 31.4 cm; H: 6.6 cm
Inv. 721

92

Three islands against a background of waves from which lotus flowers emerge; there is a branch of blossom on the central peak.

D: 31.5 cm; H: 6.1 cm
Inv. 2710

93

Medallion edged with a frieze of waves. In the centre, four steep mountains are covered in pine, bamboo and prunus blossom alternating with four large stylised waves, the whole surrounded by a row of white waves and two rows of blue waves. Insects and ducks are in flight in the sky.

D: 30.9 cm; H: 6.3 cm
Inv. 4611

The number of mountains and rows of waves were left to the decorator's imagination. The depiction of the pine, bamboo and prunus represents the allegory of the "Three Friends". This dish is one of a small, rare group of pieces all painted by the same craftsman.

94

Cavetto edged with a frieze of waves. Central medallion surrounded by a circle of trefoils. Three mountains topped with pine, bamboo, prunus branches and three rows of blue waves topped with white foam.

D: 31.9 cm; H: 6.2 cm
Inv. 2205

95

Central medallion surrounded by ring of trefoils. Three mountains with pine, bamboo and prunus branches, alternating with three small mountains, all edged with two rows of blue waves and a row of white waves.

D: 32 cm; H: 6.6 cm
Inv. 1378

96

Ring of waves on the cavetto. Central medallion surrounded by a ring of trefoils. Six mountains with pine, bamboo and prunus branches, with white lotus reversed out on a background of blue waves.

D: 31.9 cm; H: 6 cm
Inv. 1795

97

Frieze of foam-flecked waves on the cavetto. Central medallion surrounded by a ring of trefoils. Three mountains with pine, bamboo and prunus branches, all surrounded by rows of blue waves and white lotuses.

D: 31.3 cm; H: 6 cm
Inv. 322

98

Frieze of foam-flecked waves on the cavetto. Central medallion surrounded by a frieze of waves. Row of blue waves and white lotuses around four mountains converging towards the centre.

D: 31.5 cm; H: 6 cm
Inv. 314

LOST AT SEA

99

Central medallion surrounded by a frieze of waves. Row of blue waves and white lotuses around a mountain with a pine tree and bamboo.

D: 31.5 cm; H: 6.5 cm
Inv. 313

100

Ring of foam-flecked waves on the cavetto. Central medallion surrounded by a frieze of waves. Row of blue waves and white lotus around a prunus branch.

D: 32.3 cm; H: 7 cm
Inv. 1167

101

Ring of waves broken in two places on the cavetto. Central medallion surrounded by a frieze of waves. Row of blue waves and white lotus around a knotted lotus spray.

D: 31.1 cm; H: 5.6 cm
Inv. 4288

The knotted spray of lotus is symbolic of Buddhism.

102

Ring of foam-flecked waves on the cavetto. Central medallion surrounded by a frieze of waves. Rows of blue waves and white lotuses around three lotus bushes with egrets in various attitudes. An egret is in flight in the centre. Design painted in dark cobalt blue.

D: 33.4 cm; H: 6.2 cm
Inv. 1163

103

Ring of waves on the cavetto. Central medallion surrounded by a frieze of trefoil motifs. Rows of blue waves and white lotuses around lotus stems interspersed with standing or flying egrets. Designs painted in dark cobalt blue.

D: 32.1 cm; H: 6 cm
Inv. 2730

104

Rows of blue waves and white lotuses surrounding rocky mountains with pine, bamboo and prunus interspersed with fish or aquatic plants.

D: 31.8 cm; H: 6.5 cm
Inv. 311

Various species of fish are represented on porcelain from the Xuande reign onwards.

105

Ring of waves on the cavetto. Rows of blue waves and white lotuses around a fish swimming between three clumps of shrubbery.

D: 32.3 cm; H: 6.5 cm
Inv. 1171

106

Ring of waves on the cavetto. Rows of blue waves and white lotuses around a fish swimming in the waves.

D: 32 cm; H: 6.4 cm
Inv. 409

107

Ring of waves on the cavetto. Large fish against a background of blue waves and white lotuses.

D: 31.5 cm; H: 6 cm
Inv. 521

108

Three medallions set in reserve with egrets and white egret flying against a background of blue waves and white lotuses.

D: 32 cm; H: 5.8 cm
Inv. 2924

109

Central medallion surrounded by a border of trefoils. Four lotus flowers, alternating with small leaves, stems and waves set in reserve against a background of blue waves. Designs painted in dark blue.

D: 32.3 cm; H: 6 cm
Inv. 1392

110

Five lotus flowers with large leaves surrounding a central flower, set in reserve against a background of blue waves. The pattern is surrounded by a ring of white waves.

D: 32 cm; H: 6.3 cm
Inv. 2214

111

The central medallion contains a branch carrying three melons and radiating leaves.

D: 30.7 cm; H: 6.5 cm
Inv. 1779

112

On the cavetto, lotus bushes interspersed with a pair of ducks. A ring of waves surrounds the medallion and there are four clumps of lotus converging towards the centre, interspersed with egrets, each drawn differently and set in reserve against a background of blue waves.

D: 31.9 cm; H: 6 cm
Inv. 1457

113

Ring of waves around the medallion and four clumps of lotus converging towards the centre above spiralling waves, interspersed with egrets, each drawn differently, and reversed out against a background of blue waves. Designs painted in dark blue.

D: 32.2 cm; H: 6.6 cm
Inv. 1459

114

Lotus bushes interspersed with a pair of ducks above large waves on the cavetto. Small central medallion decorated with a shell, surrounded by a ring of five fantastically depicted creatures including a deer, a goat and a horse, reversed out against a background of blue waves.

D: 31.9 cm; H: 6.2 cm
Inv. 2700

LOST AT SEA

115

Lotus bushes interspersed with aquatic plants on the cavetto. Inside the medallion, a central lotus branch surrounded by two dragons with foliated bodies.

D: 32.2 cm; H: 6 cm
Inv. 1660

5.3 Large dish with trellis pattern around the rim

116

Cavetto ringed with a trellis frieze around the rim. Central medallion surrounded by a ring of waves and decorated with a descending dragon, chasing a flaming pearl amongst the clouds. On the back, dragons are depicted amongst clouds.

D: 32.2 cm; H: 6 cm
Inv. 2427

This dish is unique in the cargo. The depiction of a dragon in a descending position is typical of the period and is found on imperial porcelain.

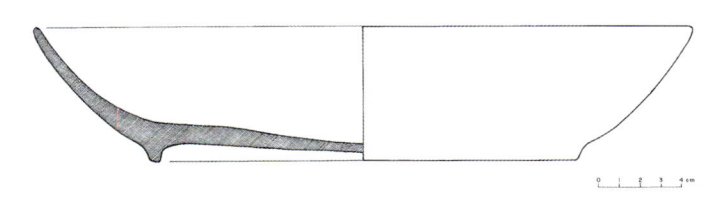

5.4 Large dishes patterned with quadrilobe medallions

These dishes are decorated inside with quadrilobed medallions generally arranged in two concentric rows around a circular central medallion. The medallions are set in reserve against a Y-shaped trellis background, sprinkled with wreaths of flowers and stylised white clouds or sometimes on a "fish roe" ground. This style of decoration is typified by a very ornamental concentric composition covering the whole surface, with a horror of white space which is contrary to the Chinese aesthetic.

The layout is new and may have been inspired by metal dishes from the Near East. The Y-shaped pattern may also have come from that part of the world. This geometric design, stemming from the rhythmic movement of Islamic art, had already appeared during the Yuan dynasty with a very rigorous composition. Yet the Chinese ethos emerges through this foreign influence, with its different beliefs and its own flora and fauna. Branches of blossom alternate with twigs bearing stylised fruit in lobed panels. The central medallion contains traditional motifs with figures, animals and flowers, or motifs reflecting Buddhist beliefs and worship of the period. A series of dishes with a central decoration in the form of a large lobed panel surrounded by eight medallions against a trellis background uses colour contrasts to great effect. Another set has a radiating cloud-collars design creating a six-pointed star. On certain pieces, the base is painted with a lion, a phoenix, a branch of blossom or the character *shou*, meaning "longevity'. These designs are generally painted in dark cobalt blue. The shiny glaze is sometimes crazed. Two hundred and fifty-four dishes in this category, whole or slightly damaged, have been recovered.

Pieces for comparison: Similar dishes are to be found in the Topkapi Saray Museum in Istanbul and various collections formed in South-East Asia. Aga-Oglu, 1982; Krahl, 1986, Vol. II; Yeo, and Martin, 1978.

117

Twelve lobed medallions with branches of fruit on a Y-shaped trellis background sprinkled with flowers and stylised clouds. The circular central medallion is decorated with a scholar standing on a fish amidst the waves.

D: 31.2 cm; H: 6 cm
Inv. 1708

A scholar sitting beneath a pine tree is depicted on another dish in the cargo whose glaze is whitish.

LOST AT SEA

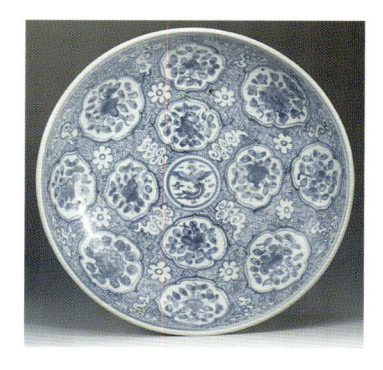

118

Central circular medallion decorated with a phoenix. Twelve lobed medallions with branches of fruit alternating with flowers against a background of a Y-shaped trellis sprinkled with flowers and stylised clouds.

D: 31.8 cm; H: 5.9 cm
Inv. 2978

119

Central circular medallion decorated with a phoenix in flight rising amidst the clouds. Twelve lobed medallions with branches of fruit against a background of a Y-shaped trellis sprinkled with flowers.

D: 31.5 cm; H: 6.4 cm
Inv. 2741

120

Central circular medallion decorated with two phoenixes in flight. Twelve lobed medallions with branches bearing two fruits against a background of a Y-shaped trellis sprinkled with flowers.

D: 31.9 cm; H: 6 cm
Inv. 4550

121

Twelve lobed medallions with floral branches against a Y-shaped trellis background sprinkled with flowers. Central circular medallion decorated with a bird on a branch.

D: 32.1 cm; H: 6.4 cm
Inv. 2225

This design of "flowers and birds" is traditional in Chinese painting.

122

Twelve lobed medallions with branches of fruit alternating with flowers against a background of a Y-shaped trellis pattern sprinkled with flowers. The circular central medallion is decorated with two birds on a branch.

D: 31.2 cm; H: 6 cm
Inv. 2224

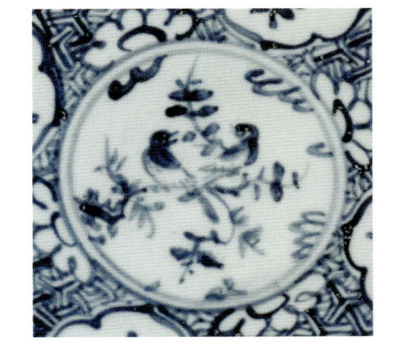

123

Central circular medallion decorated with a buck in the undergrowth. Twelve lobed medallions with branches of fruit alternating with branches of blossom against a background of a Y-shaped trellis pattern sprinkled with flowers and stylised clouds.

D: 32.3 cm; H: 5.7 cm
Inv. 3010

124

Twelve lobed medallions with branches of fruit alternating with branches of blossom and fish against the background of a Y-shaped trellis pattern sprinkled with flowers. Central medallion decorated with a fish.

D: 32.7 cm; H: 6.5 cm
Inv. 3012

125

Central circular medallion decorated with a flower. Four lobed medallions with flowers and eight with branches of fruit against a background of a Y-shaped trellis pattern sprinkled with flowers and stylised clouds.

D: 31.7 cm; H: 6.1 cm
Inv. 3385

126

Central circular medallion decorated with a white chrysanthemum against a blue background. Twelve lobed medallions with branches of fruit against a background of a Y-shaped trellis pattern sprinkled with flowers and stylised clouds.

D: 32.2 cm; H: 6.6 cm
Inv. 3655

127

Twelve lobed medallions with branches of fruit alternating with branches of blossom against a background of a Y-shaped trellis pattern sprinkled with flowers and stylised clouds. Central circular medallion decorated with a branch of blossom.

D: 31.7 cm; H: 6.9 cm
Inv. 3482

128

Central circular medallion decorated with a branch bearing three fruits. Six lobed medallions with branches of fruit against a Y-shaped trellis background sprinkled with flowers.

D: 31.3 cm; H: 6.4 cm
Inv. 902

129

Central circular medallion decorated with a branch bearing three fruits. Six lobed medallions with branches of fruit alternating with half-medallions on the rim, against a Y-shaped trellis background sprinkled with flowers. The back of the dish is decorated with a *leiwen* border and a scroll of leaves. The base is painted with a peony with radiating leaves within a circle.

D: 32.3 cm; H: 6.2 cm; Inv. 324

130

Central circular medallion decorated with a branch bearing three fruits and surrounded by white half-flowers. Six lobed medallions with branches of fruit alternating with half medallions on the rim. On the reverse, *leiwen* border and a scroll of leaves. The character *shou*, meaning "longevity", inside a circle, is painted on the base. Badly fragmented dish.

No Inv.

131

Central circular medallion decorated with a branch of blossom with radiating leaves. Six oval medallions with flowers against a cash diaper background sprinkled with flowers and stylised clouds. Reverse decorated with branches of flowers and fruits alternating with clouds.

D: 24.9 cm; H: 4.7 cm
Inv. 4621

132

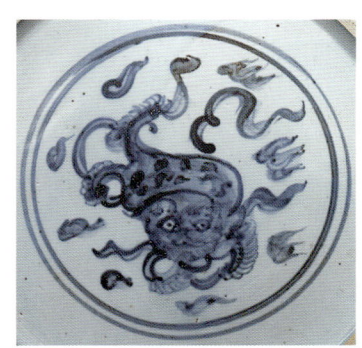

Twelve lobed medallions against a trellis background sprinkled with flowers and stylised clouds. Five of the central medallions are decorated with a lion with ribbons, the other eight contain a phoenix flying amongst clouds. A lotus scroll is on the back, each flower holding a Buddhist emblem. The base is painted with a beribboned lion.

D: 31.7 cm; H: 6.7 cm; Inv. 3406

Bases painted with a large figurative motif are exceptional on porcelain and seem to be a delightful personal flight of fancy of the artist.

133

Central circular medallion decorated with two lions playing with a beribboned ball. There are 12 lobed medallions with branches of fruits and flowers against a Y-shaped trellis background sprinkled with flowers and stylised clouds.

D: 31.5 cm; H: 7 cm
Inv. 684

134

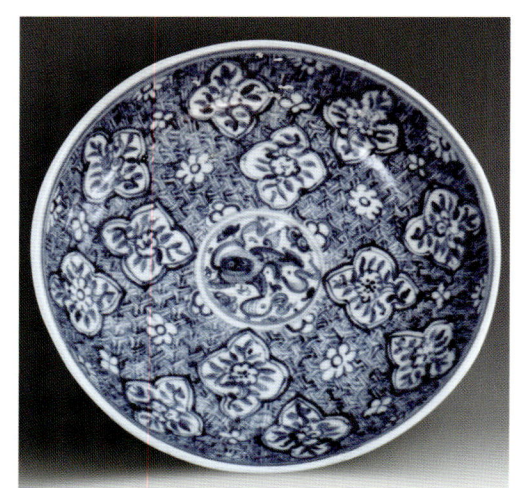

Central circular medallion decorated with a lion with ribbons. Twelve lobed medallions with flowers against a Y-shaped trellis background sprinkled with flowers and stylised clouds.

D: 31.9 cm; H: 6 cm
Inv. 2986

135

Central circular medallion decorated with a lion with ribbons, against a Y-shaped trellis background sprinkled with flowers and stylised clouds. Twelve lobed medallions with flowers.

D: 31.9 cm; H: 6 cm
Inv. 3105

136

Central circular medallion decorated with a long-eared animal, possibly an *ershu*, against a background of blue waves. Twelve lobed medallions with flowers against a Y-shaped trellis background sprinkled with flowers and stylised clouds. The central design has a Buddhist connotation.

D: 31.6 cm; H: 5.8 cm
Inv. 2982

137

Twelve lobed medallions with fruit and flowers against a Y-shaped trellis background sprinkled with flowers and stylised clouds. Central circular medallion decorated with a deer galloping against a background of blue waves.

D: 31.9 cm; H: 6.9 cm
Inv. 715

138

Central circular medallion decorated with shells against a background of blue waves. Twelve lobed medallions with flowers against a Y-shaped trellis background sprinkled with flowers.

D: 31.7 cm; H: 6 cm
Inv. 1798

139

Twelve lobed medallions with flowers against a Y-shaped trellis background sprinkled with flowers and stylised clouds. Central circular medallion decorated with a white lotus flower emerging from blue waves.

D: 31.5 cm; H: 5.9 cm
Inv. 4481

140

139: Central circular medallion decorated with a bouquet of lotus. Twelve lobed medallions with flowers against a Y-shaped trellis background sprinkled with flowers and stylised clouds.

D: 32.3 cm; H: 6 cm
Inv. 3009

141

Twelve lobed medallions with a lotus flower bearing a Sanskrit character, against a Y-shaped trellis background sprinkled with flowers. Central circular medallion decorated with a lotus scroll upholding a Sanskrit character.

D: 31.9 cm; H: 6.2 cm
Inv. 2775

142

Central circular medallion decorated with a double *vajra*. Twelve lobed medallions with flowers and fruit against a Y-shaped trellis background sprinkled with flowers and stylised clouds.

D: 32.2 cm; H: 5.5 cm
Inv. 1603

143

Central circular medallion decorated with a lion with ribbons, and surrounded by half-flowers. Seven lobed medallions with flowers against a Y-shaped trellis background sprinkled with flowers.

D: 32.8 cm; H: 5.8 cm
Inv. 2998

Certain dishes that are decorated in this way have six lobed medallions and may have stylised clouds in the background.

144

Large central lobed panel decorated with two lions playing with beribboned balls. Eight lobed medallions with a scroll of flowers against a Y-shaped trellis background sprinkled with flowers and stylised clouds.

D: 31.9 cm; H: 6 cm
Inv. 2054

145

Large lobed panel decorated with four galloping bucks between clouds around a small circular medallion containing an animal *ershu* (?) against a background of waves. Eight lobed medallions with fruit alternating with clouds against a Y-shaped trellis background.

D: 31.5 cm; H: 6 cm
Inv. 301

146

Eight lobed medallions with fruits on a Y-shaped trellis background. Wide lobed panel decorated with strings of pearls and branches of fruit around a small circular medallion with a white lotus on a background of waves.

D: 31.7 cm; H: 6.4 cm
Inv. 4484

147

Large lobed panel decorated with a scroll of chrysanthemums around a small medallion containing a Sanskrit letter. Eight lobed medallions with spiralling floral branches against a "fish roe" background, sprinkled with flowers and stylised clouds.

D: 32.2 cm; H: 6.9 cm
Inv. 1807

148

Wide lobed panel decorated with a chrysanthemum scroll around a small medallion with a floral scroll. Eight lobed medallions with spiralling floral branches against a trellis-patterned background sprinkled with flowers.

D: 31.4 cm; H: 6.5 cm
Inv. 2060

149

Eight lobed medallions with branches of fruits against a trellis-patterned background sprinkled with flowers. Large lobed panel decorated with four floral branches alternating with clouds and symbols around a small medallion containing a flower.

D: 31.3 cm; H: 6.2 cm; Inv. 331

One dish, with a whitish glaze, is decorated with bamboo stalks and pine and prunus branches, composing the theme of the "Three Friends".

150

Large lobed panel decorated with a *feiyu* winged dragon amongst clouds. Nine lobed medallions with floral branches against a "fish roe" background sprinkled with flowers.

D: 31.3 cm; H: 6.1 cm
Inv. 14

151

Eight lobed medallions with branches of blossom against a Y-shaped trellis background sprinkled with flowers. Large lobed panel decorated with two sprays of chrysanthemums on either side of a pierced rock, reversed out against a dark blue background.

D: 31.8 cm; H: 6.5 cm
Inv. 1160

152

Eight lobed medallions with branches of fruit and flowers against a Y-shaped trellis background sprinkled with flowers; lobed panel decorated with a spray of chrysanthemums and peonies on either side of a pierced rock, reversed out against a dark blue background.

D: 32.1 cm; H: 7 cm; Inv. 375

This flower painting is derived from a favourite theme in Chinese painting in which the symbolism of decorative stones with tortuous shapes, symbols of durability, are integrated into a vision of the world and the symbolism of flowers. The peony, symbol of spring is also a symbol of wealth and social success. The chrysanthemum is the flower symbol of the autumn and of longevity, and is associated with a tranquil life through the hermit poet Tao Yuanming (365–427) whose favourite flower it was. The combination of the two species expresses wishes for good fortune. The lacustrine rocks, especially the rocks of Lake Taihu, were carefully chosen and constituted an essential element in a Chinese garden. This theme is very frequent in the late fifteenth century and is found on many dishes, sometimes associated with a peacock motif.

Pieces for comparison: Krahl, 1986, Vol. II; Pope, 1956; M.-A. Pinto de Matos, 1997; Yeo, Martin, 1978.

153

Cloud collar panels with flowers radiating around a lotus corolla creating a six-pointed star against a Y-shaped trellis background sprinkled with flowers. Small medallions are decorated with emblems. On the rim of the dish there are 12 cloud collar panels pointing to the centre and containing strings of pearls and flowers. Design painted in pale blue.

D: 31.3 cm; H: 6.1 cm
Inv. 2736

154

Cloud collar panels with flowers radiating around a lotus corolla forming a six-pointed star against a Y-shaped trellis background sprinkled with flowers. Small medallions are decorated with emblems. On the rim of the dish there are 12 cloud collar panels pointing to the centre and containing strings of pearls and flowers. On the back there is a discontinuous scroll of large lotus flowers above a frieze of classic scrolls. The base is painted with a phoenix whose wings are outspread amongst clouds. Designs painted in dark blue.

D: 32.3 cm; H: 6.7 cm
Inv. 3409

The cloud collar motif was larger on ceramics produced under the Yuan dynasty. It continued to be used under the reign of Hongwu and reappeared during the reigns of Chenghua and Hongzhi. The decoration on this dish is governed by a strict geometry accentuated by colour contrasts. The patterns are linked as if there were a fear of leaving any white space. These very densely decorated dishes were designed to please a particular clientele, probably Moslem, who were used to engraved metal ware, with geometrical patterns covering the whole surface.

Pieces for comparison: Liu Xinyuan, et al., 1996, cat. 5, 22, 23, 24; Liu Xinyuan, et al., 1993, cat. B19, C49; Huang Yunpeng, Li Zhen, 1988, ill. 87.

5.5 Large dishes with all over pattern of large flower scrolls

The interior of these dishes is decorated with a small central medallion containing various motifs, surrounded by two circles of floral scrolls. The motifs are painted in dark blue, almost black on some dishes. There are nine dishes in this style, either whole or slightly damaged, which have been found in the cargo.

155

Central medallion decorated with a white buck against a background of blue waves, surrounded by two rings of chrysanthemum scrolls. There is a lotus scroll of small flowers on the exterior.

D: 32 cm; H: 6 cm
Inv. 2288

156

Central medallion decorated with a flower, surrounded by two circles of lotus scrolls. Lotus scroll with phoenixes in flight on the back.

D: 32.4 cm; H: 6.1 cm
Inv. 3379

157

Central medallion decorated with a three-flowered lotus scroll, and ringed with two circles of scrolls. Lotus scroll with phoenixes in flight on the back.

D: 32.1 cm; H: 6.5 cm
Inv. 3381

158

Central medallion decorated with a beribboned double *vajra*, and ringed with two circles of lotus scrolls. Lotus scroll with phoenixes in flight on the back.

D: 32 cm; H: 6.1 cm
Inv. 3393

159

Central medallion decorated with a conch shell against a background of blue waves, and ringed with two circles of lotus scrolls. Lotus scroll with phoenixes in flight on the back.

D: 32.2 cm; H: 6.7 cm
Inv. 3395

LOST AT SEA

5.6 Large dishes with all-over pattern of small floral scrolls

The interior surface of these deep dishes is decorated with concentric circles of scrolls of small flowers, with a plethora of leaves surrounding a central medallion which may contain a variety of designs. The same scrolls are generally repeated on the reverse of the items above a frieze. The flowers are represented facing and in profile; they are drawn with a paintbrush and then coloured in with a wash whilst the leaves are painted directly. The cobalt used is very dark, almost black on some dishes. The glaze is generally very shiny if it has not been damaged by being underwater for so long. Fifty-four dishes in this style, whole or only slightly damaged, have been found in the cargo.

Pieces for comparison: Similar dishes have been found in tombs in the Daijibu cemetery in the province of Jilin. Many examples are preserved in the Topkapi Saray Museum in Istanbul and in various collections formed in South-East Asia. Aga-Oglu, 1982; Krahl, 1986, Vol. II; Gotuaco, Tan, Diem, 1997; Yeo, Martin, 1978; *Wenwu*, 9, 1994.

160

Concentric circles of floral scrolls.

D: 31.8 cm; H: 6 cm
Inv. 3007

161

Three concentric circles of floral scrolls around a small medallion decorated with a delicate branch of blossom.

D: 31.3 cm; H: 6.5 cm
Inv. 2737

162

Medallion decorated with the "Three Friends" theme ringed with a thin floral scroll. Three concentric circles of floral scrolls surround the medallion.

D: 32.4 cm; H: 6.7 cm
Inv. 4410

163

Three concentric circles of floral scrolls around a medallion decorated with a peony and surrounded by a ring of floral scrolls.

D: 31.7 cm; H: 6 cm
Inv. 4402

164

Three concentric circles of floral scrolls around a medallion decorated with a peony flower and surrounded by a frieze with a floral scroll. The exterior is unique with a wide band of foliated scrolls below the rim and a band of small pointed leaves just above the foot.

D: 31.3 cm; H: 6 cm
Inv. 686

165

Three concentric circles of floral scrolls around a medallion decorated with a peony flower and surrounded by a frieze containing a classic scroll. The back has two circles of flowery scrolls and a ring of classic scrolls above the foot.

D: 31.3 cm; H: 6.2 cm
Inv. 290

166

Three concentric rings of floral scrolls around a medallion decorated with a white flower on a dark blue background and encircled by a border of fan-shaped designs.

D: 32.2 cm; H: 6.2 cm
Inv. 4405

167

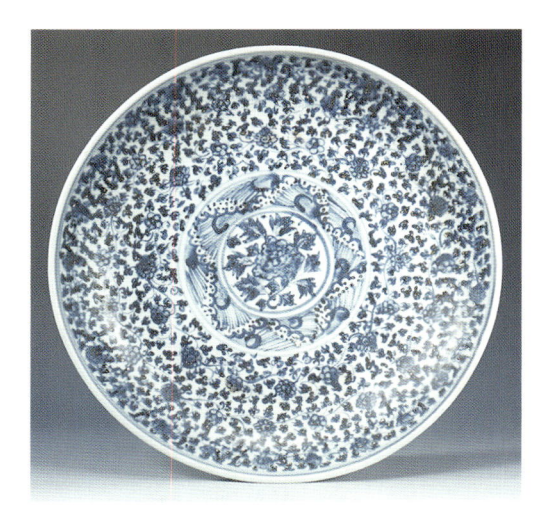

Three concentric circles of floral scrolls around a medallion decorated with a peony flower and surrounded by a ring of fan-shaped designs.

D: 32.2 cm; H: 6 cm
Inv. 4406

168

Three concentric circles of floral scrolls around a medallion decorated with a white lotus flower against a background of blue waves and surrounded by a border of floral scrolls.

D: 33.8 cm; H: 5.7 cm
Inv. 3400

169

Three concentric circles of floral scrolls surround a medallion decorated with a deer beneath a pine tree and surrounded by a band of floral scrolls.

D: 33.4 cm; H: 6.5 cm
Inv. 1725

170

Three concentric circles of floral scrolls around a medallion decorated with a white deer (?) galloping against a background of blue waves and ringed by a circular floral scroll.

D: 32 cm; H: 6.3 cm
Inv. 1034

171

Three concentric circles of floral scrolls around a medallion decorated with a galloping horse against a background of blue waves and ringed by a border of waves.

D: 33.3 cm; H: 5.6 cm
Inv. 1735

172

Three concentric circles of floral scrolls around a medallion decorated with two lions surrounded by ribbons and a band of floral scrolls.

D: 32.2 cm; H: 6 cm
Inv. 3392

173

Four concentric circles of floral scrolls around a medallion decorated with a shell and with an *ershu* (?) against a background of blue waves.

D: 33 cm; H: 7.1 cm
Inv. 3104

174

Three concentric circles of floral scrolls around a medallion decorated with a shell against a background of blue waves and surrounded by a band of floral scrolls.

D: 31.8 cm; H: 6.4 cm
Inv. 4408

LOST AT SEA

175

Three concentric circles of floral scrolls around a medallion decorated with a shell and with an *ershu* (?) against a background of blue waves, surrounded by a cash diaper pattern.

D: 31 cm; H: 6.6 cm
Inv. 3394

176

Four concentric circles of floral scrolls around a medallion decorated with a Sanskrit letter against a Y-shaped trellis background.

D: 32.2 cm; H: 6 cm
Inv. 4409

This style of religious invocation appears under the reign of Yongle. The emperors Chenghua and Hongzhi were also devout Buddhists. In such a context it is normal to find numerous religious symbols in the repertoire of the imperial manufactories and later in private workshops. Liu Xinyuan, et al., 1996, cat. 112, 120.

177

Four concentric circles of floral scrolls around a medallion decorated with a flower. Two rows of identical scrolls on the outer side.

D: 20.2 cm; H: 4 cm
Inv. 297

5.7 Small saucer-shaped dishes

These small dishes have a thin porcelain body, with the exception of a small group on which branches of blossom have been sketchily painted. They are covered with a bluish glaze. The recessed base is scored with radial marks, and the unglazed foot is generally retracted. Some of these little dishes have no foot but the cavetto extends into a recessed base. These belong to the group known as the "hole-bottom dishes". The interior design revolves around a central medallion. The cargo contained 112 such small dishes which were whole or slightly damaged.

178

Medallion decorated with a flower emerging from behind an ornamental rock surrounded by two branches of prunus. The exterior is undecorated. Thick porcelain.

D: 20.1 cm; H: 4.1 cm
Inv. 678

179

Medallion decorated with a flower. The exterior is undecorated. This saucer has no foot and the base is recessed. It is potted from thick porcelain. Crazed glaze apart from the ring at the base of the cavetto which is unglazed.

D: 9.9 cm; H: 2.6 cm
Inv. 2292

180

Overall pattern of a delicate scroll of chrysanthemums with single and double flowers. Identical scroll on the exterior. This saucer has no foot and the base is recessed with an unglazed ring at the base of the cavetto. Thin porcelain.

D: 12.7 cm; H: 3.7 cm
Inv. 523

181

Central medallion decorated with a branch of peonies and surrounded by a scroll of chrysanthemums on the cavetto. A scroll of peonies decorates the exterior. This saucer has no foot and the base is retracted with an unglazed ring at the base of the cavetto. Thin porcelain.

D: base 5.1 cm; H: 4 cm
Inv. 453

182

Central medallion decorated with a scroll of five chrysanthemums and surrounded by a scroll of chrysanthemums on the cavetto. Peony scroll on the exterior.

D: 19.3 cm; H: 4.6 cm
Inv. 4393

183

Central medallion decorated with five chrysanthemums whose stems ring an ornamental rock. There is a chrysanthemum scroll on the cavetto and a peony scroll on the exterior.

D: 19.2 cm; H: 4.6 cm
Inv. 3527

184

Central medallion decorated with a large-flowered branch (chrysanthemum or peony) emerging from behind an ornamental rock, on either side of which are small plants. A light lotus scroll decorates the cavetto inside and outside.

D: 19.6 cm; H: 4 cm
Inv. 1698

185

The central medallion is decorated with a stylised lotus flower with a Sanskrit character, surrounded by a scroll of leaves and clouds. The medallion is ringed with a trefoil pattern. There is a light lotus scroll on the cavetto below a border of *leiwen*. The exterior is decorated with a lotus scroll above a frieze of scrolls. This is a fragment of a small broken dish.

Inv. 3432

186

Central medallion decorated with cloud collar panels forming a six-pointed star set in reserve against a "fish roe" background sprinkled with half-flowers. There is a flower in the centre of the star with lotuses on long stems emerging from each petal. Around the cavetto, cloud collar panels are set in reserve against a background of dots. Inside the panels, there is an endless knot on a long stem. There are white half-flowers beneath the rim and tulip-shaped flowers at the base. Lotus scroll on the back. Design painted in pale blue.

D: 24.9 cm; H: 4.4 cm
Inv. 3445

Pieces for comparison: Addis, 1968, pl. 47; *Wenwu*, 11, 1996

6. The bowls

Bowls represent the second most important set of Chinese porcelains found in the cargo; there were 357 whole or slightly damaged bowls, and three sizes and two shapes are represented. There are large bowls with a flared rim, medium-sized bowls with a straight or flared rim and small bowls with a straight or flared rim. Similar bowls have been found at kiln sites at Jingdezhen and others are preserved in the Topkapi Saray Museum in Istanbul and various collections created in South-East Asia.

Pieces for comparison: Aga-Oglu, 1975, 1982; Krahl, 1986, Vol. II; Gotuaco, Tan, Diem, 1997; Huang Yunpeng, Li Zhen, 1988; Yeo, Martin, 1978.

187

The outside is covered with a procession of eight *hai shou* fantastic animals galloping over or emerging from the waves. There is a flying fish, a conch with a small animal, a tortoise (?) and a mollusc nestling in the waves. Flying through the clouds above them are an elephant, a goat, a horse and a *qilin*. The inside cavetto is edged with a diaper trellis and lotus stems and aquatic plants hover over blue waves. The central medallion is decorated with a shell containing an *ershu* (?), set in reserve against a background of alternating segments of waves. The animals have been drawn in with a paintbrush and are shaded to emphasise their anatomical features.

D: 26.3 cm; H: 10.2 cm
Inv. 2644

6.1 Large bowls with flared rim

These deep bowls with a rounded edge and flared rim stand on a foot that is slightly recessed at the base. They are potted in fine white porcelain coated in a transparent bluish glaze, with the exception of the foot-rim, and the design is painted in a bluish-grey cobalt. Bowls of this size are rare in the cargo, only 18 having been found. The inter-Asian market may have been less interested by this type of product than the Middle East. The bowls found on the junk were probably prestige imports destined for wealthy customers.

188

The outside is covered with large, discontinuous lotus scrolls, between a border of zigzag lines and a frieze of upright lotus panels. Inside, on the cavetto, there is a diaper trellis border with four-petalled flowers, lotus stems and aquatic plants above blue waves. The central medallion is decorated with a shell, inside which there is an *ershu* (?) set in reserve against a background of alternating segments of waves.

D: 24.3 cm; H: 9.9 cm
Inv. 3763

Discontinuous scroll patterns are also frequent on the outside of large dishes found in the cargo and are comparable to the pattern on the bowl and dish represented in Giovanni Bellini's painting, *The Feast of the Gods*, dating from 1514 (Fig. 33, p. 78). This style of scroll is typical of export porcelain and can be found on pieces in the Topkapi Saray Museum collection, the collection in the Tehran National Museum and collections formed in South-East Asia.

Pieces for comparison: Carswell, 1985, p. 89; 1995, p. 53.

189

Exterior decorated with a lotus scroll containing emblems between a trellis border and a frieze of upright petals. Inside, there is a trellis border and a lotus scroll with emblems on the side. The central medallion is decorated with a lotus sprig supporting an emblem.

D: 22.4 cm; H: 10 cm
Inv. 2648

Pieces for comparison: Krahl, 1986, Vol. II, cat. 705.

190

The outside depicts a thin lotus scroll between a trellis border and a row of lotus panels. Inside, there is a lotus scroll around the edge and the central medallion contains a flower formed by five lotus panels.

D: 19 cm; H: 8.8 cm
Inv. 1379

191

Stylised peony scroll with large flowers on the outside above a border of lotus panels. A pattern of peony scrolls covers the whole inner surface.

D: 23.5 cm; H: 9.4 cm
Inv. 1802

Pieces for comparison: Krahl, 1986, Vol. II, cat. 686.

192

The exterior depicts lotuses and aquatic plants emerging from foaming waves above a frieze of waves. Inside, there is a border of lotus scrolls and a central medallion decorated with a conch shell reversed out against a background of blue waves.

D: 18.3 cm; H: 8.5 cm
Inv. 1087

6.2 Bowls with a flared or straight rim

The largest category consists of average-sized bowls with a flared rim, of which there are 193 whole or slightly damaged bowls; there are 109 whole or slightly damaged bowls with a straight rim. There is a total of 37 small bowls and they are potted in thicker porcelain than the large bowls. Some of those that are more crudely potted have very thick sides.

193

Bowl with flared rim. The outside depicts two *kui* dragons with foliated bodies above lotus panels and small Buddhist emblems. The dragons have two front legs without claws, a nose like an elephant's trunk, rounded horns and small, curved wings. Inside, there is a trellis border and a stylised branch of blossom in the central medallion.

D: 14.5 cm; H: 7.2 cm
Inv. 1874

The *kui* dragon first appeared in China in the late fourth century and is linked to the spread of Buddhism. The emblem is carved on the walls of Buddhist caves in northern China and depicted on gold and silver vessels and ceramics during the Tang dynasty and at the start of the Song dynasty. The original ferocious animal was gradually toned down into a more benign dragon. Its reappearance in the late fifteenth century is associated with the influence of Buddhism on the emperors Chenghua and Hongzhi. The Wutasi (Temple of the Five Pagodas) built in 1473 west of Beijing, presents a very diverse range of religious motifs, including the *kui* dragon on the arch over the central gate. The dragon is often found on porcelain of the Chenghua period. Jars, bowls and dishes on which this design appears have been found in the Yudai River on the site of the imperial palace in Nanking and on the site of the imperial manufactory at Jingdezhen. Other examples have been found in the excavations on the site of the privately-owned Shibadu kilns at Jingdezhen, in Penny's Bay, Hong Kong and in the collections of the Topkapi Saray Museum and the Tehran National Museum.

Pieces for comparison: *A Legacy of the Ming*, 1996, pp. 57–8, 60–2; Liu Xinyuan, et al., 1993, pp. 211, 261, 305; P. Lam, 1989–92, pl. 21a, b, pl. 6; Krahl, 1986, Vol. II, cat. 680; Pope, 1956, pl. 62.

LOST AT SEA

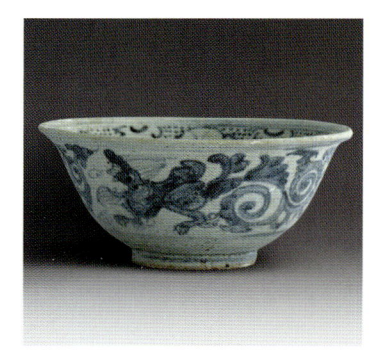

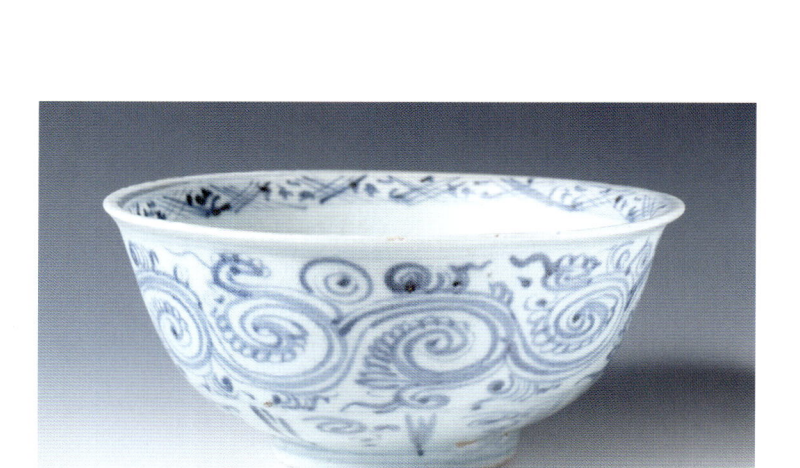

194

On the exterior surface, there are two *kui* dragons with foliated bodies hovering over blue circles. Inside, there is a beribboned double *vajra* in the central medallion and on the sides, white cloud collar panels against a background of dots, alternating with half flower-heads on the rim and tulip-shaped flowers on the base. Inside each panel there is a long stem, terminating in an endless knot.

D: 15 cm; H: 7 cm
Inv. 2965

The cloud collar design is found on imperial porcelain of the reign of Chenghua and is well-represented in the excavations on the sites of private kilns of the Hongzhi period.

Pieces for comparison: Huang Yunpeng, Li Zhen, 1988, ill. 51, 87; Liu Xinyuan, et al., 1993, cat. B19; *Ceramic Finds from the Jingdezhen Kilns (10th–17th Century)*, 1992.

195

The exterior surface is decorated with scrolls of stylised foliage above sketchily drawn lotus panels. There is a trellis frieze on the inside edge and a stylised spiralling branch of blossom inside the central medallion. The design is executed in pale cobalt blue.

D: 15.1 cm; H: 7.1 cm; Inv. 1879

The pattern of the scrolls bears some resemblance to that of the volutes of the bodies of the *kui* dragons on the previous bowls. This leaf pattern uses the decorative effects of curves and counter-curves and only seems to have been used on porcelain from privately owned kilns. Bowls of the same design have been found in excavations on the site of the imperial palace at Nanking, at the site of the privately owned Shibadu kilns at Jingdezhen and at the Penny's Bay site in Hong Kong. The sandy concretions around the foot and base indicate that the bowl was not placed on a stand, but directly on the sand packed into the bottom of the saggar. This is a feature of pieces produced at Shibadu. These bowls decorated with stylised scrolls, some of which are of a perceptibly higher quality, would have been highly prized by customers in the archipelago, as shown by the large number recovered in the cargo and the pieces in collections formed in South-East Asia.

Pieces for comparison: Aga-Oglu, 1975, p. 74, ill. 124a; 1982, p. 49, ill. 95; Lam, 1989–92, pl. 21a, b, pl. 6, p. 5; *A Legacy of the Ming*, 1996, p. 62, ill. 12; Yeo, Martin, 1978, pl. 196.

196

There are scrolls of stylised foliage on the outside above sketchily drawn lotus panels. There is a trellis frieze around the inside edge and a hastily drawn lotus bush inside the central medallion. The design is painted in pale blue-grey cobalt.

D: 14.9 cm; H: 7.4 cm
Inv. 1947

197

On the outside, foliated scrolls above sketchily drawn lotus panels. Inside, a *lingzhi* fungi scroll around the sides and a foliate scroll in the central medallion. The design is painted in pale blue-grey cobalt. The bowl has been carefully potted and is of good quality.

D: 15.8 cm; H: 7.1 cm
Inv. 3792

198

On the outside cavetto, foliated scrolls above panels of sketchily drawn lotuses. A frieze of Sanskrit characters around the inner rim and a beribboned double *vajra* in the central medallion. The bowl has a sharper outline above the foot. The design is painted in dark cobalt blue.

D: 15.4 cm; H: 7 cm
Inv. 1574

199

Bowl with straight rim. The outside cavetto is covered in stylised foliated scrolls between lotus panels and a border of chevrons. The central medallion is decorated with a white shell against a background of blue waves, surrounded by lotus flowers and aquatic plants emerging from the waves, beneath a wave pattern border. The design is painted in dark cobalt blue.

D: 14.5 cm; H: 7.2 cm
Inv. 4706

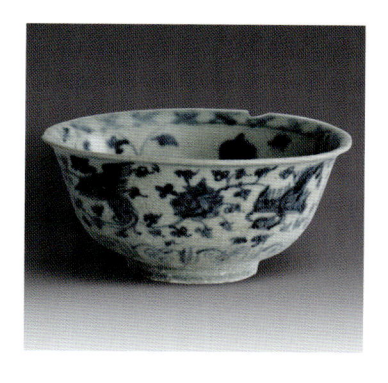

200

On the outside, four phoenixes in flight amongst a lotus scroll, a band of lotus panels beneath them. Inside, a beribboned double *vajra* in the central medallion, surrounded on the cavetto by two lotus stems dropping down from the rim and alternating with two vertical twigs. A trellis frieze on the edge. The design is painted in dark cobalt blue.

D: 15 cm; H: 7.3 cm
Inv. 2451

201

On the outside, four phoenixes in flight amongst a lotus scroll. Inside, a central flower surrounded by an overall lotus scroll. The design is painted in grey cobalt under a slightly opaque glaze.

D: 13.9 cm; H: 6.1 cm
Inv. 4389

202

A lotus flower scroll supporting Buddhist emblems and a border of chevrons on the outside. Inside, six lotus panels with a Sanskrit character form the central medallion. On the cavetto, there is a lotus flower scroll, in which each flower supports a Sanskrit character beneath a trellis border. The pattern is painted in blue-grey cobalt.

D: 16.1 cm; H: 7.1 cm
Inv. 4705

203

Bowl with straight rim. On the outside cavetto, a scroll of lotus flowers supporting Buddhist emblems between a border of chevrons and a frieze of pointed petals. Inside, the central medallion consists of six lotus panels, each framing a Sanskrit character. On the cavetto, lotus flower scrolls, each of which supports a Sanskrit character beneath a trellis border. The design is painted in dark cobalt blue.

D: 14.9 cm; H: 7.5 cm
Inv. 1672

204

Little bowl with a flared rim. On the outside cavetto, a scroll of lotus flowers supporting Buddhist emblems beneath a border of chevrons. Inside, the central medallion consists of six lotus panels each framing a Sanskrit character. On the cavetto, there are lotus flower scrolls, each of which supports a Sanskrit character beneath a trellis border. The design is painted in dark cobalt blue.

D: 13.8 cm; H: 5.5 cm
Inv. 1933

205

Bowl with flared rim. Lotus scrolls above lotus panels. Inside, a beribboned double vajra inside the wide central medallion, ringed with a double circle. The cavetto is decorated with lotus stems and twigs under a trellis border.

D: 14.5 cm; H: 7.5 cm
Inv. 2769b

206

Bowl with straight rim. Lotus flower scroll between lotus panels and a border. Inside, a beribboned double *vajra* within a small central medallion ringed by a double circle. A light lotus scroll adorns the cavetto.

D: 14.5 cm; H: 7.2 cm
Inv. 4378

207

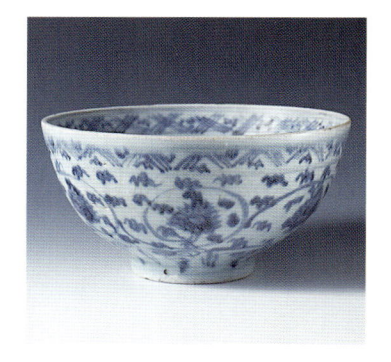

Bowl with straight rim. Lotus scroll between lotus panels and a border of chevrons. Inside, wide central medallion containing a beribboned double *vajra*, surrounded by a double circle. A light lotus scroll under a trellis border adorns the cavetto.

D: 14.5 cm; H: 7.5 cm
Inv. 4350

208

Bowl with flared rim. Lotus flower scroll with pointed petals above lotus panels. On the inside, wide central medallion containing a beribboned double *vajra* and surrounded by a double circle. There are strings of beads on the cavetto.

D: 15 cm; H: 7.3 cm
Inv. 4703

209

Scroll of large lotus flowers above lotus panels. Inside, large central medallion with a beribboned double *vajra*, surrounded on the cavetto by white cloud collar panels against a dotted background, alternating with half flower-heads on the rim and tulip-shaped flowers on the base. Inside each panel, a long stem terminating in an endless knot.

D: 16.8 cm; H: 8.3 cm
Inv. 3784

210

Bowl with straight rim. Scroll of large lotus flowers between a frieze of pointed petals and a chevron border. Central medallion decorated with a white shell against a background of blue waves, surrounded by lotus flowers and aquatic plants emerging from the waves and continuing right up to the rim of the bowl.

D: 15.7 cm; H: 8 cm
Inv. 600

211

Bowl with flared rim. Scroll of small lotus flowers between a border of chevrons and a frieze of pointed petals. The inside is completely covered with a peony scroll pattern.

D: 15.5 cm; H: 6.8 cm
Inv. 2769

212

Bowl with straight rim. Lotus flower scroll between a chevron border and a band of lotus panels. The inside is completely covered with a lotus scroll pattern.

D: 14.8 cm; H: 7.4 cm
Inv. 4383

213

Bowl with flared rim. Scroll of small lotus flowers between a border of chevrons and a frieze of lotus panels. Inside, a medallion of lotus panels decorated with thin scrolls and surrounded on the cavetto by a lotus garland supporting Sanskrit characters, under a trellis border.

D: 15.7 cm; H: 7.2 cm
Inv. 4380

214

Scroll of small lotus flowers beneath a classical scroll border. Inside, central medallion decorated with a shell with an *ershu* (?) against a background of waves, surrounded on the cavetto by thin lotus scrolls under a trellis border.

D: 13.2 cm; H: 6 cm
Inv. 4358

215

Bowl with straight rim. Scroll of small lotus flowers between a border of *leiwen* and a frieze of lotus petals. Inside, on the cavetto beneath a border of *leiwen*, four *tianma*, celestial horses with flames emerging from their shoulders, gallop amongst the clouds. Central medallion with a conch shell, inside which there is an *ershu* (?), against a background of blue waves.

D: 14.9 cm; H: 7.7 cm
Inv. 807

The theme of galloping horses appears on porcelain of the Yuan dynasty and remained very popular during later reigns, until the Qing dynasty. The horse has been a favourite subject in Chinese art since ancient times and its symbolism is extremely complex. Ancient texts contain traces of a belief in celestial horses which were the mounts of the Yellow Emperor and that conferred their exceptional longevity to their riders. These steeds were a symbol of speed and perseverance, and were one of the seven treasures of Buddhism which, according to legend, represent the attributes of a universal sovereign. The horse is one of the nine *hai shou*, marine animals often depicted on porcelain of the Xuande period, and was also used alone in the reign of Chenghua. Its association with the conch shell and the *ershu* suggests the influence of Tibetan Buddhism in the repertory of decorative arts of the period.

Pieces for comparison: Liu Xinyuan, et al., 1993, p. 237.

216

Bowl with flared rim. Scroll of sketchily drawn lotus flowers with pointed petals. Inside the bowl, central medallion with the character *fu*, "happiness". The bowl is crudely potted in thick porcelain and the base is unglazed.

D: 14.9 cm; H: 6.4 cm; Inv. 3880

This style of bowl appeared in the reigns of Hongwu Yongle, as evidenced by excavations on the kiln sites.

Pieces for comparison: Huang Yunpeng, Li Zhen, 1988, ill. 8.

217

Scroll of lotus flowers with sketchily drawn, pointed petals. Central medallion with the character *fu*, "happiness". The bowl is rather crudely potted in thick porcelain and the base is unglazed.

D: 10.1 cm; H: 4.8 cm
Inv. 1011

218

Small straight-sided bowl. Scroll of lotus flowers with sketchily drawn, pointed petals. Central medallion with the character *fu*, meaning "happiness". The bowl is rather crudely potted in thick porcelain and the base is unglazed.

D: 9.6 cm; H: 4.6 cm
Inv. 635

219

Chrysanthemum scrolls above lotus panels. Central medallion with a beribboned double *vajra* ringed by a double circle, jewelled motifs around the sides.

D: 14.6 cm; H: 7.3 cm
Inv. 2020

220

Bowl with straight rim. Camellia scroll between a trefoil pattern and a classic scroll border. Inside, beribboned double *vajra* in the central medallion, surrounded by a double circle and fine lotus scroll on the cavetto.

D: 14.4 cm; H: 7.8 cm
Inv. 2764

221

Bowl with straight rim. Camellia scroll between lotus panels and a border of chevrons, with a conch shell with a small long eared animal (an *ershu* [?]) against a background of waves in the central medallion, surrounded by lotus stems and aquatic plants emerging from the waves on the cavetto, and a frieze of waves on the rim.

D: 14.5 cm; H: 7.8 cm
Inv. SN2

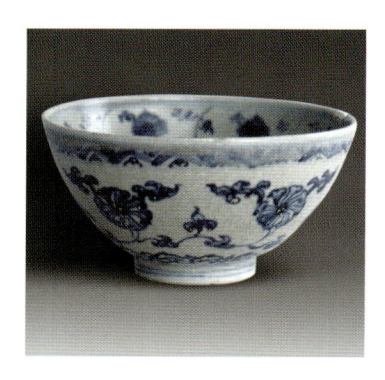

222

Bowl with straight rim. Camellia scroll between a frieze of trefoil motifs and a border of chevrons. The central medallion inside, contains a conch shell with a small long-eared animal (an *ershu* [?]) against a background of waves, surrounded by a large lotus scroll on the rim.

D: 12.2 cm; H: 6.3 cm
Inv. 1132

223

On the outside, emerging from a frieze of waves there are lotus flower stems alternating with upright lotus leaves and aquatic plants. At the rim, a band of chevron patterns. Inside, central medallion with a conch shell and a small long-eared animal (an *ershu* [?]) against a background of waves, surrounded by a thin chrysanthemum scroll on the cavetto and a trellis pattern on the rim. The design is painted in a strong blue cobalt oxide.

D: 15.3 cm; H: 6.8 cm; Inv. 2771

The stems and leaves of the lotus are accentuated by a series of dots which have probably been added to recreate the heaped and piled effect of the early fifteenth century. The lotus pattern, so popular in the reign of Chenghua (1465–87) is found on imperial porcelain. It is linked to numerous Buddhist legends, and is the symbol of perfect purity. The flower, which only grows in still waters, is also the symbol of Nirvana. It is often depicted in the caves of Dunhuang, supporting *Bodhisattvas* inside its corolla or emerging from ponds. A study of the cargo reveals that it contained goods of varying degrees of quality. There were pieces of good quality for mass export, but also a few items that were very carefully decorated and potted from a finer grade of porcelain, with a thinner glaze, of which this bowl is one of the best examples.

Pieces for comparison: Liu Xinyuan, et al., 1993.

224

Bowl with flared rim. On the outside, lotus flower stems alternating with upright lotus leaves and aquatic plants emerge from a frieze of waves. There is also a border of waves. The central medallion in the interior contains a conch shell with a small, long-eared animal (an *ershu* [?]) against a background of waves, surrounded by a wide floral scroll on the rim. The design is painted in a strong blue cobalt oxide.

D: 15.7 cm; H: 6.7 cm; Inv. 3941

225

Bowl with straight rim. On the outside, lotus flower stems, alternating with upright lotus leaves and aquatic plants emerge from a frieze of waves beneath a border of chevrons. The stems and leaves are accentuated with a series of dots. Inside, ringed by a double circle, the medallion is formed by six lotus panels, each framing a Sanskrit character. The flowers of lotus scrolls support Sanskrit characters around the cavetto beneath a trellis frieze. The design is painted in a strong blue cobalt oxide.

D: 14.7 cm; H: 7.3 cm; Inv. 4354

Such decoration based on written characters of religious significance was very popular at the end of the reign of Chenghua. The inscription represents various syllables which correspond with a particular mandala. Excavations at the site of the imperial manufacture at Jingdezhen have revealed numerous pieces of porcelain decorated with Buddhist writings or symbols. Originally, these designs would have been used on porcelain vessels destined for religious use, but they then passed into the decorative vocabulary of potters from the private kilns. It is clear that the foreign clientele did not perceive such a connotation and only saw them as exotic, graphic designs.

Pieces for comparison: Liu Xinyuan, et al., 1993.

226

Bowl with straight rim. On the outside, emerging from a frieze of waves, stems of lotus flowers alternating with upright lotus leaves and aquatic plants. There is a border of chevrons. Inside, large central medallion decorated with a beribboned double *vajra*, surrounded by a light lotus scroll on the cavetto. The design is painted in a strong blue cobalt oxide.

D: 14.2 cm; H: 7.7 cm
Inv. 1983

227

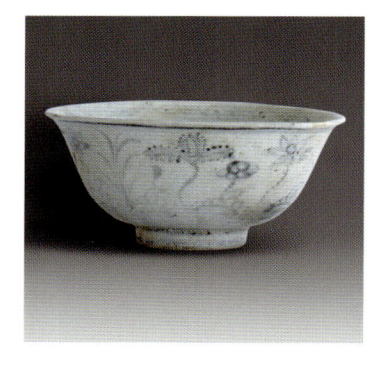

Small bowl with flared rim. On the outside, emerging from a frieze of waves, lotus flower stems alternate with upright lotus leaves and aquatic plants. On the inside, central medallion decorated with a conch against a background of waves, surrounded by lotus flower stems and aquatic plants emerging from a frieze of waves on the cavetto, edged with a trellis band. The glaze is slightly opaque.

D: 13 cm; H: 6 cm
Inv. 4359

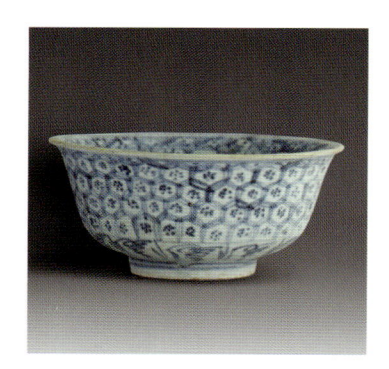

228

Above lotus panels, the outside is entirely covered with a honeycomb pattern. Inside, in the central medallion, four cloud collar panels radiate around a cash diaper pattern on a "fish roe" background, alternating with a white half flower-head. Each panel contains a long lotus stem. On the cavetto, white cloud collar panels against a dotted background alternating with half flower-heads at the rim and tulip-shaped flowers at the base. Inside each panel, a long stem ends in an endless knot. Trellis border.

D: 15 cm; H: 7 cm
Inv. 1571

229

Above lotus panels, overall honeycomb pattern. Inside, large central medallion with a beribboned double *vajra*. White cloud collar panels on the cavetto alternating with half flower-heads and tulip-shaped flowers at the base, against a spotted background. Inside each panel, a long stem ends with an endless knot. Trellis border.

D: 14.4 cm; H: 7.3 cm
No Inv. SN

230

Above lotus panels, overall honeycomb pattern. Inside, large central medallion with a beribboned double *vajra*. Sanskrit characters on the rim.

D: 13.1 cm; H: 6.6 cm
Inv. 4702

231

On the outside, wide band decorated with spiralling clouds. Inside, in the central medallion, a large four-petalled flower has been hastily drawn. The decoration has been applied in blue-black cobalt. This is a crudely potted bowl with a straight foot and unglazed base.

D: 15.1 cm; H: 6.5 cm; Inv. 1126

This style of bowl appeared in the reigns of Hongwu and Yongle, as witnessed by the excavations at the kiln sites.

Pieces for comparison: Gotuaco, Tan, Diem, 1997, cat. M1; Huang Yunpeng, Li Zhen, 1988, ill. 6.

232

On the outside, small spiralling scrolls under a border of criss-crossed lines. Inside, medallion formed by five lotus panels. White cloud collar panels on the cavetto alternating with half flower-heads and tulip-shaped flowers at the base, against a spotted background. Inside each panel, a long stem ends with an endless knot. Trellis border.

D: 13.1 cm; H: 6 cm
Inv. 4219

233

On the outside, *lingzhi* scrolls, the immortality fungus, above spearhead patterns. Inside, small central medallion decorated with a *lingzhi* and surrounded by a frieze of flowerets. Good quality piece and carefully painted design in very dark cobalt blue.

D: 13.3 cm; H: 6.1 cm
No Inv.

The *lingzhi* fungus motif has been used on porcelain since the reign of Hongwu and is well represented on the porcelain of the Chenghua period.

Pieces for comparison: *Yuan's and Ming's Imperial Porcelains*, 1999, cat. 19, 28, 58, 62, 87, 127, 129, 162, 354–5.

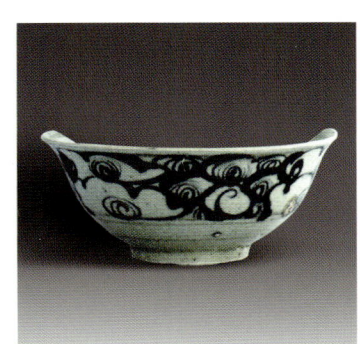

234

Exterior decorated with two branches of blossom, alternating with a small moon (?) design and twigs. Inside, medallion of six lotus panels and a frieze of Sanskrit characters around the edge.

D: 12.8 cm; H: 6.4 cm
Inv. 608

This delicate design of a branch of blossom is also represented in the cargo on an oval box and a small jar and in a secondary design on the large ewers. It is typical of imperial porcelain of the end of the reign of Chenghua and can be found on the ceramics of private kilns of the reign of Hongzhi.

Pieces for comparison: Huang Yunpeng, Li Zhen, 1988, ill. 67, 78, 83; Liu Xinyuan, et al., 1993, cat. C58, C106, C115, C117.

235

Exterior decorated with four stylised clouds. Central medallion with the character *fu*, meaning "happiness". This bowl is rather crudely potted in thick porcelain and has an unglazed base.

D: 12.2 cm; H: 5.2 cm
Inv. 4302

This style of bowl emerged in the reigns of Hongwu–Yongle, as shown by excavations on the kiln sites.

Pieces for comparison: Huang Yunpeng, Li Zhen, 1988, ill. 8.

236

Little bell-shaped cups used for alcohol, decorated respectively on the outside with flowers or characters in Sanskrit, with a character inside.

D: 5.7 cm; H: 4.5 cm
Inv. 2106, Inv. 4424

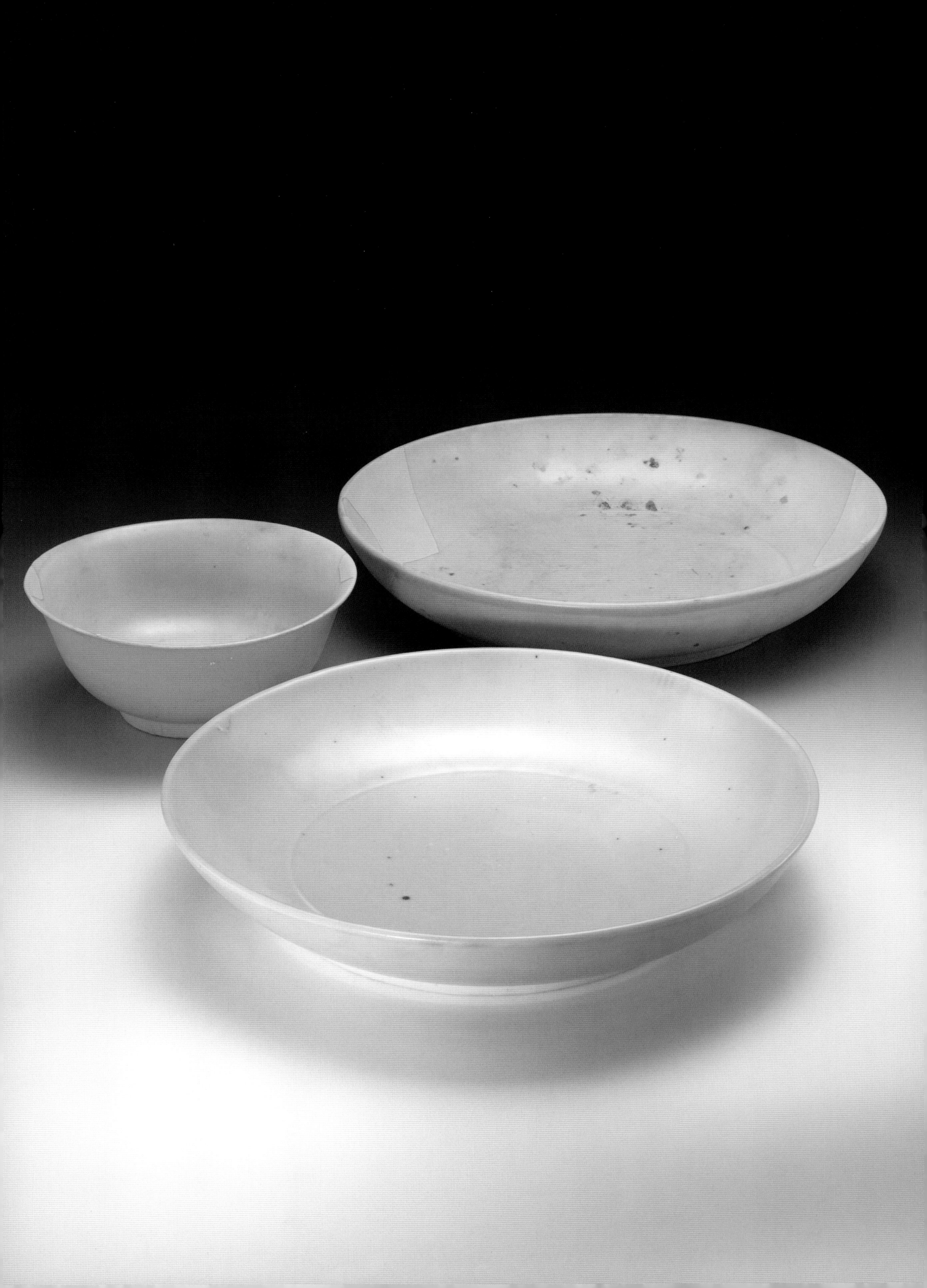

7. Monochrome white porcelain, enamelled porcelain and *fahua* stoneware

7.1 Monochrome white porcelain

A total of 10 intact or slightly damaged monochrome white pieces were found in the cargo, including dishes, bowls and a small bell-shaped cup. The saucer-shaped dishes were potted in a thick white porcelain covered in a glaze that was more opaque on plain white wares than on those which had incised decoration. They stand on a straight foot and unlike the blue and white ware, the base is unglazed. The average-sized dishes decorated with incisions have a glazed base and a foot that is slightly undercut at the junction with the base. The bowls and cup are of a finer quality. Similar pieces are to be found in the Topkapi Saray Museum in Istanbul.

Pieces for comparison: Krahl, 1986, Vol. II.

237

Large monochrome white saucer-shaped dish. The surface has a ferruginous stain on the surface.

D: 32.8 cm; H: 6.3 cm
Inv. 1651

238

Large monochrome white saucer-shaped dish with incised decoration. Inside, a branch of blossom in the centre and a plain cavetto. A lotus scroll adorns the outside cavetto. The glaze is fairly opaque.

D: 26 cm; H: 4.8 cm
Inv. 296

239

Plain white bowl with flared rim. Straight foot and base covered with glaze.

D: 19.7 cm; H: 8.6 cm
Inv. 729

LOST AT SEA

7.2 Enamelled porcelain

Only one dish has been found with traces of polychrome enamelling in red, green and yellow. It has been potted in thick porcelain and stands on a straight foot. It is glazed, except on the base. A few examples of enamelled pieces are to be found in the collection of Chinese porcelain owned by the Turkish sultans of Istanbul, others have been found in excavations in the Daijibu cemetery in the commune of Fuyu in Jilin province.

Pieces for comparison: Krahl, 1986, Vol. II, pp. 571–2; *Wenwu*, 9, 1994; 4, 1995.

240

Large saucer-shaped dish. Inside, a central medallion is surrounded by petals and decorated with four lotuses converging towards the centre. The cavetto has a border of *leiwen* from which blossom hangs. On the back, there is a floral scroll and a border of chevrons punctuated with small flowers. There are traces of enamel on the dish and on the concretions detached from the dish.

D: 34.5 cm; H: 7.5 cm
Inv. 1641

241

Monochrome white bell-shaped cup with traces of enamelled floral decoration. Small, slightly sloping foot, slightly recessed unglazed base.

D: 5.3 cm; H: 4.6 cm
Inv. 2606

7.3 *Fahua* stoneware

Shards of buff stoneware bearing traces of turquoise, dark blue and yellow enamel were found in the cargo. These fragments were probably part of a small jar with a reticulated pattern on the outside. This is indicated by the shape of the shards and the smooth, undecorated band. The fragment of handle must have belonged to a ewer.

242

Moulded and incised flowers and a scroll of leaves, coloured in yellow and turquoise, separated by a plain band originally in plain blue. Ewer handle partially coated with a green glaze.

No Inv.

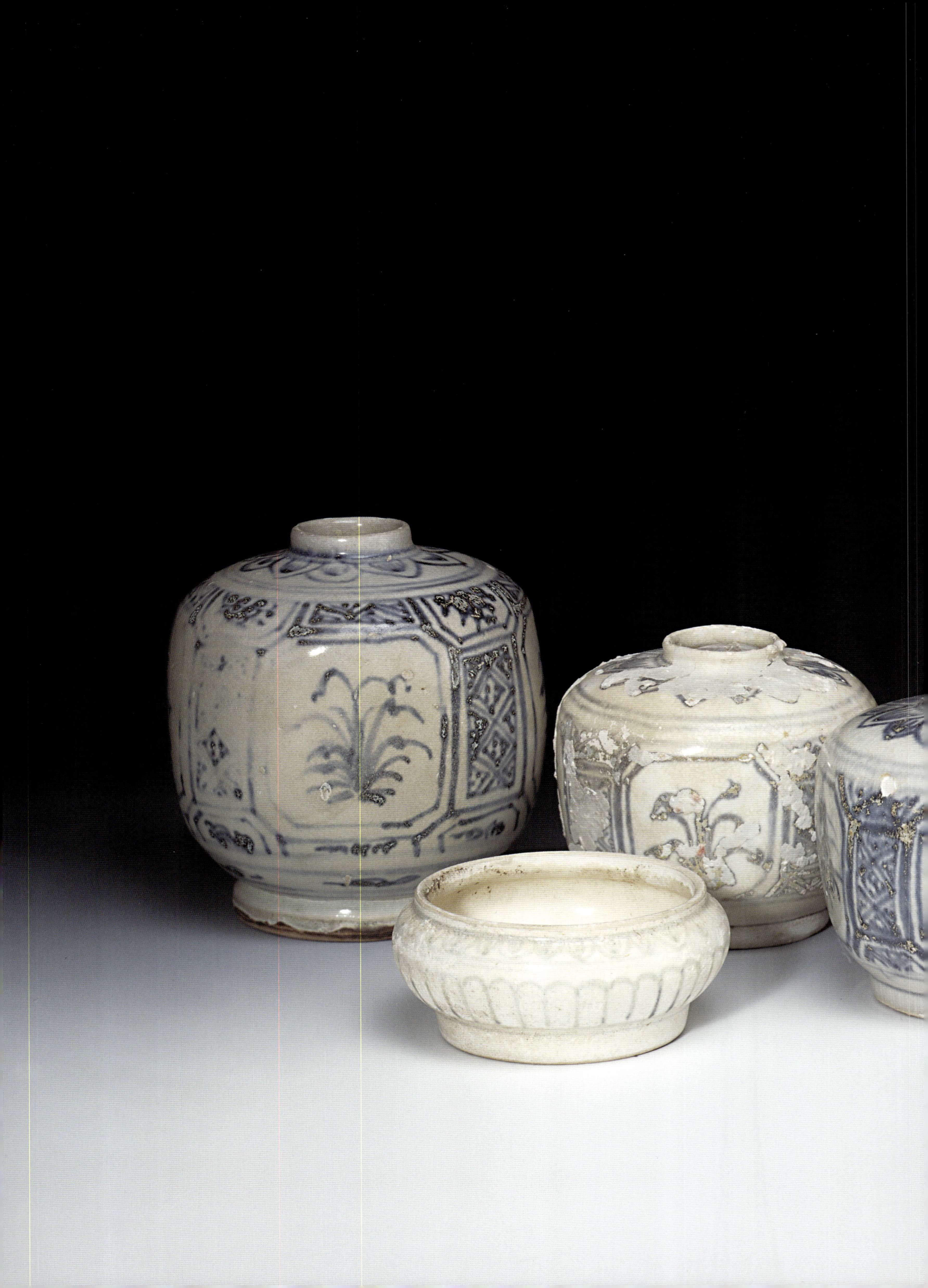

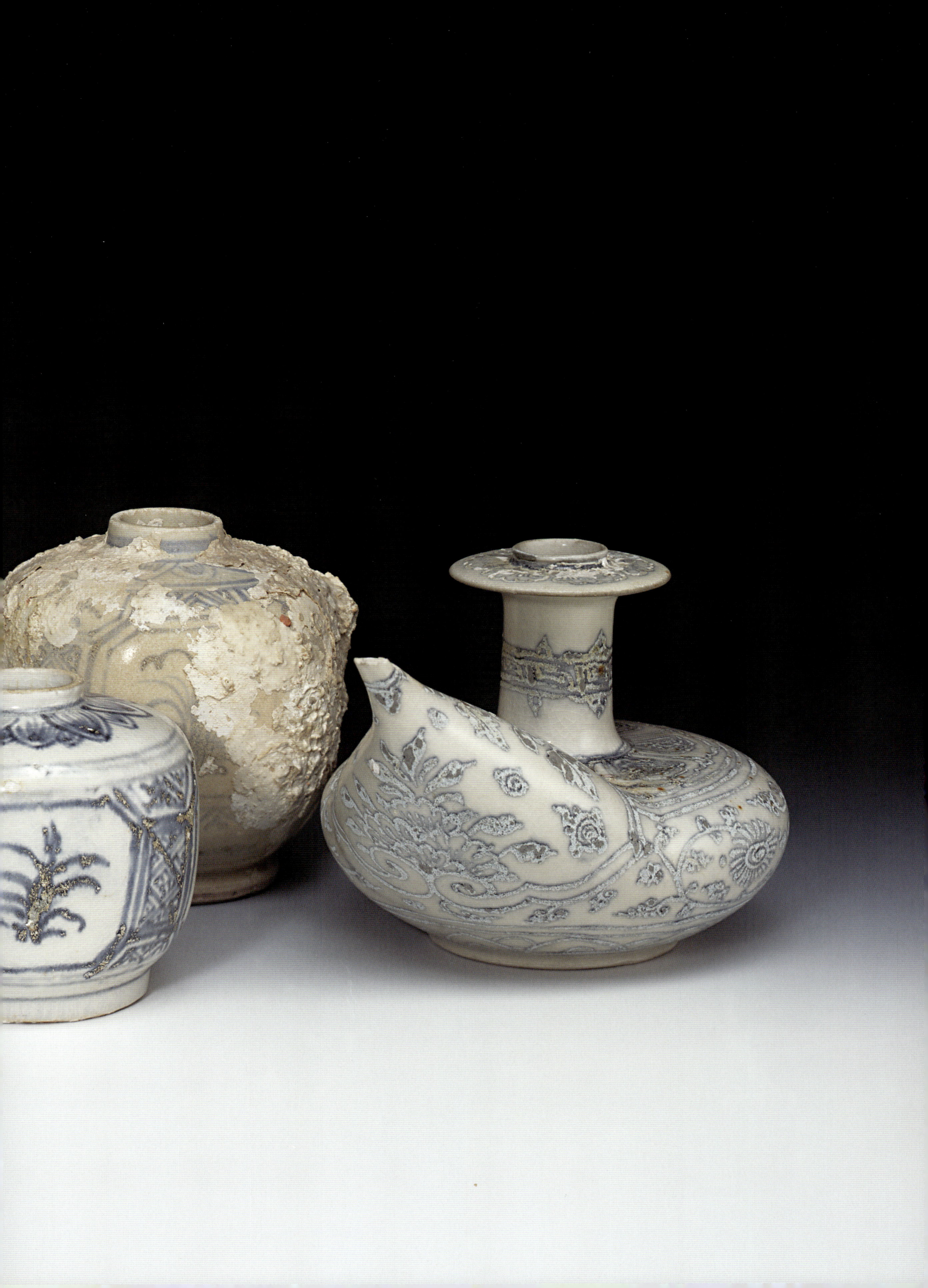

8. Vietnamese porcelain

There were only 28 whole or slightly damaged pieces of Vietnamese porcelain in the cargo. These consisted of a bottle, a *kendi*, a bowl, jarlets and boxes. With the exception of a small jar, all of the Vietnamese porcelain is decorated in underglaze cobalt blue. This type of Vietnamese ceramic is familiar in South-East Asia and is perfectly suited to the needs of the islanders, but the exact site at which they were made long remained unknown. Vietnamese archaeologists began researching in 1983 and the first excavations began in 1986. It was only then established that they had been produced in the Hanoi Delta region, in the Chu Dâu kilns in Hai Hu'ng province.

The production of blue and white wares began in that region in the fourteenth century, and was heavily modelled on Chinese porcelain, which also influenced the repertoire of decorative elements. Production increased rapidly in the fifteenth and sixteenth centuries but declined from the seventeenth century. Ceramics other than blue and white wares were also manufactured. Kaolin

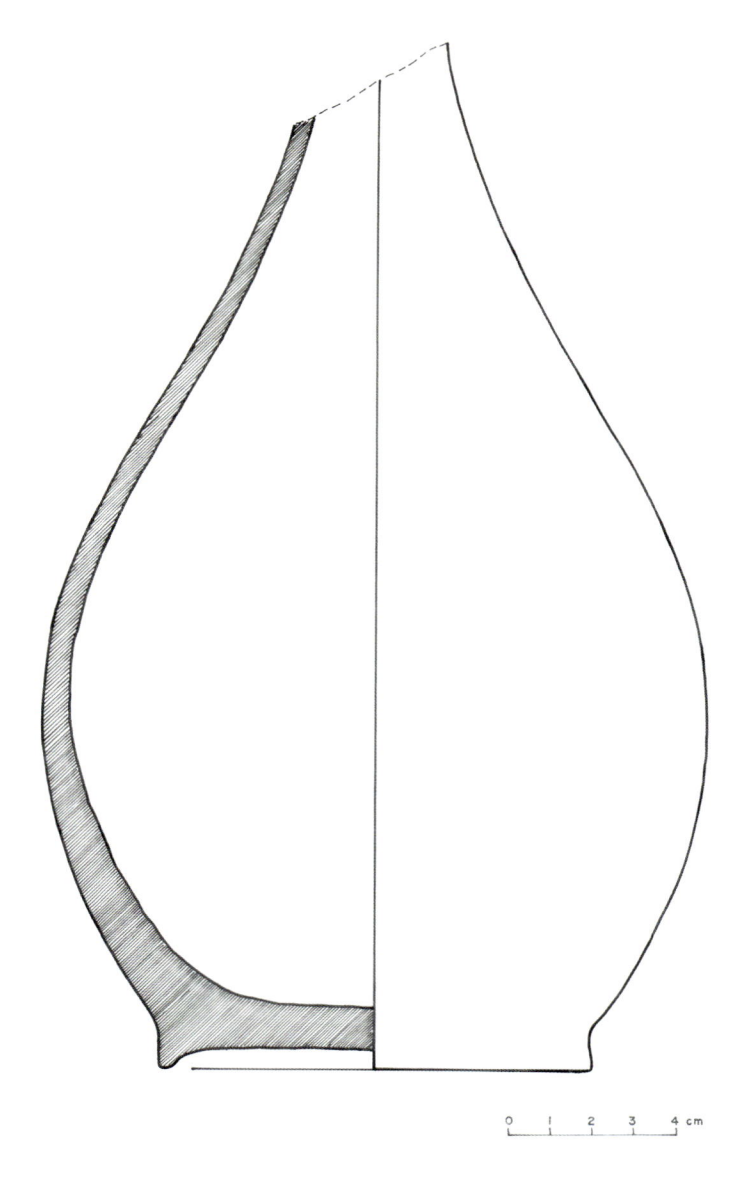

243

Large pear-shaped bottle with truncated neck, of the so-called *yuhuchun ping* type, a copy of a Chinese model. Lotus panel border around the base and around the bulb, wide band of medallions decorated with branches of blossom, set in reserve against a background of stylised waves. Identical flowers in the panels around the neck. Slightly recessed base painted brown. The design is painted in grey-blue cobalt.

Max. D: 15.8 cm; H: 25.5 cm
Inv. 2148

mines were conveniently close, as was a supply of good quality clay. The site was easily accessed from the Kinh Thay and Thai Binh rivers which facilitated the despatch of the finished products to the capital Thang Long and the international port of Vân Dôn, and in the seventeenth century to Phô Hiên. Boxes, jars and bottles are typical products of these kilns and those found in the cargo were made of fine-textured, creamy white porcelain, covered in a fine, transparent, crazed glaze. The foot was carefully finished and some pieces have the chocolate-coloured base which is characteristic of Vietnamese ceramics.

Pieces for comparison: R. Brown, *The Ceramics of South-East Asia: Their Dating and Identification*, Oxford University Press, Singapore, 1977, 1988; J. Guy, *Ceramic Traditions of South-East Asia*, Oxford University Press Ltd, Singapore, 1989; *Vietnamese Ceramics, A Separate Tradition*, Avery Press, 1997; D. Richards, *South-East Asian Ceramics: Thai, Vietnamese and Khmer. From the Collection of the Art Gallery in South Australia*, Oxford University Press, Kuala Lumpur, 1995; *South-East Asian and Early Chinese Export Ceramics*, William Sorsby Ltd, London, 1974; Tang Ba Hoanh, et al., *Gôm Chu Dâu*, Bao Tang Tinh Hai Hu'ng, 1993; *Vietnamese Ceramics*, Southeast Asian Ceramic Society, Singapore, 1982; W. Willets, *Ceramic Art of Southeast Asia*, The Southeast Asian Ceramic Society, Singapore, 1971.

8.1 Blue and white porcelain

244

Kendi with a flattened globular body and a long cylindrical neck terminating in a disc below the circular opening. The spout has a flattened funnel shape with a small pointed opening. The base is flat and unglazed. Chrysanthemum scroll pattern on the sides between a row of pointed petals around the base and lotus panels on the shoulder. Frieze of *leiwen* around the neck and a crown of petals around the opening. A branch of blossom and clouds decorate each side of the spout. The design is very carefully painted in pale cobalt blue.

D: max. width 13.2 cm; H: 12 cm
Inv. 2145

245

Small octagonal jar with flat shoulder. The foot is slightly bevelled, and the recessed base is partially painted brown. Crown of petals around the small opening and on the body, four main octagonal panels decorated with a stem of bamboo, alternating with smaller panels decorated with a trellis or stylised waves. There are small spaced scrolls above the foot.

D: max. 11.2 cm; H: 12.1 cm
Inv. 2083

246

Small octagonal jar with flat shoulder. Straight foot and recessed base. Crown of petals around a small opening and on the body, four main octagonal panels decorated either with an orchid-like plant or a stem of bamboo, alternating with smaller panels decorated with a trellis.

H: 9.8 cm
Inv. 2311

247

Small octagonal jar with a flat shoulder. Straight foot and recessed base. Around the small opening and the body, octagonal panels decorated with an orchid-like plant, alternating with panels decorated with geometrical designs.

D: 7 cm; H: 6 cm
Inv. 2127

248

Small shallow bowl with rounded cavetto, resting on a straight foot that is very carefully potted. The recessed base is unglazed. Border of pointed petals around the rounded rim and a row of petals arranged vertically on the sides. The bowl has an unglazed rim and must have been designed to be fitted with a lid.

D: opening 7.8 cm; H: 4.3 cm
Inv. 2859

249

Small, round box with a slightly recessed base and flat lid. There is a branch of blossom inside a circular medallion on the top of the lid and six vertical panels on the sides of the lid corresponding to those on the base, decorated with twigs and strapwork. The design is painted in grey-blue cobalt and the glaze is slightly opaque. The base of a smaller box with the same design was also found.

Lid Inv. 2442, H: 1.7 cm; D: 7 cm
Base Inv. 2716, H: 3.9 cm; D: 7 cm

8.2 White monochrome porcelain
One small jar was found in the cargo. It is covered with a smooth white glaze, apart from the rim and base which are unglazed.

250

Small jar with rounded body narrowing at the base.

D: 7 cm; H: 8.5 cm
Inv. 2859

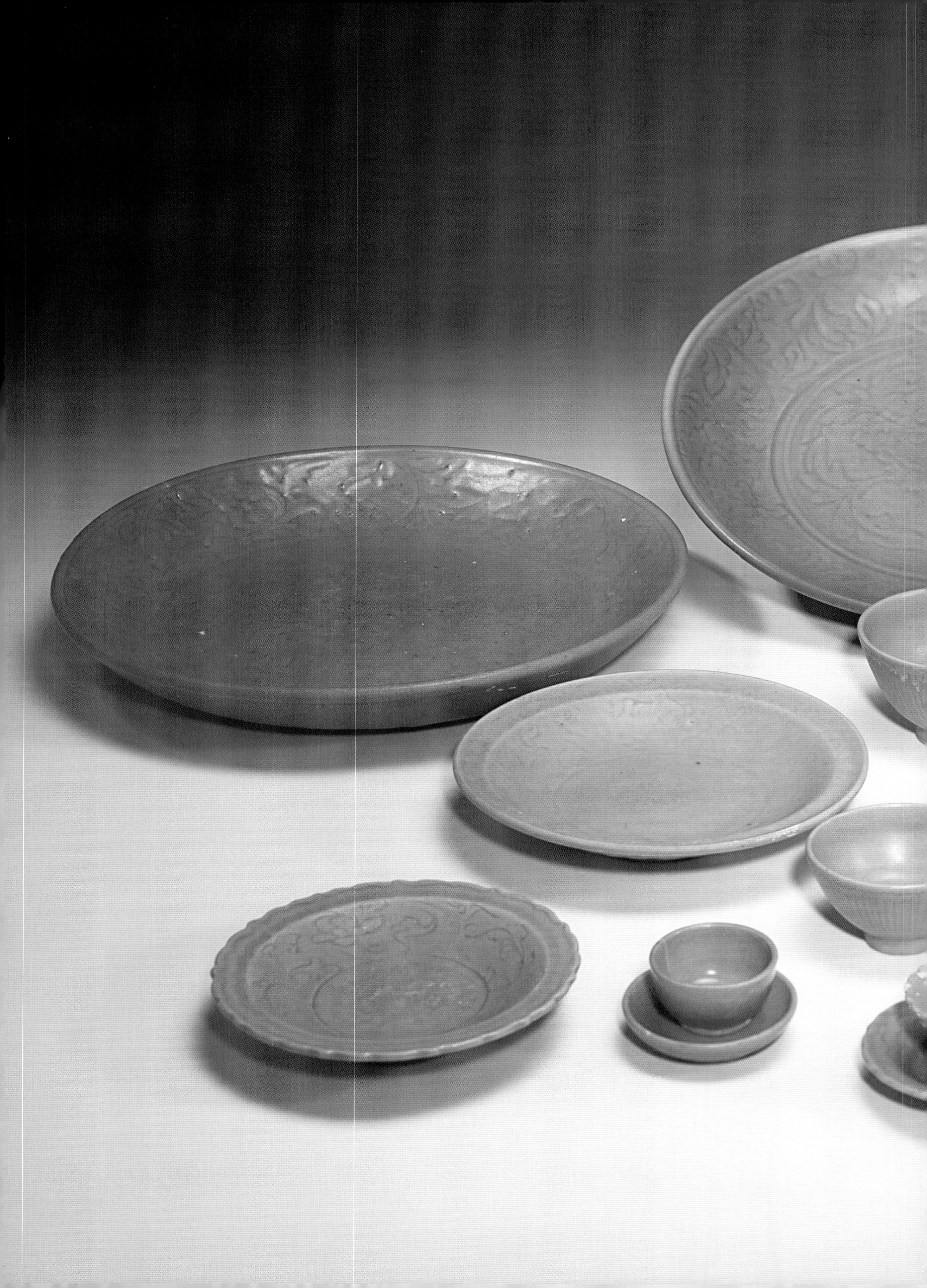

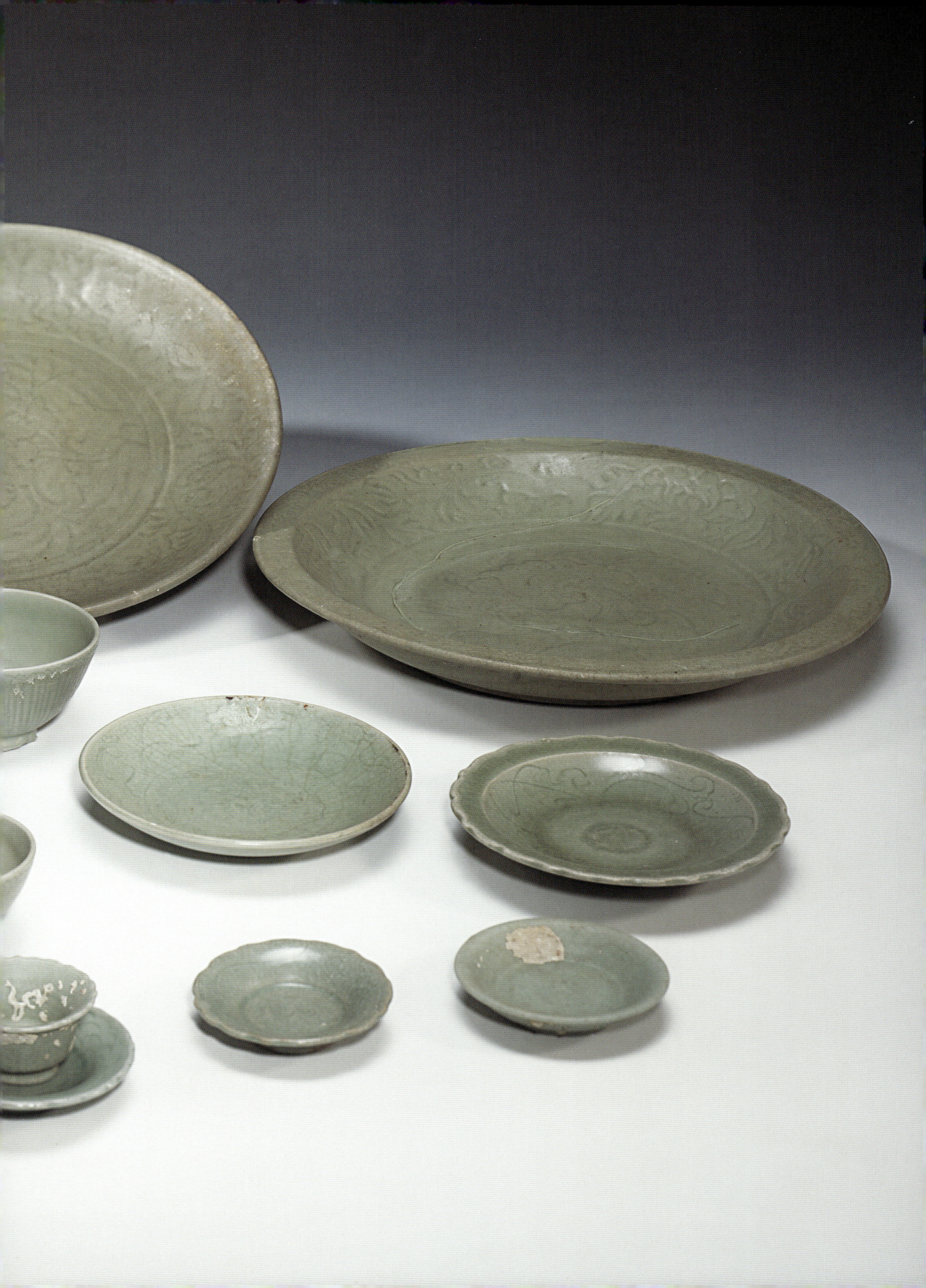

9. Chinese stoneware

9.1 Celadon ware

The stoneware cargo with a green celadon glaze was produced in the Longquan kilns. It consisted of 37 whole or slightly damaged pieces of various shapes, including dishes, saucers, bowls, cups and a jarlet. The dishes have straight or lobed edges and are only decorated on the inside, with the exception of dishes with a fluted well. Fragments of dishes which survived from the pillage that took place prior to the scientific excavation have an incised scroll design on the outside wall. Most have been potted from thick, solid, pale grey stoneware. Similar ceramics are preserved in the Middle East in the Topkapi Saray in Istanbul, the Sadberk Hanim Museum, the Tehran Museum and collections in South-East Asia.

Only nine pieces of celadon ware do not present a glaze and a body typical of the wares produced at Longquan. The provenance of three dishes is still uncertain. The bowls, on the other hand, imitate the decorative style of the Longquan kilns, with incised vertical petals. These might have been produced by the Huiyang, or the Sancun kilns in the village of Xin'an in Guangdong.

Pieces for comparison: J. Carswell, 1995; R. Krahl, 1986, Vol. I; J. Pope, 1956; *Chinese Celadons and Other Related Wares in Southeast Asia*, Southeast Asian Ceramic Society, Singapore, 1979; *Archaeological Finds from the Five Dynasties to the Qing periods in Guangdong*, The Art Gallery, The Chinese University of Hong Kong, 1989.

251

Saucer-shaped dish with straight edge. Peony branch with a large, incised flower inside an incised double circle, surrounded by a large peony scroll drawn with double or triple outlines on the cavetto. There are traces of a circular firing support on the base. The glaze has been eroded. Other dishes were decorated with a large lotus stem or flower corolla.

D: 44.2 cm; H: 7 cm; Inv. 4194

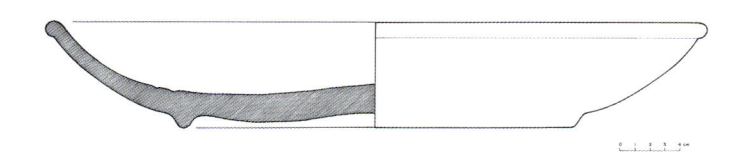

Inv. 4195

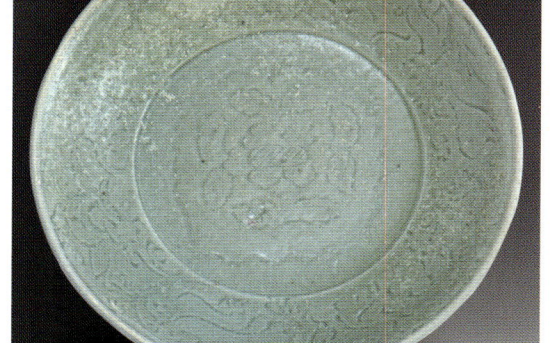

252

Saucer-shaped dish with straight edge. Five-petalled flower surrounded on four sides by a group of two leaves inside a lobed, incised medallion. Incised lotus scroll on the cavetto. Trace of a circular firing support on the base. The glaze is damaged.

D: 36.3 cm; H: 6.3 cm
Inv. 2589

253

Saucer-shaped dish with straight edge and a branch of blossom in the centre. The trace of a circular firing support appears on the base. The erosion of the glaze makes it hard to identify the decoration.

D: 35.8 cm; H: 6.8 cm
Inv. 3817

254

Saucer-shaped dish with straight rim. Peony flower in light relief printed in the centre of the dish inside an incised, lobed medallion. Flower scroll incised on the cavetto. Transparent crazed glaze, uneven on the outside. Narrow base with a small circle of glaze only in the centre.

D: 21.6 cm; H: 4.7 cm
Inv. 1401

255

Saucer-shaped dish with straight edge. Cash diaper pattern printed in the centre, and five-petalled flower scroll incised on the cavetto. Trace of a circular firing support on the base.

D: 45.4 cm; H: 7.2 cm
Inv. 4195

256

Saucer-shaped dish with straight edge. Cash diaper pattern printed in the centre, inside a lobed incised panel, and peony scroll with double lines deeply incised on the cavetto. Trace of a circular firing support on the base.

D: 44.7 cm; H: 7 cm
Inv. 4547

257

Saucer-shaped dish with straight edge. Medallion with printed cash diaper pattern inside an incised lobed panel and flower scroll on the cavetto. Trace of a circular firing support on the base.

D: 31.6 cm; H: 6.9 cm
Inv. 3153

258

Saucer-shaped dish with straight edge. Small medallion with a printed cash diaper pattern inside an incised, lobed panel. Glaze roughened and eroded, making it hard to discern the pattern. Narrow base with small circle of glaze only in the centre.

D: 29 cm; H: 6 cm
Inv. 3043

259

Saucer with flared rim, decorated in the central medallion with a printed cash diaper pattern. Small circle of glaze in the centre of the base.

D: 12.8 cm; H: 3.2 cm
Inv. 2051

260

Saucer with flared rim, no decoration. Small circle of glaze in the centre of the base.

D: 12.8 cm; H: 2.6 cm
Inv. 544

261

Large deep dish with flat rim. Broad incised flower with large petals, surrounded by a floral scroll on the cavetto and scrolls on the rim. Trace of a circular firing support on the base.

D: 45.3 cm; H: 7 cm
Inv. 4544

262

Deep dish with flat rim and ridged lip. Small lobed medallion in the centre with a cash diaper pattern, inside a large panel with five brackets. Incised lotus scroll on the cavetto and a double wavy line incised on the rim. Trace of a circular firing support on the base.

D: 36 cm; H: 6.2 cm
Inv. 348

263

Deep dish with flat rim. Large lobed panel with an illegible central design. Floral scroll incised on the cavetto and three parallel incised wavy lines on the rim. There is a ferruginous mark in the glaze and sandy adhesions. Trace of a circular firing support on the base.

D: 34.5 cm; H: 6.5 cm
Inv. 349

264

Deep dish with flat rim. Incised scroll of foliage on the rim and a lotus scroll on the cavetto. A peony flower is printed in the centre of the dish, inside an incised lobed medallion. The reverse is fluted. Trace of a circular firing support on the base.

D: 27.1 cm; H: 5.3 cm
Inv. 2430

265

Deep dish with flat rim. Floral design printed on the centre of the dish, inside a lobed, incised medallion. There are irregular grooves on the cavetto. The back is undecorated with the exception of a line incised under the rim. Trace of a circular firing support on the narrow base.

D: 29.2 cm; H: 6 cm
Inv. 394

266

Deep dish with a scalloped rim emphasised by incised bracket lobes. The cavetto is fluted and incised with floral scrolls. There is a peony flower printed in the centre of the dish, inside a large incised lobed medallion. The external wall is fluted. Trace of a circular firing support on the base.

D: 35.8 cm; H: 6.6 cm
Inv. 343

267

Dish with scalloped edge emphasised by incised bracket lobes and a ridged lip. Floral wreath incised on the cavetto. A large peony flower is printed in the centre of the dish. The reverse is fluted. Trace of a circular firing support on the base.

D: 21.6 cm; H: 4.4 cm
Inv. 3844

268

Dish with scalloped edge emphasised by incised bracket lobes and a ridged lip. A lotus scroll is incised on the cavetto. A peony flower is printed in the centre of the dish inside a large, lobed medallion. The reverse side is fluted. Trace of a circular firing support on the base.

D: 22 cm; H: 4.5 cm
Inv. 4427

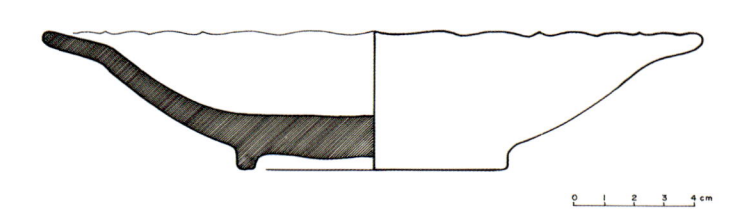

269

Small dish with scalloped edge emphasised by incised bracket lobes. There is a light lotus scroll on the walls. A small flower is printed in the centre of the dish. Trace of a circular firing support on the base. The glaze is uneven, shiny and translucent, allowing the decoration to show through.

D: 21.6 cm; H: 4 cm; Inv. 1175

Although the glaze is different on this dish, the archaeologist Zhu Boqian has stated that it can be attributed to kilns in the Longquan region.

270

Small dish with lobed rim, angular profile and flared walls. Inside, there are bracket lobes emphasised by three incised lines and walls decorated with incised petals or waves. The central medallion contains a printed seal mark, reading "Gushi", which is surrounded by a lobed, incised panel. The reverse is decorated with wide incised petals. Trace of a circular firing support on the base.

D: 13.1 cm; H: 2.9 cm; Inv. 540

Identical seals, which consist of the potter's name, have been found at the kiln sites of Dayao and Fengtang as well as in Penny's Bay in Hong Kong.

271

Small dish with lobed rim, angular profile and flared walls. There are bracket lobes on the interior emphasised by three incised lines and the walls are decorated with a light scroll. Spiral design inside a circle incised in the centre of the dish. The reverse is undecorated. Trace of a circular firing support on the base. The glaze is shiny and transparent and has been partially wiped off the foot.

D: 13.6 cm; H: 2.8 cm
Inv. 1420

272

Small dish with lobed rim, with an angular profile and flared walls. Inside, there are bracket lobes emphasised by three incised lines and a twig design incised in the centre of the dish. The reverse is undecorated. The foot and base are unglazed, and there is a trace of a circular firing support.

D: 11 cm; H: 2.7 cm
Inv. 884

273

Small dish with lobed rim, with an angular profile and flared walls. Inside, there are bracket lobes emphasised by three incised lines. A circle is incised in the bottom of the dish and the centre of the dish is unglazed. The back is undecorated. The foot and base are unglazed.

D: 11.8 cm; H: 2.7 cm; Inv. 885

The unglazed ring on the inside of the saucers appears to indicate that they would have been piled on top of each other, separated by a pontil, during firing. Although this set of similar dishes is glazed in a different type of glaze than that normally used on Longquan celadon ware, according to the archaeologist Zhu Boqian, it is attributable to the kilns in the Longquan region.

274

Saucer decorated with a floral design printed in the centre and with diagonal fluting on the cavetto. The foot is rounded and the base unglazed. The very thin glaze is aquamarine in colour.

D: 10.3 cm; H: 3.1 cm
Inv. 3015

275

Small cup with unglazed foot and base. The very thin glaze is aquamarine in colour.

D: 7.6 cm; H: 3.4 cm
Inv. 2131

276

Little cup with convex, flared walls and bracket lobed rim, emphasised by incisions. The reverse is fluted. The foot is rounded and there is the trace of a circular firing support on the base.

D: 8.7 cm; H: 5.4 cm
Inv. 2049

277

Bowl with rounded sides and straight rim, standing on a straight, narrow foot. The exterior is incised with long, thin petals and the interior with a large flower corolla in the centre. The rounded foot is glazed. The base has a small circle of glaze in the centre.

D: 13.4 cm; H: 8.1 cm; Inv. 576

278

Bowl with rounded sides and straight rim, standing on a straight, narrow foot. The exterior is incised with long, thin petals and the interior with a large flower corolla, with two Chinese characters in the centre, one of which is readable as *ji*, meaning "lucky". The rounded foot is glazed. The base has a small circle of glaze in the centre.

D: 11.8 cm; H: 6.8 cm; Inv. 3988

279

Spherical jarlet moulded in two parts, the join being clearly visible. The small, short neck is flanked by two round lugs. A moulded floral scroll surrounds the widest part of the body with chrysanthemums, lotuses, and peonies, between a frieze of lotus petals moulded in relief around the base and a row of petals on the shoulder. The unglazed base is slightly concave.

D: 11.9 cm; H: 9.9 cm
Inv. 3631

280

Bowl with flared walls and straight rim, standing on a wide foot and potted from pale buff stoneware. The outside is covered in long, thin incised petals. The bowl is covered with a thin, uneven, pale green glaze. The rounded foot is glazed. The unglazed base shows the trace of a circular firing support. Guangdong kiln.

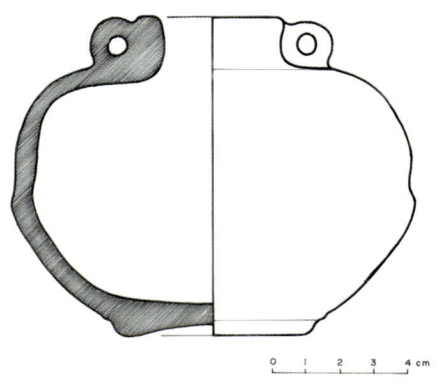

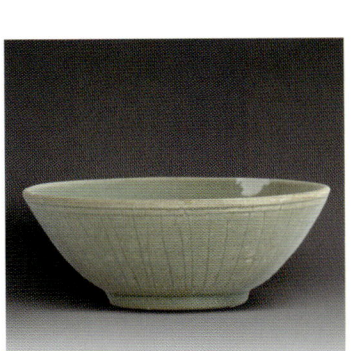

D: 17.8 cm; H: 7.1 cm; Inv. 2466

281

Straight-sided bowl, resting on a narrow foot. The outside is covered in long, thin incised petals. The bowl is covered with a thin, uneven, dark green glaze. The rounded foot is glazed, but the base is unglazed. The bowl is potted in beige stoneware and comes from a Guangdong kiln.

D: 13.8 cm; H: 6.4 cm; Inv. 2390

282

Small dish with flat rim and ridged lip. On the inside, the walls are fluted and there is a flower corolla printed in the centre of the dish. The reverse is undecorated. The glaze ends before the foot. The foot and base are unglazed and have turned rust-coloured. Buff stoneware.

D: 16.8 cm; H: 4.8 cm
Inv. 2291

283

Deep dish with flat rim and ridged lip. The inside and outside walls are delicately fluted. There is a thin and uneven pale green glaze that peels around the edges. The foot is unglazed. The retracted base shows radial marks and is coated with a thin white glaze. The dish is potted from cream-coloured stoneware. The kiln cannot be determined with certainty.

D: 26 cm; H: 4.5 cm; Inv. 3766

284

Deep dish with a very thick, flat rim which is square in section and has a ridged lip. Incised double wavy line on the rim and flowering plant incised with double lines in the centre. The walls on the reverse side are fluted. The uneven glaze is thin, pale green and transparent and has accumulated in the incisions, running into droplets under the rim. The unglazed foot is sharply defined at the edge. The retracted base has radial marks and is covered in a thin glaze. The stoneware is buff-coloured. The kiln cannot be determined with certainty.

D: 21.2 cm; H: 4 cm
Inv. 1640

9.2 Brown-glazed stoneware

With the exception of the jars described in another chapter, the cargo of brown-glazed stoneware was not important. These are the sort of utilitarian wares for which it is usually hard to ascribe a specific kiln of origin, since there are no pieces with which to compare them. These are attributable, however, to the kilns in the southern provinces of Fujian or Guangdong because of the style in which they are potted and the properties of the stoneware and glaze.

285

Spherical ewer of pale buff stoneware, with a high, flat shoulder, evenly coated with an attractive, dark brown glaze which ends at the straight foot. The shoulder extends into a small neck with flared rim. On the opposite side to the curved spout there is a vertical handle between the shoulder and the edge of the neck. There are also two small horizontal lugs on either side of the shoulder, one of which is damaged.

H: 15.2 cm
Inv. 2115

Piece for comparison: L., C. Locsin, and a smilar ewer was found at Calatagan, ill. 184.

286

Small ovoid jar, the body extending into a short, flared neck, potted from beige stoneware. There are two horizontal, protruding lugs on the shoulder. The piece is glazed with an uneven brown glaze which covers two-thirds of the body. The base is flat.

H: 10.3 cm
Inv. 2314

287

Small jar similar to 286, but the body is more slender. Some jarlets have a glaze that is greenish but remains brown underneath. The green colour could thus be due to a deterioration of the surface of the glaze due to the material being left underwater.

H: 10.3 cm
Inv. 2458

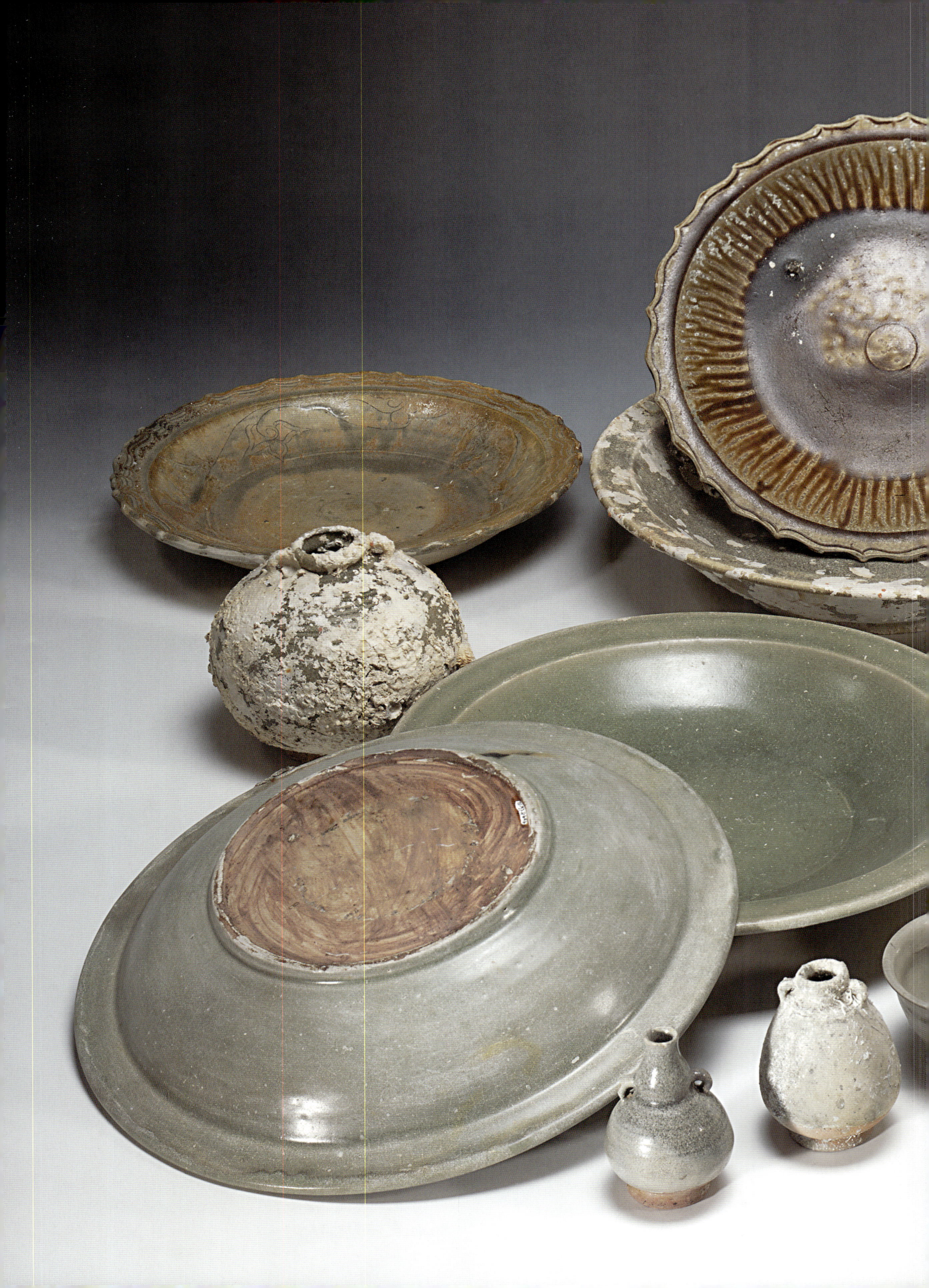

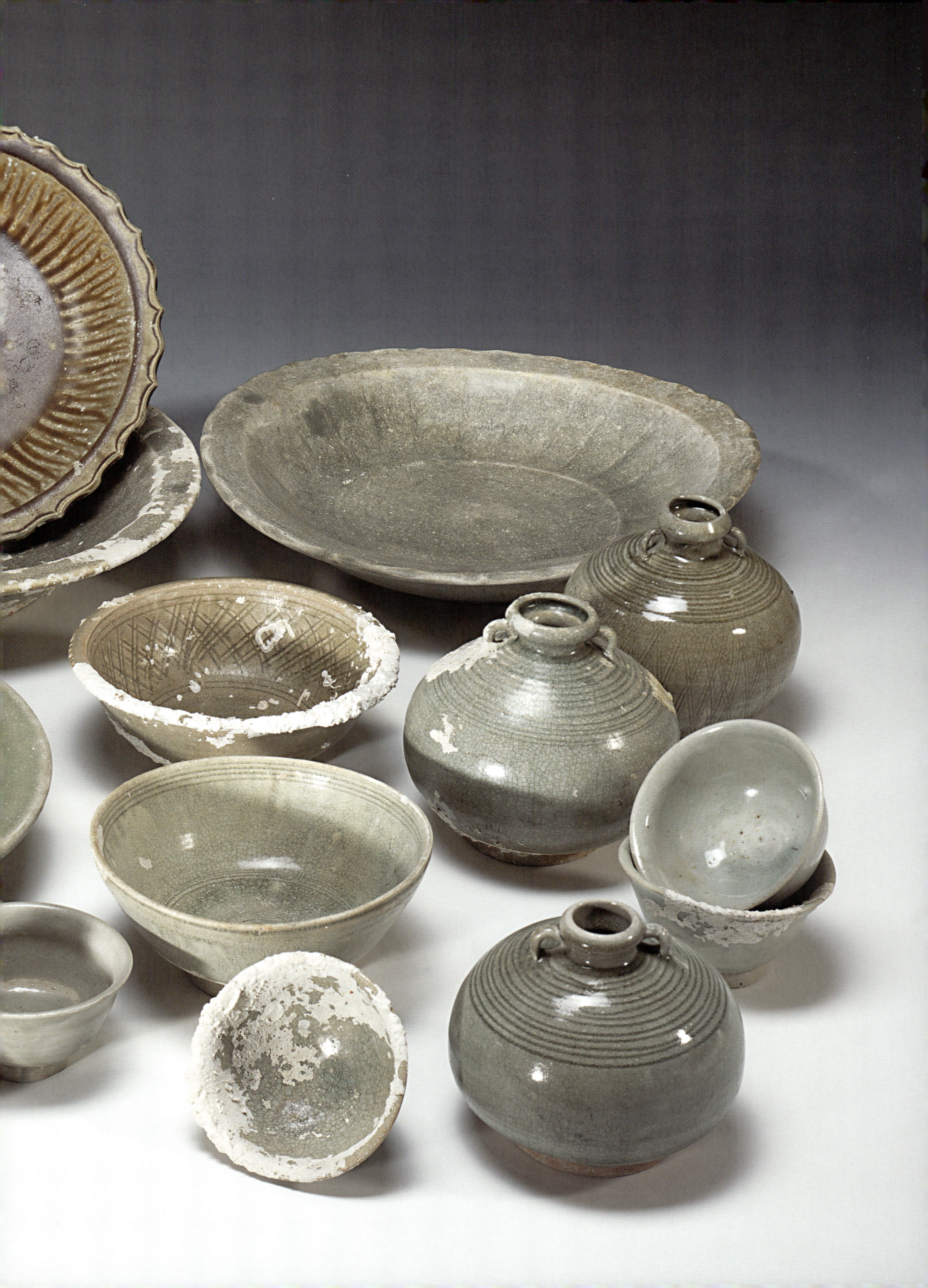

10. Thai stoneware

10.1 Celadon ware

The green-glazed stoneware found in the cargo consisted of dishes with flat or bracket-lobed rims, bowls, bottles and jars. Some of the bowls and the spherical jars, known locally as "coconut jars", of which there were nearly 400 in the cargo, were of a type known to have been produced by the Si Satchanalai kiln complex, also known as Sawankhalok, in the heart of Thailand. A large proportion of the stoneware in the cargo also came from the northern provinces, and is very different in style to the Sawankhalok ceramics.

The green-glazed ceramics of Sawankhalok are potted from a thick grey clay in which black specks have been incorporated into the paste. They are glazed with a shiny, vitreous green glaze which accumulates in large droplets on the outside of the pieces, or in highly vitrified "puddles" in the interior. The glaze ends in irregular rivulets above the foot-rim and the base shows the dark marks of the pontil. The clay tends to turn orange where the surfaces are exposed and unglazed. These ceramics are often represented in South-East Asian collections and have also been found in Thai wrecks.

The green-glazed ceramics from northern Thailand have been potted from a very fine-grained, cream-coloured clay. The dishes in the cargo are glazed all over, with the exception of the base. The glaze is finely crazed, smooth, and dark green with an oily look and it tends to deteriorate easily in an underwater environment. All the dishes show faint marks of a round pontil on the base, although these marks are different from the blackish indentations on the wares from Si Satchanalai. The clay has turned orange-red on the exposed surfaces and the bases of some of the dishes have been coated with a layer of brownish paint. These dishes could have been fired in the kilns of the Kalong complex. A series of bowls coated with a brilliant, crazed, pale aquamarine glaze were also produced at these sites. Other bowls with thick sides and an uneven glaze were fired in the Phan kilns in the Chiang Rai province, near the borders of Burma and Laos. These pieces are not often found in the cargo and are under-represented in the collections of South-East Asia. Yet in view of the fact that such a large quantity of plates and bowls from the Kalong kilns were found on board, they must have been popular and much in demand among the inhabitants of the islands. They are unsophisticated and easily breakable in comparison with the solid, compact earthenware of Si Satchanalai, so they were probably used as standard household crockery which would gradually have disappeared through being in daily use.

Pieces for comparison: R. Brown, *The Ceramics of South-East Asia: Their Dating and Identification*, Oxford University Press, Singapore, 1977, 1988; J. Guy, *Ceramic Traditions of South-East Asia*, Oxford University Press Ltd, Singapore, 1989; K. Itoi, *Thai Ceramics from the Sosai Collection*, Oxford University Press Ltd, Singapore, 1989; D. Richards, *South-East Asian Ceramics: Thai, Vietnamese, and Khmer. From the Collection of the Art Gallery in South Australia*, Oxford University Press, Kuala Lumpur, 1995; J. Shaw, *Northern Thai Ceramics*, Oxford University Press, 1981; W. Willets, *Ceramic Art of Southeast Asia*, The Southeast Asian Ceramic Society, Singapore, 1971; *Chinese Celadons and Other Related Wares in Southeast Asia*, Southeast Asian Ceramic Society, Singapore, 1979; *South-East Asian Ceramics from the Collection of Margot and Hans Ries*, Pacific Asia Museum, Pasadena, 1989; *South-East Asian and Early Chinese Export Ceramics*, William Sorsby Ltd, London, 1974; *Thai Ceramics, the James and Elaine Connell Collection. Asian Art Museum of San Francisco*, Oxford University Press, Kuala Lumpur, 1993.

288

Straight-sided bowl of black-flecked grey stoneware, covered in a shiny grey-green glaze which ends in irregular rivulets and large droplets at the base of the walls. The foot is straight and the base recessed, displaying the mark of a pontil which has left blackish indentations. The lines incised on the rim, inside and out, are the only decoration. The glaze has puddled in the bottom of the bowl. Si Satchanalai kilns.

D: 19.9 cm; H: 9.2 cm
Inv. 832

289

Straight-sided bowl of black-flecked grey stoneware, covered in a shiny, crazed, grey-green glaze which ends in irregular rivulets at the base of the walls. The foot is straight and the base recessed, displaying the mark of a pontil and blackish indentations. Long petals are incised in the interior cavetto of the bowl. There is a small central medallion containing what appears to be a character stamped in relief. Si Satchanalai kilns.

D: 21 cm; H: 9.2 cm
Inv. 3644

290

Bowl of black-flecked grey stoneware with a rounded, scalloped rim, covered with a crazed, dark olive glaze that ends at the base of the walls. The foot is straight and the base is recessed, displaying the marks of the pontil and blackish indentations. A trellis pattern is incised on the cavetto inside the bowl. Si Satchanalai kilns.

D: 20.8 cm; H. 9.4 cm
Inv. 3152

Bowls similar to the series found in the cargo were made in the Ban Pa Yang kiln in the Si Satchanalai complex.

291

Short-necked, globular jar of black-flecked grey stoneware, flanked by two ring-shaped lugs coated in a crazed, green glaze that ends at base of the walls. Foot straight and base slightly recessed, displaying the pontil mark and blackish indentations. Concentric circles incised on the shoulder and deep grooves on the widest part of the body. One lug is missing. Si Satchanalai kilns.

D: max. 16 cm; H: 15.5 cm
Inv. 1350 (?)

292

Short-necked globular jar of black-flecked grey stoneware, flanked by two ring-shaped lugs coated in a shiny, crazed green glaze that ends at the base of the walls in irregular rivulets that have formed droplets. The foot is straight and the base is recessed, displaying a pontil mark and blackish indentations. Concentric circles are incised at the top of the shoulder. Si Satchanalai kilns.

D: max. 16.1 cm; H: 15.6 cm
Inv. 1791

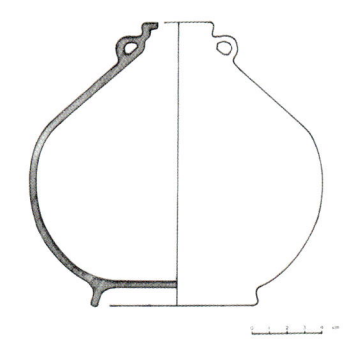

293

Globular jar flanked by two ring-shaped lugs on either side of the neck, potted from black-flecked grey stoneware and covered in a crazed green glaze that ends at the base of the walls. Foot slightly sloping and base recessed, displaying a pontil mark and blackish indentations. Concentric circles incised near the widest part of the sphere. Si Satchanalai kilns.

D: max. 16.5 cm; H: 15.9 cm
Inv. 1224

294

Short-necked, squat, globular jar with two ring-shaped lugs on either side of the neck, potted from black-flecked grey stoneware and covered in a shiny, crazed green glaze that ends in irregular rivulets at the bottom of the body. The foot is straight and the base recessed, displaying a pontil mark and blackish indentations. Concentric circles are incised at the top of the shoulder. Si Satchanalai kilns.

D: max. 17.3 cm; H: 15.5 cm
Inv. 2507

295

Short-necked, squat, globular jar with two ring-shaped lugs on either side of the neck, potted from black-flecked grey stoneware and coated with a crazed green glaze which ends at the bottom of the widest part of the body. Foot straight and base retracted, displaying a pontil mark and blackish indentations. An incised band of trelliswork stops at the widest part of the body, between two borders of incised concentric circles. Si Satchanalai kilns.

D: max. 18.5 cm; H: 15.2 cm
Inv. 742

296

Short-necked, squat, globular jar with two ring-shaped lugs on either side of the neck, made of black-flecked grey stoneware with a shiny crazed green glaze that ends in irregular rivulets forming large, vitrified droplets at the bottom of the widest part of the body. Foot straight and base recessed, displaying a pontil mark and blackish indentations. The widest part of the body is decorated with a band of incised concentric circles and trelliswork. Si Satchanalai kilns.

D: max. 15.9 cm; H: 16 cm; Inv. 1269

297

Large, short-necked, squat, globular jar with two ring-shaped lugs on either side of the neck, made of black-flecked grey stoneware with a shiny, crazed green glaze that ends at the bottom of the body. Straight foot and recessed base displaying a pontil mark and blackish indentations. A band of concentric circles incised on the shoulder. Si Satchanalai kilns.

D: max. 14.2 cm; H: 21 cm; Inv. 3968

298

Small, short-necked ovoid bottle with two ring-shaped lugs on either side of the neck, made of black-flecked grey stoneware and coated with a green glaze that ends below the widest part of the body. Straight foot and retracted base, displaying a pontil mark and blackish indentations. Concentric circles incised under the handles. Eroded glaze. Si Satchanalai kilns.

D: max. 7.8 cm; H: 12 cm
Inv. 2276

299

Small, pear-shaped, short-necked bottle with two ring-shaped lugs, made of black-flecked grey stoneware. The bottle is covered in a green glaze that ends at the bottom of the body. The sides are deeply fluted and the grooves are filled with the shiny pale green glaze. A small bronze bracelet is attached to the bottle by a concretion. Si Satchanalai kilns.

D: max. 6.5 cm; H: 7.7 cm
Inv. 2045

300

Small double-gourd bottle, originally with two ring-shaped handles, made of black-flecked grey stoneware and covered in a green glaze that ends at the bottom of the body. The foot is sloping and the base is recessed, displaying a pontil mark and blackish indentations. Concentric circles incised on the shoulder. The glaze has been eroded and one handle is broken. Si Satchanalai kilns.

D: max. 7.8 cm; H: 12 cm
Inv. 4071

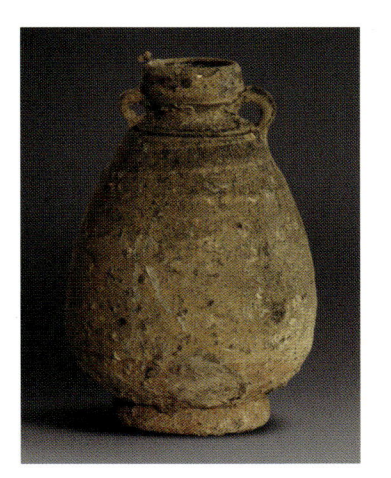

301

Large baluster-shaped jar of beige stoneware. The short neck ends in a large straight-sided opening. Two vertical loop-shaped handles stand erect on the shoulder. The glaze, which is visible in places under the concretions, is a translucent, uneven aquamarine. Sankampaeng kilns, in northern Thailand.

H: 33.5 cm
Inv. 2320

Pieces for comparison: R. Brown, 1977, pl. S.4; D. Richards, 1995, ill. 90; J. Shaw, 1981, ill. 106, C29.

302

Large, flat-rimmed, deep dish of fine-grained cream stoneware, covered with a crazed green, oily glaze, with the exception of the base. Rounded foot and slightly recessed base painted brown. The unglazed base has a pontil mark. Possibly produced by the Kalong kiln complex in northern Thailand.

D: 38 cm; H: 7.8 cm; Inv. 646

Pieces for comparison: Some dishes produced in the Kalong, kilns at the Pa Dong and Payoom sites have a base coated in a chocolate-coloured paint. J. Shaw, 1981, p. 44, ill. C22D.

303

Large flat-rimmed deep dish of fine-grained cream stoneware, completely coated in dark green oily glaze, except for the base. Rounded foot and slightly recessed base. There is a pontil mark under the base. The glaze has been eroded. Possibly from the Kalong kiln complex in northern Thailand.

D: 39.5 cm; H: 8.2 cm
Inv. 353

Pieces for comparison: W. Willets, 1971, pl. 342; *Chinese Celadons and Other Related Wares in Southeast Asia*, 1979, pl. 273.

304

Large flat-rimmed, bracket-lobed deep dish of fine-grained cream stoneware, entirely covered with an uneven dark green oily glaze, with the exception of the base. The rim is emphasised by means of incised bracket lobes. On the back, the design of a standing phoenix is incised on the base. The foot is rounded and the base is slightly recessed and bears a pontil mark. Unidentified kiln.

D: 44.5 cm; H: 8.7 cm
Inv. 4549

305

Large, flat-rimmed, bracket-lobed deep dish of fine-grained cream stoneware, entirely covered with a crazed dark green oily glaze, with the exception of the base. The interior wall is fluted. The foot is rounded and the base slightly recessed. There is a pontil mark on the base. The glaze has been eroded. Unidentified kiln.

D: 42.2 cm; H: 9.2 cm
Inv. 356

306

Large, flat-rimmed, bracket-lobed deep dish of grey stoneware, entirely coated in a thin, crazed eroded glaze. The rim is emphasised by incised bracket lobes on the inside and reverse. A simplified lotus scroll pattern is incised on the wall. The foot is rounded and the base slightly recessed. The base has a pontil mark. Unidentified kiln.

D: 34 cm; H: 6.5 cm
Inv. 2432

307

Flat-rimmed, bracket-lobed deep dish of grey-beige stoneware entirely covered with a thin, eroded, crazed glaze. The rim is emphasised by incised bracket lobes on the inside and there are three spur marks in the centre. The foot is rounded and the base slightly recessed. There is a pontil mark on the base. Unidentified kiln.

D: 34 cm; H: 6.9 cm
Inv. 2433

308

Large deep dish of pale grey stoneware with a ridged, scalloped rim. The whole dish is covered in a thin, uneven, yellowish glaze with areas of thicker dark green glaze. The foot is rounded and the unglazed base slightly recessed. There is a pontil mark on the base. Wang Nua kiln (?) in the Kalong complex.

D: 32.2 cm; H: 5.8 cm
Inv. 2435

Pieces for comparison: R. Brown, 1977, pl. 42, ill. 137; 1988, pl. 54c; J. Shaw, 1981, C20.

309

Large deep dish with a flat, ridged rim made of pale grey stoneware entirely covered in a thin, uneven yellowish glaze with areas of thicker dark green glaze. The foot is rounded and the unglazed base slightly recessed. There is a pontil mark on the base. Unidentified kiln.

D: 29.5 cm; H: 5.6 cm
Inv. 2428

310

Bowl with rounded sides and thick, flat straight rim, made of grey-beige stoneware and covered in an uneven pale green glaze down to the straight, thick foot. A line is incised under the rim. The base is deeply recessed and unglazed and has a pontil mark. This bowl is from the Phan kiln, in Chiang Rai province, northern Thailand.

D: 14.3 cm; H: 7.7 cm; Inv. 2803

Pieces for comparison: K. Itoi, 1989, pl. 91; *Thai Ceramics*, 1993, pl. 157, 158.

311

Bowl with rounded sides and thick, flat straight edge, made of buff stoneware and covered in an uneven brown glaze down to the straight, thick foot. The glaze has become eroded and peels easily through lack of adhesion to the body. The unglazed base is very recessed, displaying a pontil mark. Kalong kiln in northern Thailand.

D: 13.7 cm; H: 7.4 cm; Inv. 4126

Pieces for comparison: J. Shaw, 1981, C19.

312

Bowl with rounded cavetto and thick straight rim, potted from whitish stoneware and covered with a uniform pale green glaze which ends just above the straight, thick foot. The glaze is crackled. The base is slightly recessed and unglazed, and there is no pontil mark. Unidentified kiln.

D: 13.7 cm; H: 7.4 cm
Inv. 4125

313

Bowl with rounded walls and flared rim, made of grey stoneware and covered with a shiny, crackled aquamarine glaze that ends above the straight, thick foot. The foot is irregular in shape, and the base slightly recessed and unglazed, displaying a pontil mark. Kalong kilns.

D: 12.3 cm; H: 6.5 cm
Inv. 1052

Pieces for comparison: K. Itoi, 1989, pl. 59, 60; J. Shaw, 1981, ill. 35.

314

Bowl with rounded sides and flared rim, made of grey stoneware covered in a shiny, bluish-green glaze that ends above the thick, straight foot. The foot is irregular in shape. The unglazed base is slightly recessed and has no pontil mark. Kalong kiln.

D: 12.5 cm; H: 6.5 cm
Inv. 962

Pieces for comparison: K. Itoi, 1989, pl. 59, 60; J. Shaw, 1981, ill. 35.

10.2 Brown-painted stoneware and brown-glazed stoneware

315

Jarlet with flared neck, made of grey stoneware covered in buff slip. The shoulder is decorated with incised petals in reserve on a brown ground painted with iron oxide. The translucent glaze has been eroded. Kiln of Si Satchanalai.

D: max. 6.6 cm; H: 6.9 cm
Inv. 2155

316

Pear-shaped, long-necked bottle of grey, black-flecked stoneware. The brown glaze, which stops at the widest part of the body has been eroded. Si Satchanalai kiln.

D: max. 11 cm; H: 19.8 cm
Inv. 2121

317

Short-necked jar with squat spherical body, of grey, black-flecked stoneware. Two rounded lugs attached to either side of the neck. The brown glaze ends in the centre of the body and flows in irregular rivulets. Si Satchanalai kiln.

D: max. 16.6 cm; H: 14 cm
Inv. 3062

318

Dish with bracket-lobed ridged rim. Potted in pale buff stoneware and covered with a shiny, thin brown glaze which runs in rivulets ending in thick droplets which have vitrified on the reverse and have puddled in the centre of the dish. Decorated with incisions around the rim and shallow grooves on the cavetto. The unglazed base is slightly recessed and shows a pontil mark. Unidentified kiln.

D: 37.7 cm; H: 7.3 cm
Inv. 2562

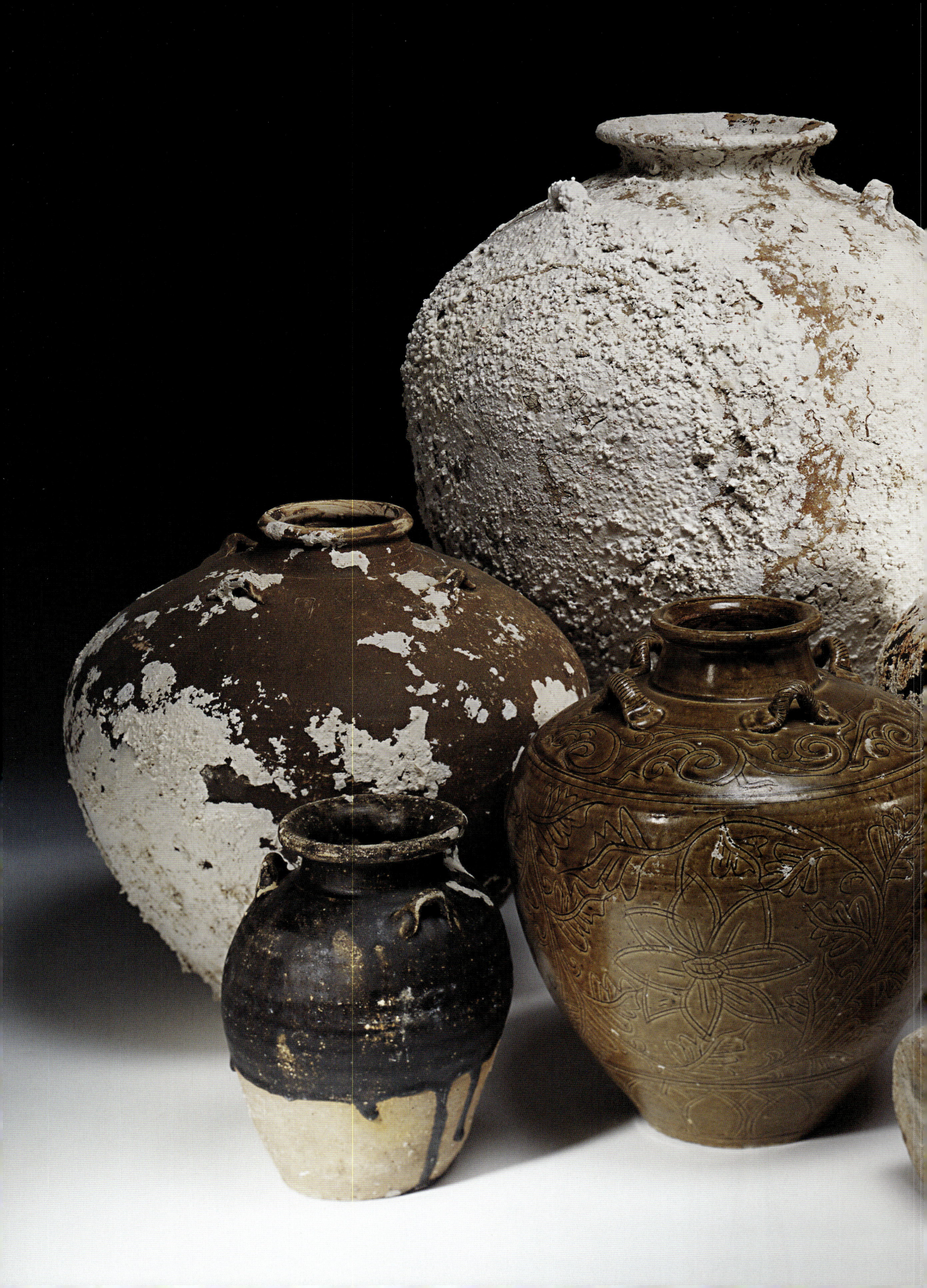

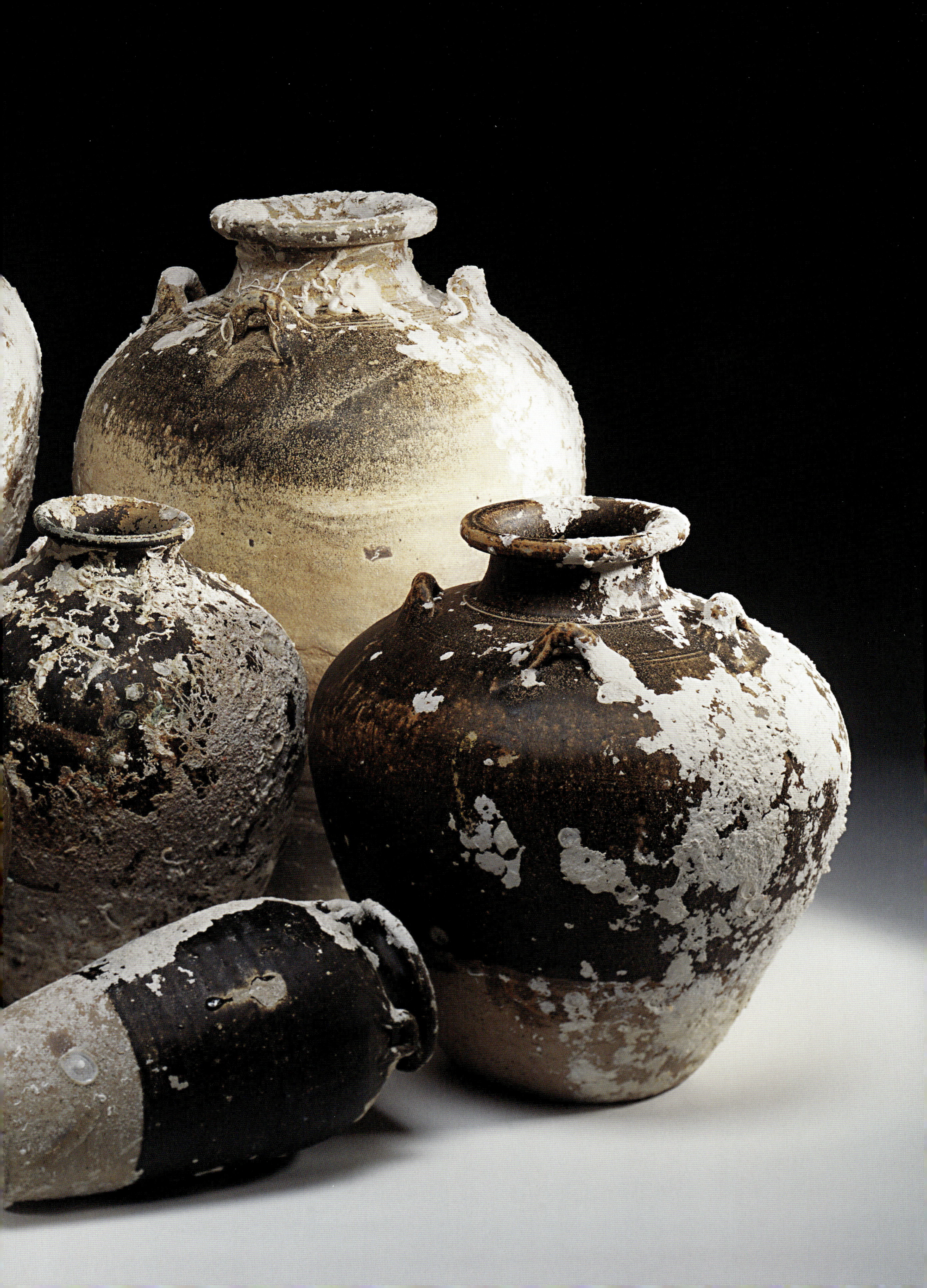

11. The martaban jars

In Asia, the jar was used as a utilitarian vessel for holding water and food, and jars were imported for this purpose to the Philippine archipelago. When transported in junks, these large storage jars also served as containers for other goods, such as cups, jarlets, glass beads or spices. Large stoneware jars are part of the history of the Philippines. They were probably brought to the islands on foreign vessels from the ninth century onwards and were valued for their practical and aesthetic qualities.

When the Spaniards first made contact with the natives after their arrival in the Philippines in 1521, they noticed the presence of these jars and mentioned them in their writings. The chronicles of these expeditions relate that Magellan was presented with "three porcelain jars covered with leaves and filled with rice wine" from the chief of an islet near Leyte and that numerous jars of wine were brought to a reception held by the rajah of the island of Cebu on 7 April 1521. When Pigafetta visited the king, he found him sitting in front of four jars of palm wine covered with aromatic herbs. He saw similar vessels suspended inside houses on the island of Mindanao. The native inhabitants considered them to be sufficiently valuable to warrant being despatched by the local chiefs to the Spanish authorities as presents for the king of Spain. Thus, enduring customs were already attested by the sixteenth century.

Jars were very popular for storing wines and spirits for traditional ceremonies and were a part of daily life. Aduarte reports in 1640 that they were also used in funerary rites. He mentions the discovery by a ship's crew of jars used as funerary urns in the Batan Islands. The jars have various names in the Philippines, depending upon the usage to which they are put, but are generally known as *gusi* or *tapayan*. Among native tribes, the jars were symbols of wealth and social status. They were handed down from generation to generation, and their origin as well as their powers sometimes became magical. Some of them were alleged to have an independent existence, able to travel or warning of imminent danger. They married and even had children. Such stories abound in local legend in South-East Asia. From being mere utility vessels, the jars became an integral part of the local culture in the countries in which they were distributed.

Pieces for comparison: S. Adhyatman, A. Ridho, *Tempayan-Martavans in Indonesia*, the Ceramic Society of Indonesia, Jakarta, 1984; F-C. Cole, *Chinese Pottery in the Philippines*, Field Museum of Natural History, Publication 162, Anthropological Series, Vol. XII, No. I, Chicago, 1912; B. Harrisson, Pusaka, *Heirloom Jars of Borneo*, Oxford University Press, Singapore, 1986; C. O. Valdes, K. Nguyen Long, A. C. Barbosa, *A Thousand Years of Stoneware Jars in the Philippines*, Jar Collectors (Philippines), Manila, 1992.

11.1 The Chinese jars

These jars were found in large quantities in the cargo and are made of a fairly thin beige stoneware, coated with a thin glaze which varies in colour from olive-green to golden-brown and forms rivulets at the bottom of the walls. They were traditionally made in south China in the provinces of Fujian and Guangdong. Most of them are elongated ovoid in shape with high shoulders, a short neck and rounded lip, standing on an unglazed concave base. A few of the jars are globular in shape and entirely covered with a dark brown glaze, with the exception of the concave base.

319

Ovoid jar covered in golden-brown glaze.

D: max. 29.2 cm; H: 34 cm
Inv. 3805

320

Ovoid jar, covered in pale brown glaze, with four small horizontal lugs attached to the top of the shoulder.

D: max. 31.5 cm; H: 35.5 cm
Inv. 3806

321

Ovoid jar, covered in greenish-brown glaze, with four small horizontal lugs and a vertical handle attached to the top of the shoulder.

D: max. 29.9 cm; H: 34.7 cm
Inv. 847

322

Ovoid brown-glazed jar with three small horizontal lugs and a vertical lug attached to the top of the shoulder. Covered in concretions.

D: max. 24 cm; H: 27.2 cm
Inv. 1785

323

Spherical jar, covered with dark brown glaze, with four small horizontal lugs attached to the top of the shoulder. Potter's mark impressed on the shoulder.

D: max. 39.8 cm; H: 36.2 cm
Inv. 3808

Piece for comparison: Valdes, Nguyen Long, Barbosa, 1992, fig. 14, cat. 49.

LOST AT SEA

11.2 The Vietnamese jars

These jars were also found in large numbers in the cargo. They are made of fine, close-grained cream-coloured stoneware and are decorated with incised floral patterns. The walls are thin and coated to the base with a thin, shiny glaze which varies in colour from golden-brown to olive green. They have been attributed to the kilns of central Vietnam or to kilns in southern China.

Pieces for comparison: J. Guy, 1997, cat. 316, 318; Valdes, Nguyen Long, Barbosa, 1992, cat. 50, 51.

324

Guan jar with short neck, flared rim and rounded lip, coated in golden-buff glaze. The incised patterns are arranged in three registers: upright pointed petals around the base, a six-petalled flower scroll on the widest part of the body and a foliated scroll on the shoulder.

D: max. 25 cm; H: 28.7 cm; Inv. 268

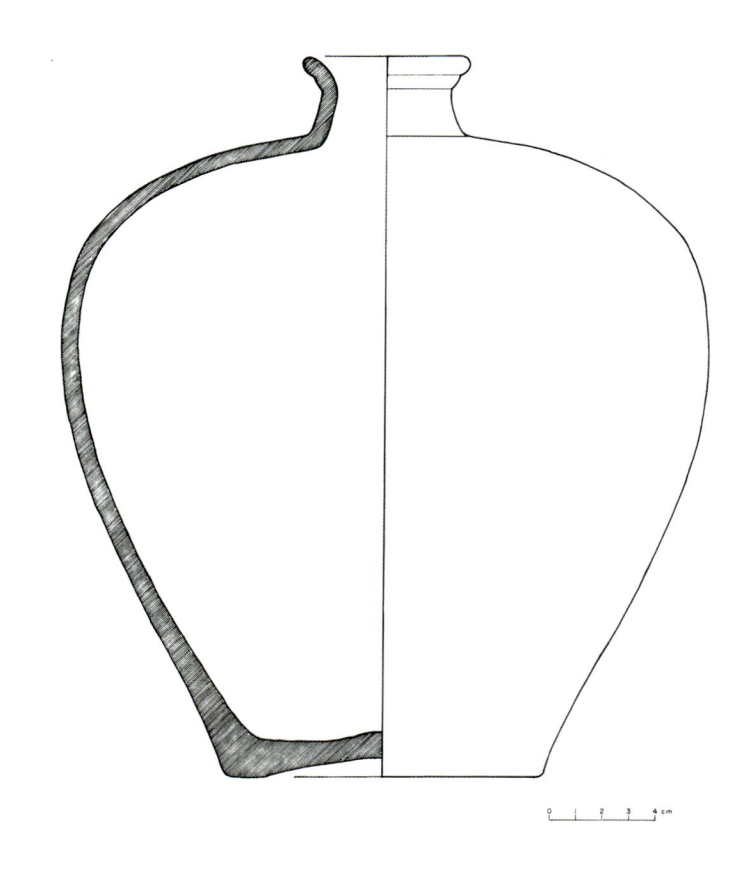

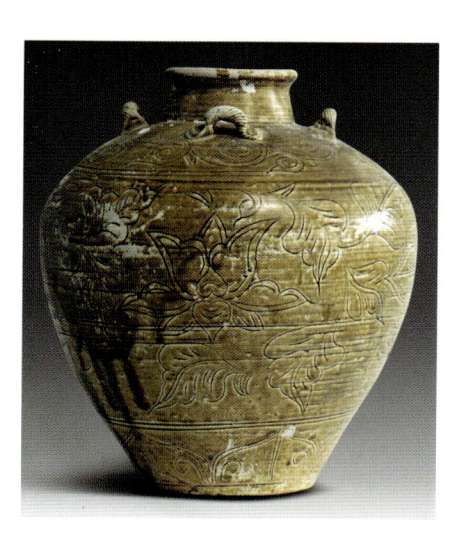

325

Bulbous jar with short neck and rounded lip, coated in golden-brown glaze. There are four striated horizontal lugs on the shoulder, which are interlinked by incised lines. The incised patterns are arranged in three registers: upright pointed petals around the base, a lotus flower scroll on the widest part of the body and a foliated scroll on the shoulder.

D: max. 31.9 cm; H: 35.2 cm
Inv. 615

326

Bulbous jar with a short neck and rounded lip, covered in olive-green glaze. There are four striated horizontal lugs on the shoulder, which are interlinked by incised lines. The incised patterns are arranged in three registers: upright pointed petals around the base, a flower scroll on the widest part of the body, and four galloping horses between Buddhist symbols and clouds on the shoulder.

D. max. 30.4 cm; H. 34.6 cm
Inv. 2195

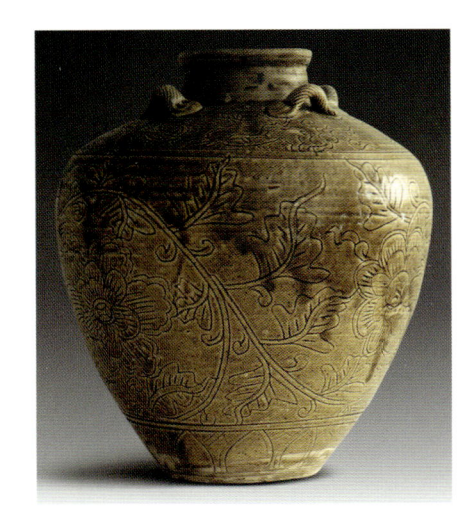

327

Fragment of jar with floral scroll on the widest part of the body and design of human figures on the shoulder.

Inv. 2473

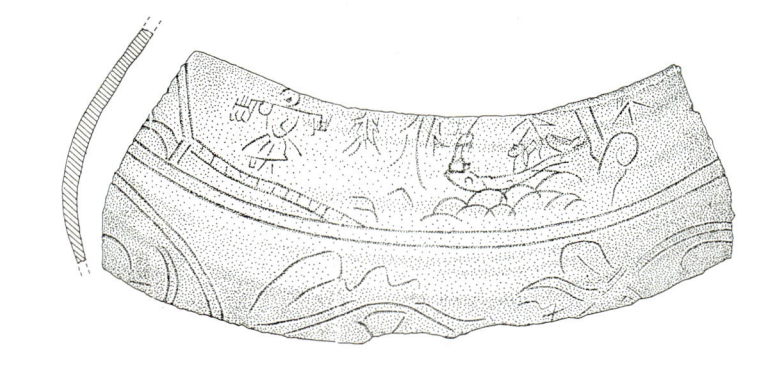

328

Top of large bulbous jar with short neck and rounded lip, covered in golden-brown glaze. The four striated horizontal lugs on the shoulder are interlinked by incised lines, and there is an incised design of a foliated scroll.

Inv. 4086

LOST AT SEA

11.3 Thai jars
These jars are made of thick, solid black-flecked grey stoneware, and are covered in a brownish-black glaze. The large jars with four lugs and a neck with a rounded lip were fired in the kilns of Tao Maenam Noi in Singburi province and in the kilns of Si Satchanalai. The largest of them is more than 60 cm tall. The jars with an elongated oval shape were a typical product of the Tao Maenam Noi kilns.

329

Elongated ovoid, short-necked jar with straight rim, with brownish-black glaze on the upper part. There are four horizontal lugs on the shoulder.

D: max. 18.2 cm; H: 30.2 cm; Inv. 2253

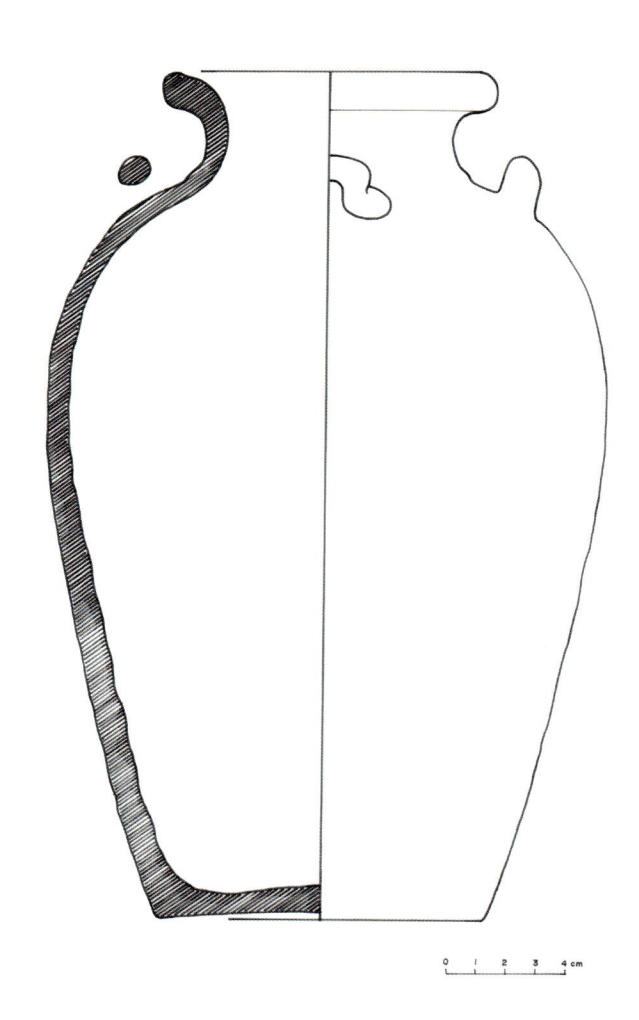

330

Ovoid jar with short neck and straight rim, covered in a blackish-brown glaze on the upper half of the body. There are four horizontal lugs on the shoulder. It is covered in concretions.

D: max. 18.5 cm; H: 31.2 cm
Inv. 1295

331

Elongated ovoid, almost cylindrical short-necked jar with a blackish-brown glaze on the upper half of the body. There are four horizontal lugs on the shoulder.

D: max. 16.8 cm; H: 32.1 cm
Inv. 1786

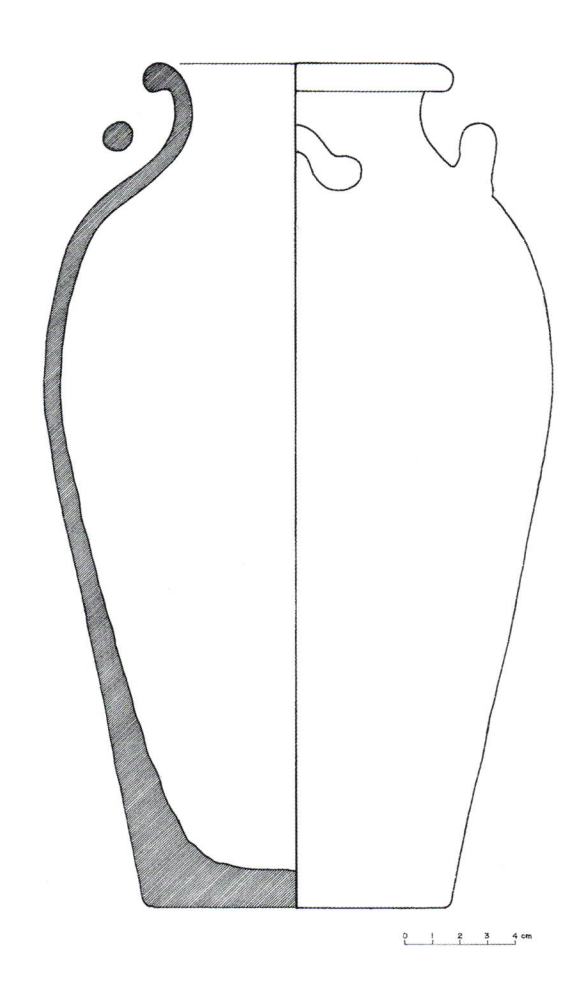

332

Bulbous, short-necked jar with rounded lip, with blackish-brown glaze over two-thirds of the body. There are four horizontal lugs on the shoulder.

D: max. 37.3 cm; H: 39.4 cm
Inv. 4292

LOST AT SEA

11.4 Burmese jar
This grey stoneware jar is covered in a blackish-brown glaze to the base. It is ovoid in shape with high shoulders and decorated with vertical and horizontal lines in relief, which have the effect of dividing the body into two registers of superimposed panels.

333

Jar with damaged rim.

D: max. 53 cm; H: 75 cm
Inv. 1560

11.5 The lids
The lids are made of brownish or buff-coloured clay and are of various sizes. They are concave and have a central round knob.

334

D: 13.4 cm; H: 3 cm
Inv. 2294

335

D: 8.8 cm; H: 3 cm
Inv. 2602

D: 14.1 cm; H: 3.6 cm
Inv. 406

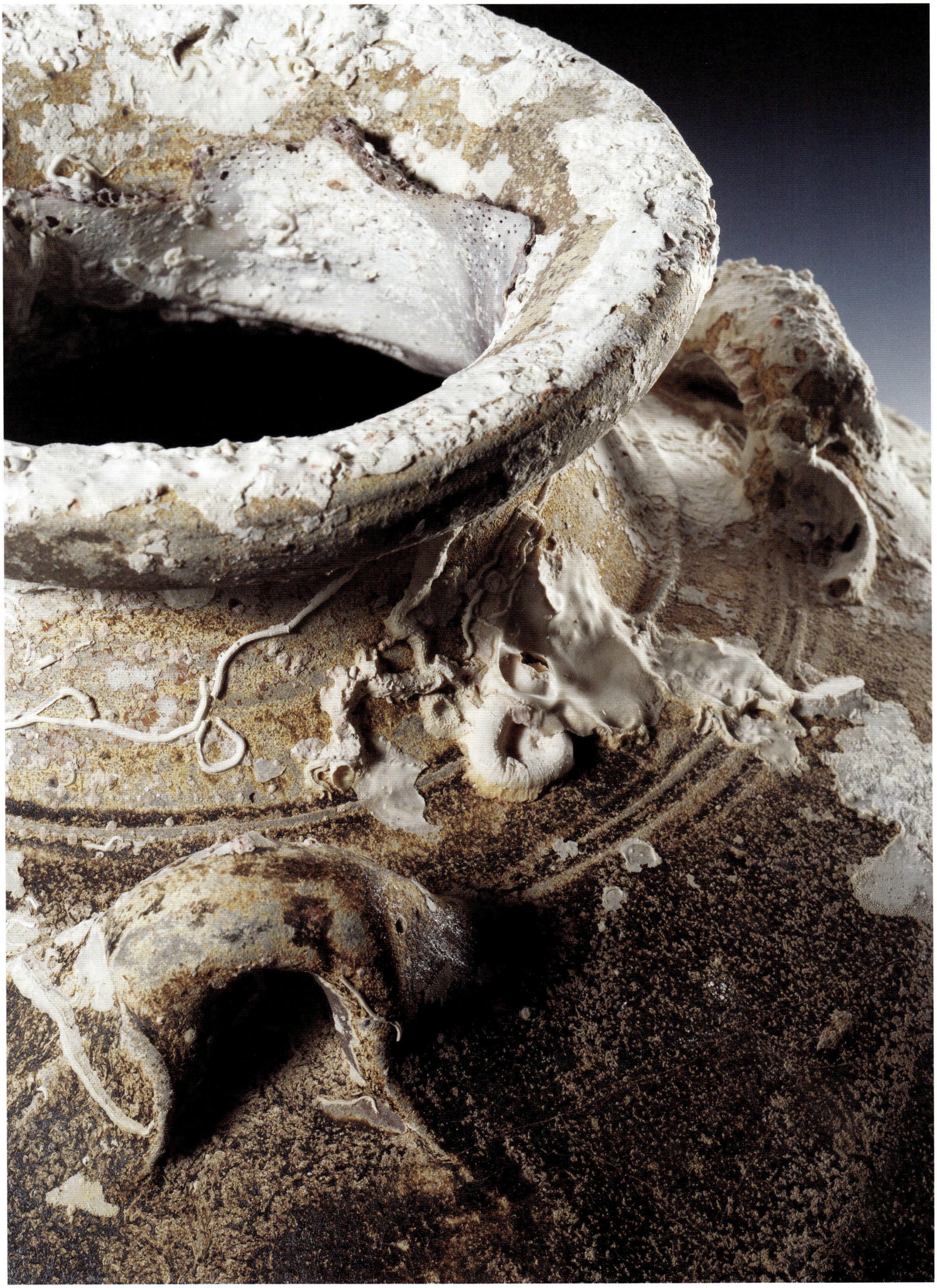

12. Terracotta and ceramics of indeterminate origin

12.1 Thai terracotta

336

Neck of a large jar with a flared neck, potted in reddish clay. There are traces of horizontal incised lines. Unglazed jars were fired in the kilns of Suphanbur and at Singburi in central Thailand.

Inv. 3862

Pieces for comparison: D. Richards, 1995, ill. 7; C. O. Valdes, K. Nguyen Long, A. C. Barbosa, 1992, cat. 152–4.

337

Buff terracotta, short-necked vessel with flared rim and convex base. Design of printed patterns, including a continuous frieze of pipal (*Ficus religiosa*) leaves on the shoulder.

H: 25cm
Inv. 3304

12.2 Filipino terracotta

338

Cooking pot with convex base, vertical walls and flared rim. Decorated with incised lines.

Inv. 4091

339

Miniature cooking pot with convex base, vertical walls and flared rim, decorated with incised lines.

D: 9 cm; H: 4.3 cm
Inv. 2461

340

Dish with flared walls, rounded rim and flat base.

D: 30.5 cm; H: 9.6 cm
Inv. 3684

341

Globular jar with flared rim, standing on low foot.

D: max. 15.4 cm; H: 14.2 cm
Inv. 1589

342

Spherical ewer with flared rim and short spout. The base is convex and there is a line in relief on the shoulder.

D: max. 21 cm; H: 16 cm
Inv. 728

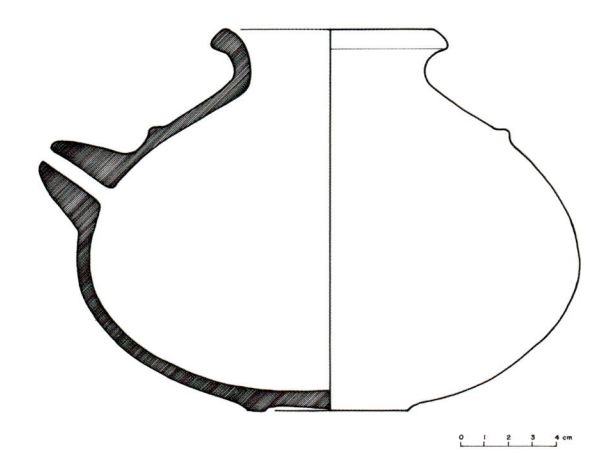

LOST AT SEA

343

Convex lid with hollow knob.

D: 13 cm; H: 3 cm
Inv. 2548

12.3 Ceramics of indeterminate origin

344

Kendi with flattened body and polished surface potted from dark grey clay, resting on a flat base. The long neck ends in a bulb. Two lines are incised on the shoulder.

H: 15.9 cm
Inv. 2689

345

Spherical jarlet with flat shoulders and rounded rim, potted from fine, grey clay and resting on a slightly flared foot. The convex base is recessed. The jar is moulded and copies a metal shape and decoration. The body is lobed and there is a decoration of petals in relief on the shoulder. A fragment of another jar made from the same clay seems to have been coated with a very thin layer of green glaze.

H: 7 cm
Inv. 3603

346

Fragments of a spherical jarlet with a rounded rim made of fine-grained ochre clay. The base is flat and the surface polished.

Inv. 17/4159

347

Circular basin made of grey clay. The interior has been hastily coated with brown glaze. Crudely fashioned basins of this type were made in southern China, Vietnam and Thailand.

D: 29.9 cm; H: 7.8 cm
Inv. 4086

Photo 63. The Jade Temple, the cast-iron pagoda near Tang-Yang Hsien in the province of Hopei. It was built in 1061 (after Boerschmann).

13. Iron artefacts
Franck Goddio

13.1 Pig-iron

The iron ingots were of an average length of 25 cm. They were in a very poor state of preservation, making it impossible to isolate specimens, so measurements had to be made in situ on the accretions.

Chinese metallurgy seems to have begun around the sixth century AD.[1] and the art of making cast iron, which requires the complete liquefaction of the metal, was mastered by the Chinese in the fourth century BC – nearly 17 centuries before it was discovered in the West – and was used to manufacture agricultural implements and weaponry. Chinese architects began using iron as a construction material at an early stage. From the seventh century, iron suspension bridges and the framework of pagodas were built of cast iron.[2]

Photo 64. Bridge suspended on iron chains in the province of Yunnan (photo : Potts-Popper).

Iron was cast in innumerable small furnaces throughout the length and breadth of the empire. Iron ore was heated under conditions which would raise the temperature of the molten metal to more than 1130°C. The metal could then be poured into moulds in order to obtain pigs or ingots. Pig-iron is a hard, brittle material which is not malleable and cannot be welded. Pig-iron was exported in the form of pigs (ingots) or as finished products.

One speciality of Chinese craftsmen was the making of large cast iron pans of a very thin gauge and remarkable quality. The master-craftsmen were often Taoist monks working in their monasteries.

A military compendium, the *Wu Pien*, written c. 1550 indicates precisely where the main centres of production were situated. "Cast iron was produced mainly in Guangdong and Fujian. The fire inside the furnaces transforms the iron into a molten liquid like copper or tin in fusion. Nowadays, men make utensils such as pans and three-legged cauldrons".

China exported ingots and iron utensils such as the large pans as part of the Nanhai trade. The fact that the provinces of Guangdong and Fujian lay on the coast and had large ports must have been a factor that facilitated the export of these heavy goods. We have been able to show how much of this type of product was exported over the centuries through the discovery of five junks dating from between the eleventh and sixteenth centuries. Archaeological excavations of these junks all show cargoes of ingots and cast iron pans.[3]

On the Lena Shoal junk, numerous cast iron pans of various sizes were found resting on a bed of iron ingots. The pans were stacked in piles of 10 arranged by size. They were particularly numerous in band I at references 31, 27.7 and 32.2.

We were able to detach some of them from the metal accretion formed by the ingots and separate them into individual pans. The bottom of each pan has a small

---

[1] J. Needham, "Remarks on the history of iron and steel technology in China", *Acts of the International Colloquium on Iron*, Nancy, 1956. BEFEO M4247

[2] The monument called the "Celestial Axis, Commemorating the Virtue of the Great Chou Dynasty and its Myriad of Regions", is made entirely of cast iron and was erected in 695. It was built on a base of 50 m circumference and is 7 m high, consisting of an octagonal column 32 m high and 3 m in diameter topped by an amazing capital 10 m in circumference supporting four dragons, also made of cast iron. A 13-storey temple with a metal structure designed by Yu Chuan Su at Tang-Yang Hsien in the province of Hopei, dates from the year 1061.

[3] Goddio, *Discovery and Archaeological Excavation of a 16th Century Trading Vessel in the Phillipines*, WWF, Manila, 1988; Goddio and Dupoizat, *Investigator Shoal Wreck: Southern Song-Yuan Dynasty*, 1993 and *Breaker Reef Wreck: Northern Song Dynasty*, 1993; Goddio, 1997.

Photo 65. Metal accretion of iron needles found inside a little porcelain vase, Inv. 2128.

LOST AT SEA

indentation like a tiny dome. Sometimes there were vestiges of short iron protuberances, the remains of the lugs. The extraordinarily thin gauge of these pans showed that their contents could be heated very quickly to high temperatures and they were thus very energy-efficient.

348

Diameter of large pans: 63 cm
Height: 23 cm
Thickness: 0.4 cm

Diameter of the small pans: 30 cm
Height: 15 cm
Thickness: 0.3 cm

13.2 Needles
Needles made of wrought iron (Inv. 2128 bis) were found in a little blue and white porcelain vase (Inv. 2128). They had formed a small accretion from which the needles could be extracted.

349

The maximum length of the needles preserved was 48 mm and their diameter was 0.9 mm.

Iron needles were a traditional Chinese export product for the Nanhai trade. Zhao Rugua wrote that: "Foreign merchants barter for porcelain, gold, iron censers, lead, glass beads and iron needles".[4]

Antonio de Morga, First Oïdor of the Audiencia Royal of the Philippines, states that needles were still being imported into the Philippines by Chinese merchants in the late fifteenth century, when they were first colonised by Spain.[5]

The production of iron nails, wire and needles was a speciality of small plants.[6] Once the iron had been cast, it was refined by oxidation; beating the pig-iron with a hammer and heating it with a lot of hot air from a bellows. The pure iron could then be forged. Forged or wrought iron is very different from pig-iron or cast iron. It is tougher, fibrous and malleable, lending itself perfectly to the manufacture of wire, nails, needles and tools of all types.

A few needles have been detached from the accretion.

---

[4] Op. cit.
[5] A. Morga, *Successos de las Islas Filipinas*, Mexico, 1609, ch. 8.
[6] Thien Kung Khai Wu, 1637.

14. Bronze artefacts
Franck Goddio (gongs and bracelets), *Javier Mártin López* (cannon)

14.1 Gongs
Four whole gongs (Inv. 1124, 2550, 2594, 2595), and three fragments were discovered at references 17 and 18. Each was of a different size.

350

Inv. 2550
Maximum diameter: 36.7 cm
Diameter at the base: 28.5 cm
Height: 6 cm

Inv. 2594
Maximum diameter: 37.2 cm
Diameter at the base: 29.7 cm
Height: 6.7 cm

Inv. 1124
Maximum diameter: 38.2 cm
Diameter at the base: 29.5 cm
Height: 7 cm

351

Inv. 2595
Maximum diameter: 54.5 cm
Diameter at the base: 43.4 cm
Height: 14.4 cm

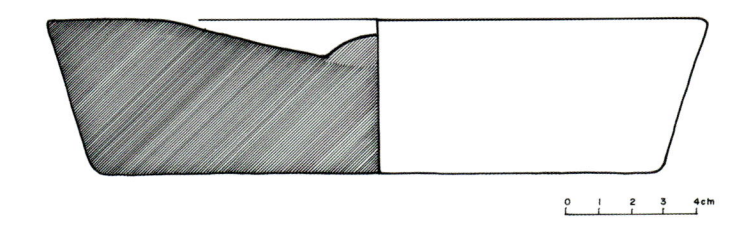

The gongs are disc-shaped, with a small domed indentation in the centre. The sides slope outwards towards the top and there are two holes in the sides for a strap on which they could be hung.

According to literary tradition, the gong was introduced into China at the dawn of the sixth century. It was brought by the "barbarians" who lived west of the empire. The country of origin is designated by the name "Hsi-Yu", probably eastern Turkestan. The Chinese encyclopaedia, *Ku chin T'u Shu chi ch'eng* states, "In the last part of the Wei dynasty, in the reign of Emperor Hsuan Wu (498–501), music-loving peoples who had come from the frontiers of the empire introduced into the capital the five-stringed guitar and the bronze gong (*t'ung-lo*)".[7]

These flat percussion instruments soon became popular for music-making in China and throughout the Asian world. The Chinese soon became gong-manufacturers and decided to sell their gongs throughout South-East Asia. Trade in these brass instruments with Gili (Bali), Timor and Pahang (Malaysia) is mentioned in Wang t'a Yuan's *Tao-i chih-lueh*, written in 1350.

Thirty years after the sinking of the Lena Shoal junk, Pigafetta, who accompanied Magellan on his visit to Sultan Homahon on the island of Cebu, reported seeing a young girl beating two brass gongs of Chinese manufacture.[8] Shortly thereafter, while in Mindanao (Philippines), he saw four gongs in a local home and was informed that every year, six or seven junks would reach the Philippine archipelago from Liukiu (China).

---

[7] Tsai Ping Liang, *Chinese Musical Instruments in Pictures*, Taibei, 1970. Other traditions claim that the brass gong was called "sha-lo", see H. Simbriger, "Gong und Gongspiele", in *Internationales Archiv für Ethnographie*, Vol. XXXVI, Leiden, 1939.

[8] Pigafetta, *Voyage autour du monde*, Ms. Fr. 24224 B.N., Paris.

Gongs of a type similar to those found in the wreck are still in current use in China and throughout Asia. They are mainly used for civil and religious ceremonies, especially Buddhist rites. They have also long been ritual or musical instruments among the Dayaks of Borneo and numerous tribes on the island of Java. "When the inhabitants of P'o-ni (Borneo) hold a celebration, they beat drums, sound gongs, sing and dance."[9] The possession of gongs was also one the most reliable indications of wealth in these lands.[10]

Gongs were also used on board ship. Once the ship was at sea, a gong sounded the hours.[11] Gongs also had another use: "In the southernmost islands of the Philippines archipelago, Chinese junks would drop anchor quite a distance from the coast and beat large gongs to attract the attention of any natives who wanted to trade with them".[12]

Gongs were usually made from a copper-rich alloy and this is also true of the gongs found in the wreck. This type of alloy is often mentioned in China under the name of "sounding brass". Some gongs appear to have been made from the recycled remains of old gongs.

The alloy was smelted in furnaces capable of reaching high temperatures. There then followed several purification phases, and the molten metal thus obtained was poured into a round iron mould. The metal was hammered while still red-hot so as to create the basic shape and size. It was then reheated and rehammered several times. Once the central part was complete, the edge of the brass plate was heated on its own so that it could be rounded and bent under. Once the definitive form had been attained, the gong was cleaned, polished and sometimes decorated.

The strength and the purity of tone of a gong were carefully tested before it was sold. To lower the note of the ring, the central dome was flattened; to make the note higher, the flat surface of the gong was filed down. The secrets of manufacture were jealously guarded and each gong-maker had his own special techniques for creating the best sound for his gongs. To improve the timbre, Javanese and Balinese makers added gold to the alloy.[13] On the basis of the nature of the sound produced and its intensity, the

Fig. 42. Woman playing a gong.

Chinese would describe a gong as being "male" or "female". Pictorial representations show that these gongs were sometimes struck with a padded hammer.

It is not possible to determine the site of the workshops that made the gongs found on the wreck. There were many places in China where such gongs were made, although Suzhou was one of the most important.

The fact that China had many copper mines facilitated the manufacture of gongs, which corroborates texts claiming the instruments were products manufactured especially and traditionally for the Nanhai trade. However, it cannot be stated with absolute certainty that the gongs on the ship were made in China. Other underwater archaeological excavations have produced bronze gongs[14] dating from the early and late seventeenth century.

---

[9] Zhao Rugua (Chau Ju-kua), 1911.

[10] M. Colanie, "Essai d'ethnographie comparée", *BEFEO*, Vol. XXXVI, 1936.

[11] Chóu K'ü-feï, *Ling-wai-tai-ta*, 3, 10–11. Written in 1178.

[12] Chau Ju-kua, 1911.

[13] M. Honneger, *Dictionnaire des sciences de la musique : techniques, formes instruments*, Paris, 1976.

[14] Goddio, 1997; 1988; see also *Weisses Gold*, 1997.

14.2 Cannon

From the pioneer writings of Fêng Chia-Shêng and J. R. Partington[15] onwards, a new current of thought, purged of chauvinistic sentiment, led to an acceptance of the Chinese origin of gunpowder as well as of firearm use, in the sense of a metal appliance capable of launching a projectile propelled by a gunpowder detonation.

This re-evaluation lead to the acknowledgement of a Chinese origin for practically all surviving fourteenth century cannon (*phao*, or *huo phao*), as well as for the majority of those from the fifteenth century.[16] In addition, most such Chinese specimens are dated, while early European pieces rarely are before the sixteenth century. The precise characteristics of this early Chinese repertoire, consisting of more than 50 pieces, mostly in Chinese museums, lend themselves to formulating a classification scheme.

The earliest surviving specimens are from the first half of the fourteenth century.[17] They frequently feature a cup-shaped muzzle, like a plumber's plunger, or the trumpet profile of a nineteenth century blunderbuss, without rings or any other decoration. The bore is often wider at exit than inside.

Another common feature of the oldest Chinese cannon is the bulbous charge chamber, with the walls thickened to resist the stress of discharge. The touch-hole is on top, sometimes with a pronounced lip to form a sort of nipple.

Instead of a cascabel, there is usually an end-mounted socket for a wooden stock, for manoeuvring the weapon. Although inscriptions are not invariably found, there are plenty from all periods, recording the year of manufacture (emperor and dynasty), the destination of the piece (naval units or frontier posts), the weights and even the officer in charge of foundry operations.

Last but not least, are the barrel-stiffening rings. They first appear in the mid fourteenth century, and continue until the nineteenth century.[18] However, in some cases their function appears to be as adornment rather than reinforcement, since by the early 1400s bronze foundry techniques were sufficiently evolved for there to be no danger of a casting malfunction or burst cannon in their absence, particularly as the rings were cast in, rather than being hammered on, as in their European wrought iron counterparts of the fifteenth and sixteenth centuries. The rings and the stock socket show the consistancy of Chinese features in the development of the design and decoration of firearms.[19]

Some of these features appear in the five bronze cannon or hand-guns recovered from the Lena Shoal wreck: the flared muzzle, the barrel stiffening rings, the bulbous chamber, and the stock socket.[20] Even though characteristics remain fairly constant, they lead eventually to evolution.

The Lena Shoal junk cannon, however, lack two quintessentially Chinese features. One relates to the shape of the barrels: the Lena Shoal pieces have evolved away from the original vase shape associated with early cannon in both East and West. Also, the muzzle enlargement features in only one of the pieces, while in other cases it is reinforced by a single moulding ring (Inv. 4011 and 4009), and elsewhere there is a simple cut-off (Inv. 4012).

The Lena Shoal junk cannon are also distinctive in other respects. The side-mounted lug diverges from what is found in other pieces. In all cases the lug is mounted so as not to impede firing operations, and has the typically Chinese shape that persisted until the end of the seventeenth century.[21] This type of lug has so far not been found in Chinese weapons older than the beginning of the sixteenth century. China then started to imitate the Portuguese breech-loading *versos*, whose interchangeable breech chambers have a handle.

The influence of the Portuguese cannon may even be suspected in South-East Asia slightly earlier and the Lena cannon may be connected with this.[22] 1522 is the generally accepted date of the first exchanges between the

---

[15] J.R. Partington, *A History of Greek Fire and Gunpowder*, Cambridge, 1960.

[16] Excepting the oldest two, undated European examples – Germany's so-called Tannenberg Cannon, datable before 1399, and the Loshult Cannon from Sweden, attributed to the same century without further precision.

[17] The earliest dated is of 1332, although there is another hand cannon found in excavations in the Heilungchiang Province (Manchuria), attributed to 1288–1290.

[18] For example, those preserved in England in the Royal Armouries, such as xix-184, dated 17 August 1841, which is 3.2 m long and has 11 rings.

[19] Compared at least with the transformations found in Europe, where, between the first efforts depicted by Walter de Milamete (1327) and the end of the 15th century, there was a genuine design and production revolution.

[20] Bronze cannon: Inv. 2901, calibre 9.4 cm, length 30.8 cm; Inv. 4008, calibre 7 cm, length 55.5 cm; Inv. 4009, calibre 6 cm, length 30.8 cm; Inv. 4010, calibre 6 cm, length, 27 cm; Inv. 4011, calibre 6.4 cm, length 35.5 cm; Inv. 4012, calibre 2.7 cm, length 58 cm. There are no surviving marks on the guns.

[21] M. Flecker, "Excavation of an Oriental Vessel of c. 1690 off Con Dao, Vietnam", *International Journal of Nautical Archaeology*, 1992, vol. 21, pp. 221–44. In the 1991 excavation two breech-chambers were found, one with a handle of similar design. Although not explicitly identified as such, the vessel was probably Chinese. The resemblance of the handles fits the unchanging pattern of Chinese types described above.

[22] The Xuande wreck cannon, known to have been cast in Asia, yet to a totally Portuguese design, antedate the arrival of the Portuguese, who reached Calicut in 1498, the Malacca Straits in 1509 (Malacca was taken in 1511) and China around 1514.

LOST AT SEA

Chinese Empire and the Portuguese Crown. According to Needham, however, the Chinese used Portuguese-style *versos* (*Fo-lang-Chi*) to put down revolts around 1519 or even earlier.[23]

A probable dissemination route for this type of firearm ran from Malaysia to both the Chinese Empire and the Philippines archipelago. Thus, the brief interval between the first contact of the Portuguese expeditions with the South-East Asian peoples and the definitive establishment of relations with China, a few years after, is likely to be the background of the Lena Shoal cannon.

The Chinese diaspora was also a channel for the spread of ideas; commercial and cultural contacts between the mainland empire, the Philippine archipelago and the Malacca Straits were highly developed by the end of the fifteenth century, as was the spread of firearms.

There were highly productive copper and tin mines not just in China, but also in South-East Asia (north of Vietnam). Some were owned by Chinese entrepreneurs, who processed the metal and produced artefacts which may have included armaments.[24]

The hand-gun dimensions of the five Lena Shoal junk cannon suggest that they were launchers of metal tipped incendiary darts, installed on the junk's gunwales, and aimed with the leverage of the stock and the lug. According to Chinese sources of 1464 and 1496, dart-firing guns were still in use on China's interior frontiers and in merchant junks to repel pirate attacks on the seas of Asia.

The following descriptions of three of the cannon retrieved from the Lena Shoal are based on photographs alone.

---

[23] Needham mentions the suppression of the Fukien rebellions in 1510. J. Needham and R. D. S. Yates, *Science and Civilisation in China: vol. V, Part VII*, Cambridge, 1994, pp. 372–3.

[24] A. Reid, *South-East Asia in the Age of Commerce, 1450-1680: vol. I*, Yale University Press, New Haven and London, 1988, p. 116.

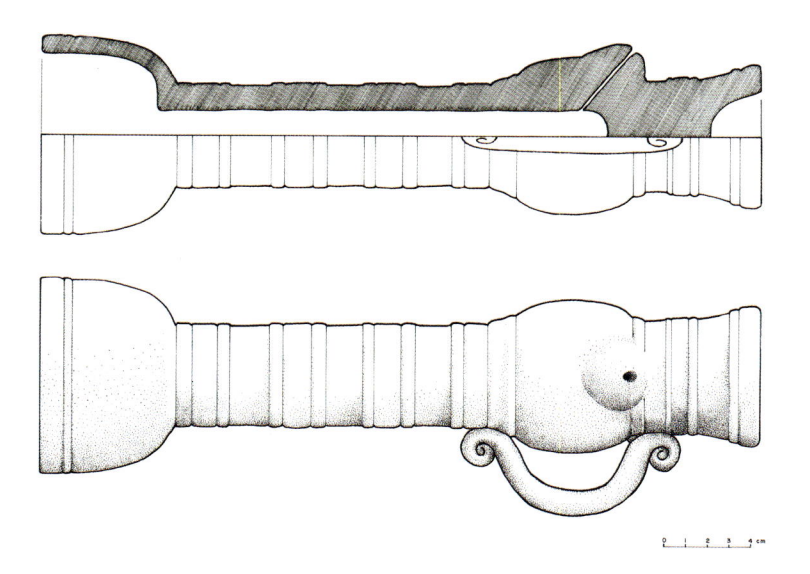

352

Inv. 2901
Cast bronze muzzle-loading gun with the barrel divided by three wide bands of rings that continue at the socket for a wooden stock (missing). The flared shaped muzzle sticks out from the rest of the pieces and remind us the dart-firing guns of the fourteenth and fifteenth centuries.

353

Inv. 4009
Cast bronze muzzle-loading gun with the barrel in four sections defined by five raised bands of clustered rings. The three central ones are formed of triplicate rings, while at the muzzle and breech extremities the rings are simply in pairs. The charge chamber is bellied out bulbously, with a rearward tilted touch-hole drawn out to form a spout. There is a curly side-mounted lug for manhandling the piece. Where a cascabel might otherwise be formed, there is a socket for a wooden stock (missing). Its rim has grooves which appear to be decorative.

354

Inv. 4011
The barrel of the gun is divided into three sections. The muzzle enlargement is reinforced by a simple moulding ring. The shapes of the lug and the bulbous chamber are almost the same as in the other cases. The main important difference between this and Inv. 4009 is the prominent stock socket at its rear end.

14.3 Bracelets
Plain: two plain, continuous brass bracelets were found (Inv. 3042 and 2045 bis) near the packing-case at reference 29-D. Diameter of the bracelets: 6.5 cm; diameter of the wire: 0.5 cm

355

Spiral bracelets: 30 spiral bracelets were excavated, with a major concentration near the packing-case at 26-C. Some were attached to the remnants of wood on the packing-case, others scattered nearby.

15. Copper artefacts
Franck Goddio

15.1 Copper vessels

Copper vessels of various shapes were unearthed crushed near the little cannon at 26-I. The repoussé decoration of some of these artefacts indicates that they came from South-East Asia, perhaps from the Malay peninsula.

356

Inv. 4013 A
Cup on a narrow foot decorated with repoussé work in three reversed out bands edged with rows of beading. The upper band consists of a reversed out lotus frieze. The middle band is undecorated. The lower band contains groups of four arcs.

Four little rings are attached to the lowest row of beading. One of them still has a chain attached to it with a copper fastening in the form of a stylised lotus flower. The chain is so long that the fastening extends beyond the level of the base of the foot. The upper row of beading also has four rings fixed to it which are staggered in relation to the lower set of rings. A chain is still attached to one of them.

Diameter at the rim: 17 cm
Diameter at the foot: 7.5 cm
Height: 8 cm

357

Inv. 4779
Round bowl with flared rim and narrow neck.

Diameter at the rim: 31 cm
Diameter of the body: 28 cm
Height: 32 cm

358

Inv. 4530
Round bowl with flared rim.

Diameter at the rim: 36.5 cm
Diameter of the body: 28 cm
Height: 30 cm

359

Inv. 4013 C
Round bowl with flared rim.

Diameter at the rim: 38 cm
Diameter of the body: 37.5 cm
Height: 25 cm

360

Inv. 4097
Cover of flattened bowl with radiating decoration in the form of five stylised lotus flowers. In the centre of the motif, there is a dome and a five-pointed star.

Diameter: 24 cm
Height: 25 cm

361

Inv. 4013 E
Shallow bowl with central floral decoration.

Diameter: 21 cm
Internal diameter: 14 cm
Height: 2.5 cm

362

Inv. 4532 A
Part of plate with central floral decoration. Rim with decoration on the sides.

Internal diameter: 14 cm

363

Inv. 4013 J
Undecorated plate.

Diameter: 25 cm
Height: 2.3 cm

LOST AT SEA

364

Inv. 4013 D
Fragment of deep bowl with decoration on the sides.

Diameter of whole plate: 21 cm
Height: 2.3 cm

365
Inv. 2462
Undecorated plate.

Diameter: 25 cm
Height: 2.3 cm

366

Inv. 4013 G

Flared goblet with rounded base.

Diameter at the rim: 12 cm
Diameter at the foot: 10 cm
Height: 11 cm

367

Inv. 4532 B
Bulbous goblet with tall base.

Diameter at the rim: 13 cm
Diameter at the foot: 10 cm
Height: 11 cm

368

Inv. 4013 B
Flared goblet with domed base decorated with a double row of beading.

Diameter at the rim: 16 cm
Diameter at the foot: 11 cm
Height: 15 cm

369

Inv. 4014 A
Flared goblet with domed base, decorated with a line of repoussé beading.

Diameter at the rim: 15 cm
Diameter at the foot: 11 cm
Height: 15 cm

370

Inv. 4013 F
Deep cup with rounded base.

Diameter at the rim: 15 cm
Diameter at the foot: 11 cm
Height: 13 cm

371

Inv. 4532 C
Round basin on cylindrical stem with flat base.

Maximum diameter: 10 cm
Diameter of the base: 5 cm
Height: 11 cm

372

Inv. 4013 I
Round basin on cylindrical stem with flat base.

Maximum diameter: 8 cm
Diameter of the base: 6 cm
Height: 7 cm

373

Inv. 4532 D
Large bowl or cauldron with domed bottom.

Diameter at the rim: 35 cm
Diameter at the base: 30 cm
Height: 35 cm

LOST AT SEA

374

Inv. 4013 K
Small bowl decorated with arcs.

Diameter: 10 cm
Height: 3.5 cm

375

Inv. 4013 N
Decorated plaque showing two lotuses in flower and two in bud in a vase standing on a base. Radiating quarter circle at the two bottom corners.

Length: 26 cm
Width: 16 cm

376

Inv. 4014 B
Rectangular bowl.

Length: 8 cm
Height: 3.5 cm

377

Inv. 4013 L
Two-handled cooking pan.

Diameter: 26 cm
Height: 8 cm

378

Inv. 4532 F
Square lid with remains of knob handle.

Measurement of side: 8 cm

379

Inv. 4532 E
A lug, circular in section with flattened extension of the attachment containing two rivets on each side.

Total length: 9 cm
Section of handle: 0.5 cm

380

Inv. 4013 M
Flattened lug with extended attachment point and evidence of two rivets.

Total length: 8 cm
Height: 0.3 cm

15.2 Coins

Only three coins were recovered (Inv. 2110, 2028, 121).

381

Inv. 2110
Hongwu tongbao, currency in circulation during the reign of Hongwu (1368–1398).

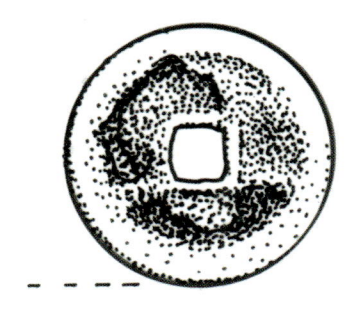

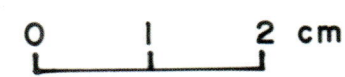

16. Tin goods

Franck Goddio

A cargo of more than 187 tin ingots was discovered and they were distributed in various parts of the ship. Analysis revealed that they were made of pure tin. (Analysis 98-1-0199-43 performed by the Department of Science and Development, Manila, using an energy dispersal spectrometer. Kevex Sigma X-ray Detector, 15 Kev.)

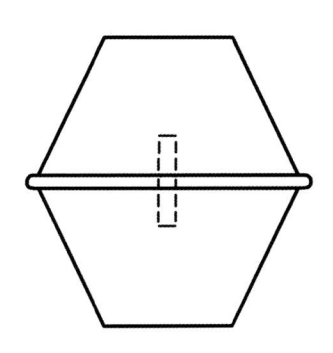

The ingots consist of two sections stuck together at the base. Each section is shaped like a truncated pyramid. The upper part is concave and sometimes decorated with a four-lobed design. There is an extension at the base of the truncated half-pyramid. The vestige of a thin strip of wood was discernible in the centre of the base of each part.

382

Measurement at the base: 6 cm
Measurement at truncated top: 5.4 cm
Height of one section: 4 cm
A complete ingot is 8 cm high.

The production of tin in South-East Asia is confined to eastern Sumatra, the island of Banca, the Malay peninsula and the little islands that lie off it.[25] Trade in this raw material was extremely important because it is used in the composition of brass, an alloy of copper and tin.

According to Zhao Rugua,[26] "The land of Kien-pi[27] (Kampar, on the east coast of Sumatra) produces tin, elephant tusks and pearls". This author provides an insight into the contents of the Lena Shoal junk since he states that tin was imported into San-sü (identified as the islands of Calamian, Busuanga and the Palawan region).

The following items were bartered: porcelain, black damask and other silks, glass beads of all colours, lead weights for fishing nets and tin.

---

[25] Crawfurd, *History*, III.
[26] Zhao Rugua (Chau Ju-kua), 1911.
[27] According to Peliot (*BEFEO*, IV, 344) Kien-pi is the kingdom of Kampé mentioned in the Javanese chronicles of the 15th c. as a dependency of the Majapahit Empire.

17. Plant and animal remains

Franck Goddio

Forty-one elephant tusks of various sizes were raised to the surface during the excavation. This quantity bears no relation to the total amount in the cargo because a large number of tusks, estimated at 30 or so, had been removed by the pillagers. In addition to these tusks, some were attached to metal accretions at map reference 31 and could not be extracted (about 10 or so that we could see).

The cargo of ivory on the Lena Shoal junk is thus estimated at a minimum of 80 tusks of various sizes and weights. Zhao Rugua provides interesting information about trade in this product[28] and shows that the ivory came from various countries such as the Malay peninsula, Sumatra, Java and the Coromandel coast. He states, "the large specimens can weigh from 50–100 catties.[29] The straight, pale-coloured tusks with delicate striations come from Ta-shï (land of the Arabs); while those from Chön-la (Cambodia) and Chan-ch'öng (Annam) consist of two small tusks that are reddish in colour and only weigh 10 to 20 or 30 catties, and the tips of these tusks only are used to make perfume vials".

---

[28] Ibid.
[29] One catty = 605 g.

We know that under the Song dynasty, the importation of this product was heavily regulated. An import duty of 10 per cent was levied on ivory tusks weighing 30 catties or more and they had to be sold on the official market because they could only be bought under licence. "Merchants who had large tusks and intended to sell them through other channels, had to cut their tusks into sections weighing three catties or less in order to escape the official market. The official market price was low and the products for which 'licences' were needed were so devalued that the merchants were very unhappy."[30]

---

[30] P'ing-chou-k'o-t'an.

Photo 66. Pepper was found inside a porcelain box, Inv. 2618.

Only five intact tusks were found on the Lena Shoal wreck.

383

Inv. 428; length: 85.2 cm; diameter at the base: 32 cm
Inv. 469; length: 61 cm; diameter at the base: 29 cm
Inv. 3187; length: 56 cm; diameter at the base: 26 cm
Inv. 3995; length: 63 cm; diameter at the base: 30 cm
Inv. 3999; length: 62 cm; diameter at the base: 21 cm

The tusks had been subjected to physical and chemical changes due to their immersion, making their weight unrepresentative.

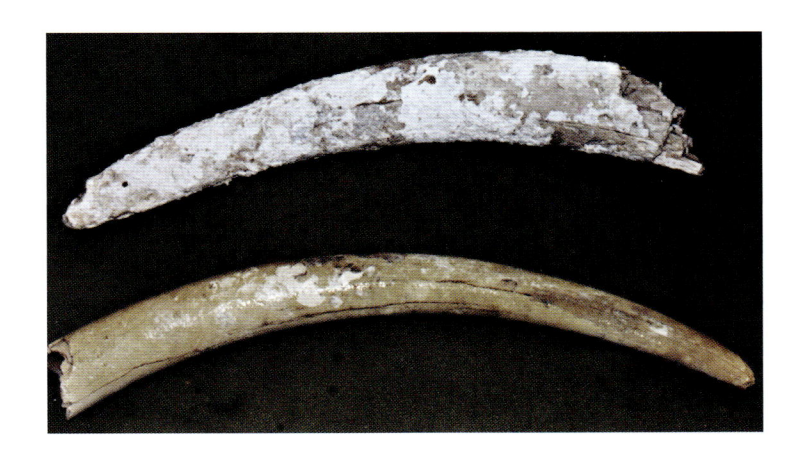

18. Glass beads
Franck Goddio

Several thousand glass beads were unearthed during the excavations, weighing a total of 3.8 kg, including some accretions. They had been packed into small ovoid Sawankhalok jars from the kilns of Tao Maenam Noi. Seven of these little jars were found intact with their content of glass beads (at 20-K, 22-L, 23-K, 27-L, 27-C, 29-O, 30-F and 32-L). Other beads were found scattered on the sand but they were always associated with shards of these jars.

This type of glassware was a traditional Nanhai trade good also destined for the Philippines. The following items were bartered: porcelain, gold, iron censers, glass beads of every colour and iron needles.[31] To Borneo, the merchants brought gold and silver, imitation silk brocade, Kien-yang brocades, other types of shiny silk and glass beads.[32]

Asian glass beads, especially those from China, were directly influenced by Western beads from the sixth or seventh century BC onwards. In fact, many glass beads from the Han (206 BC–220 AD) or post-Han periods found in China are of Mediterranean origin. The greatest period for western and Romanised oriental beads exported to Asia was between the second and fourth centuries AD.[33]

These foreign manufactured goods were soon emulated locally in a more primitive fashion, at first in slavish imitation of the originals, but subsequently generating new prototypes that were imitated in their turn throughout the Far East. Thus, in the course of time, the patterns and designs became universal and the origin of such products can no longer be determined with accuracy. Nor is the manufacturing technique a reliable criterion for identifying the geographical origin of glass beads, since it was almost identical from one county to the next.

---

[31] Zhao Rugua (Chau Ju-kua), 1911, § 40, Ma-i (the Philippines).
[32] Ibid; § 39, P'o-ni (Borneo).
[33] *The Annals of the Han* and *Wei-lio* composed during the period of the Three Kingdoms (AD 221–64) attribute the origin of coloured glass to Ta-Ts'in, that is to say, the eastern Roman Empire. Concerning the export of glass beads to Asia, see also G.B. Gardner, "Ancient beads from the Johore river as evidence of an early link by sea between Malaya and the Roman Empire", in the *Journal of the Royal Asiatic Society*, London, 1937.

LOST AT SEA

Manufacture generally begins by blowing a tube of glass that is worked over heat by pulling or twisting. Depending on the decorative effect desired, the glass-blower can create stripes or spirals.

The tube is fixed on a stem and is worked by being rotated on a small gearwheel. The craftsman uses a small wire to pinch a bunch of glass rods together. When the molten glass cools, the beads can be separated by breaking them at the point where they were pinched together. Almost exactly the same method of manufacture, with a few minor modifications, was used in India, the Mekong Delta, the Philippines and China.[34]

It is therefore hard to recognise the origin of an Asian glass bead by examining the method of manufacture. Chemical analysis, on the other hand, can be useful in this instance. The presence of a high level of lead and barium in the composition of the glass of a bead tends to indicate a Chinese origin.[35]

Spectrographic analysis demonstrated the role of metal oxides in colouring the glass. For instance, adding copper to molten glass will colour it green or red, depending on how it is tempered, and copper and cobalt together will colour the glass blue. Iron will turn it yellow and zinc and lead will produce opaque or translucent whites, depending on the proportions used. Caution must be excercised, however, in dealing with glass beads found on a wreck after it has been under water for several centuries. Bacterial action following the sinking could have changed the colour of certain of these artefacts by breaking down the metal oxides in the paste.[36] The glass beads recovered during the excavation can be divided into six categories of shape.

---

[34] Van der Hoop, *Megalithic Remains in South Sumatra*, Sutphen, 1932; and L. Malleret, *L'archéologie du delta du Mékong, Vol. III, La culture du Fou-nan*, Paris, 1962.

[35] C.G. Seligman and H.C. Beck, "Far-Eastern glass: some Western origins", *The Museum of Far Eastern Antiquities*, No. 10, Stockholm, 1938.

[36] Cf. Guyot de Saint Michel, "Conservation of material", § 6, in Goddio and Guyot de Saint Michel, 1999.

18.1 Octahedral beads
Consisting of two pyramids of four facets joined at the base, the top sometimes being flattened at the points where the bead has been perforated. Only one type of bead falls into this group, a royal blue translucent glass bead.

384

Inv. 446
Dimensions: 13 mm long and 8 mm wide at the base.

18.2 Cylindrical beads
There is only one example of this type of tubular or cylindrical bead which is made of a Prussian blue opaque paste.

385

Inv. 4464
Dimensions: 5 mm long and 5 mm in diameter.

18.3 Olive-shaped beads
There is only one example of this type. The paste is white and translucent with spiralling opaque white striations.

386

Inv. 4460
Dimensions: 15 mm long, with a maximum diameter of 10 mm.

18.4 Rounded elongated beads
Most of the beads were of this shape and the total weight of the several thousand such beads was 3.07 kg. The paste is semi-opaque, the colour varying from black to blackish-brown and burnt sienna.

387

Average dimensions: 9 to 11 mm in length with diameters of 8 to 10 mm.

The beads were separated from each other when the narrow strip that joined them was broken. A few samples remained connected and form a series of multiple spherical or tubular beads.

18.5 Faceted discoid beads
This group includes several sub-groups of various dimensions and colours.

18.5.1 – Dimensions: 7 to 9 mm in diameter and with thicknesses of 4 to 6 mm. This sub-group includes hundreds of different types. The weight is not significant because so many of the beads are attached to calcareous and metallic accretions. The opaque paste is turquoise in colour. The beads became detached from each other as the thin strip between them broke. A few samples remained connected and form strings of disc-shaped beads.

18.5.2 – Dimensions: about 6 mm in diameter with a thickness of 4 mm. There were 134 beads and 32 identifiable fragments of this type. The paste is opaque and turquoise blue in colour.

18.5.3 – Dimensions: 3 to 4 mm in diameter with a thickness of 2.5 to 3 mm. This sub-group includes 367 intact beads and 123 identifiable fragments made of an opaque turquoise blue paste as well as 97 intact beads and 23 identifiable fragments of translucent white paste with opaque white spiral striations.

18.6 Round beads

388

Dimension: 9 mm in diameter.

This group contains about 100 black paste beads stuck in a metallic accretion and 21 unattached examples, all found only in jar Inv. 4284.

19. Stone and shell goods
Franck Goddio

Several carved stone or shell objects were unearthed. In some cases, their purpose remains unclear.

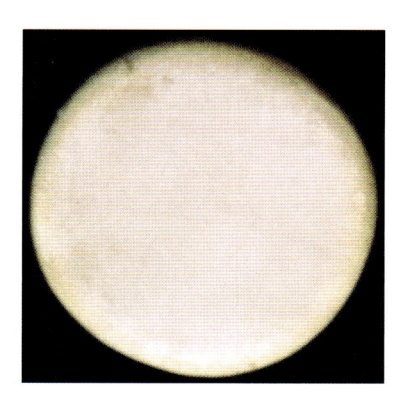

389

Inv. 4443
A large disc of pale green stone (a type of jadeite), semi-polished and chamfered on both sides. It has two holes in it, presumably so that it could be hung on a cord.

Maximum diameter: 100 mm
Diameter of polished surfaces, not including the chamfered edges: 90 mm
Thickness: 18 mm

390

Inv. 4163
A white marble disc in the centre of which there is a narrow strip of what appears to be lead. Both sides are polished, with sharply chamfered edges.

Maximum diameter: 56 mm
Diameter of polished surfaces, not including the chamfered edges: 43 mm
Thickness: 25 mm

391

Inv. 4166
A white marble disc with rounded edges, polished on both sides.

Diameter: 57 mm
Thickness: 16 mm

392

Inv. 4250
Four white marble discs (Inv. 3834, 3835, 3827, 4250), with polished and chamfered surfaces.

Maximum diameter: 36 mm
Diameter of the polished surfaces, not including the chamfered edges: 26 mm
Thickness: 15 mm

393

Inv. 4247
Four white marble discs (Inv. 4247, 4248, 4251, 4252), with polished, chamfered surfaces.

Maximum diameter: 25 mm
Diameter of the polished surfaces, not including the chamfered edges: 19 mm
Thickness: 19 mm

394

Inv. 4449
A shell disc, with polished surfaces and rounded edges.

Diameter: 15 mm
Thickness: 6 mm

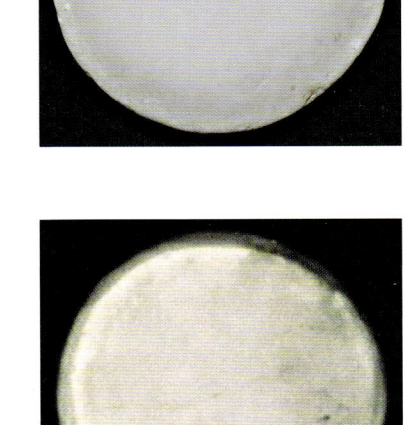

395

Inv. 4164
A white marble disc, with polished surfaces and chamfered edges.

Maximum diameter: 21 mm
Diameter of polished surfaces excluding the chamfered edge: 19 mm
Thickness: 10 mm

396

Inv. 4444
A shell disc, both sides polished and with rounded edges. There are five dots in the centre of each side, four arranged in a square and the fifth in the centre.

Diameter: 48 mm
Thickness: 16 mm

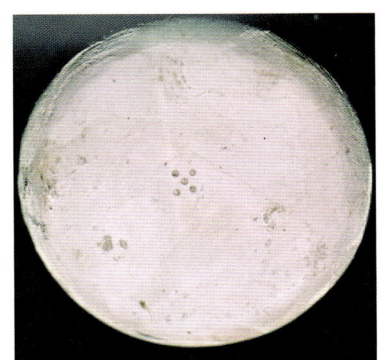

LOST AT SEA

397

Forty-three hemispherical pieces of shell.
Diameter: between 35 and 37 mm
Thickness: between 8 and 10 mm

These were probably used as counters in the game of *weiqi*, known as "go" in Japan. It is a game that dates from antiquity. It is played by two players on a chequerboard consisting of 19 horizontal lines and 19 vertical lines creating 361 intersections. The opponents have counters – one player has black counters and his opponent has white ones – which they place on the intersections, attempting to define the territories, encircling the adversary or destroying him. The aim is to occupy the largest amount of space possible on the chequerboard. The beauty and subtlety of the game, which requires that the players act as strategists and tacticians and wage psychological warfare, made it a challenging pastime that was, and remains, very popular in China.

Fig. 43. Chinese painting from the end of the 16th c. depicting a game of *weiqi*. Private collection, Paris.

398

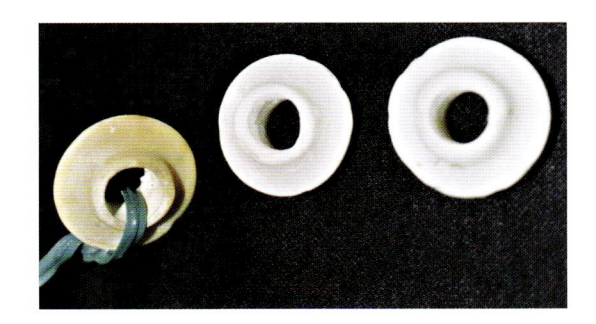

Inv. 4681 A, B, C
Three items of polished white marble, with perforations along the axis.

Maximum diameter: 18 mm
Diameter at the central perforation: 8 mm
Diameter at the extremities: 11 mm
Thickness: 7 mm

399 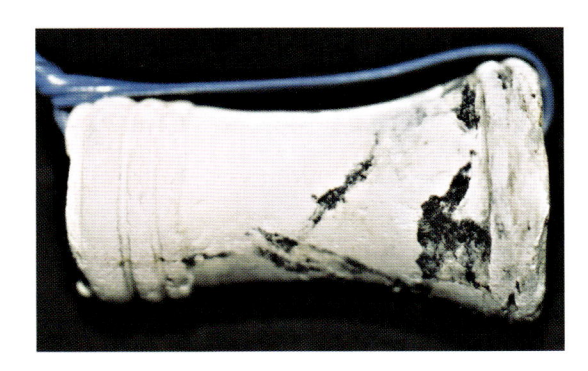
Inv. 2095
One item of polished white marble perforated along its axis, with two convex rounded mouldings at one end.

Length: 38 mm
Diameter at the plain end: 20 mm
Diameter at the moulded end: 18 mm
Diameter of the perforations along the axis: 10 mm

400

Inv. 4136
A stone grinding roller.

Diameter: 5 cm
Length: 17.5 cm

401

Inv. 4732
A grinding stone.

Base: 17 x 8 cm
Upper surface: 20 x 11 cm
Height: 5.5 cm.

402

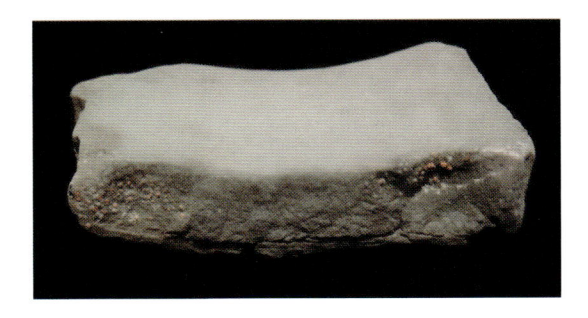

Inv. 1352
Sharpening stone.

Length: 24 cm
Thickness: 18.7 cm
Height: 5.7 cm

A ceramic cooking plate was retrieved: external diameter: 8 cm; internal diameter: 4.6 cm; height: 1 cm.

A few scattered ballast stones were revealed, near remains of wood. The sailors preferred to use iron ingots for ballast instead of stones since the iron bars could later be sold at a good price. The stones that were found, which were large smooth river boulders, had probably been forgotten in the bottom of the hold when the ballast was discharged.

20. Lacquerware
Rosemary Scott

Chinese lacquer is made from the sap of the lacquer tree *rhus verniciflua*, which in ancient times was indigenous to a wide area of China, and is still today found in central and south China. Early texts speak of attempts to reintroduce lacquer trees to Henan province as early as the Eastern Han dynasty (25–220 AD).

Chinese craftsmen appear to have been the first to recognise and use lacquer's remarkable properties. Early wooden objects covered with a coating of coloured lacquer have been found at Neolithic sites in Zhejiang, Jiangsu and Shanxi provinces.

Although the lacquer sap itself is dark grey, it is usually coloured – either red using mercuric sulphide, or black using carbon or iron oxide. Other colours were also produced, for example green, brown and yellow, but some pigments could not be combined with the lacquer sap, so that, for instance blue lacquer could not be made. Red and black, however are the most favoured colours and the mythical founder of the Xia dynasty, Emperor Yu, is supposed to have used vessels for sacrifice which were red on the interior and black on the exterior.

While one reason for using lacquer in these early times was as a paint, lacquer actually had other, more important, properties. The lacquer sap is an oil in water emulsion, an essential ingredient of which is urushiol. The latter is a hydrocarbon ($C_{14}H_{18}O_2$), which polymerises on exposure to oxygen and becomes, what is in effect, a natural plastic. Lacquer is resistant to heat, water, acids and termites, and can be used as an adhesive. It is therefore a very useful material with which to provide organic materials such as wood, bamboo, leather and even cloth with a protective coating.

Lacquer can also provide extra strength and, when applied with care, can take on a beautiful glossy sheen. It has only two disadvantages. The first is that it can only be applied in very thin layers (0.03–0.05 mm), as only the lacquer in immediate contact with the air will set, and so the lacquer has to be applied in many layers allowing it to fully set between applications. The second disadvantage is that the lacquer tree is a relative of poison ivy and the sap in its raw state produces serious skin reactions.

The laborious manner in which lacquer had to be applied was one of the contributing factors ensuring that lacquer wares were very expensive – a lacquered vessel costing as much as 10 times more than a bronze one. Nevertheless lacquer was very popular, not only for sacrificial vessels, such as those used by Emperor Yu, but in the late Bronze Age, for instance, to strengthen and decorate leather shields. Indeed, the Warring States and Han dynasties saw all manner of objects painted with intricate designs in differently coloured lacquer. The Bronze Age also saw the use of lacquer to pick out carved and pierced designs on wood, and as an adhesive for precious metal, shell and bone inlays.

Photo 67. Underside of a lacquered box, on which can be read a Chinese character.

As early as the Tang dynasty there is evidence that lacquer was being applied in layers of different colours and then linear designs cut into the lacquer with a knife held at an oblique angle, thus revealing the bands of colour. Fragments using this technique, previously referred to by the Japanese term "guri" lacquer, but now usually known as either "tixi" (literally "carved rhinoceros") or carved marbled lacquer have been found among the Tang dynasty ruins at Fort Miran in Turkestan. Here the technique had been applied to lacquered leather plaques, which were originally fastened together to form armour. It is also from the Tang period onwards that beautiful designs using carefully-shaped pieces of mother-of-pearl inlaid into a lacquer ground are seen.

Photo 68. A woman's lacquerware comb still in excellent state of preservation.

The Song dynasty saw further developments in lacquer technology. *Tixi* lacquer developed several characteristic scrolling designs, which showed the colour layering to its best advantage. The application of gold to lacquer also seems to have been popular at this time. There were several ways in which gold could be applied. As early as the late Bronze Age patterns had been incised into the surface of lacquer, but in the Song period gold was inlaid into the incisions creating a rich brocade-like design. Gold foil was also inlaid in larger sections, sometimes to form the background of a carved design.

Gold was also painted onto the surface of the lacquer, using one of two methods. The first involved the required design being painted on to the surface using liquid lacquer and then gold powder was sprinkled into the design, so that it adhered to the wet lacquer. The other method was more straight forward, and involved mixing the gold powder with liquid lacquer and then using it in the same way as paint to apply the design.

Perhaps the most important development in the Song period, however, was pictorial carved lacquer. In order to be carved effectively, the lacquer had to be very thick. Since each individual layer of lacquer could only be very thin, this meant that many layers of lacquer had to be applied before carving could even begin. Nevertheless, carved lacquer was to become perhaps the most popular of all the lacquer techniques. Indeed, when most people in the West think of Chinese lacquer, they imagine carved red lacquer.

Recent investigations have shown that carved lacquer was being made at least as early as the Song dynasty, but it became firmly established in the Yuan period, when the names of famous carvers, such as Yang Mao and Zhang Cheng from Zhejiang province are recorded. It is also from the Yuan period that we see an excellent example of the endurance of lacquer. In 1323 a ship from China went down off the coast of Korea on its way to Japan. Its cargo mainly consisted of ceramics, with some metalwork and other materials, but it also included a small carved red lacquer jar, which in the 1970s was retrieved from the wreck and still looked fresh and bright despite its 600 years on the sea bed.

Areas of South East Asia also made use of lacquer to preserve and decorate items made of various organic materials. The lacquer pieces found in the cargo of the Lena Shoal junk are likely to be of South-East Asian origin.

Photo 69. Lacquerware container with lid.

Photo 70. Lacquerware container.

Photo 71. Underside of lacquerware container.

CONCLUSION
The route taken by the junk and the position of the wreck
Franck Goddio

The position of the shipwreck and its itinerary, which we have been able to retrace according to the objects found on board, suggest three possible hypotheses on the final destination of the junk. The geographical location of where the junk sank also enlightens us as to the probable cause of its sinking.

The wreck was found 600 m south of a shoal that lies only 7 m under water at the point at which it is closest to the surface. In view of its size, the junk ought not to have had a draught of more than 2.5–3 m below the waterline. Its position appears to indicate that it had hit the reef during a tempest which created a heavy swell. It is significant that the waters in which the ship was wrecked are known to be particularly difficult to navigate due to the heavy swell that forms quickly in bad weather. This fact was known in the twelfth and thirteenth centuries: "The coast lies on a south-westerly axis and during the monsoon when a sou'wester blows, the swell breaks on the shore and huge rollers form so quickly that vessels are unable to anchor in these waters. The sea here is littered with jagged rocks, their tips as sharp as sword or spear; when ships reached these waters they would steer out to sea to avoid them".[1]

If the exact destination of the Lena Shoal junk remains a puzzle, we can nonetheless reconstruct its itinerary. Indeed, in view of the type of cargo she was carrying, part of her route since leaving China can be guessed at with a fairly large measure of certainty.

After loading ceramics, including those from the kilns of Jingdezhen, Longquan and Guangdong, as well as miscellaneous goods such as gongs and brass bracelets, copper bowls, iron pans and lead ingots, the ship was probably provisioned at a port in Zhejiang or Fujian. The junk then made for southern China where various types of jars were loaded on board. It then called in at Annam where more jars and a few porcelain items were added to its cargo. Finally the junk called at a port in Siam where large quantities of pottery from various kilns, such as those of Sawankhalok, Kalong, Tao Maenam Noi, Pa Dong, Payoom and Phan were loaded into the holds. It might also have touched the coasts of the Malay peninsula and Sumatra where perhaps the tin ingots and copper utensils were loaded. On the other hand, it probably never reached the Burmese coast because there is only one Martaban jar in the cargo, indicating that this receptacle was not part of a set. In any case, these jars were used extensively throughout South-East Asia.

There are three main hypotheses as to the final destination of the cargo, and the goods on board the junk certainly seem to indicate that the probable destination was a large port such as Malacca.

The presence of Siamese goods on the shipwreck suggests that the junk followed the coastal route along the Chinese borders in order to get to Malacca where the cargo would then be exported towards the Middle-East. It is thus surprising to find this wreck lying to the north-east of Palawan, nearly 2,000 nautical miles from a Siamese port or the Malacca Straits.

The high quality of some of the ceramic items, especially the large dishes, the ewers, boxes and writing-cases, would indicate that a large part of the cargo was destined for a very selective market, such as Persia, the Mameluke Empire or the Ottoman Empire. This supposition is borne out by the presence of similar items in the collections of the Ardebil Shrine in Tehran and the Topkapi Saray Museum in Istanbul.[2] The sophisticated court of Timur (Tamburlaine), who ruled Khorasan and Transoxiana from 1405 to 1507, was extremely fond of this blue and white ware.

It is also known that many ceramics of that era which are preserved in the Istanbul museum come from collections created by Selim I (1512–20) which were kept in the Tabriz palace of the Shah Isma'il I of Persia and from the collections of the Mameluke sultans, which were transferred to Istanbul by the Ottomans when they captured Cairo in 1517.[3] Consequently, the probable destination of the junk was a large port such as Malacca, whence these precious items would have been re-exported to ports such as Hormuz and Aden, and thence to those distant regions. Ceramics of lesser quality, iron pans, iron and tin ingots would have been loaded on board for the purpose of barter at stops along the way at the sultanates of the Moluccas or on the return route via the Philippine archipelago.

---

[1] Zhao Rugua (Chau Ju-Kua), 1911, paragraph on the islands of Calamian, Busuanga and Palawan.

[2] J-P. Desroches, *Topkapi à Versailles, Les collections de céramiques chinoises*, exhibition catalogue, RMN, AFAA, Paris, 1999.

[3] The inventories which were periodically conducted of the collections in the Topkapi Saray are evidence of their progressive enrichment. See J. Raby and Ü. Yücel in R. Krahl and J. Ayers, *Chinese Ceramics in the Topkapi Saray Museum, Istanbul*, Sotheby's Publications, London, 1986.

Another theory is that the cargo was destined for the Muslim sultanates of the islands in the Philippine archipelago, the large island of Borneo or the Moluccas. However, its itinerary towards the southern Philippines after loading in a Siamese port and the Malay peninsula, does not indicate a logical route through the north-east of Palawan. This remains a mystery. The fact that the holds contained numerous goods which were very popular in these sultanates, such as Siamese and Annamese ceramics, glass beads, bracelets and bronze gongs, as well as iron ingots and pans would seem to support this theory. A few rare pieces of high quality, similar to those produced by the wreck, are still preserved in collections created in these regions and offer an additional reinforcement for this theory.

In this instance, however, the position of the wreck off the north-eastern coast of the large island of Palawan is also strange. The position could be explained if this were a vessel coming from China and making for the southern end of the Philippine archipelago by following a route west of Palawan after crossing the China Sea. We have been able to prove the existence of such a trading route thanks to four discoveries and archaeological excavations of wrecks dating from the eleventh to the sixteenth century on which we worked from 1985 to 1997. Yet the junk's position is still difficult to explain for a vessel which had clearly called at Siam and the Malay peninsula and was aiming for the Sulu sea or the Celebes. It would have been more logical to take the Balabac Strait between Palawan and Borneo[4] or the Karimata Strait between Borneo and Sumatra, rather than returning to the north-east.

Nor is the theory of a trip to the northern end of the Philippine archipelago explained by the location of the discovery. If this had been the case, the merchants would have off loaded the valuable goods taken on board in South China before returning northwards to barter the goods bought in Siam and the Malay peninsula. In particular, the presence of Chinese merchandise on the shipwreck suggests an unexpected event must have prevented the junk from unloading its cargo in the ports of southern China.

Futhermore, the fact that the wreck was found at the southern end of the Lena Shoal – which probably caused it to founder – suggests the junk was heading south. In view of the presence on board at the time of the sinking of goods from China and Siam, we must resign ourselves to considering that unforeseen circumstances, perhaps connected with the weather, forced the junk far from any logical route.

Each hypothesis presents a coherent itinerary, however none seem to entirely explain its position to the North-East of Palawan. The mystery remains to be solved.

---

[4] *Shun Fêng Hsiang Sung*, Laud MS, Or. 145, Bodleian Library, Oxford.

Appendix 1

METALS INDUSTRY RESEARCH AND DEVELOPMENT CENTER
Department of Science and Technology
Science Community Complex, MIRDC Compound, Gen. Santos Ave.
Bicutan, Taguig, Metro Manila, Philippines
Tel. Nos.: 837-0431 to 38 local 480, 481, 482 or 460/Fax No.: 837-0430

ANALYSIS, TESTING AND INSPECTION DIVISION

BPS
PNS 1600/ISO/IEC GUIDE 25

CERTIFICATE

NATIONAL MUSEUM
P. Burgos Street, Manila

Attention : Engr. ORLANDO ABINION

Job Description   : QUALITATIVE ANALYSIS
Customer's Sample Description: Metal Sample
Date Received   : 27 October 1998
Date Tested   : 28 October 1998

TEST METHODS:

Surface of the as-received sample was qualitatively analyzed using an Energy Dispersive Spectrometer.

Detector   : Kevex Sigma X-ray Detector
Voltage   : 15 KeV

TEST RESULT/S:

Lena Shoal metal samples

Element Detected
Tin (Sn)

Note : Please refer to the accompanying spectrum

JOSELITO MARTIN C. CAPARAS
Engineer III
PML

AGUSTIN M. FUDOLIG, Dr. Eng.
Division Chief

Certificate No. : 98-1-0199-43
Date   : 05 November 1998

This certificate shall not be reproduced except in full, without the written approval of the Laboratory.

Appendix 2

METALS INDUSTRY RESEARCH AND DEVELOPMENT CENTER
Analysis Testing and Inspection Division
Physical Laboratories Section – Physical Metallurgy Laboratory
MIRDC Compound, Gen. Santos Ave.
Bicutan, Taguig, M.M.
Tel. (632) 837-0431/38 loc. 484   Fax: (632) 837-0430

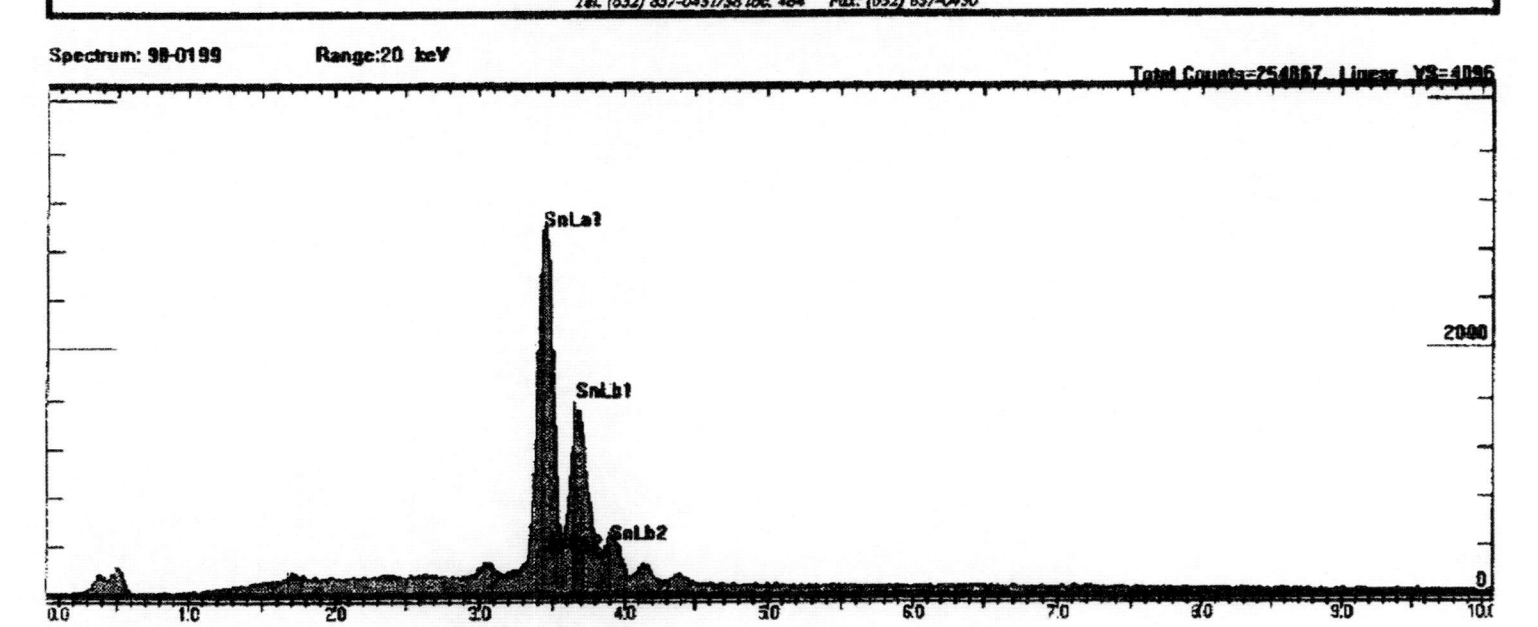

Spectrum: 98-0199   Range: 20 keV   Total Counts=254867, Linear YS=4096

Peaks labeled: SnLa1, SnLb1, SnLb2

JEO NUMBER	: 98-1-0199-43
TEST DESCRIPTION	: Energy Dispersive Spectrometry (Qualitative Analysis)
SAMPLE DESCRIPTION	: METAL SAMPLE *from Lena shad*
SAMPLE DESIGNATION	: METAL SAMPLE
DATE ANALYZED	: 28 October 1998

Appendix 3
Analysis of a bracelet from the Lena Shoal junk

1. Item sent for analysis

This consists of a bangle from the Lena Shoal junk, marked with the reference number 4668. It is oval in shape (7 cm at its longest point), and is about 5 mm in diameter.

2. Analyses performed

These consisted in determining the metal parts, using a scanning electron microscope (SEM) attached to an EDX microanalyser. The sample is bombarded with an electron beam and emits X-rays specific to each element present. A quantitative approach is also feasible.

This analysis requires a small amount of preparation of the bangle (scraping off a few mm^2 to produce a flat surface) in order to make the bombardment perpendicular to the surface of the object. The formation of verdigris (copper carbonate from corrosion) did not affect the analysis.

3. Results

The three elements highlighted on the attached graph were:
- copper (Cu on the graph)
- zinc (Zn on the graph)
- tin (Sn on the graph)

These three elements could be quantified by weight, to the nearest percentage:
- Copper: 79%
- Zinc: 17%
- Tin: 4%.

The analysis was repeated at three different sites of the prepared surface and produced identical results, with percentage variations of less than 1%.

The item is therefore made of brass, an alloy of copper and zinc, also containing a small amount of tin. The brass seems to be homogeneous, at least in the surface section that was analysed.

Note that tin has been found in abundance, in the form of cassiterite, in the Malayan peninsula (nowadays known as Western Malaysia), where copper deposits were also known to exist.

Zinc is also found in Vietnam, Thailand and China.

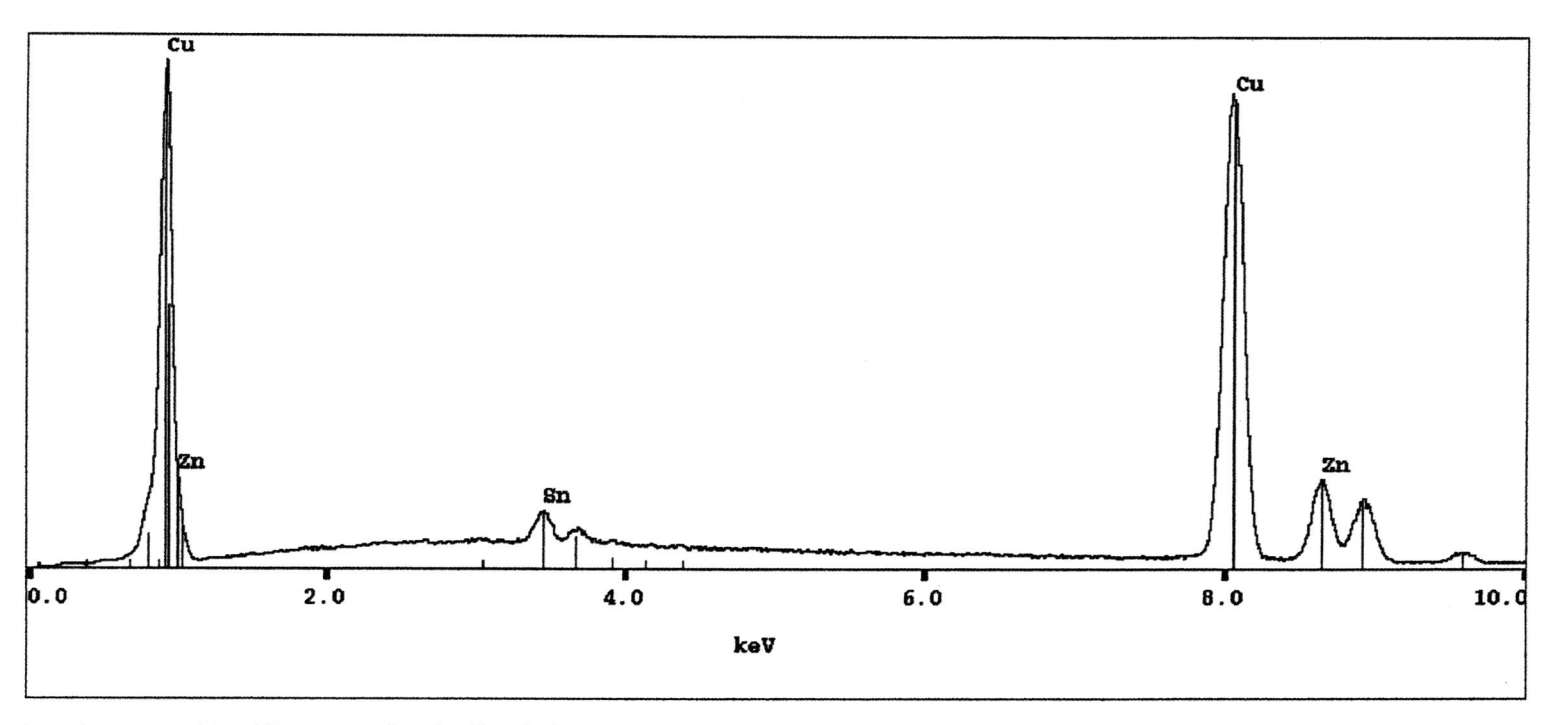

Bracelet: composition (Cu: copper; Sn: tin; Zn: zinc).

Appendix 4
Analysis of the composition of beads from the Lena Shoal junk

1. Material for analysis

The material consists of six batches of beads originating from the Lena Shoal junk. The batches of beads are eroded and damaged to a greater or lesser extent.

No. 3126

Two dark beads, 10 mm in diameter and some fragments. They are quite badly eroded, without apparent decoration. The composition of the paste is heterogeneous, consisting of a thin dark outer layer, a pale beige intermediate layer (1 mm thick) and a heterogeneous core (dark green to white paste).

Two pale beige beads, each 9 mm in diameter. They are very eroded, without apparent decoration. The composition of the paste seems to be fairly homogeneous.

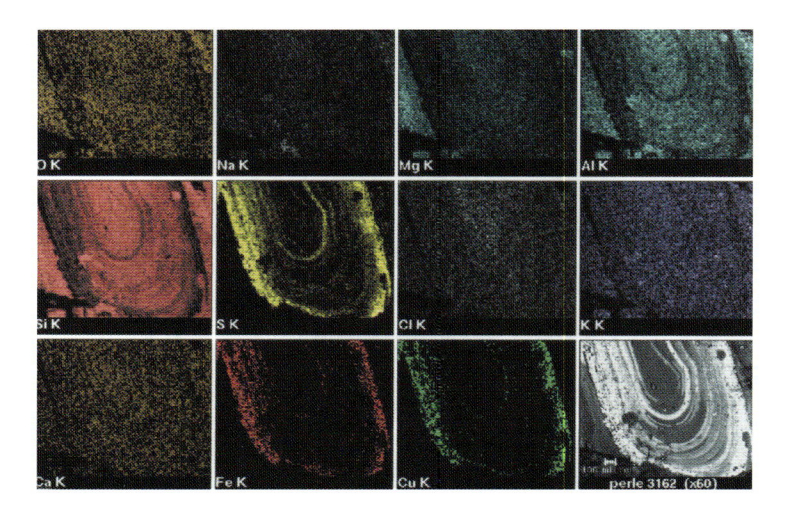

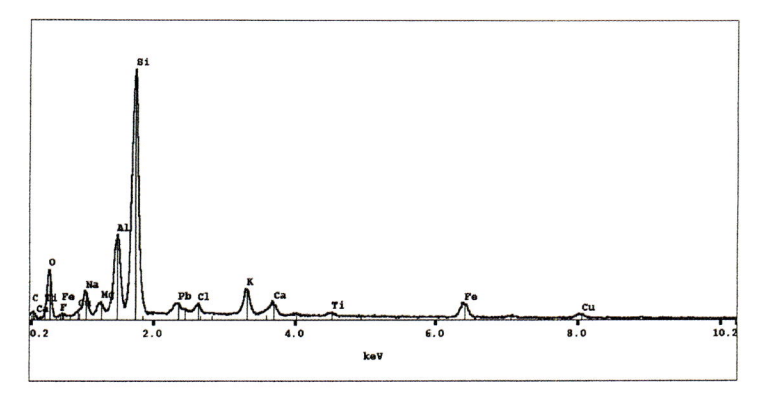

No. 3162, bead: composition of the outer zone.

No. 4157

Two dark brown beads, 10 mm in diameter. They are only slightly eroded, and lack apparent decoration. The composition of the bead is heterogeneous, with a thin dark-brown external layer, beneath which there is a green to beige paste. The interior is not visible.

One beige bead 8 mm in diameter. It is very eroded and does not show decoration. The composition of the paste seems to be homogeneous.

Four brown beads, 8 to 9 mm in diameter, of which two are stuck to each other. They are badly eroded, without apparent decoration. The composition of the bead shows a thin outer dark brown layer and a lighter heterogeneous inner part (beige to green).

No. 4158

Five blue beads, 6 to 7 mm in diameter. They are fairly seriously eroded, sometimes slightly encrusted, decorated with shallow grooves. The composition of the paste is homogeneous throughout the thickness of the bead.

No. 4267/1 (small blue beads)

Four blue beads, 5 to 6 mm in diameter and three fragments. They are very badly eroded, decorated with shallow grooves. The composition of the paste is homogeneous throughout the thickness of the bead.

No. 4267/2 (white beads and dark beads)

Three dark brown beads, 9 mm in diameter. They are only slightly eroded, without apparent decoration. They have a thin outer dark brown layer and an inner greenish-grey part.

One greyish-beige bead, 8 mm in diameter. It is slightly eroded, without apparent decoration. It seems to be composed of a thin outer brown layer and an inner beige part.

One creamy-white bead, 7 mm in diameter. It is slightly eroded, without apparent decoration. The composition of the paste shows a thin outer creamy-white layer and an inner white nacreous layer.

One nacreous white bead, 7 mm in diameter. It is slightly eroded, without apparent decoration. The composition of the paste seems to be homogeneous throughout the thickness of the bead.

No. 4681

Five blue beads, 7 to 8 mm in diameter, and a small fragment. They are only slightly eroded and incised with deep grooves. The composition of the paste is homogeneous throughout the thickness of the bead.

2. Analysed material

The time allocated for making these analyses was short. We prioritised two analyses corresponding to two different types of bead:

- brown beads made of heterogeneous paste (No 3162);
- blue beads made of homogeneous paste (No 4681).

3. Analyses performed

These consisted in determining the elements under a scanning electron microscope (SEM) attached to an EDX micro-analyser. The sample was bombarded by an electron beam to cause it to emit the X-rays specific to each element present.

3.1 No. 3162

For the brown beads (No. 3162), we selected a small fragment consisting of two layers, an intermediate pale-beige layer and a heterogeneous core. Preparation involved coating the surface with a layer of carbon, so as to make the sample conductive.

3.2 No. 4681

For the blue beads (No. 4681), minor preparation had been done on one of the beads (scraping off a few mm² to make a flat surface) so as to make the bombardment perpendicular to the surface of the object. The surface was also been covered with a thin carbon film.

4. Results
4.1 Brown beads (No. 3162)

The SEM revealed at least three different zones in the analysed fragment:
- an outer, dark-grey zone, at the right and left margins of the picture, that corresponds to the intermediate pale beige layer described previously (see paragraph 3.1);
- intermediate striped white to light grey zone;
- central dark grey zone.

These two latter zones correspond to the heterogeneous core described before (see paragraph 3.1). The corresponding graphs are attached.

4.1.1 Outer dark grey zone
The elements revealed were:
- silicon (Si on the graph)
- aluminium (Al on the graph)
- potassium (K on the graph)
- calcium (Ca on the graph)
- sodium (Na on the graph)
- magnesium (Mg on the graph)
- iron (Fe on the graph)
- copper (Cu on the graph)
- lead (Pb on the graph)
- titanium (Ti on the graph)
- fluorine (F on the graph)
- chlorine (Cl on the graph)
- oxygen (O on the graph)
- carbon (C on the graph).

The carbon derives in whole or in part from the film applied to the sample during preparation.

Oxygen has combined with other elements to form oxides.

The elements found were too numerous for us to be able to assess their respective proportions.

4.1.2 Intermediate striped zone
The elements found at a specific point in this zone (the most central white vein) were:
- silicon (Si on the graph)
- sulphur (S on the graph)
- aluminium (Al on the graph)
- potassium (K on the graph)
- calcium (Ca on the graph)
- sodium (Na on the graph)
- magnesium (Mg on the graph)
- iron (Fe on the graph)
- copper (Cu on the graph)
- titanium (Ti on the graph)
- chlorine (Cl on the graph)
- oxygen (O on the graph)
- carbon (C on the graph).

Lead is probably present, but masked by the sulphur line that is very prominent here.

The previous remarks apply.

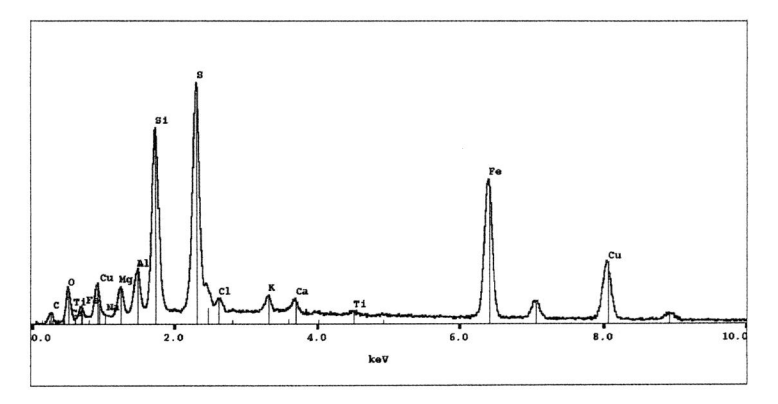

No. 3162, bead: composition of the striped intermediate zone.

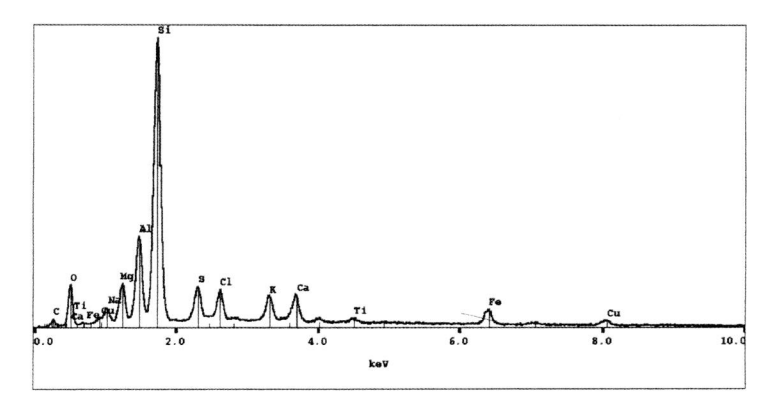

No. 3162, bead: composition of the central zone.

The composition of this zone is not identical to the previous one. Sulphur has been added and there are higher proportions of iron and copper.

4.1.3 Central dark grey zone
The elements found were:
- silicon (Si on the graph)
- sulphur (S on the graph)
- aluminium (Al on the graph)
- potassium (K on the graph)
- calcium (Ca on the graph)
- sodium (Na on the graph)
- magnesium (Mg on the graph)
- iron (Fe on the graph)
- copper (Cu on the graph)
- titanium (Ti on the graph)
- chlorine (Cl on the graph)
- oxygen (O on the graph)
- carbon (C on the graph).

Here again, lead is probably present, but hidden by the line of sulphur.

The previous notes are still valid.

The composition of this zone is very similar to that of the outer zone, except for the sulphur that is present in small amounts.

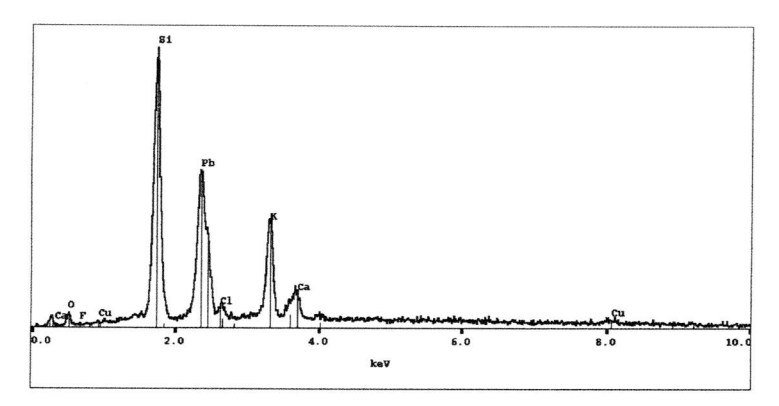

No. 4681, bead: composition of the matrix.

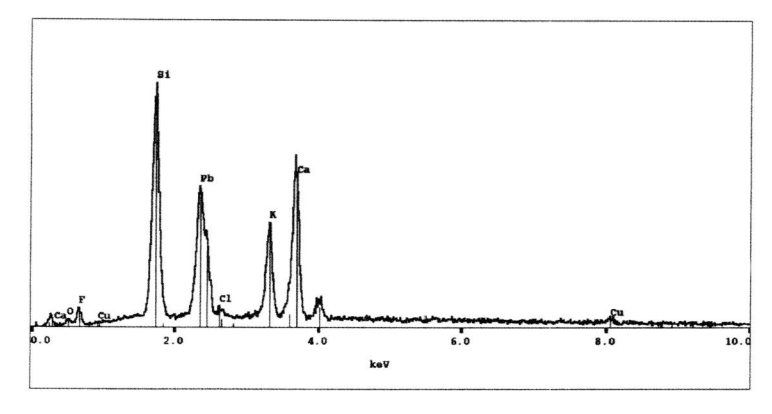

No. 4681, bead: composition of the angular chips.

4.1.4 Mapping the various elements on the analysed sample
The map is shown in the graph attached hereto. It indicates the relative concentrations of the elements in relation to the zones in which they were found. The codes of the elements are:
- O: oxygen
- Na: sodium
- Mg: magnesium
- Al: aluminium
- Si: silicon
- S: sulphur
- Cl: chlorine
- K: potassium
- Ca: calcium
- Fe: iron
- Cu: copper.

The following facts are noticed:
- elements such as sulphur, iron and copper are mainly concentrated in the intermediate striped zone. This explains its naturally dark colour (light zone on the SEM photograph);
- elements such as silicon and aluminium are concentrated in the outer and central zones;
- magnesium seems to be more heavily present in the outer zone.

The other elements show no or little restriction to particular zones.

4.1.5 Interpretation
This type of bead shows great complexity in its internal structure, as well as in its composition. The composition is a glass (silica) containing a great number of compounds that are difficult to combine.

In theory:
- aluminium could be combined with silicon and potassium and may derive from felspars such as potash felspar ($KalSi_3O_8$), used in glass-making;
- potassium carbonate (K_2CO_3 or potash obtained from wood ash) and sodium carbonate (Na_2CO_3 or soda obtained from algae ash) were used to lower the melting temperature and the viscosity of the glass;
- lime (CaO) and dolomite ($CaMg(CO_3)_2$) were added to stabilise the mix that is to make glass;
- elements such lead, iron and copper were probably combined with sulphur and derived from sulfides or sulfates;
- titanium probably derived from ilmenite ($FeTiO_3$) and, in this case, was associated with iron.

4.2 Blue beads (No. 4681)
Under the SEM, the composition of the analysed bead indicated a matrix in which small chips of material were

floating. The analyses centred on both these chips and the graphs for them are reproduced and attached hereto.

4.2.1 Matrix
The elements found were:
- silicon (Si on the graph)
- lead (Pb on the graph)
- potassium (K on the graph)
- calcium (Ca on the graph)
- chlorine (Cl on the graph)
- copper (Cu on the graph)
- fluorine (F on the graph)
- sodium (Na on the graph)
- oxygen (O on the graph)
- carbon (not mentioned on the graphs, the line furthest to the left).

The percentages of certain elements can be stated approximately:
- silicon: 23%
- lead: 5%
- potassium: 9%
- calcium: 3%
- copper: 0.3%.

Oxygen makes up the rest, to add up to 100%.

The carbon derives totally or partially from the film covering the sample during the preparation.

4.2.2 Chips
These chips floating in the matrix are identical to the previous ones. Only the percentages vary. It should be noted that the percentages of silica and lead decrease in favour of fluorine and especially calcium. The percentages of the other elements do not seem to vary.

4.2.3 Interpretation
Most of the material is silica (SiO_2) that has been melted at high temperature. Potassium is reputed to lower the melting temperature and the viscosity, and can derive either from potash (potassium carbonate K_2CO_3) derived from wood ash, or potassium chloride (KCl).

The behaviour of calcium seems to be linked to that of fluorine. It is thus possible that the chips of matter are rich in fluorite (CaF_2), another flux used mainly in the production of enamels.

Lead is very likely to have been introduced as lead monoxide or litharge (PbO). It is a crystalline yellow powder obtained by heating lead in presence of air and is used in the production of leaded glass (also called crystal, and sparkling and very clear in its known form).

Finally, copper in the form of copper oxide (CuO) may be present in order to colour glass green.

The bead is thus composed of melted glass (silica). Components such as potassium and fluorite were introduced to lower the melting point, and the lead was there to give the glass a sparkling appearance. The very small quantity of copper is a colourant.

There remains the problem of the blue colour of the beads. Could the green colouration due to the presence of copper oxide react with other compounds present to produce the blue colour? According to the literature, the blue colouration of glass is obtained by adding cobalt oxide.

Appendix 5
Analysis of the composition of a fragment of a gong

1. Item offered for analysis
This consisted of a fragment of a gong. The fragment measured 15 x 14 cm and about 1 mm thick.

2. Analyses performed
These consisted in examining the metal parts under a scanning electron microscope (SEM) attached to an EDX micro-analyser. When the sample is bombarded with an electron beam, it emits X-rays specific to each element present. A quantitative approach is also feasible.

This analysis was performed on a cross-section of small fragment measuring a few mm^2. The fragment was coated with a resin and then polished in order to make the bombardment perpendicular to the surface to be analysed.

3. Results
3.1 Mapping the elements
An SEM photograph of the analysed cross-section is attached. It shows three zones characterised by grey shading:
- a fissured, dark-grey peripheral zone which corresponds to the corroded surface area;
- a pale, homogeneous central zone;
- some small pale grey patches included in the central zone.

The peripheral zone is composed of tin, in the form of an oxide or hydroxide. Copper is no longer present, it has probably been dissolved out.

The two last areas, which had not been corroded, were quantitatively analysed.

3.2 Analysis of the non-corroded zones
The two elements found were:
- copper (Cu on the graph)
- tin (Sn on the graph).

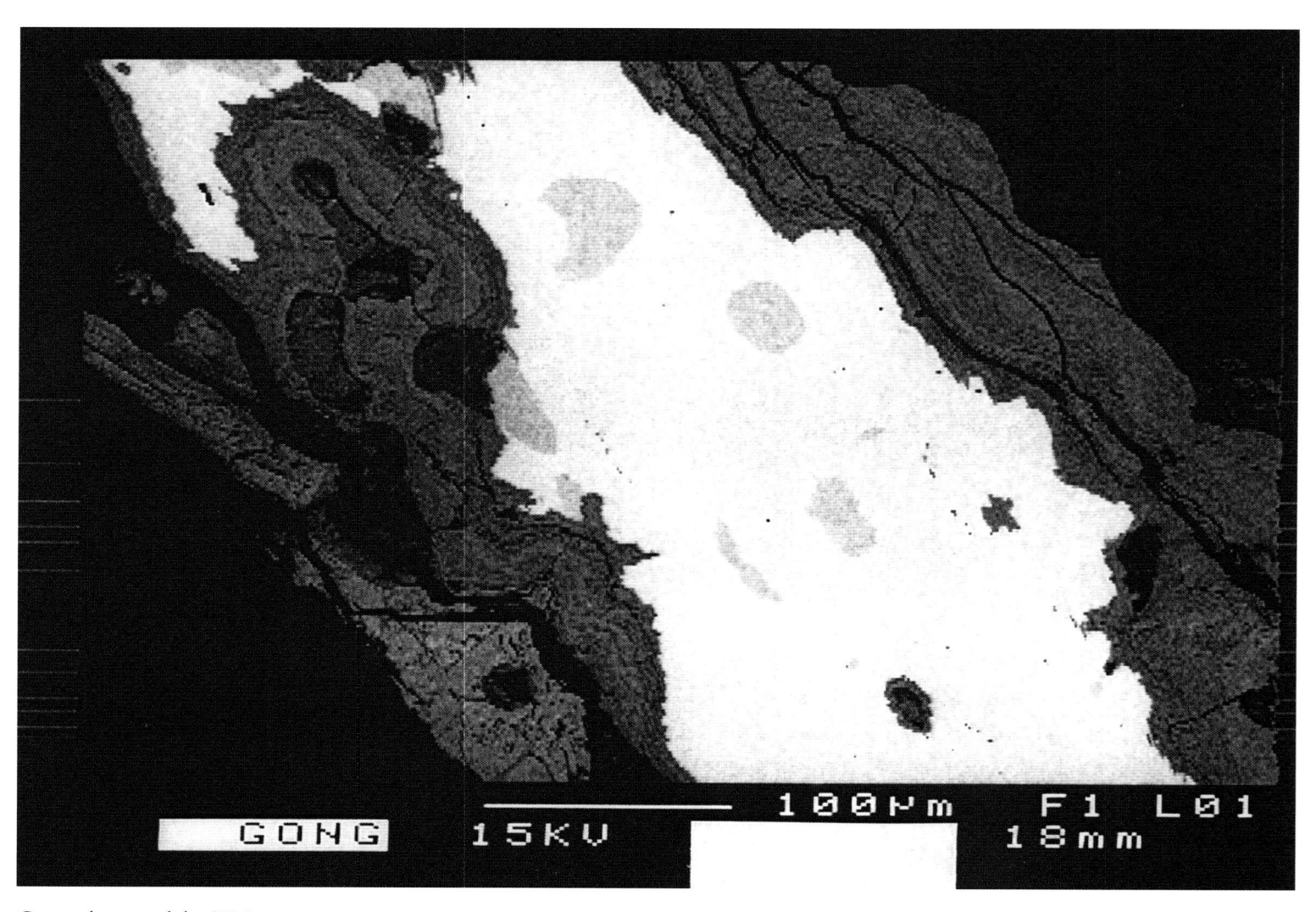

Gong: photograph by SEM.

Both elements show variable percentages in mass, depending on the zones. The graphs corresponding to the zones are attached.

In the pale, homogeneous central zone, the proportions are:
- copper: 61%
- tin: 39%.

In the light grey patches, proportions are:
- copper: 74%
- tin: 26%.

These proportions are accurate to the nearest percentage point and were tested at several sites on both the aforesaid zones.

The fragment is therefore made of bronze, an alloy of copper and tin, consisting of two phases in which the proportions of these two elements are noticeably different.

The commonest types of bronze contain 80 to 90% of copper by weight, but this object has a particularly high tin content. It would appear that the addition of tin hardens bronze and lowers its melting point.

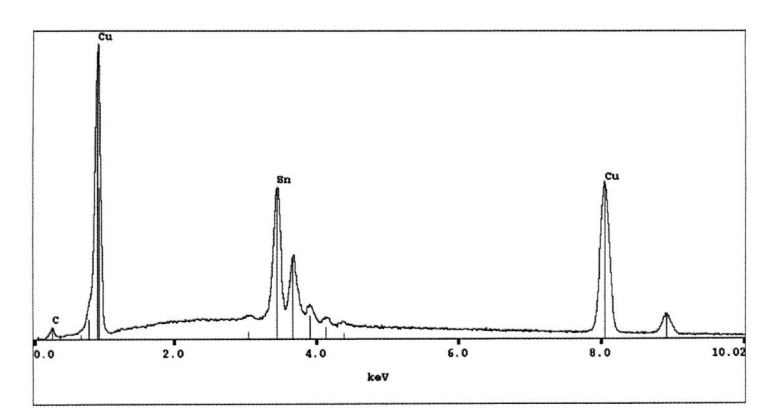

Gong: composition of the pale central zone (Cu: copper; Sn: tin).

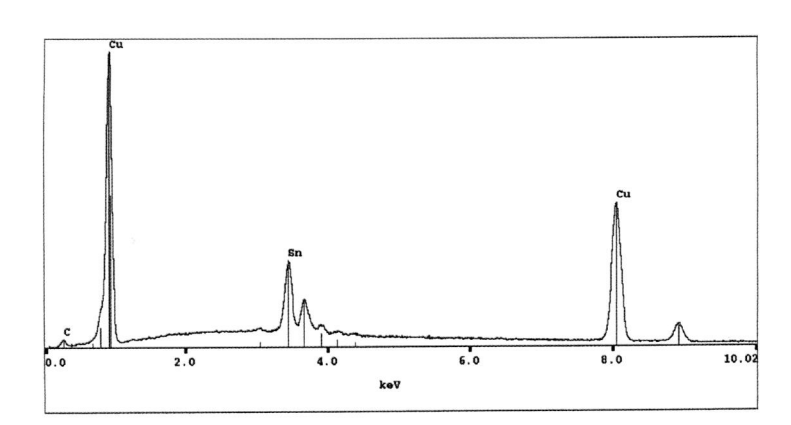

Gong: composition of the pale grey spots (Cu: copper; Sn: tin).

SELECTED BIBLIOGRAPHY

ADDIS, J. M., *Chinese Ceramics from Datable Tombs*, Sotheby Parke Bernet, London, 1978.

ADHYATMAN, S. and ABU RIDHO, *Tempayan-Martavans in Indonesia*, the Ceramic Society of Indonesia, Jakarta, 1984.

AGA-OGLU, K., *The Williams Collection of Far Eastern Ceramics*, Museum of Anthropology, University of Michigan, Ann Arbor, 1972.

ALLAN, J. W., "Later Mamluk Metalwork-II, A Series of Lunch-Boxes", *Oriental Art*, vol. XVII, No. 2, Summer 1971.

ATWELL, W., "Ming China and the Emerging World Economy, c. 1470–1650", *The Cambridge History of China, Vol. 8*, Twitchett and Mote, eds, Cambridge University Press, 1998.

AYERS, J. and KRAHL, R., *Chinese Ceramics in the Topkapi Saray Museum, Istanbul*, Sotheby's, London, 1986.

BLAIR, E. H. and ROBERTSON, J. A., *The Philippine Islands (1493–1898)*, vols II, III, XXXIII, Cleveland, Ohio, 1903–09.

BROWN, R., *The Ceramics of South-East Asia: Their Dating and Identification*, Oxford University Press, Singapore, 1977, 1988.

CARSWELL, J., *Blue and White Chinese Porcelain and Its Impact on the Western World*, The University of Chicago, The David and Alfred Smart Gallery, 1985.

CHAN, A., *The Glory and Fall of the Ming Dynasty*, Oklahoma, 1982.

CHANG FOUNDATION, *Imperial Hongwu and Yongle Porcelain Excavated at Jingdezhen*, Chang Foundation, Taibei, 1996.

CHANG FOUNDATION, *Xuande Imperial Porcelain Excavated at Jingdezhen*, Chang Foundation, Taibei, 1998.

CHEN CHING-KUANG, "Sea Creatures on Ming Imperial Porcelains", *The Porcelains of Jingdezhen*, Colloquies on Art & Archaeology in Asia, No. 16, R. Scott, ed., Percival David Foundation, London, 1993.

CHEN DA-SHENG and KALUS, L., *Corpus d'inscriptions arabes et persanes en Chine, I, Province du Fujian*, Bibliothèque d'études islamiques, Paris, 1991.

CHEN GAOHUA and CHEN SHANGSHENG, *Zhongguo haiwei jiaotongshi* (History of Chinese Overseas Communications), Wenjin chubanshe, Taibei, 1997.

CHEN JIARONG, et al., *Gudai Nanhai diming huishi* (A Dictionary of Place Names in the Nanhai Region), Zhonghua shuju, Beijing, 1986.

CHEN WENSHI, *Ming Hongwu Jiajing jian de haijin zhengce* (The Sea-Faring Prohibition Policy in the Early Ming Dynasty), Arts Faculty, National Taiwan University, Taibei, 1966.

CHINESE UNIVERSITY OF HONG KONG, *Archaeological Finds from the Five Dynasties to the Qing Periods in Guangdong*, The Art Gallery, the Chinese University of Hong Kong, 1989.

CHUAN HAN-SHENG, "The Overseas Trade of Macao after the Mid-Ming Period", *The Journal of the Institute of Chinese Studies of the Chinese University of Hong Kong*, vol. 5, No. 1, 1972.

CHUAN HAN-SHENG, "The Trade Between China and the Philippines during the Late Ming Period", *The Journal of the Institute of Chinese Studies of the Chinese University of Hong Kong*, vol. 1, 1968.

CLUNAS, C., *Superfluous Things*, Polity press, Cambridge, 1991.

COLOMBUS MUSEUM OF ART, *Shadow of the Dragon, Chinese Domestic and Trade Ceramics*, Colombus Museum of Art, 1982.

DARS, J., *La marine chinoise du Xe siècle au XIVe siècle*, Etudes d'histoire maritime 11, Economica, Paris, 1992.

DEFRÉMERY, C. and SANGUINETTI, B. R., *Voyages d'Ibn Battuta*, Paris, 1854.

DIAS, P., *Symbols and Images of Christianity on Chinese Porcelain*, Museu de São Roque, Lisbon, 1996.

DUPOIZAT, M-F., "Investigator Shoal wreck, Southern Song-Yuan dynasty", *Archaeological Report*, Paris, 1993

FAY-COOPER COLE, *Chinese Pottery in the Philippines*, Field Museum of Natural History, Publication 162, Anthropological Series, vol. XII, No. I, Chicago, 1912.

FOX, R. B., "The Calatagan Excavations", *Philippine Studies*, vol. 7, 1968.

FREESTONE, I. and GAIMSTER, D., eds, *Pottery in the Making*, British Museum Press, London, 1997.

FUNG PING SHAN MUSEUM, *Ceramic Finds from the Jingdezhen Kilns (10th–17th Century)*, exhibition catalogue, The Fung Ping Shan Museum, The University of Hong Kong, 1992.

GERNET, J., *Le monde chinois*, A. Colin, Paris, 1972.

GODDIO, F. et alii, *Royal Captain, a ship lost in the abyss*, Periplus Publishing London Ltd, London, 2000

GODDIO, F. and DUPOIZAT, M. F., "Breaker Reef wreck, Northen Song dynasty", *Archaeogical Report*, Paris, 1993.

GODDIO, F. and GUYOT DE SAINT MICHEL, E. J., *Griffin, on the Route of an Indiaman*, Periplus Publishing, London Ltd, London, 1999.

GODDIO, F., *Discovery and Archaeological Excavation of a 16th Century Trading Vessel in the Philippines*, Manila, 1988.

GODDIO, F., *Dossier Histoire et Archéologie, No. 113*, Archéologia, Quetigny/Turin, February, 1987.

GODDIO, F., *Weisses Gold*, Steidl Verlag, Göttingen, 1997.

GOODRICH, L. C. and CHAOYING FANG, *Dictionary of Ming Biography 1368–1644*, Columbia University Press, New York and London, 1976.

GOTUACO, L., TAN, R. C., DIEM, A. I., *Chinese and Vietnamese Blue and White Wares found in the Philippines*, Makati City : Bookmark, 1997.

GUY, J., *Ceramic Traditions of South-East Asia*, Oxford University Press Ltd, Singapore, 1989.

GUY, J., et al., *Thai Ceramics: the James and Elaine Connell Collection*, Asian Art Museum of San Francisco, Oxford University Press, Kuala Lumpur, 1993.

GUY, J., *Vietnamese Ceramics: A Separate Tradition*, Avery Press, 1997

HARRISSON, B., *Pusaka, Heirloom Jars of Borneo*, Oxford University Press, Singapore, 1986.

HARRISSON, B., *Asian Ceramics*, Princessehof Museum, Leeuwarden, 1986.

HIGGINS, R. L., "Privates in Gowns and Caps: Gentry Law-breaking in the Mid-Ming", *Ming Studies*, 10, Spring, 1980.

HUANG SHIJIAN, ed., *Zhongxi guangxi shi nianbiao* (A Chronological Table of Sino-Western Relations), Zhejiang renmin chubanshe, Hangzhou, 1994.

HUANG YUNPENG, et al., "Provincial Blue and White Porcelain from Jingdezhen", *Zhongguo Taoci Chuanji*, vol.19, Kyoto, 1983.

HUANG YUNPENG and ZHEN LI, *Jingdezhen minjian qinghua ciqi* (Jingdezhen Porcelains from Private Kilns), Renmin Meishu Chubanshe, 1988.

ITOI, K., *Thai Ceramics from the Sosai Collection*, Oxford University Press Ltd, Singapore, 1989

JUNKER, L. L., "Archaeological Excavations at the Late First Millenium and Early Second Millenium A.D. Settlement of Tanjay, Negros Oriental : Household organization, Chiefly Production and Social Ranking", *Philippine Quarterly of Culture and Society*, 21, 1993.

KACMERER, A., "La découverte de la Chine par les Portugais", *T'oung Pao*, 1944.

KRAHL and AYERS, *Chinese Ceramics in the Topkapi Saray Museum, Istanbul*, vols I & II, Sotheby's Publications, London, 1986.

LAM, P. Y. K., "Late 15th to Early 16th Century Blue and White Porcelain from Penny's Bay, Hong Kong"; "Ceramic Finds of the Ming Period from Penny's Bay. An Addendum.", *Journal of the Hong Kong Archaeological Society*, XIII, 1989–1992, Hong Kong Archaeological Society.

LAU, C., "Ceremonial Monochrome Wares of the Ming Dynasty", Colloquies on Art & Archaeology in Asia, No. 16, R. Scott, ed., Percival David Foundation, London, 1993.

LEDDEROSE, L., *Ten Thousand Things: Module and Mass Production in Chinese Art*, Princeton, 2000.

LEVENSON, J. A., ed., *Circa 1492: Art in the Age of Exploration*, National Gallery, Washington, 1991.

LI JINMING, *Mingdai haiwai moyi shi* (History of Overseas Trade in the Ming Period), Zhongguo shehui kexue chubanshe, Beijing, 1990.

LIN RENCHUAN, *Ming mo Qing chu siren haishang moyi* (Private Maritime Trade in the Late Ming and Early Qing). Huadong Shifan daxue chubanshe, Shanghai, 1987.

LION-GOLDSCHMIDT, D., *La Porcelaine Ming*, Office du Livre, Fribourg, 1978.

LIU XINYUAN, et al., *A Legacy of Chenhua*, The Jingdezhen Institute of Ceramic Archaeology and the Tsui Museum of Art, Hong Kong, 1993.

LIU XINYUAN, et al., *Imperial Hongwu and Yongle Porcelain Excavated at Jingdezhen*, exhibition catalogue, Chang Foundation, Taibei, 1996.

LOCSIN, L. C., *Oriental Ceramics Discovered in the Philippines*, Charles E. Tuttle Co, Vermont & Tokyo, 1967.

LOVINCY, C., *The Pearl Road: Tales of Treasure Ships*, Asiatype, Makati City, 1996.

MARCO POLO, *Le Devisement du monde. Le livre des merveilles. La Découverte*, éditions François Maspero, Paris, 1980.

MC ELNEY, B., "New Discoveries and Dating Concerning Some Blue and White Ceramics in the Museum's Collection", *The Museum of East Asian Art Journal*, vol. V, 1999.

MEDLEY, M., "Organization and Production at Jingdezhen in the Sixteenth Century", *The Porcelains of Jingdezhen*, Colloquies on Art & Archaeology in Asia No. 16, Rosemary Scott, ed., Percival David Foundation, London, 1993.

MEDLEY, M., *The Chinese Potter*, London, 1976.

MUSEUM OF ANTHROPOLOGY, UNIVERSITY OF MICHIGAN, *The Williams Collection of Far Eastern Ceramics: Tonancour Section*, Ann Arbor, 1975.

NANJING MUSEUM, *A Legacy of the Ming*, exhibition catalogue, Nanjing Museum and the Art Museum, The Chinese University of Hong Kong, 1996.

NEEDHAM, J., *Science and Civilisation in China*, Cambridge University Press, Cambridge, 1971.

ORIENTAL CERAMIC SOCIETY OF HONG KONG, *South East Asian and Chinese Trade Pottery*, exhibition catalogue, The Oriental Ceramic Society of Hong Kong, Hong Kong, 1979.

PACIFIC ASIA MUSEUM, *South-East Asian Ceramics from the Collection of Margot and Hans Ries*, Pacific Asia Museum, Pasadena, 1989.

PENG SHIFAN, ed., *Dated Qingbai Wares of the Song and Yuan Dynasties*, Ching Leng Foundation, 1998.

PINTO DE MATOS, M.-A., *Azul e Branco da China, Porcelana ao Tempo dos Descobrimentos*, IPM, Lisbon, 1997.

PINTO DE MATOS, M.-A., *Chinese Export Porcelain from the Museum Anastacio-Gonçalves*, IPM & Philip Wilson Publishers, Lisbon, 1996.

POPE, J. A., *Chinese Porcelains from the Ardebil Shrine*, Freer Gallery of Art, Smithsonian Institution, Washington D.C., 1956.

POPE, J. A., *Chinese Porcelains from the Ardebil Shrine*, Sotheby's, London, 1981.

RICHARDS, D., *South-East Asian Ceramics : Thai, Vietnamese, and Khmer from the Collection of the Art Gallery in South Australia*, Oxford University Press, Kuala Lumpur, 1995.

ROCKHILL, W., "Notes on the relations and trade of China with the eastern archipelago and the coast of the Indian Ocean during the fourteenth century", *T'oung Pao*, vol. XVI, Leyden, 1913.

SCOTT, R. and KERR, R., *Ceramic Evolution in the Middle Ming Period: Hongzhi to Wanli (1488–1620)*, Percival David Foundation, London, 1994.

SCOTT, R. and PIERSON, S., *Flawless Porcelains: Imperial Ceramics from the Reign of the Chenghua Emperor*, Percival David Foundation, London, 1995.

SCOTT, R., "The Imperial Collections, Collecting Chinese Art: Interpretation and Display", Colloquies on Art and Archaeology in Asia No. 20, Stacey Pierson, ed., Percival David Foundation, London, in press.

SCOTT, R., *Elegant Form and Harmonious Decoration: Four Dynasties of Jingdezhen Porcelain*, Percival David Foundation and Sun Tree Publishing, London/Singapore, 1992.

SCOTT, R. and KERR, R., *Ceramic Evolution in the Middle Ming Period*, Victoria & Albert Museum/Percival David Foundation, London, 1994.

SHAW, J., *Northern Thai Ceramics*, Oxford University Press, 1981.

SHEN GUANGYAO, *Zhongguo gudai duiwai moyi shi* (History of Overseas Trade in Ancient China), Guangdong renmin chubanse, Guangzhou, 1985.

SHEN LIXIN, ed., *Zhongwai wenhua jiaoliu shihua* (History of Cultural Exchange between China and Foreign Countries), Huadong shifan daxue chubanshe, Shanghai, 1991.

SMART, E., "Fourteenth Century Chinese Porcelain from a Tughlaq Palace in Delhi", *Transactions of the Oriental Ceramic Society*, vol. 41, 1975–77.

SOUTHEAST ASIAN CERAMIC SOCIETY, *Chinese Celadons and Other Related Wares in Southeast Asia*, Southeast Asian Ceramic Society, Singapore, 1979.

SOUTHEAST ASIAN CERAMIC SOCIETY, *Vietnamese Ceramics*, Southeast Asian Ceramic Society, Singapore, 1982.

SPRIGGS, A., "Oriental Porcelain in Western Paintings", *Transactions of the Oriental Ceramic Society*, 1964–66.

SUNG YING-HSING, *Chinese Technology in the Seventeenth Century*, Pennsylvania State University Press, 1966.

TANG BA HOANH, et al., *Gôm Chu Dâu*, Bao Tang Tinh Hai Hu'ng, 1993, 1999.

TSUI MUSEUM OF ART, *A Legacy of Chenghua*, The Tsui Museum of Art, Hong Kong, 1993.

TWITCHETT, D. and MOTE, F., eds, *The Cambridge History of China, Vol. 8: The Ming Dynasty, 1368–1644*, Cambridge University Press, Cambridge, 1998.

URBAN COUNCIL, HONG KONG, *Imperial Porcelain of the Yongle and Xuande Periods Excavated from the Site of the Ming Imperial Factory at Jingdezhen*, Urban Council, Hong Kong, 1989.

VALDES, C. O., NGUYEN LONG, K., BARBOSA, A. C., *A Thousand Years of Stoneware Jars in the Philippines*, Jar Collectors (Philippines), Manila, 1992.

VEHBI KOÇ FOUNDATION, *Chinese Ceramics in the Sadberk Hanim Museum*, Vehbi Koç Foundation-Sadberk Hanim Museum, Istanbul, 1995.

WANG GUANZHUO, *Zhongguo guchuan* (Ancient Chinese Ships), Haiyang chubanshe, Beijing, 1991.

WANG GUNGWU, "Early Ming Relations with Southeast Asia: A Background Essay", in J.K. Fairbank, *The Chinese World Order, Traditional Chinese Foreign Relations*, Harvard University Press, Cambridge, 1968.

WANG JIENAN, *Zhongguo yu Dongnan Ya wenhua jiaoliu shi* (History of the Cultural Exchange between China and Southeast Asia), Shanghai renmin chubanshe, Shanghai, 1998.

WANG YI-T'UNG, *Official Relations between China and Japan, 1368–1549*, Harvard University Press, Cambridge, 1953.

WANG YUDE, ed., *Ming Shilu neisu, shewai shiliao zhuan* (Classified Veritable Records of the Ming: Volume on Foreign Matters), Wuhan chubanshe, Wuhan, 1991.

WHEATLEY, P., "Geographical Notes on Some Commodities Involved in Sung Maritime Trade", *Journal of the Malay Branch of the Royal Asiatic Society*, vol. 32, 1959.

WIESNER, U., *Chinesische Keramik auf den Philippinen,* Museen der Stadt Köln, Museum für Ostasiatische Kunst.

WIESNER, U., *Seladon Swatow Blauweiss*, Museen der Stadt Köln, Museum für Ostasiatische Kunst, 1983.

WILLETS, W., *Ceramic Art of Southeast Asia*, The Southeast Asian Ceramic Society, Singapore, 1971.

WIRGIN, J., "Sung Ceramic Designs", *The Museum of Far Eastern Antiquities Bulletin*, No. 42, Stockholm, 1970.

WOOD, N., *Chinese Glazes*, London, 1999.

WU CHI-HUA, "Basic Foreign-policy Attitudes of the Early Ming Dynasty", *Ming Studies*, 12, Spring, 1981.

YAN-HUANG ART MUSEUM, *Yuan's and Ming's Porcelains unearthed from Jingdezhen*, Yan-Huang Art Museum, exhibition catalogue, Cultural Relics Publishing House, Beijing, 1999.

YEO, S. T., MARTIN, J., *Chinese Blue and White Ceramics*, Arts Orientalis, Singapore, 1978.

ZHANG JINGYUE, et al., *Shangshi tongjian* (A Chronological Record of Commerce in China), Jiuzhou tushu chubanshe, Beijing, 1996.

ZHANG WEIHUA, *Mingdai haiwai moyi jianlun* (A Brief Introduction to the Overseas Trade in the Ming Dynasty), Shanghai renmin chubanshe, Shanghai, 1956.

ZHAO RUGUA, *Chu-fan-chï* (description of the barbarian peoples), translated by F. Hirth and W. Rockhill, *Académie impériale des Sciences*, St. Petersburg, 1911.

ZHONGSHAN DAXUE, DONGNANYA LISHI, YANJIU SUO, eds, *Zhongguo guji zhong youguan feilubin ziliao huibian* (A Collection of documents on the Philippines Found in Ancient Chinese Texts), Zhonghua shuju, Beijing, 1980.

ZHU BOQIAN, *Celadons from Longquan Kilns*, Yishujia, Taibei, 1998.

LIST OF PLATES

Photo 1. The IEASM research vessel, *Kaimiloa*, used for magnetic surveying. 12

Photo 2. The barge *Thania* anchored by six anchors over the site. 13

Photo 3. The tumulus of the junk lay at a depth of 48 m. 14

Photo 4. Condition of the site at the start of archaeological excavations. 15

Photo 5. A label is completed by the diver at the time of discovery and is attached to a recovery net. Another label is attached to the object at the time it is recorded. 16

Photo 6. Close-up of labels. The lower is attached by the diver on finding an object; the upper when the find is recorded. 16

Photo 7. Recording search information on the database. 16

Photo 8. The porcelains are placed in plastic crates for recovery to the surface. 17

Photo 9. Rolls of porcelain bowls. 18

Photo 10. Piles of plates being discovered. 19

Photo 11. Remains of the bottom of the hull. It is possible to discern the double-lined construction. 22

Photo 12. The best preserved section of the hull's bottom. 23

Photo 13. A split between the planking reveals the lateral fastening at the joints. 24

Photo 14. Sections of a planking streak meeting in a Jupiter joint. 25

Photo 15. A section of the Lena Shoal junk's hull. 27

Photo 16. Rolls of porcelain bowls at 25-H. 29

Photo 17. Piles of dishes stacked horizontally and vertically at 24-L. 30

Photo 18. Piles of porcelain dishes lying directly on the wooden hull at 23-H. 31

Photo 19. The remains of a packing case with high quality porcelain pen boxes and pitchers. 32

Photo 20. Small, globular jars from Sawankhalok. 33

Photo 21. A jar from the kilns of Tao Maenam Noi. 34

Photo 22. Glass beads found inside a jar. 35

Photo 23. Detail of glass beads. 35

Photo 24. Examples of Siamese celadon ware. 36

Photo 25. Chinese celadon ware. 37

Photo 26. Vietnamese jars as found during the archaeological excavation. 38

Photo 27. Tin ingots and half-ingot. 39

Photo 28. Spiral brass bracelet 40

Photo 29. Imprint of braided palm leaves forming racks on which the bundles of iron pigs were stored. 40

Photo 30. Remains of a bamboo tie in an accretion of ingots. 40

Photo 31. Elephant tusks. — 41

Photo 32. Dish with underglaze cobalt blue decoration, Ming dynasty, Xuande mark and period, AD1426–35. Percival David Foundation of Chinese Art; PDF B679. — 59

Photo 33. Lobed vase with *qingbai* glaze. Song dynasty, late eleventh to early twelfth century. Percival David Foundation of Chinese Art; PDF A496. — 62

Photo 34. Pair of temple vases, the "David vases", with underglaze cobalt blue decoration. Yuan dynasty, dated 1351. Percival David Foundation of Chinese Art; PDF B613, B614. — 64

Photo 35. Ewer with underglaze copper red decoration, Ming dynasty, Hongwu period, late fourteenth century. Percival David Foundation of Chinese Art; PDF A696. — 65

Photo 36. Monk's cap ewer with incised decoration and *tian bai* glaze. Ming dynasty, Yongle period, 1403–24. Percival David Foundation of Chinese Art; PDF A426. — 66

Photo 37. Jar with underglaze blue and overglaze enamel decoration in *doucai* style, Ming dynasty, Chenghua mark and period, 1465–87. PDF 797. — 67

Photo 38. Bowl with copper red glaze, Ming dynasty, Xuande mark and period, 1426–35. Percival David Foundation of Chinese Art; PDF A529. — 67

Photo 39. Jar with enamel-on-biscuit decoration in *fahua* style, Ming dynasty, Hongzhi period, 1488–1505. Percival David Foundation of Chinese Art; PDF 759. — 68

Photo 40. Warming bowl with underglaze blue decoration, Ming dynasty, Hongzhi period, 1488–1505. Percival David Foundation of Chinese Art; PDF A623. — 69

Photo 41. Bowl with underglaze blue decoration, Ming dynasty, Chenghua mark and period, 1465–87. Percival David Foundation of Chinese Art; PDF A650. — 69

Photo 42. Ming temple vase from the Hongzhi period, 1496. Height: 62.1 cm. Percival David Foundation of Chinese Art; PDF 680. — 70

Photo 43. Blue and white water-dropper modelled as a mandarin duck. Inv. No. 165, from *Yuan's and Ming's Imperial Porcelains Unearthed from Jingdezhen*, Yan-Huang Art Museum, Beijing, Cultural Relics Publishing House, Beijing, 1999. — 72

Photo 44. Underwater photograph showing blue and white porcelain duck ewer with oval boxes. — 73

Photo 45. Porcelain pen box. Ming, Xuande period, 1426–1435. Length: 31.2 cm. Percival David Foundation of Chinese Art; PDF A629. — 74

Photo 46. Brass pen box, 1281. Designed by Mahmud ibn Sunqur. The British Museum (Inv. 91 6-23 5). — 75

Photo 47. Brass pen box (as above). — 75

Photo 48. Brass casket, engraved and inlaid with silver. Syrian, 15th c. The Metropolitan Museum of Art, The Edward C. Moore Collection, bequest of Edward C. Moore, 1891 (91.1.538). — 76

Photo 49. Brass tray, inlaid with silver, c. 1290. Made for Yusuf, Rasulid sultan of Yemen. Inv. No. 15153. Museum of Islamic Art, Cairo. — 76

Photo 50. Detail of brass tray (as above). — 76

Photo 51. Brass candle holder for Ahmad Shah *al naqqash*, Shiraz (?), third quarter of the 14th c. Pierre et Maurice Chuzeville/Musée du Louvre. Département des Antiquités Orientales, section Islam. No. OA7530. — 77

Photo 52. Detail of the central medallion of a blue and white porcelain dish from the Lena Shoal junk cargo. Inv. No. 2924. — 77

Photo 53. Large dish with peony decoration in the central medallion. — 79

Photo 54. *Ding* plate, 13th c. Diameter: 22.1 cm. Percival David Foundation of Chinese Art; PDF 171. — 80

List of plates

Photo 55. Large blue and white dish painted with a sea creature, Ming dynasty, Xuande mark and period. Jingdezhen Institute of Ceramic Archaeology, Jingdezhen, Jiangxi province, China. — 82

Photo 56. Central detail of a blue and white dish with an elephant from the Lena Shoal junk. — 83

Photo 57. Porcelain stem cup, 15th c., Ming dynasty, Xuande period, 1426–35. diameter: 10 cm. Percival David Foundation of Chinese Art; PDF B638 — 84

Photo 58. Tripod perfume-burner with mountains and waves decoration, Ming porcelain, Yongle period. Jingdezhen Institute of Ceramic Archaeology, Jianxi, China. — 84

Photo 59. Plate, *ding* ware, 11th to 12th c. diameter: 28.7 cm. Percival David Foundation of Chinese Art; PDF 117. — 85

Photo 60. Dayao village at the foot of the kiln sites. — 87

Photo 61. This river, running by Longquan, was used for transportation and had higher water levels at the time of production. — 87

Photo 62. Blue and white porcelain bottle decorated with the symbols of the Passion. Height: 38.5 cm. British Museum (Brook Sewell Bequest 1963.5-20.7). — 90

Photo 63. The Jade Temple, the cast-iron pagoda near Tang-Yang Hsien in the province of Hopei. It was built in 1061 (after Boerschmann). — 234

Photo 64. Bridge suspended on iron chains in the province of Yunnan (photo: Potts-Popper). — 235

Photo 65. Metal accretion of iron needles found inside a little porcelain vase, Inv. 2128. — 235

Photo 66. Pepper was found inside a porcelain box, Inv. 2618. — 249

Photo 67. Underside of a laquered box, on which can be read a Chinese character. — 256

Photo 68. A woman's lacquerware comb still in excellent state of preservation. — 256

Photo 69. Lacquerware container with lid. — 257

Photo 70. Lacquerware container. — 257

Photo 71. Underside of lacquerware container. — 257

Fig. 1. Detail of map of Asia (VE94). Reproduced by permission of the Controller of Her Majesty's Stationary Office and the United Kingdom Hydrographic Office. — XIV

Fig. 2. River boats. Detail of Riverside Scene at the Qingming Festival in Kaifeng by Zhang Zeduan, Northern Song dynasty, 12th c. Collection of the Palace Museum, Beijing. — 3

Fig. 3. River boat by a bridge. Detail of Riverside Scene at the Qingming Festival in Kaifeng by Zhang Zeduan, Northern Song Dynasty, 12th c. Collection of the Palace Museum, Beijing. — 3

Fig. 4. Map of maritime routes employed by junks in the 15th c. — 5

Fig. 5. Page from the *Shun Fêng Hsiang Sung* (Laud MS, Or. 145 folio 53 v.). Reproduced by permission of the Bodleian Library, Oxford University. — 7

Fig. 6. Map showing the positions of wrecks discovered by l'IEASM in the vicinity of the island of Palawan. — 8

Fig. 7. Map AC 4058, reproduced by permission of the Controller of Her Majesty's Stationary Office and the Hydrographic Offices of France and the UK. — 9

Fig. 8. Map (Casa No. 70) from the Atlas de Fermão Vaz Dourado, 1571. Reproduced by permission of the Instituto dos Arquivos Nacionais/Torre do Tombo, Lisbon. — 10–11

Fig. 9. Diagram of the grid laid over the Lena Shoal wreck site showing the location of the various artefacts. — 20–21

Fig. 10. Section of planking on the Lena Shoal wreck. — 23

Fig. 11. Fastening between two rows of planking. — 24

Fig. 12. Diagram of a Jupiter joint. — 25

Fig. 13. Official portrait of Zhu Youtang (1470–1505), the Hongzhi emperor who reigned 1488–1505. Hanging scroll, ink and colour on silk. 209.8 x 115 cm. Collection of the National Palace Museum, Taibei. — 42

Fig. 14. Nanjing, the Ming southern capital with the Treasure Ship Yard. A page from *Zheng He hanghai tu* (Maritime Maps of Zheng He). Woodblock illustration reprint from Wubei zhi, 1628. — 44

Fig. 15. A page from a 15th c. navigation logbook supposedly used by the Zheng He team from the *Zheng He hanghai tu* (Maritime Maps of Zheng He). Woodblock illustration reprint from Wubei zhi, 1628. — 45

Fig. 16. Chinese description of the Sulu Islands. A page from *Xiyang chaogong dian lu* (A Record of Tribute States from the Western Oceans) by Huang Shengzeng, preface dated 1520. — 47

Fig. 17. Woodblock illustrations from a 16th c. travel book. Reprinted from *Tuxiang nanbei liangjing lucheng* (Illustrated travel guide from Nanjing to Beijing). Published by Qinxian shutang, 1535. — 48

Fig. 18. City scenes of Nanjing, the southern capital of the Ming dynasty by a 16th c. painter. Section from a handscroll, ink and colour on silk. Height: 44 cm. Collection of the Chinese Museum of History, Beijing. — 49

Fig. 19. Detail from Fig. 18. — 49

Fig. 20. Portrait of Ferdinand Magellan (1480–1521). © Corbis Agency. — 51

Fig. 21. Entry on Sulu from a 15th c. Chinese publication. A page from *Da Ming yitong zhi* (Historical Geography of the Great Ming). Compiled by Li Xian in 1461. — 52

Fig. 22. Barbarian couple from Sulu. Woodblock from *Huang Qing zhigongtu* (Pictures of Tribute Bearers to the Great Qing Empire). Reprinted from *Siku chuanshu* (The Siku Encyclopedia), 1782. — 53

Fig. 23. Spanish couple in Luzon. Woodblock illustration from *Huang Qing zhigongtu*. Reprinted from *Siku chuanshu*, 1782. — 53

Fig. 24. The Treasure Ship Yard in Nanjing. Woodblock illustration from the 1553 edition of the *Longjiang Chuanchang zhi*. — 54

List of plates

Fig. 25. Drawing of a five-masted freighter to give some indication of the probable type of build of the much larger Treasure Ships of the fleet of Zheng He in the 15th c. — 55

Fig. 26. A Shachuan freighter in full sails. — 56

Fig. 27. A large Fujian warship. Woodblock illustration from a Ming treatise. — 56

Fig. 28. A Guangdong warship. Woodblock illustration from a Ming treatise. — 56

Fig. 29. Drawing of a Shachuan freighter. — 57

Fig. 30. A *Fengzhou*, government ocean-going junk. Woodblock illustration from the 1757 *Liuqiu guo zhilue*. — 57

Fig. 31. Map of Chinese kiln sites. — 58

Fig. 32. *Suihan sanyou tu* (The Three Friends of Winter) by Zhao Mengtian (1199–1264), National Palace Museum, Taibei, Taiwan. — 78

Fig. 33. *The Feast of the Gods* by Giovanni Bellini, oil on canvas, 1.702 x 1.880 m, National Gallery of Art, Washington. Widener Collection. — 78

Fig. 34. *Sui zhao tu* (Flowers of the New Year) by Zhao Chang (active 960–1016), Northern Song dynasty, painted on silk scroll. National Palace Museum, Taibei, Taiwan. — 79

Fig. 35. *Two Carps Leaping among Waves*, anonymous, Yuan dynasty, 14th c., hanging scroll. Reproduced courtesy of the Museum of Fine Arts, Boston, all rights reserved. — 80

Fig. 36. *Qiupu shuangyuan* (Two Birds in the Autumn) attributed to Huichong (965–1017), Northern Song dynasty. National Palace Museum, Taibei, Taiwan. — 80

Fig. 37. *Kumu zhu shi* (Old tree with a Bird, Bamboo and Rock), attributed to Zhao Mengfu (1254–1322), Yuan dynasty. National Palace Museum, Taibei, Taiwan. — 81

Fig. 38. *Scholar Seated under a Tree*, Wu Wei, Ming dynasty. Reproduced courtesy of the Museum of Fine Arts, Boston. — 81

Fig. 39. *Deer in an Autumnal Wood*, anonymous, Five Dynasties, 10th to 11th c. National Palace Museum, Taibei, Taiwan. — 85

Fig. 40. *Renwu* (Portrait of a Scholar), anonymous, 11th c., Northern Song dynasty. National Palace Museum, Taibei, Taiwan. — 85

Fig. 41. Still-life oil painting depicting *kraak* porcelain bowls holding fruit, attributed to Osias Beert. Rijkmuseum, Amsterdam; Inv. A2549. — 94

Fig. 42. Woman playing a gong. — 238

Fig. 43. Chinese painting from the end of the 16th c. depicting a game of *weiqi*. Private collection, Paris. — 254

PHOTOGRAPHIC CREDITS

Frederic Osada

Photo Nos
1, 2, 3, 4, 5, 6, 7, 8, 9, 10, 11, 12, 13, 14, 15, 16, 17, 18, 19, 20, 21, 26, 27, 28, 29, 30, 44, 19, 20, 21, 69, 70, 71.

Typology Nos
6, 7, 8, 13, 15, 36, 37, 38, 39, 40, 41, 42, 43, 44, 53, 54, 57, 58, 61, 66, 67, 70, 78, 81, 83, 85, 95, 99, 107, 116, 126, 127, 128, 129, 130, 134, 135 136, 137, 138, 139, 140, 141, 142, 143, 144, 145, 148, 149, 151, 153, 155, 156, 157, 158, 159, 163, 164, 165, 168, 169, 170, 173, 174, 175, 189, 196, 227, 228, 230, 243, 244, 245, 246, 253, 254, 256, 257, 258, 260, 261, 265, 268, 271, 277, 278, 280, 282, 288, 290, 291, 292, 293, 294, 295, 296, 297, 298, 299, 300, 301, 302, 306, 307, 308, 309, 310, 311, 312, 313, 314, 315, 316, 317, 319, 320, 321, 322, 323, 324, 325, 326, 328, 329, 330, 331, 332, 333, 334, 335, 336, 337, 338, 339, 340, 341, 342, 344, 345, 347, 348, 350, 355, 356, 357, 358, 359, 360, 361, 362, 363, 364, 365, 366, 367, 368, 369, 370, 371, 372, 373, 374, 375, 376, 377, 378, 379, 380, 381, 382.
© HILTI Foundation - Franck Goddio.

IEASM

Photo Nos
22, 23, 31, 65, 66, 67, 68.

Typology Nos
349, 352, 353, 354, 383, 384, 385, 386, 387, 388, 389, 390, 391, 392, 393, 394, 395, 396, 397, 398, 399, 400, 401, 402.
© HILTI Foundation - Franck Goddio.

Marian Gerard Photographs

Photo Nos
24, 25, 53

Page Nos
96–97, 114–115, 135, 185, 190–191, 196–197, 209–210, 220–221, 229.

Typology Nos
1, 3, 5, 9, 11, 12,14, 28 , 33, 34, 35, 50, 51, 51, 52, 55, 56, 60, 62, 63, 64, 65, 68, 69, 71, 77, 80, 84, 86, 89, 93, 96, 106, 112, 117, 118, 119, 120, 121, 122, 123, 124, 125, 146, 147, 150, 152, 154, 167, 172, 176, 177, 186, 187, 188, 193, 195, 197, 207, 211, 215, 219, 221, 223, 225, 226, 229, 233, 234, 237, 239, 240, 242, 251, 252, 255, 266, 267, 269, 275, 276, 283, 284.
© HILTI Foundation - Franck Goddio.

Monique Crick

Photo No.
56.

Typology Nos
4, 10, 16, 17, 18, 22, 23, 24, 25, 26, 27, 29, 30, 31, 32, 45, 46, 47, 48, 49, 71b, 72, 73, 74, 75, 76, 79, 87, 88, 90, 91, 92, 94, 97, 98, 100, 101, 102, 103, 104, 105, 108, 109, 110, 111, 113, 114, 115, 131, 160, 161, 162, 166, 171, 178, 179, 180, 181, 182, 183, 184, 185, 190, 191, 192, 194, 198, 199, 200, 201, 202, 203, 204, 205, 206, 213, 214, 208, 209, 210, 212, 213, 214, 216, 217, 218, 220, 222, 224, 227, 228, 231, 232, 235, 236, 238, 241, 247, 248, 249, 250, 259, 262, 263, 264, 270, 272, 273, 274, 279, 281, 285, 286, 287, 289, 303, 304, 305, 343, 346.

Monique Crick would like to thank Sophie Chéry for her enormous work in assembling and cleaning the images used in the typology.

Dirk Reinartz

Typology Nos
2, 59, 132, 133.
© Dirk Reinartz.

FENTRESS BRADBURN ARCHITECTS
MUSEUMS + THEATERS

EDIZIONI PRESS

COPYRIGHT (C) 2003 *by* EDIZIONI PRESS, INC.
All rights reserved. No part of this book may be reproduced in any form
without written permission of the copyright owners.
All images in this book have been reproduced with the consent of the artists
concerned and no responsibility is accepted by producer,
publisher or printer for any infringement of copyright or otherwise, arising
from the contents of this publication. Every effort has been
made to ensure that credits comply with information supplied.

FIRST PUBLISHED IN
THE UNITED STATES OF AMERICA

by EDIZIONI PRESS, INC.
469 WEST 21ST STREET
NEW YORK, NEW YORK 10011
WWW.EDIZIONIPRESS.COM

ISBN: 1-931536-32-5
PORTIONS OF THIS VOLUME FORMERLY APPEARED IN:
ISBN: 1-931536-00-7
LIBRARY OF CONGRESS CATALOGUE
CARD NUMBER: 2001086704
PRINTED *in* ITALY

DESIGN AND COMPOSITION: Ethan Trask, Adam Michaels
COVER: Carl Dalio
BACK COVER PHOTO: Nick Merrick/Hedrich-Blessing

■ INTRODUCTION

4-7 TOWARD A CRITICAL REGIONALISM
DAVID DILLON

8-11 DESIGNING PUBLIC SPACE: PROCESS/CONCEPTS/IDEAS
CURT FENTRESS, FAIA

■ MUSEUMS + THEATERS

14-19 NATIONAL MUSEUM OF WILDLIFE ART *JACKSON, WYOMING*

20-27 THE NATIONAL MUSEUM OF THE MARINE CORPS
AND HERITAGE CENTER *QUANTICO, VIRGINIA*

28-31 DRAPER MUSEUM OF NATURAL HISTORY
BUFFALO BILL HISTORICAL CENTER *CODY, WYOMING*

32-35 WHITNEY GALLERY OF WESTERN ART
BUFFALO BILL HISTORICAL CENTER *CODY, WYOMING*

36-39 BUFFALO BILL HISTORICAL CENTER
RENOVATION & EXPANSION *CODY, WYOMING*

40-47 NATIONAL COWBOY AND WESTERN HERITAGE MUSEUM
OKLAHOMA CITY, OKLAHOMA

48-53 MUSEUM OF WESTERN ART *DENVER, COLORADO*

54-57 BLACK AMERICAN WEST MUSEUM AND HERITAGE CENTER
DENVER, COLORADO

58-61 LEGACY OF FLIGHT *SPRINGFIELD, MISSOURI*

62-67 PEERY'S EGYPTIAN THEATER
AND THE DAVID ECCLES CONFERENCE CENTER *OGDEN, UTAH*

68-71 THE AUDITORIUM
COLORADO CONVENTION CENTER PHASE II EXPANSION
DENVER, COLORADO

72-73 ARVADA CENTER FOR THE ARTS AND
HUMANITIES EXPANSION *DENVER, COLORADO*

■ APPENDIX

74 CREDITS

75 ACKNOWLEDGMENTS
JIM BRADBURN, FAIA

TOWARD A CRITICAL REGIONALISM
DAVID DILLON

THE DESIGN OF THE GREAT HALL IN MADRID/BARAJAS AIRPORT (MADRID, SPAIN) INCORPORATED THE ARCH BOTH AS AN ARCHITECTURAL REFERENCE AND A STRUCTURAL MEMBER.

THIS SECTION OF THE MADRID BARAJAS AIRPORT MODEL SHOWS THE APPROACH ROAD (FRONT), THE TRAIN STATION (RIGHT) AND THE GREAT HALL (TOP CENTER).

Fentress Bradburn Architects was launched in 1980 by two young architects who felt that they had learned what they could from prestigious East Coast firms and wanted to try something different, "out West," where precedent has a less tenacious grip on the imagination.

Curt Fentress, then 32, had spent six years at I.M Pei and Partners before moving across town to fledgling Kohn Pedersen Fox. His partner Jim Bradburn, only two years older, had worked for Roche Dinkeloo, the successor to Eero Saarinen's celebrated firm in Hamden, Connecticut. They had big ideas, substantial experience and no money, which in the "Shoot the Moon" '80s passed for a business plan.

Twenty years later, Fentress Bradburn Architects has 90 employees, 30 of whom are architects, and projects around the world, including airports, museums, convention centers and office buildings. Two-thirds of the firm's work is public, with an increasing amount located in the new frontier that is the Middle East. To each project the firm brings solid modernist credentials coupled with an unusual sensitivity to place and enthusiasm for the expressive potential of technology.

Adventurous without being avant-garde, Fentress Bradburn has designed more than 100 careful, sophisticated buildings, many for clients who are more inclined toward expediency than art. And they have done it without devolving into just another characterless corporate office with a detail kit and a slick brochure. Their work is typically bold and graphic yet it is not enslaved to geometry. At the same time, Fentress Bradburn has no signature style, no single big idea or theoretical mantra that drives its designs. Each project is an exploration of a particular problem in a particular circumstance, and, consequently, takes on a character of its own. Their goal is pragmatic problem-solving, without the imposition of a signature look.

"After all these years, it still feels like a couple of guys having fun," says Jim Bradburn.

But the early days were anything but fun. Initially buoyed by Denver's oil and gas boom, Fentress Bradburn's fortunes fell as dramatically as energy prices. Speculative office development, fueled by dreams of $50 a barrel oil, dried up overnight, leaving the firm with little work and looming bankruptcy. Rescue came in the form of the Colorado Convention Center in Denver, a 1987 competition project for which the firm's primary qualification was dire need. Through shrewd urban analysis, the architects determined that a downtown convention center, only two blocks from the 16th Street Mall, would be more profitable and generate more new development than one located on the fringes, where the other competitors had chosen sites. The city fathers agreed and awarded them the contract over, among others, I.M Pei and Partners.

The finished building seems stolid and bunkerish when compared to Fentress Bradburn's later work, but it came in on time and under budget and gave the struggling firm the necessary credentials for large public work. Shortly thereafter, Fentress Bradburn was hired to redesign the main terminal of the new Denver International Airport.

"We got DIA by persuading the city that an airline terminal was like a convention center," Fentress recalls. "Both are two or three stories tall, with long spans, huge traffic volumes and lots of daily wear and tear."

But that was only part of the story. The original terminal design, by another firm, was a prosaic steel-and-glass ziggurat that had all the excitement of a pound cake. It was over budget and behind schedule. With critics howling and time running out, the city told Fentress Bradburn to come up with an image that would put Denver on the map by capturing the excitement and romance of travel— and to do it in three weeks.

WHEN OFFICIALS WANTED TO MINIMIZE WINDOW SPACE ON THE COLORADO CONVENTION CENTER (DENVER, COLORADO), THE DESIGNERS FUNNELED ALL FENESTRATION TO THE BUILDING'S TWO ENTRANCES.

Their solution was a cable-stretched fabric roof configured into an abstract profile of the Rocky Mountains. The forms are apparitional, a congeries of late 20th century technology in a 19th century prairie setting, but the basic concept had been around since the early 1950s, when Frei Otto and others began experimenting with tensile structures for pavilions and theaters.

"We didn't do that roof just to be different," insists Bradburn. "Given the budget problems and the schedule, it was the simplest and most economical solution."

Drawing on his experience at Roche Dinkeloo, Bradburn and his team visited fabric manufacturers, tested glues and cables, studied the effects of wind and snow loads, even discovered how to bleach the yellow out of the fabric to make it look snowier. The roof turned out to be light, scenographic and energy efficient, admitting enough daylight by which to read a newspaper, then acting as a gigantic reflector at night. Down below, instead of a blandly efficient passenger terminal, the architects created a dramatic civic space, divided into three large rooms and filled with trees, benches, several tiers of shops, even a bronze statue of local aviation pioneer Elrey B. Jeppesen. The firm's other airports have comparable spaces, as do major civic buildings such as the Clark County and Jefferson County government centers.

DIA put both Denver and Fentress Bradburn on the map, enhancing its reputation for making sophisticated technology work for clients. Although it avoids the label "green architects," the firm continues to excel at environmental design.

"We've come to like the complex stuff and the associations with other disciplines that it makes possible," says Fentress. "It allows us to grow intellectually."

The State of Washington Natural Resources Building in Olympia, Washington, completed in 1992, won numerous awards for its sophisticated air quality and energy conservation programs, including its comprehensive use of recyclable materials and the installation of nearly 200 air monitors throughout the building.

The David E. Skaggs Research Center in Boulder, Colorado, headquarters for the National Oceanic and Atmospheric Administration, was shaped by a different set of environmental imperatives. A long, low Colorado sandstone structure — four stories and nearly 900 feet — meanders along the banks of a historic waterway while preserving views of the Flatiron Mountains to the west. (The front half of the site was donated to the city for a park.) To reduce its apparent mass, the architects broke it into four crisp blocks and marked the joint with expressed staircases and terraces. All laboratories and support spaces are in the center of the building; the exterior walls were reserved for offices and conference rooms. Even basement offices look out to gardens and landscaped patios.

The Skaggs Building underscores Fentress Bradburn's search for what it calls "a contextual regionalism." This is not the regionalism of shed roofs and peanut brittle rock work, a lick and stick regionalism that is primarily about style. It is the kind of regionalism that is rooted in place and local cultural tradition; that is symbolic, as well as literal; and that acknowledges what is intimated and unsaid, as well as what is expressed. It is a regionalism that considers the individual building as part of a larger whole.

At Denver International Airport, the big picture includes mountains, prairie and enveloping sky coming together in a place where there is no middle distance, only near and far. For the Doha International Airport in Qatar, the architects adapted the form of a traditional wooden fishing ship, a *dhow*, for the main terminal and public spaces, using its low masts and triangular sails to suggest a vessel in motion. Elsewhere, they used traditional Qatari patterns for floor tiles and as frits around windows and skylights. These details, together with native trees and plants, create a national gateway, not just a point of entry.

In the new Seoul Incheon International Airport in Seoul, South Korea, the architects appropriated the base,

CURBSIDE CANOPIES AT DENVER INTERNATIONAL AIRPORT (DENVER, COLORADO) ARE MADE OF THE SAME TENSILE-MEMBRANE FABRIC AS THE PEAKS OF ITS GREAT ROOF.

THE UPPER FLOORS OF THE NATURAL RESOURCES BUILDING (OLYMPIA, WASHINGTON) ARE SUPPORTED BY PILLARS DESIGNED AS ABSTRACT TREES.

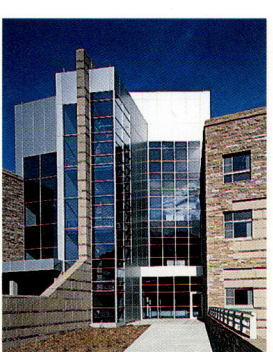

THE STAIRWELLS AND ENTRYWAYS OF THE DAVID E. SKAGGS FEDERAL BUILDING (BOULDER, COLORADO) ARE CONSTRUCTED OF ALUMINUM AND GLASS, MATERIALS WHICH SPEAK OF THE SCIENTIFIC ACTIVITIES WITHIN THE FACILITY.

CLERESTORIES IN THE ROOF OVER THE GREAT HALL AT SEOUL INCHEON INTERNATIONAL AIRPORT (SEOUL, KOREA) ADMIT ENOUGH LIGHT TO SUPPORT TREES GROWING INSIDE THE BUILDING.

A NEW CONFERENCE ROOM LEVEL AT 421 BROADWAY (DENVER, COLORADO) IS DESIGNATED ON THE EXTERIOR BY ALUMINUM CLADDING AND TOPPED BY A PYRAMID-SHAPED SKYLIGHT.

THE NATIONAL MUSEUM OF WILDLIFE ART (JACKSON, WYOMING) BLENDS INTO ITS CONTEXT ON THE SIDE OF A ROCKY BLUFF.

column and catenary system of the traditional Korean temple for the passenger concourses and the roof of the main terminal. Traditional Korean gardens, placed strategically throughout the terminal, soften the effect of all the steel and glass. Yet, in each case, the traditional elements go beyond mere mimicry of familiar details to create a fresh synthesis of past and future.

The most striking example of this contextual regionalism is the National Museum of Wildlife Art in Jackson, Wyoming, completed in 1996. Local pressure to produce a nostalgic, board-and-batten frontier look was intense. What was the frontier West if not that? Instead, the architects found their inspiration in the Tetons and in the Native-American history of the area. The completed building resembles an outcropping of rock, most of it tucked into the hillside and the remainder sculpted into an abstraction of a cliff dwelling. Native grasses grow up to the walls on three sides, merging their edges with the surrounding landscape. The stone that covers the exterior reappears inside as walls and staircases; logs from the Yellowstone fire of 1988 were recycled into beams and posts.

Some visitors complain that the museum is so discreet that they drive right past it, a complaint that underscores Fentress Bradburn's subtlety as it occasionally irritates curators. The National Museum of Wildlife Art is not a self-important object, architecture with a capital 'A'; it does not engage in hand-to-hand combat with its exhibits. Rather, it makes a case for the importance of place, context, appropriateness and the conservation of resources.

Since the late 1980s, public work played a central role in Fentress Bradburn's practice, not only because of its programmatic complexity and formal challenges, but also because the partners genuinely enjoy it; they even enjoy the interminable public meetings and Byzantine negotiations with government agencies. Over the years, they have learned to listen, to question and to respond to the public's concerns and criticisms. This is not a process that can be faked or undertaken half-heartedly.

"A lot of architects are scared of it," says Fentress, "but it fits the way we like to work. We try not to impose solutions. We prefer to pull ideas from the place and the people who live with and work in our buildings. No matter how sophisticated the design, if it doesn't work for the users, it's a failure."

The design of the Clark County Government Center in Las Vegas, for example, responds to the wishes of residents, who did not want the city equated with The Strip and the postwar culture of gambling. "We are not all cocktail waitresses and Black Jack dealers," they told the architects. So Fentress Bradburn created a village of four buildings grouped around a large circular courtyard. The form is that of an encampment, with the arms of the building and the concentric rings of the circle creating a defined civic space in the middle of a vast open landscape. The buildings are dense, like pueblos, and at the heart of the complex is a kiva-like rotunda for important ceremonial occasions. The Clark County Center says nothing about The Strip, but speaks eloquently about the historical roots of the community.

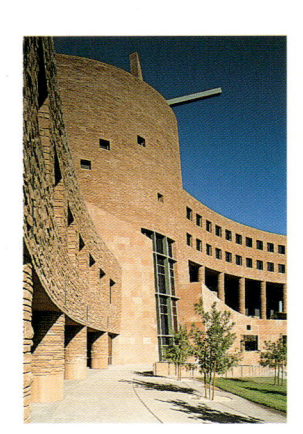

The Jefferson County Government Center appropriates the dome and rotunda of classical architecture to create a new civic heart for a sprawling and largely anonymous area west of Denver. It is not a spec office building that reflects only the gyrations of the real estate market. Its familiar forms and rich materials — granite, marble, cherry paneling with gleaming brass trim — make a strong statement about the importance of the government and the law. People coming to pay their taxes or to attend a hearing enter a tall, handsomely detailed rotunda that directs them to courts and city offices. These spaces open out to galleries and patios with views of the mountains; the design is entirely appropriate in the West, where the weather is beautiful for much of the year. People leave feeling good about their community.

THE DESIGN FOR THE CLARK COUNTY GOVERNMENT CENTER (CLARK COUNTY, NEVADA) INCORPORATES DESERT IMAGERY TAKEN FROM THE FACILITY'S NEVADA SETTING.

The site plan is almost baroque in its use of curves and partial views. Instead of a direct axial approach, visitors must slowly circle the building, viewing it from this angle, then from that, before arriving at the front door. This circuitous approach helps to disguise the enormous scale of the building — 550,000 square feet — and, by slowing the visitor's pace, also underscores the impor-

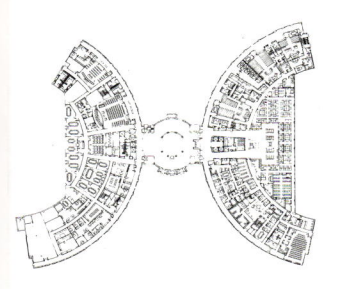

THE VARIOUS FUNCTIONS AT JEFFERSON COUNTY COURTS AND ADMINISTRATION BUILDING (GOLDEN, COLORADO) ARE SEPARATED INTO TWO ARCS THAT ARE JOINED BY A CENTRAL ROTUNDA.

tance of what takes place within. "It is important to go beyond the walls and create a setting for a building," says Fentress. "I.M Pei was brilliant at standing back and looking at the big picture in order to make a total environment. This might involve adding a few trees or changing the direction of an approach, but it made a huge difference. Using berms at Jefferson County and a long armature of trees in Las Vegas are my way of doing the same thing."

Fentress Bradburn got the Larimer County and Clark County commissions through competitions, which have buttressed the practice from the beginning. Competitions are risky ventures, the architectural equivalent of roulette, in which enormous amounts of capital and emotional energy are bet on a single roll of the dice. On the other hand, winning a major competition can propel a firm from obscurity to celebrity almost overnight.

Fentress Bradburn parlayed their initial success in the Colorado Convention Center competition into the commission for the Denver International Airport, which in turn generated other airport commissions around the world. Competitions are collaborative efforts that bring the firm together, and generate invaluable creative capital that, even in a loss, can be deposited in an intellectual savings account for future use.

"They're essential for sharpening your design skills," says Fentress. "There's nothing like a competition to get the juices going and remind you of why you became an architect."

A graduate of I.M Pei's office and one of the first employees of Kohn Pedersen Fox, Curt Fentress learned how to grow a firm from experts. At Pei, he discovered the importance of collaboration and the value of such apparent luxuries as a model shop, which Fentress Bradburn has. At Kohn Pedersen Fox, he learned how to think like a client, how to use the office as a sales tool — the model gallery in the lobby of Fentress Bradburn's office was inspired by a similar space at KPF — and how to take chances.

THE NEW ATRIUM, AT CENTER, AT THE NATIONAL COWBOY HALL OF FAME (OKLAHOMA CITY, OKLAHOMA) BLENDS WITH THE EXISTING FACILITY.

In Denver, Curt is the principal who directs design while Jim oversees production. Bradburn describes the division of labor like this: "Curt is the principal in charge of promises and I'm the principal in charge of delivery." But the line between design and production is not nearly as rigid as it was at Roche Dinkeloo. The architects work in project teams instead of studios. Each team functions as a sort of office, to which the principals serve as critics and advisors. Bradburn meets regularly with each team to assess the status of projects, including whether or not it is making money. "It's fascinating to me to know where every project is every day, financially as well as architecturally. I got that from John Dinkeloo." The firm has also completed ten design-build projects, starting with the Colorado Convention Center, which have expanded the range and versatility of the practice.

Fentress Bradburn expects to grow to 150 employees within the next few years. Although the firm continues to expand, it refuses to grow fat and complacent. The work that is coming out of the firm these days is as diverse and ambitious as that of many large coastal firms. Courthouses, office buildings and convention centers continue to be a major part of the mix. (The firm recently won the commission for a $270 million expansion of the Colorado Convention Center.) And the firm continues to be one of the leading airport designers in the world, with recent designs for projects in Seattle/Tacoma, Vienna, Madrid and Tenerife-Sur. Their new stadium for the Denver Broncos football team is a sculptural contemporary design that bucks the current retro craze in sports architecture. Design is underway for an $80 million air museum in Springfield, Missouri, along with several office buildings, the conversion of a former rubber factory into an e-commerce incubator and a number of major planning studies.

Instead of finding a comfortable niche and settling in, Fentress Bradburn continues to reinvent itself, expanding into new areas and rethinking its place in familiar ones.

"It still feels like a big experiment," insists Bradburn. "There's a youthful questioning quality to much of what we do, and I hope that continues."

THE BOWL OF THE BRONCO STADIUM (DENVER, COLORADO) BEGINS TO TAKE SHAPE AS THE AUGUST 2001 OPENING DATE APPROACHES.

AN EARLY DESIGN CONCEPT FOR THE SEATTLE-TACOMA INTERNATIONAL AIRPORT (SEATTLE, WASHINGTON).

DAVID DILLON INTRODUCTION | 7

DESIGNING PUBLIC SPACE
PROCESSES/CONCEPTS/IDEAS
CURT FENTRESS, FAIA

A passion for designing to region and context has figured significantly in our work, but the true importance of this approach lies in the higher ideal it serves: humanism. Tying buildings to their region and context strengthens the human sense of structures and puts users at the center of the design.

The rigors of public architecture have been the crucible in which we have tested our ideas about humanizing architecture. Civic buildings tend to be larger, to have more users, to encompass a greater number of purposes. Designers must therefore give these buildings a comfortable scale and a clear plan. But the greatest design challenge is in symbolism, which in the best civic architecture manifests as a ceremonial quality that provides a felt connection with community.

A building's aesthetics and the emotional response it evokes should work on behalf of this human need to connect—for instance, by embodying the welcoming arms of open and accessible government. But, in addition to such universal forms and gestures, this need can be addressed through the use of native materials, references to context or the introduction of design elements that are evocative of region and culture. All of these aesthetic elements enrich the experience of a building, heightening users' awareness of the space and how it connects with the landscape and the collective civic spirit. Designed well, a public building reinforces and enhances the experience of community.

Our concern with both the humanistic and functional issues of design makes public work a natural choice for Fentress Bradburn Architects. However, even these natural affinities were only a beginning for us. Each project has taught us about the process of creating public structures and, over time, certain constants have emerged. These are less guideposts than they are touchstones—ideas that continue to surface each time our designs for public structures begin to take shape.

Our experience can be distilled into seven ideas: four design concepts that put the user foremost and three humanistic ideas that have guided us from the first. I believe that in order to design successful public architecture, one must:

1) USE CONTEXT TO CREATE AN IDENTITY.
An architect can learn from a public building's context how to express its purpose. One may be inspired by landforms, use natural materials from the region or match the colors and textures of the environment. But one must keep foremost in mind the purpose of the building, the function it serves and its identity.

This can be done with soaring shapes for an airport, with more earth-bound forms to show solidity in government or in more subtle and playful ways. Let me give two examples from our work: We housed the Regional Flood Control District at Clark County, Nevada, within undulating "canyon" walls, which bring to mind the volatile resource that agency regulates. At the National Museum of Wildlife Art, we evoked the experience of discovery in wildlife observation by making the museum mysterious on first approach, blending it into the background as a natural stone outcropping.

2) LET CULTURE GUIDE DESIGN.
The culture—whether it's the culture of an entire country, that of a region or a corporate culture—can direct the architect. When designing airports in Qatar and Korea, we were led by cultural markers, including local sailing vessels, the lines of which helped us sustain the imagery of transit.

At the David E. Skaggs Research Center, which houses the National Oceanic and Atmospheric Administration's research laboratories in Boulder, Colorado, we punctuated walls of locally quarried stone with atriums and stairwells constructed of sleek aluminum columns that bespeak the facility's scientific culture.

In the city of Oakland, California, we re-wove the city fabric by creating new administration buildings that were inspired and rooted in the traditions of the area's historic buildings, bringing new life to the area while still honoring the culture that already existed there.

3) CELEBRATE THE ENTRY.

To function well, a building must be easy to read from the outside, as well as from the inside. Users must know at a glance where to enter and, once inside, they should be directed with a minimum of graphics. At the same time, the architect should give users a moment of repose, to tell them they have arrived and to explain how the building works—a moment when, in a sense, the building greets the user.

The front door of the original National Cowboy and Western Heritage Museum was very difficult to find. With our addition, we created a completely new entry that is prominent on the exterior. Inside, we placed the museum's largest sculpture on an axis with the entrance, emphasizing the atrium's heroic scale. This kind of detail helps to center the user within the building.

To create a sense of arrival in government facilities, we have used entries and rotundas, points from which the building radiates or branches out or encircles the user. We have made many of these glassy and bright, but some situations have called for other solutions. Las Vegas is surrounded by desert, where one seeks shade and rest from the light. For this reason, we made the central point of the Clark County Government Center a solid kiva-like form.

Inside Denver International Airport, users experience a sense of arrival upon entering the Great Hall, the openness

A FABRIC CANOPY SHADES THE NATIONAL COWBOY AND WESTERN HERITAGE MUSEUM'S ARRIVING PATRONS AND CLEARLY DEFINES THE MUSEUM'S NEW ENTRANCE.

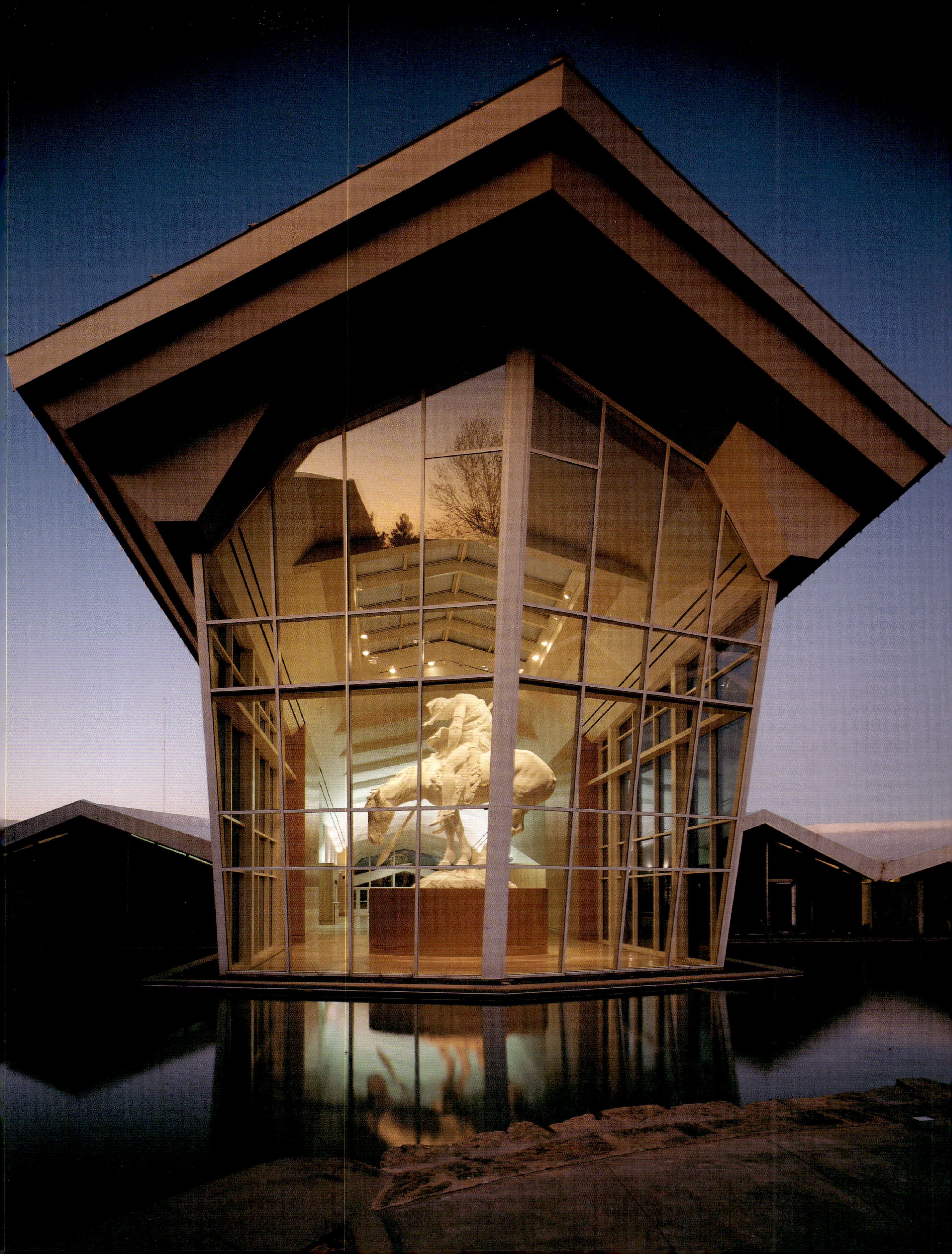

of which also helps people find their way. We placed taller skylighted masts at the two bridges that cross the cathedral-like interior of Denver International Airport to help organize the space for travelers.

4) DISCOVER THE NATURAL ORDER.
Many buildings with complex programs become mazes, simply by fulfilling all the needs called for to make them functional. The challenge for the architect of complex large-scale projects is to make it easy for users to find their way around. To do this, one must discover the natural order of the elements and organize them in a simple manner. In Jefferson, Larimer and Clark counties, we organized agencies based on the amount of public contact they have: The services used most often were made most accessible by putting those offices on the lowest floors.

5) STAY FOCUSED.
The public process tends to be long, protracted, bureaucratic, complex and vulnerable to political upheaval. Public buildings bring together many personalities and agendas, which make misunderstandings and conflicts much more likely. It is necessary for the architect to practice patience on all fronts and avoid getting swept up in the process itself, which can be halting in its progress and frustrating at times. The architect should remain open to all communication while cultivating an understanding that the public process is simply more intense than other design processes.

6) LISTEN CLOSELY.
For the architect, creating public architecture is not a tidy package or a simple task and it is seldom an easy process. The architect is answerable not just to one owner or a board of directors but to an entire community. At the same time, public architecture is one of the most exciting arenas in which an architect can work, balancing aesthetics and utilitarian concerns with program, public input and one's own inspiration.

Public input is a large part of the process of creating a civic building. There needs to be a relationship of trust and respect between the architect and the people who will work in the building, use the building, live near the building and pay for the building. We are often inspired by these people's thoughts, which usually reach our ears in public meetings, rather than in letters or reports or even notes.

This is an important point: These are people who literally want a voice in the design of the building. These people take the time to come to a meeting organized by the city or county or agency in question, and they find the courage to speak; to voice their passions, their desires and their frustrations; to take a stand; to offer their insight; and to invest their emotions. Part of the task of an architect of public buildings is to acknowledge these personal acts of community and to embody these voices.

At a reception before the competition for the government center in Clark County, Nevada, I heard people say, "We're not all showgirls or gamblers or dealers." They wanted an alternative to the Las Vegas Strip; they wanted a place with dignity, where they could gather as a community of citizens. This is where the inspiration to add an amphitheater to the facility originated. If you go there to hear a classical music concert, you'll come away with a very different impression of those who live in Las Vegas than you would if you simply visited the casinos.

The public process can either kill a building or make great architecture. It can be a part of the creation of art, just as the potter's wheel is essential to the creation of pottery. But it is a tool one must learn how to use. The architect must understand the public process and respect it as a means to do more than just build a functional building. There's a certain flow to the process. You can see in many buildings of the '50s, '60s and '70s that the community and the architect suffered with this process. Without a good process, you don't get a good building.

7) RESTRAIN THE EGO.
A building's presence should speak. It should make a statement, but not a statement that overpowers the building's purpose, its operation, its landscape, its culture or the users who come to it. A building's statement should emerge from those very elements, and the architect should serve as their contact point. The moment of creativity for the architect should be neither a flight of fancy away from earthly or quotidian concerns nor a retreat into intellect and theory. Instead, the moment of creativity should be pure alchemy, a time when the user becomes central, when the place and the people and the program are allowed to speak through the architect, coming together to create a compelling structure.

FACING PAGE:
ON AXIS WITH THE ENTRANCE, THE NATIONAL COWBOY AND WESTERN HERITAGE MUSEUM'S LARGEST SCULPTURE JUTS INTO A LARGE, CENTRAL COURTYARD.

MUSEUMS + THEATERS

"Designed well, a cultural facility reinforces and enhances the experience of gathering together for reasons that are other than purely functional. A building's aesthetics, the emotional response it evokes, should work on behalf of this need to connect."
  - Curt Fentress

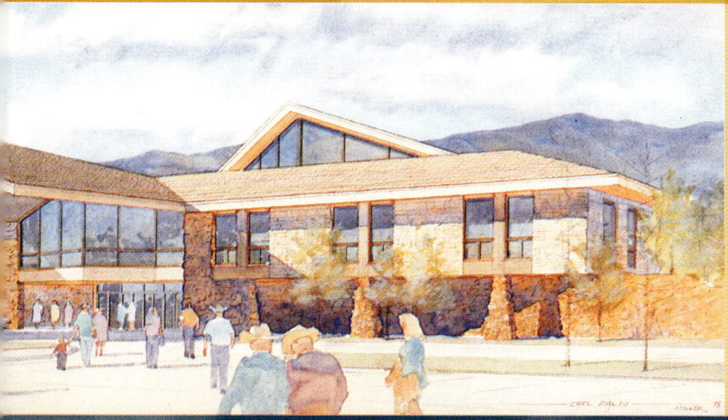
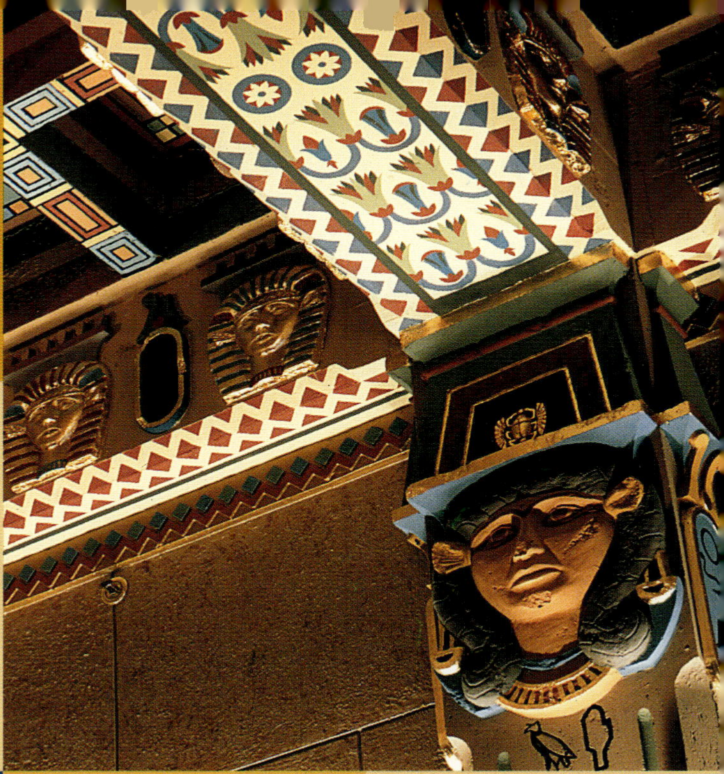
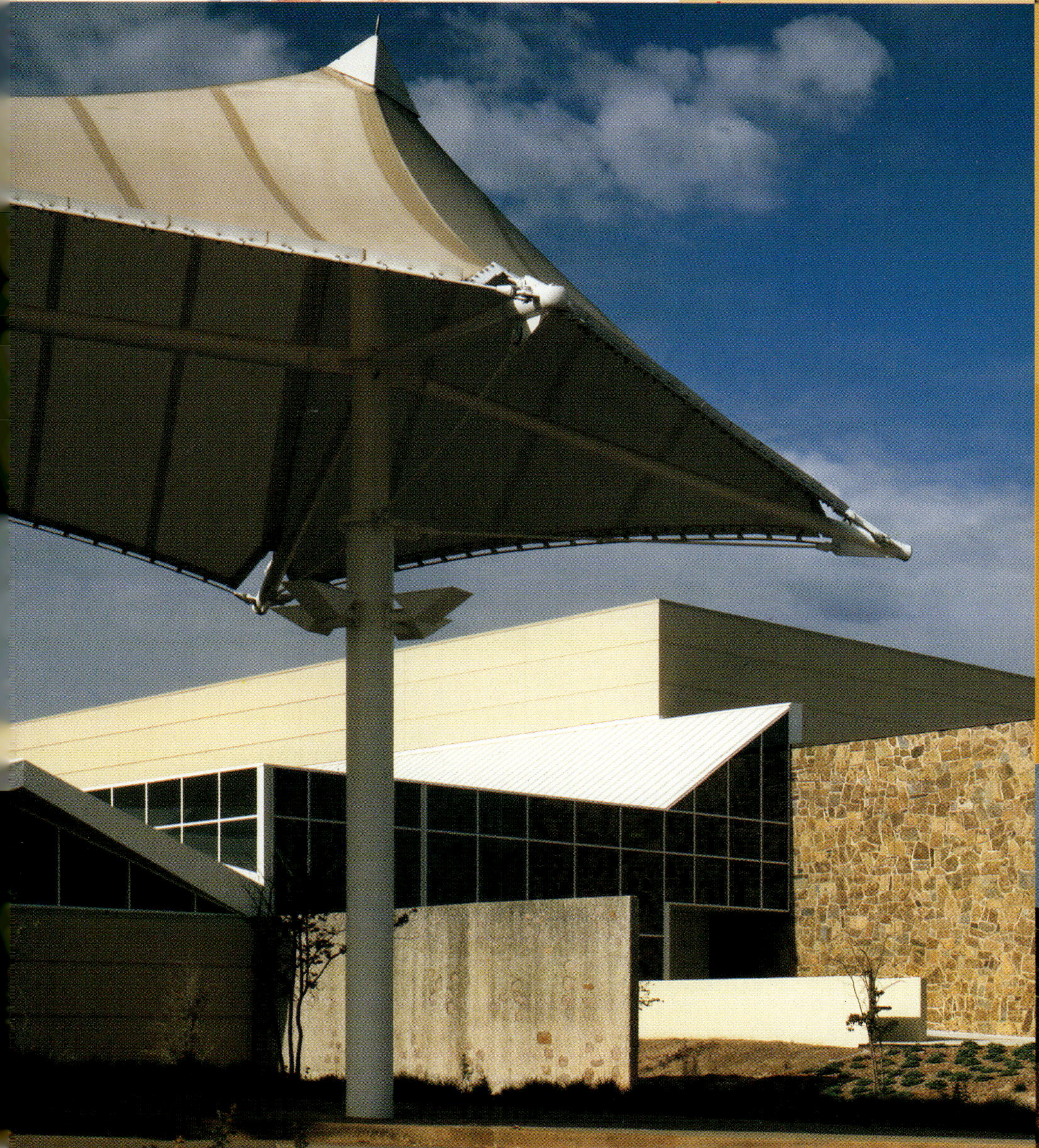
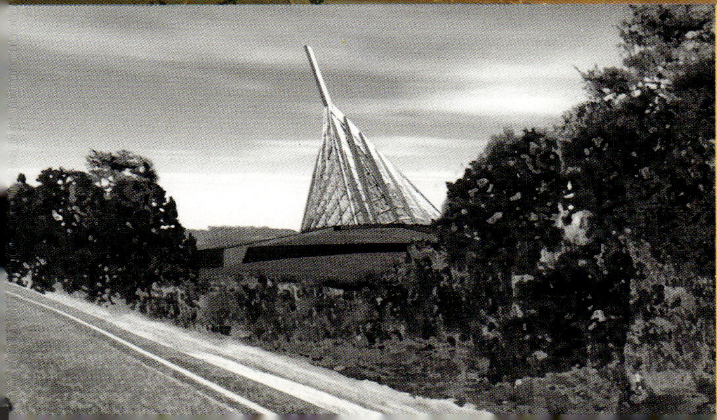
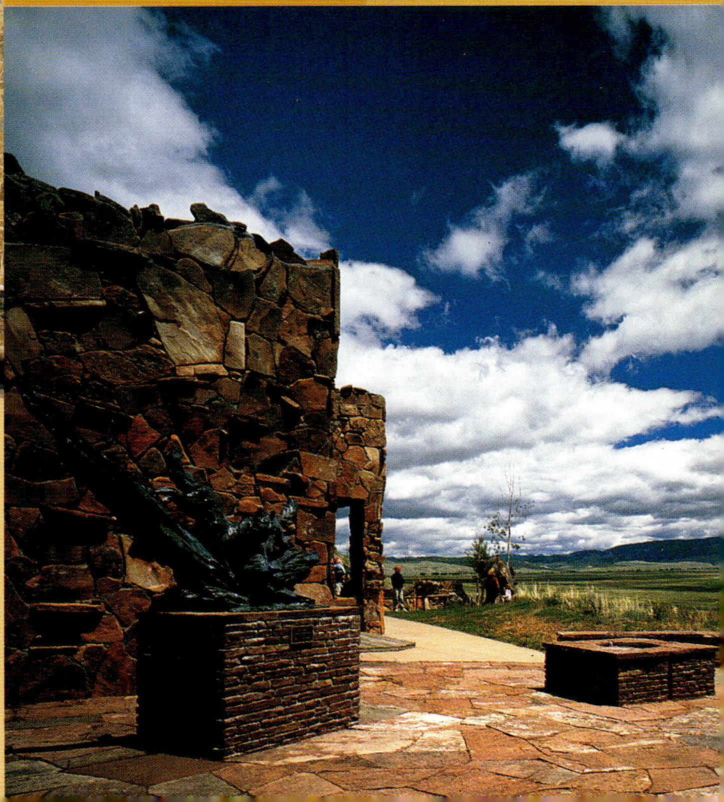

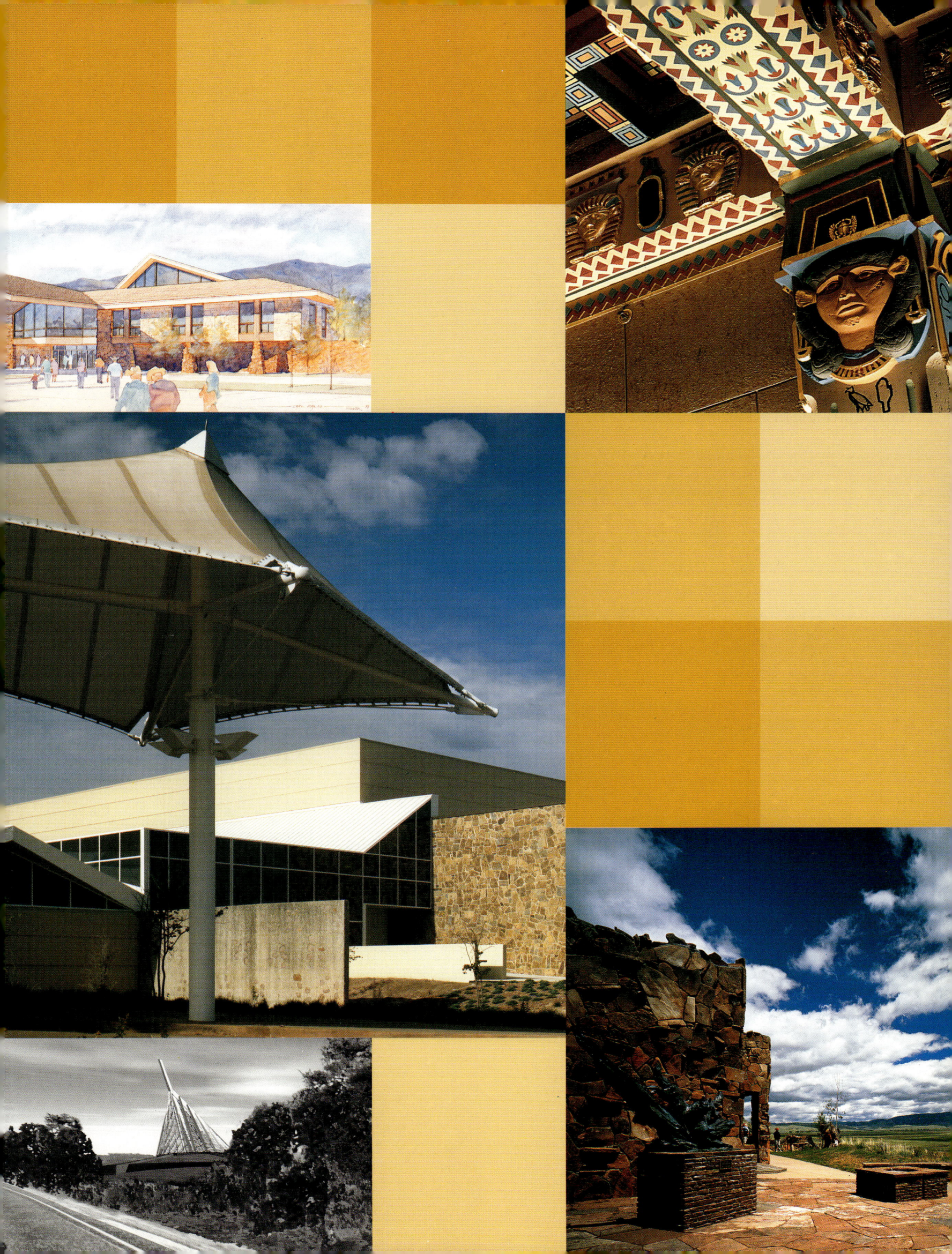

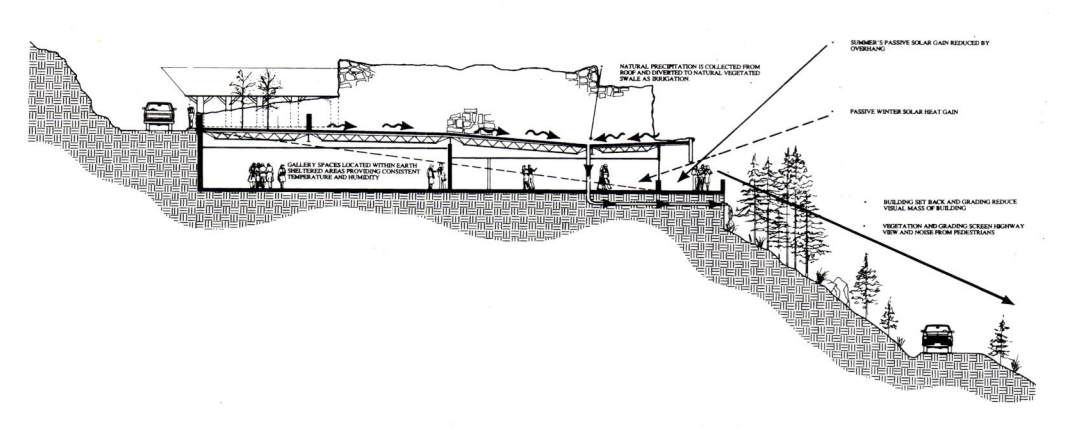

TOP:
THIS SECTIONAL DRAWING OF THE BUILDING ILLUSTRATES THE DRAINAGE SYSTEM AND SEASONAL SOLAR PENETRATION.

ABOVE:
ON FIRST APPROACH, THE BUILDING APPEARS AS A NATURAL OUTCROPPING OF ROCK.

RIGHT:
SEVERAL BRONZE WILDLIFE SCULPTURES ARE LOCATED OUTSIDE THE MUSEUM.

14 | **MUSEUMS+THEATERS** NATIONAL MUSEUM OF WILDLIFE ART

NATIONAL MUSEUM OF WILDLIFE ART
JACKSON, WYOMING

On a dramatic cliff overlooking the National Elk Refuge, the National Museum of Wildlife Art emerges from the earth like a natural outcropping of rock. The museum's location, coupled with the collection of artwork that pays tribute to wildlife, provides a rare opportunity to view wildlife in its natural habitat. Constructed out of rough stone, the building blends seamlessly into the native terrain, capturing the natural beauty of Jackson, Wyoming. The end result is an original, contextually relevant and timeless design.

In an effort to create a unique museum, the Fentress Bradburn team was sensitive to place and purpose. The practical, functional and aesthetic design highlights the Grand Tetons site and the art collections offered inside. The unobtrusive structure captures the subtlety of the landscape and natural light and features canyon-like interior spaces that house the collections on display.

The museum's roofline slowly emerges over the rocky terrain, welcoming visitors as they approach. The structure

LEFT and CENTER: STONE CLADDING ON THE BUILDING'S EXTERIOR HELPS IT BLEND INTO THE ROCKY BLUFF.

has a playful nature. It first appears to be a natural formation, before revealing itself as a building.

Fentress Bradburn realized energy savings by setting the western side of the building into the hillside. The design allows for careful heat and humidity control in the galleries and storage spaces by placing those areas along the buried western portion of the building. Thus, temperatures remain stabilized and food service, retail, conference and private office areas enjoy windows and outdoor terraces for the observation of wildlife, outdoor dining and educational programs. By bringing the outdoors into the museum, the architects created an open natural environment appropriate to the collections on display.

The team carefully chose exterior and interior details that coincide with the museum collection. An open-entrance lobby features animal tracks etched into the floor and a bronze mountain lion peering over a stone stairwell wall. The window-lined lobby allows natural light to flood the space. Its position also works to divide the space of the galleries and maintain temperature and humidity control in that area.

The architectural design of the museum had to address many important issues including concerns about the impact of developing a pristine wilderness area, the desire to create a building that embraces the spirit of the Grand Tetons region and the challenge of placing a structure within its site. Fentress Bradburn has crafted an extension of nature by designing a state-of-the-art museum facility with a unique awareness of environmental and ecological concerns.

THIS PAGE
ABOVE RIGHT:
THE ENTRYWAY WAS CONSTRUCTED FROM PINE TREES THAT WERE SALVAGED FROM THE YELLOWSTONE FIRE OF 1988.

CENTER RIGHT:
OUTDOOR TERRACES ARE PROVIDED FOR THE OBSERVATION OF WILDLIFE.

BELOW:
SOUTH FAÇADE: THIS SECTIONAL DRAWING ILLUSTRATES THAT THE GALLERIES WERE POSITIONED IN THE LOWER PORTION OF THE BUILDING AND ORIENTED TOWARD THE HILLSIDE TO AID LIGHT AND HUMIDITY CONTROLS.

FACING PAGE:
THE CEILING GRID ADDS ORDER AND RHYTHM WHILE ALLOWING FOR MAXIMUM FLEXIBILITY IN GALLERY CONFIGURATION.

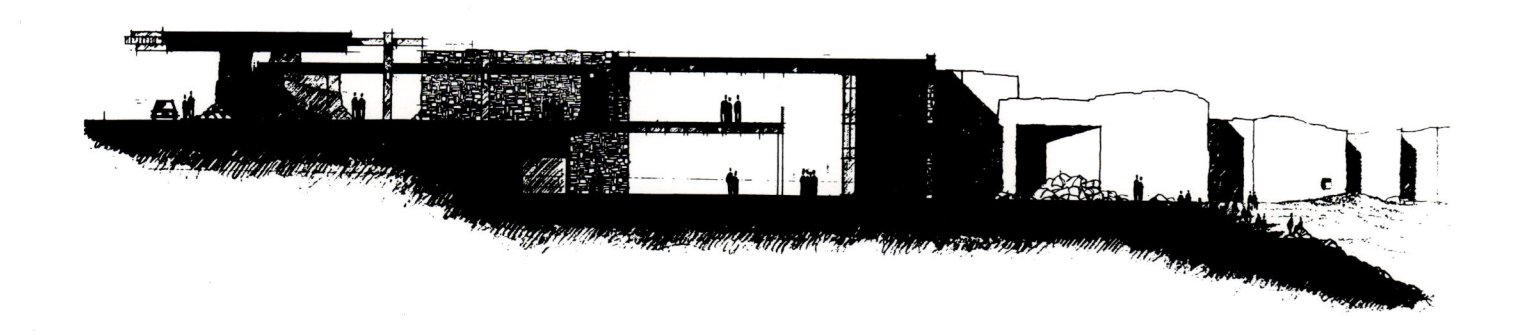

16 | MUSEUMS+THEATERS NATIONAL MUSEUM OF WILDLIFE ART

"When the buffalo saw their day was over and they could no longer protect the people, survivors gathered in Council. One side day a young woman looked through the mist toward the herd appearing like a spirit dream and walking in an opening in Mount Scott. Inside, the world was as fresh and green as it once had been. Into this beauty the buffalo walked, never to be seen again."

— Kiowa Legend

THE MUSEUM'S TOTEM POLE IS HOUSED IN THE TURRETED PORTION OF THE STRUCTURE.

18 | **MUSEUMS+THEATERS** NATIONAL MUSEUM OF WILDLIFE ART

ABOVE:
A BRONZE MOUNTAIN LION OVERLOOKS THE CANYON-LIKE LOBBY OF THE MUSEUM.

BELOW LEFT:
STORAGE AND CURATORIAL AREAS ARE LOCATED ON THE LOWER FLOORS OF THE BUILDING, AWAY FROM WINDOWS.

BELOW RIGHT:
THE MUSEUM FEATURES A SMALL AUDITORIUM.

NATIONAL MUSEUM OF WILDLIFE ART   MUSEUMS+THEATERS | 19

THE NATIONAL MUSEUM OF THE MARINE CORPS AND HERITAGE CENTER
QUANTICO, VIRGINIA

Of all the imagery associated with the U.S. Marine Corps, the flag-raising at Iwo Jima is perhaps the best known and most enduring symbol. Iwo Jima is widely seen as both the turning point in the World War II battle for the Pacific as well as a defining moment for the Marine Corps. It is this image that provides the central architectural theme for the design of the National Museum of the Marine Corps. Expressed in a 210-foot-tall soaring form that is the museum's most visible element, the image becomes a tilted, conical, glass-encased lobby gallery focused around a great mast grounded in the earth but sweeping up toward the sky. This grand gesture also evokes imagery of the bayonet, the sword and even artillery.

The dramatic composition of structural lines creates a poised image of strength and stability that so clearly epitomizes the spirit of the United States Marine Corps. It is Fentress Bradburn's clarity in design and message that ultimately led to their selection as winner in the national design competition for the Heritage Center complex.

The museum's intention is to inspire, educate and inform over 400,000 annual visitors about the 230-year history of the Marine Corps. The site is organized to give its soaring central feature high visibility from adjacent Interstate 95. Visitors first see the central atrium prominently displayed on the hill, followed by a series of increasingly dramatic views through the trees as they approach. The museum is approached from the south end of the site, which encompasses Semper Fidelis Memorial Park, where unit memorials and individual remem-

ABOVE LEFT:
ARTIST'S RENDERING SHOWING VISIBILITY OF MUSEUM FROM I-95.

LEFT:
SITE MODEL SHOWING VISIBILITY OF MUSEUM FROM I-95.

ABOVE RIGHT:
SECTION WITH OVERLAY OF IWO JIMA FLAG RAISING.

NATIONAL MUSEUM OF THE MARINE CORPS

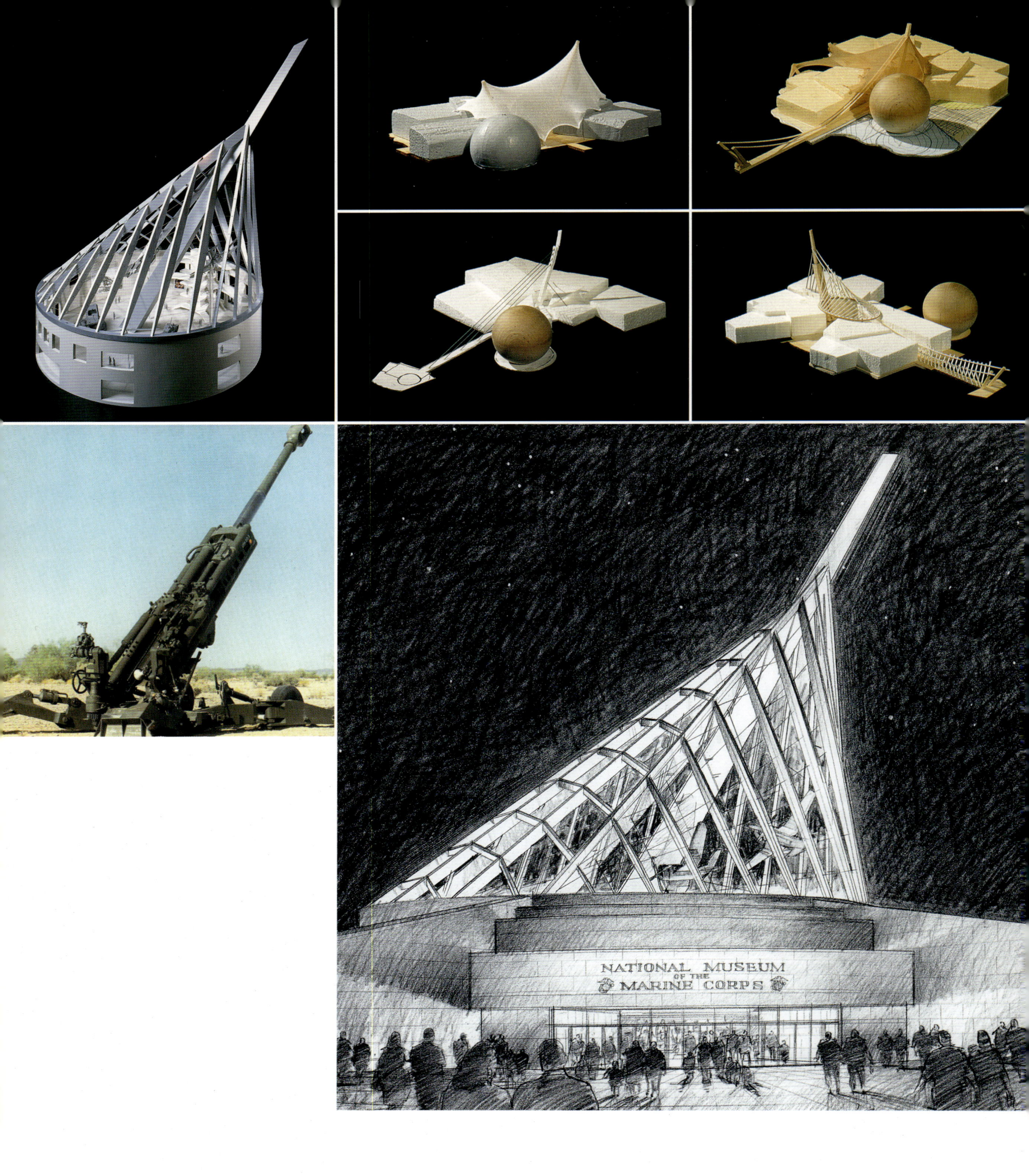

22 | **MUSEUMS + THEATERS** NATIONAL MUSEUM OF THE MARINE CORPS

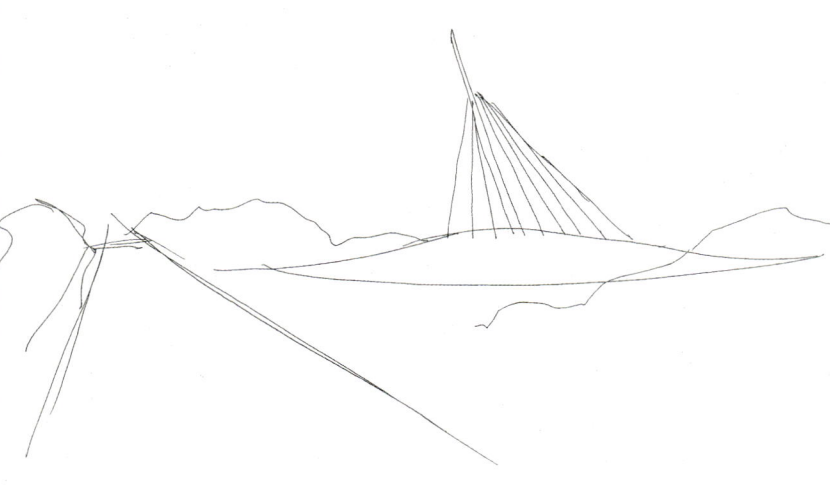

brances will honor the Marines' service. Parades, ceremonies and Marine Band concerts will take place on the parade grounds near the museum.

Earth integration of the building not only provides for significant energy savings, it also helps evoke a bunker-like image, and leaves intact the lush foliage of the 135-acre site. The design features many other sustainable concepts to support construction of a responsible building that is energy efficient, easy to maintain and physically secure, all of which work to minimize long-term operating costs.

As visitors enter the museum, they arrive through a guest services lobby to reach the 180-foot-tall, glass-enclosed central gallery space. Here, visitors find an introduction to the Marine Corps story celebrated in imagery and exhibits. Functioning as the main circulation hub, this central feature directs visitors to galleries as well as the facility's gift shop and orientation theater.

In addition to defining both the building's organization and form, the circular plan of the 110,000-square-foot facility provides ultimate flexibility for future expansions. Phase 2 will add an IMAX theater to the facility that is directly accessed from the museum's main level. On the second level, overlooking the central atrium, are meeting and classroom spaces for Marine, community and fraternal organizations, museum and foundation offices and a restaurant, with views to the entry plaza and the central gallery below.

FACING PAGE
TOP LEFT:
STUDY MODEL OF CENTRAL GALLERY.

TOP RIGHT:
CONCEPTUAL MODELS DEVELOPED DURING DESIGN COMPETITION.

BOTTOM LEFT:
INSPIRATION IMAGES INCLUDED HOWITZER CANNONS.

BOTTOM RIGHT:
ARTIST'S RENDERING OF MUSEUM ENTRANCE.

THIS PAGE
TOP:
ARTIST'S RENDERING OF CENTRAL GALLERY INTERIOR.

ABOVE LEFT:
CURT FENTRESS' SKETCH OF THE MUSEUM.

24 | **MUSEUMS +THEATERS** NATIONAL MUSEUM OF THE MARINE CORPS

FACING PAGE
VIEW FROM DROP-OFF AREA TO A HALF-INCH EQUALS ONE-FOOT SCALE MODEL OF THE MUSEUM.

THIS PAGE
VIEW FROM SECOND STORY RESTAURANT TO A HALF-INCH EQUALS ONE-FOOT SCALE MODEL OF THE MUSEUM

NATIONAL MUSEUM OF THE MARINE CORPS *MUSEUMS + THEATERS* | 25

26 | **MUSEUMS + THEATERS** NATIONAL MUSEUM OF THE MARINE CORPS

TOP LEFT:
SITE PLAN

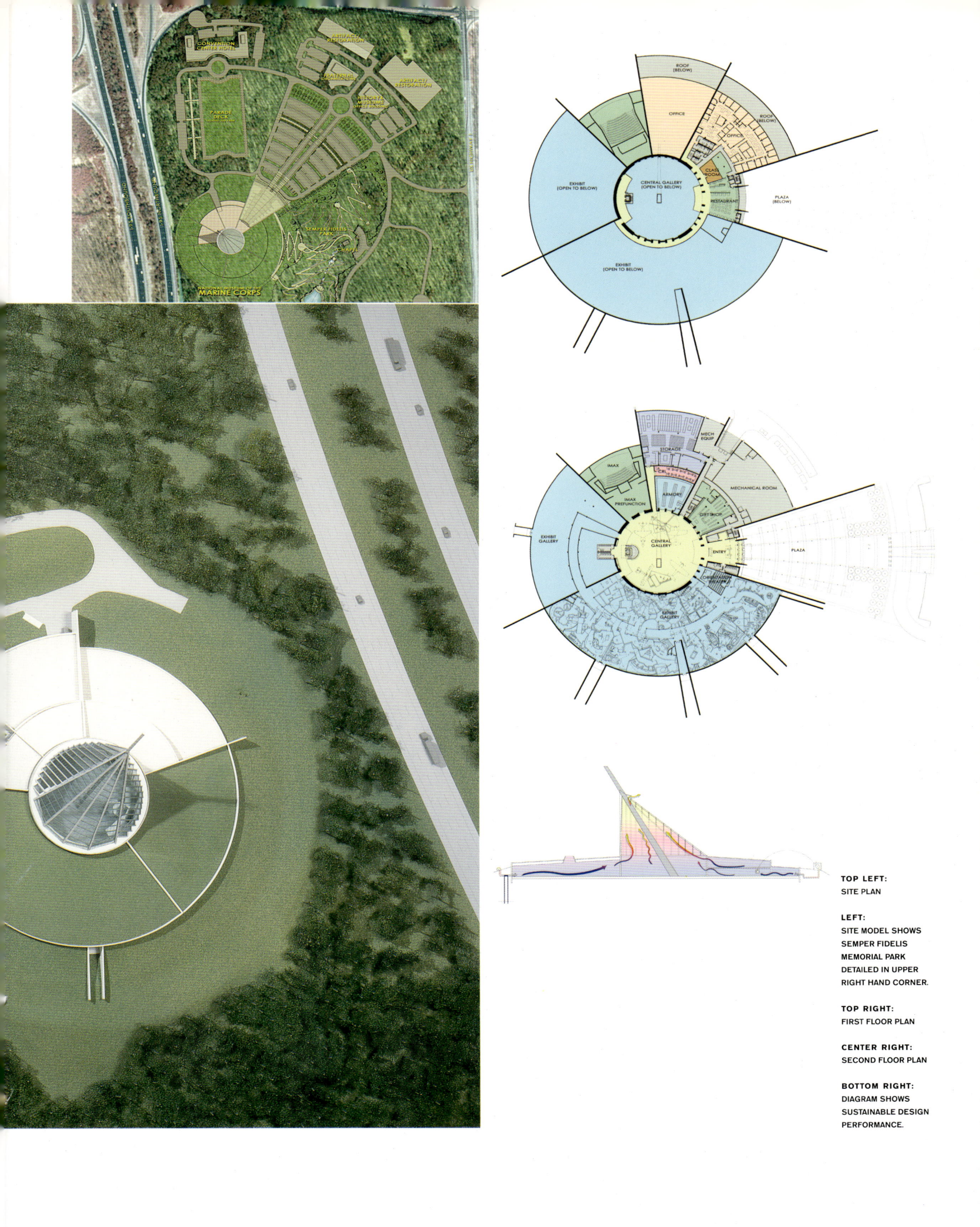

LEFT:
SITE MODEL SHOWS
SEMPER FIDELIS
MEMORIAL PARK
DETAILED IN UPPER
RIGHT HAND CORNER.

TOP RIGHT:
FIRST FLOOR PLAN

CENTER RIGHT:
SECOND FLOOR PLAN

BOTTOM RIGHT:
DIAGRAM SHOWS
SUSTAINABLE DESIGN
PERFORMANCE.

NATIONAL MUSEUM OF THE MARINE CORPS **MUSEUMS + THEATERS** | 27

DRAPER MUSEUM OF NATURAL HISTORY
BUFFALO BILL HISTORICAL CENTER
CODY, WYOMING

The 50,000-square-foot Draper Museum of National History is the first natural history museum of the 21st century. Draper joins the Buffalo Bill Historical Center's four internationally acclaimed museums—the Whitney Gallery of Western Art, the Buffalo Bill Museum, the Plains Indian Museum and the Cody Firearms Museum—as the final element in a comprehensive portrayal of the West.

Fentress Bradburn's design for the Draper Museum is responsive to program, sympathetic to context and distinctive in expression. The new museum actively contributes to the strength of Yellowstone's tourism industry by stirring interest in the subject on local and national levels. Visitors become explorers in their journey through the museum, as they find it to be friendly, familiar and educational.

While the Draper Museum mirrors the Firearms Museum in plan and elevation, its circular form embraces the front door drop-off area and provides a counter element to the center's otherwise linear and symmetrical massing. Entry elements include a spacious orientation area with two small ranger cabins—one a typical ranger cabin with tools and furnishings and the other housing interactive computer terminals. Beyond the entry is a 4,000-square-foot flexible exhibition hall designed to display artwork and play host to any number of events including dinners and lectures.

Once past the entry elements, visitors enter the main space, which is spatially akin to a small version of the Solomon R. Guggenheim Museum in New York City with four quadrants that cascade vertically down. The levels are developed in response to the Yellowstone area's natural habitat from Alpine at the top, through Forest and Meadow, to Plains at the bottom level, where a T.D. Kelsey bronze sculpture of a buffalo jump penetrates a 30-foot-long window. Lamps in four colors alternate up-lighting the domed fabric ceiling, simulating the changing seasons. Opposite the domed ceiling and set into the floor is a circular regional mosaic map created using one-inch tiles. Halfway through the quadrants an arched doorway provides entrance to an adjacent wing, which houses the museum's 4,900-square-foot educational area with a small theater, dress-up area and a classroom. On the ground level, prior to exit, the Discovery Gallery comprises an additional 1,500 square feet of flexible exhibit space.

The Draper Museum's interactive exhibits, state-of-the-art displays and mood lighting create an exciting environment for people of all ages. A myriad of wildlife including bears, bison, moose and wolves compose large, open displays. The only exhibits of wildlife found behind plexiglass in this museum are beavers, snakes and fish, which spot the museum's floor, as if to appear underground, in their real-life habitats.

DRAPER'S CIRCULAR FORM ACTS AS A COUNTER ELEMENT TO THE CENTER'S OTHERWISE LINEAR FORM.

30 | **MUSEUMS + THEATERS** DRAPER MUSEUM OF NATURAL HISTORY

FACING PAGE

TOP:
THE MAIN EXHIBIT SPACE IS SPATIALLY AKIN TO THE GUGGENHEIM MUSEUM IN NEW YORK CITY.

BOTTOM LEFT:
A BREAK-OUT ROOM OFF THE MAIN SPACE HOUSES EDUCATIONAL FORUMS.

BOTTOM RIGHT:
A LARGE MULTIPURPOSE VENUE IS LOCATED JUST INSIDE THE ENTRANCE.

THIS PAGE
FENTRESS BRADBURN WORKED COLLABORATIVELY WITH DMCD, EXHIBIT DESIGNERS, TO ENHANCE THE RELATIONSHIP BETWEEN ARCHITECTURE AND EXHIBITS.

DRAPER MUSEUM OF NATURAL HISTORY **MUSEUMS + THEATERS** | 31

ABOVE LEFT AND RIGHT: THE GALLERY LAYOUT AFFORDS A FLEXIBLE AND EASILY NAVIGABLE ENVIRONMENT FOR THE VIEWING OF BOTH PAINTINGS AND SCULPTURES.

32 | **MUSEUMS + THEATERS** WHITNEY GALLERY OF WESTERN ART

WHITNEY GALLERY OF WESTERN ART
BUFFALO BILL HISTORICAL CENTER
CODY, WYOMING

Located in the nationally acclaimed Buffalo Bill Historical Center, the 6,000-square-foot Whitney Gallery of Western Art contains masterpieces by such famed artists as Albert Bierstadt and Frederic Remington.

In the late 1980s, as the Center gained in popularity, Fentress Bradburn was asked to create a more ideal viewing experience for patrons. As the design team set out to create a neutral and contemporary backdrop for the gallery's fine arts and artifacts, they paid careful attention to lighting, security, signage and seating.

The gallery's articulated ceiling adds order and rhythm, while its matching floors and walls create the illusion of a more voluminous space. Gallery lighting is tucked away in the ceiling grid for subtle illumination of both art and sculpture. A screened partition at the far end of the gallery protects the artwork from exterior light and eases the indoor viewing experience. Just beyond the partition, patrons may view the sculpture garden. Barriers, signage and direct lighting clearly guide patrons through the space and enhance the gallery's security. Designated seating areas provide places to relax without interfering with the established circulation patterns.

ABOVE LEFT AND RIGHT: THE GALLERY IS ORGANIZED AS A SERIES OF INTERCONNECTING SPACES.

34 | **MUSEUMS + THEATERS** WHITNEY GALLERY OF WESTERN ART

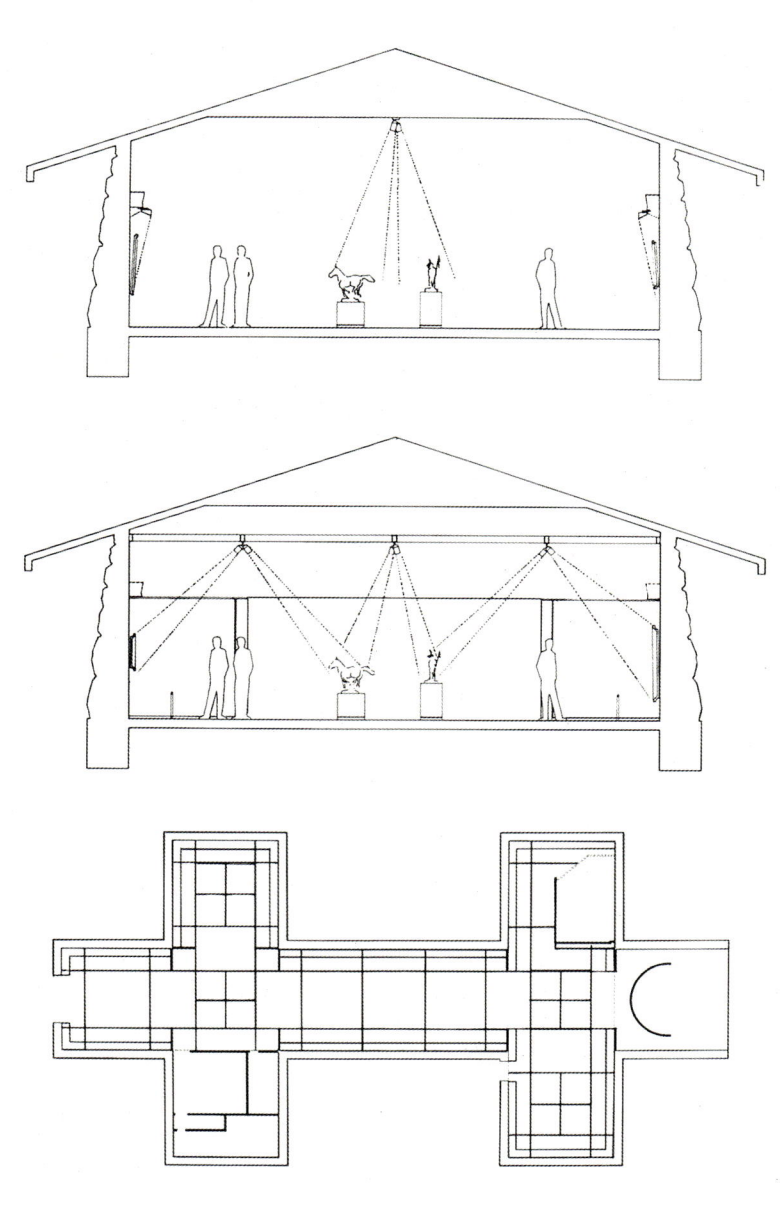

TOP AND CENTER DRAWINGS: ORIGINAL LIGHTING CONDITIONS; LIGHTING CONDITIONS AFTER RENOVATION.

BOTTOM DRAWING: THIS FLOOR PLAN DETAILS LIGHTING AND DISPLAY AREAS.

WHITNEY GALLERY OF WESTERN ART *MUSEUMS+THEATERS* | 35

BOARD ROOM | EXPANDED KRIENDLER GALLERY

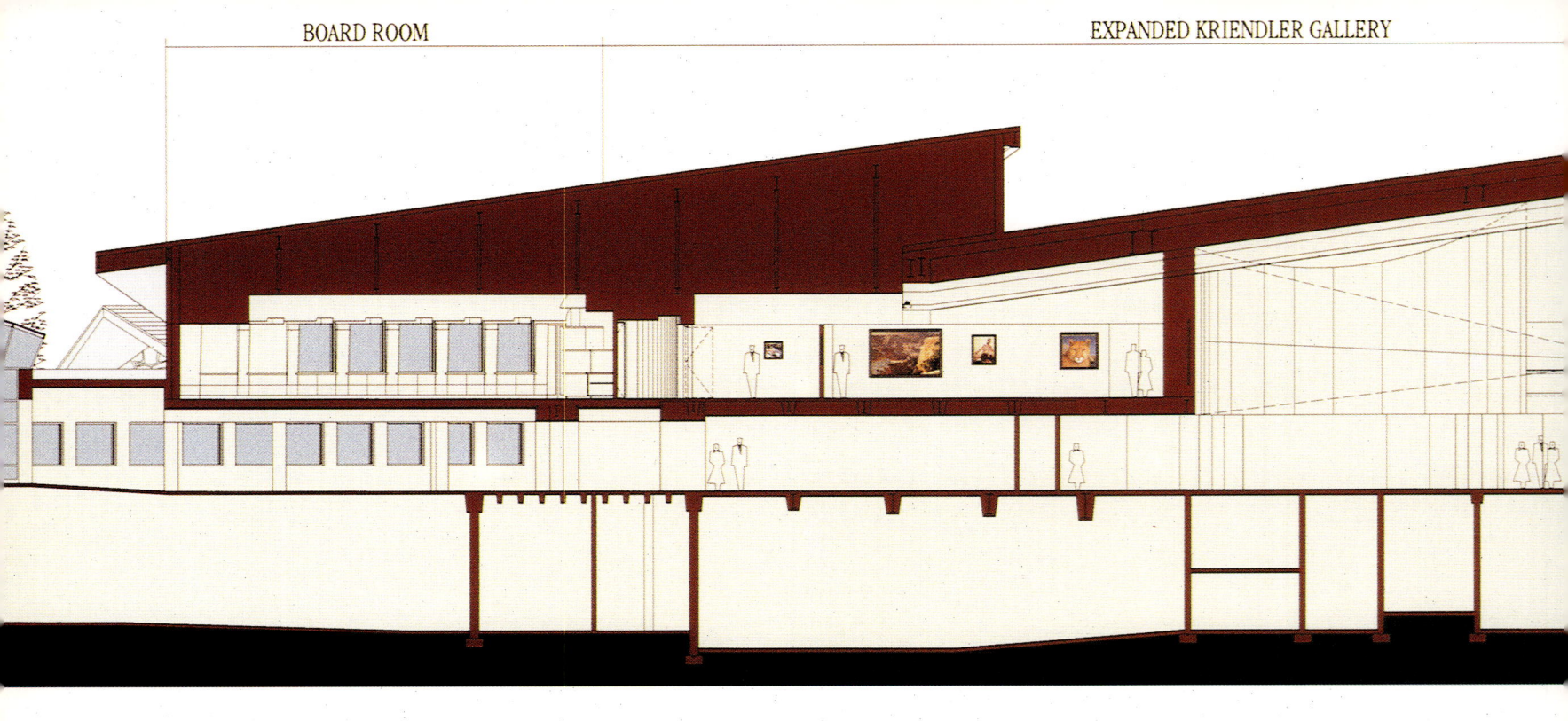

BUFFALO BILL HISTORICAL CENTER RENOVATION AND EXPANSION
CODY, WYOMING

TOP: FENTRESS BRADBURN'S ADDITION TO THE MUSEUM INCLUDES A 50,000-SQUARE FOOT NATURAL HISTORY WING, AN ORIENTATION THEATER AND COLLECTION CARE FACILITIES.

The 237,000-square-foot Buffalo Bill Historical Center sits on a bluff overlooking the Shoshone River in northwestern Wyoming. Located 52 miles from Yellowstone National Park's East Gate, the Center is widely regarded as America's finest Western gallery, featuring the Harold McCracken Research Library and four internationally acclaimed collections: the Whitney Gallery of Western Art, the Buffalo Bill Museum, the Plains Indian Museum and the Cody Firearms Museum. Fentress Bradburn's addition to the Center would include a new 50,000-square-foot Natural History Museum wing, an orientation theater and collection care facilities. The design also reorganizes the entry drive and parking facilities. The Fentress Bradburn team redesigned the lobby to give it monumental scale, transforming it into a central orientation area for visitors, as well as communicating the uniqueness of the center and providing a site for special events.

Named after William Frederick Cody, commonly known as Buffalo Bill, the museum captures his vibrant and multi-faceted life as a Colorado "59er," Pony Express rider, stagecoach driver, Civil War soldier, hotel manager, scout and actor. For design inspiration, Fentress Bradburn looked to statements Cody made in his later years. "All my interests are still in the West, the modern West," he said. Cody envisioned a new West, "with its waving grain fields, fenced flocks and splendid cities, drawing upon the mountains for the water to make it fertile and upon the whole world for men to make it rich." The new museum asserts the importance of the Western causes for which Cody crusaded, such as conservation and civil rights for Native Americans and women. Just as Cody helped transform the West, Fentress Bradburn transformed this space to reflect the spirit of the Old West with the technology of a new West.

The Board of Directors for the Buffalo Bill Historical Center had the foresight to authorize work on mechanical and electrical system master plans. Review of the existing infrastructure determined its capacity to accommodate this major expansion and develop a long-range strategy for consolidating engineering systems into a central location. By replacing obsolete equipment, the museum will reduce energy and maintenance costs. Overall, the design features elements of beauty and functionality that work together to form a cohesive whole.

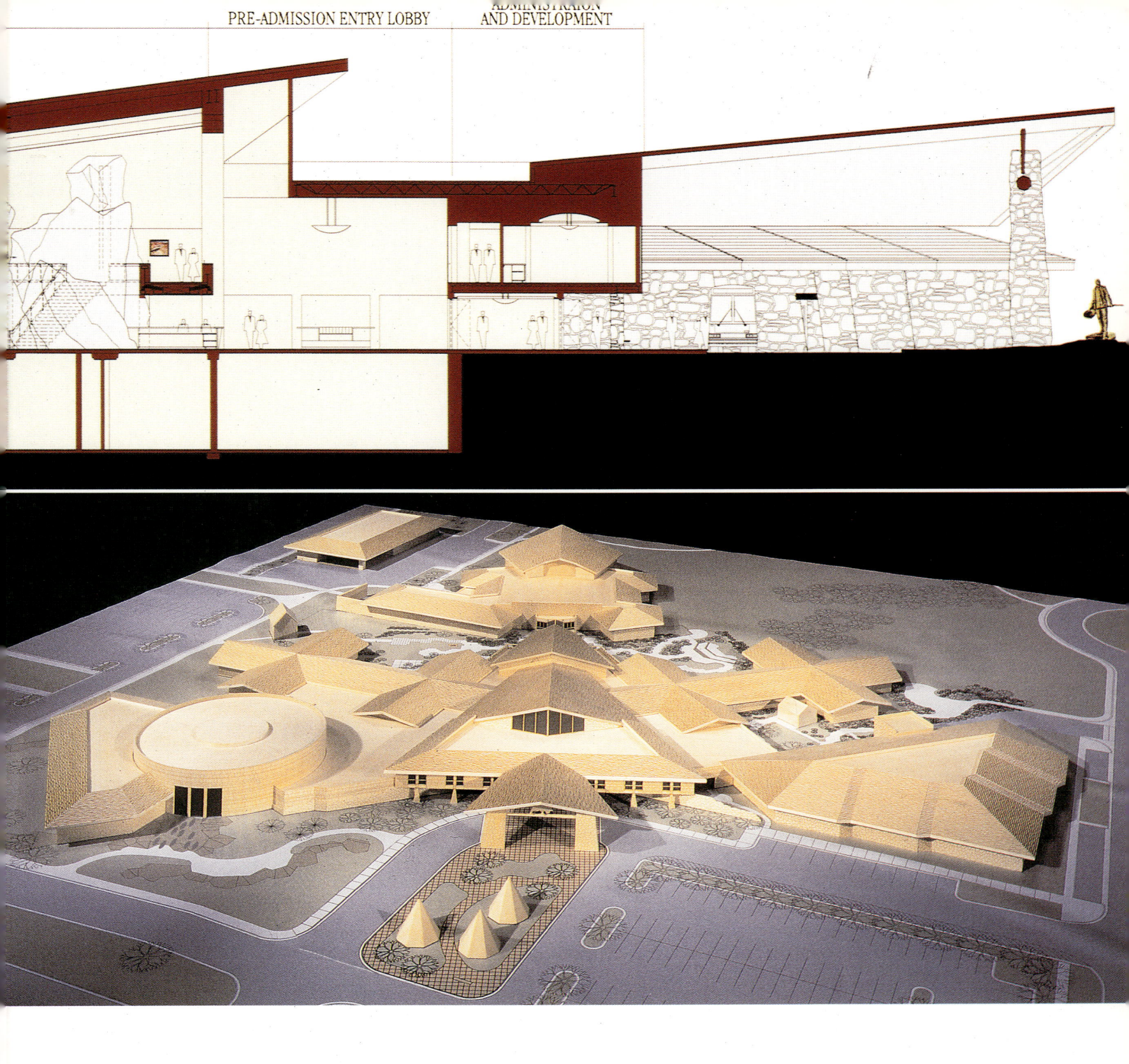

PRE-ADMISSION ENTRY LOBBY   ADMINISTRATION AND DEVELOPMENT

ABOVE:
AT FULL BUILD-OUT, THE MUSEUM WILL FEATURE AN EXPANDED AND RENOVATED LOBBY (CENTER).

BUFFALO BILL HISTORICAL CENTER **MUSEUMS+THEATERS** | 37

ABOVE:
THE DESIGN STRENGTHENS THE CENTRAL ENTRY AND CREATES AN INVITING FRONT DOOR DROP-OFF.

RIGHT:
THIS SITE PLAN SHOWS THE EXISTING CODY FIREARMS MUSEUM (TOP), BEFORE THE ADDITION OF THE DRAPER NATURAL HISTORY MUSEUM.

ABOVE:
THE EXPANDED LOBBY WILL PROVIDE THE MUSEUM WITH A GRAND ENTRY, WHICH ORIENTS VISITORS.

LEFT:
DETAIL OF LINKAGE BETWEEN THE PLAINS INDIAN MUSEUM (AT LEFT) AND THE LOBBY

BUFFALO BILL HISTORICAL CENTER **MUSEUMS+THEATERS** | 39

NATIONAL COWBOY AND WESTERN HERITAGE MUSEUM
OKLAHOMA CITY, OKLAHOMA

Fentress Bradburn won the national design competition for renovation and expansion of the National Cowboy and Western Heritage Museum in Oklahoma City, Oklahoma. The Museum sought a design that would increase its size and enhance the appearance of its Hall of Fame to give it a heroic and monumental presence. The National Cowboy and Western Heritage Museum design was required to address several key issues: the establishment of a new and exciting image for the museum, the creation of a functional building plan that would provide clear pathways through the exhibits and the flexibility to expand. Growth is always a challenge, and planning for logical growth and expansion within the framework of an established facility is doubly so.

Prior to Fentress Bradburn's major expansion, the Museum consisted of a two-level, 77,000-square-foot gallery, an exhibit hall and an administrative facility. The 163,000-square-foot addition allowed for the rearrangement of gallery and curatorial spaces. All gallery space was placed on the main level and all curatorial and storage functions were relocated to the lower level. This plan expanded the entire facility to 240,000 square feet. The new arrangement allowed for over 75,000 square feet of state-of-the-art flexible gallery and exhibit space and created an excellent forum for the display and integration of art within the building.

The National Cowboy and Western Heritage Museum contains galleries devoted to the American cowboy, firearms, Native Americans, the Lynn Hickey Rodeo and the children's cowboy corral, as well as galleries named for patrons Arthur and Shifra Silberman and William S. and Ann Atherton. The architects faced the challenge of strengthening the cohesiveness of this vast collection, while creating an iconic representation of the West and its history. Fentress Bradburn Architects recognized the merits of the original building and expanded upon them metaphorically and physically. This meant calling upon the established design inspirations of Oklahoma—namely, the covered wagons and camp tents that peppered the West during its early settlement, as well as rolling prairie forms. These inspirations primarily materialized into the rooflines.

The architects created a new museum entrance with a sweeping, peaked, curved canopy that is inviting to visitors.

A CANOPY NEAR THE ENTRYWAY FRAMES PART OF THE ADDITION TO THE MUSEUM.

40 | MUSEUMS+THEATERS NATIONAL COWBOY AND WESTERN HERITAGE MUSEUM

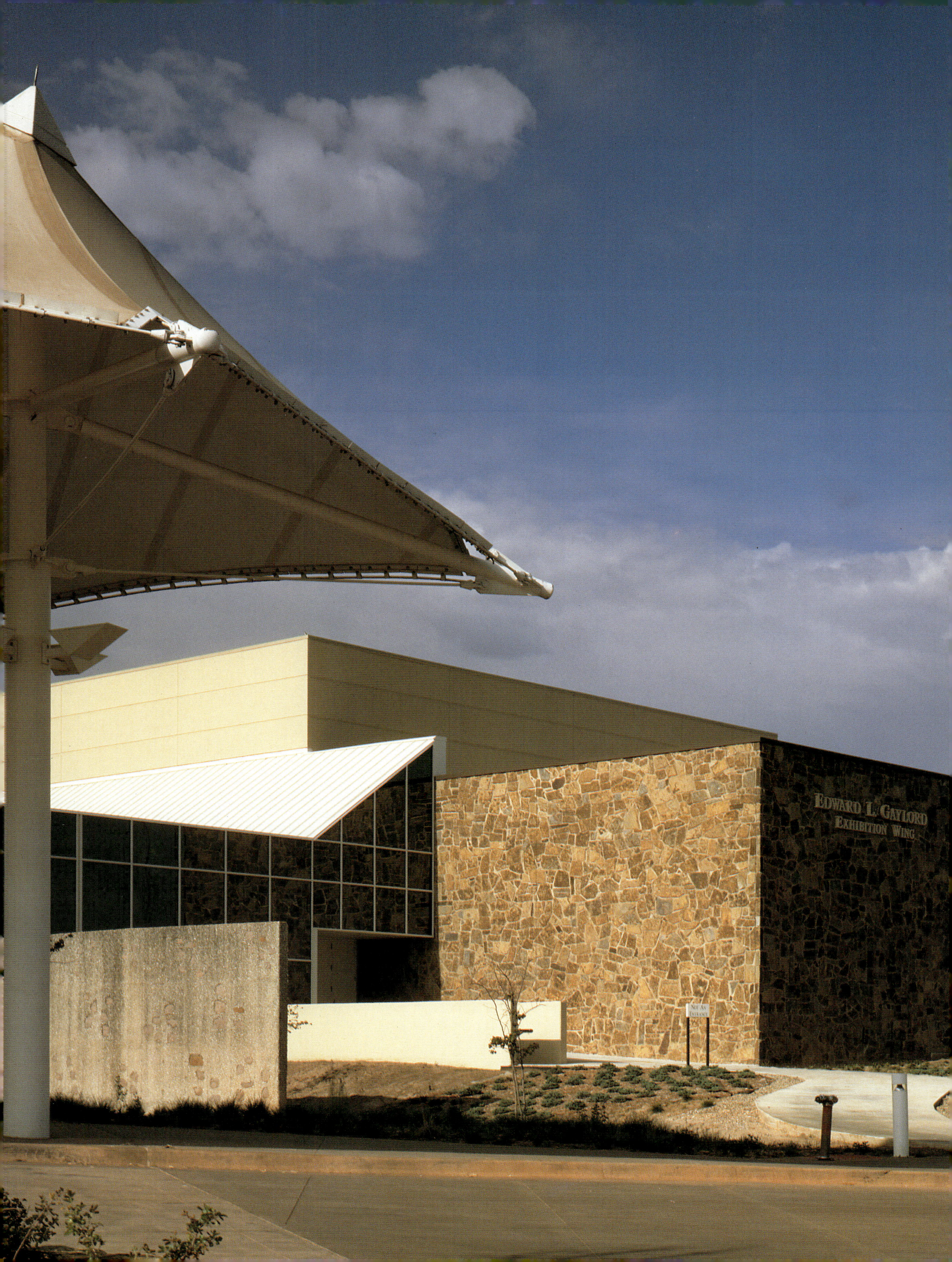
EDWARD L. GAYLORD
EXHIBITION WING

This architectural gesture reinforces a sense of entry that was not present within the original layout, while emphasizing the original reflecting pool and sculpture garden courtyard. The National Cowboy and Western Heritage Museum image is created in part by Leonard McMurray's magnificent Buffalo Bill Memorial. His work has been strategically placed to dramatize its scale and attract potential visitors traveling along the adjacent interstate highway. Inside, the firm's comprehensive design encompasses large, brightly-lit exhibition spaces and clearly defined passageways.

Many other works of art within the museum unify the structure and the surrounding environment. Evidence of this is clearly seen in "The Remuda" by artist Tom Ryan. The exhibition wing generated a 400-foot-by-26-foot wall. To integrate the character of the museum's architecture with the artwork, and to break up the monolithic quality of such a large façade, the architects separated the wall into five planes. Ryan's work now graces the five bays of the west wing and depicts 30 galloping horses and two cowhands, one leading and the other waving a lasso and following behind. "The Remuda" allowed the artist to expand and

ABOVE:
THE NEW ATRIUM BLENDS WITH THE EXISTING MUSEUM.

RIGHT:
THE LINES OF THE WINDOWS CREATE A GRID THAT PLAYS OFF THE TRIANGULAR ROOFLINE.

42 | MUSEUMS+THEATERS NATIONAL COWBOY AND WESTERN HERITAGE MUSEUM

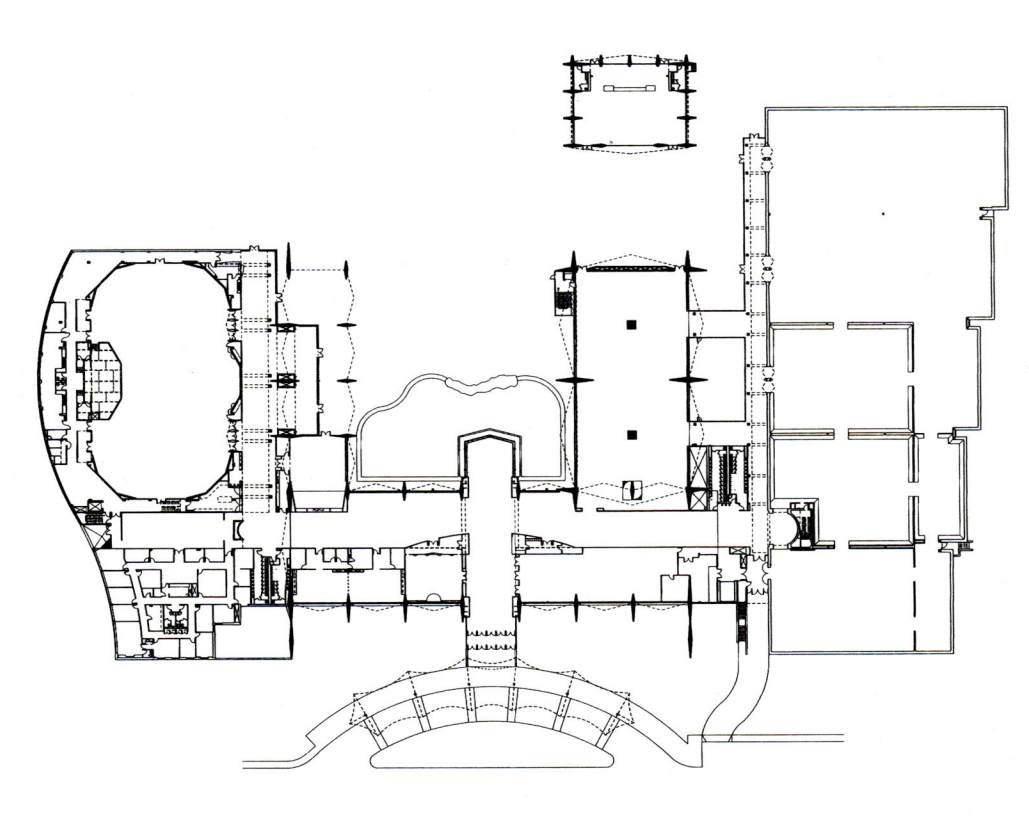

ABOVE:
THE CURVILINEAR SHAPE OF THE EXPANSION SERVES TO SOFTEN THE LINES OF THE BUILDING.

LEFT:
THE NEW ENTRYWAY (CENTER) FACES A NARROW ATRIUM THAT HELPS ORIENT VISITORS TO THE MUSEUM.

NATIONAL COWBOY AND WESTERN HERITAGE MUSEUM **MUSEUMS+THEATERS** | 43

RIGHT:
BRONZE STATUES OF HORSES AT FULL GALLOP STAND OUTSIDE THE BUILDING, FACING THE ATRIUM.

BELOW:
THE NEW ATRIUM CAN BE SEEN THROUGH THE WINDOWS OF THE EXISTING GALLERY.

ABOVE:
A POOL WITH FOUNTAINS SURROUNDS THE NEW ATRIUM.

LEFT:
THE RENOVATION AND EXPANSION CENTERED ON THE CREATION OF A GRAND ATRIUM, WHICH ORIENTS VISITORS.

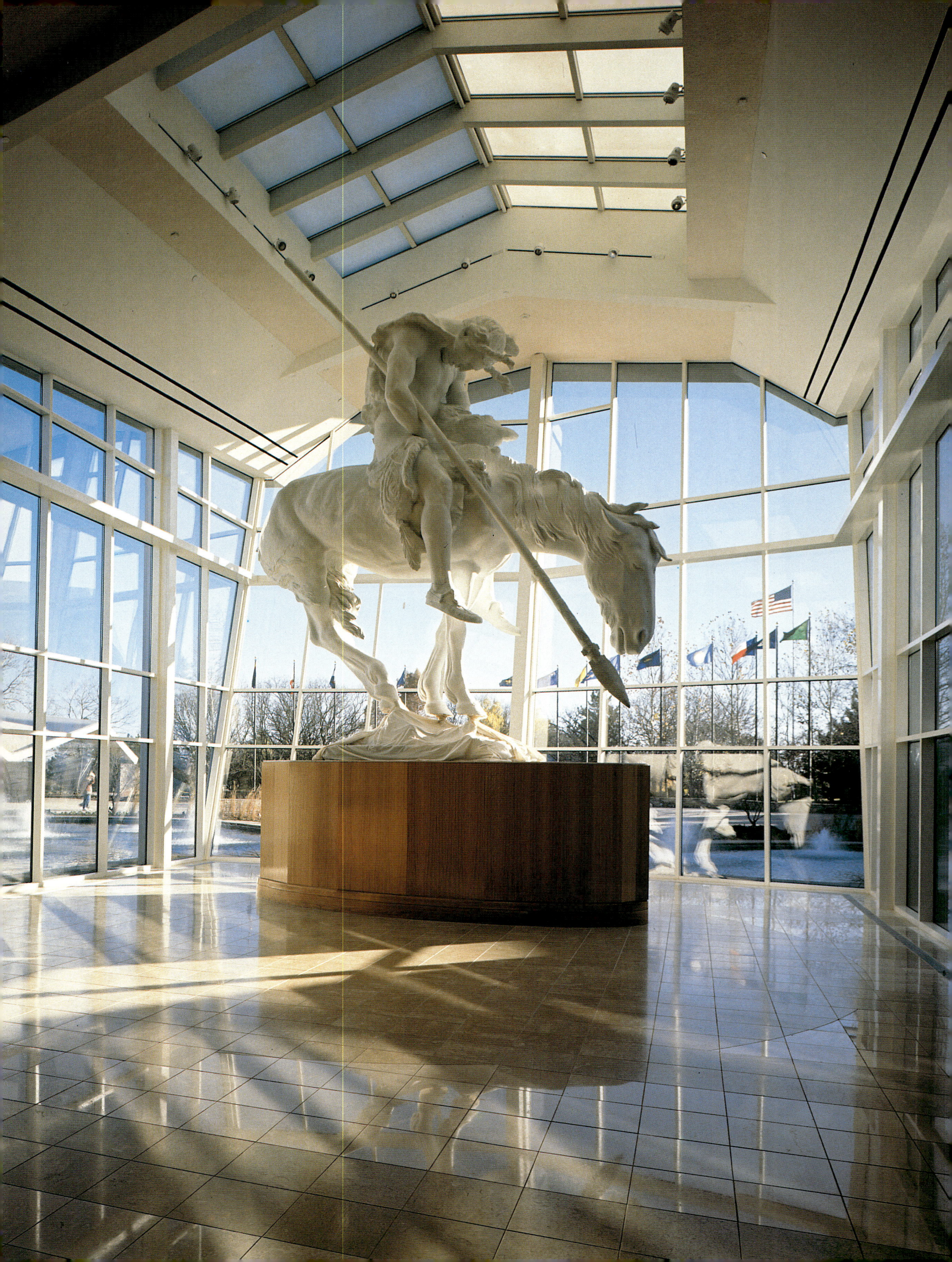

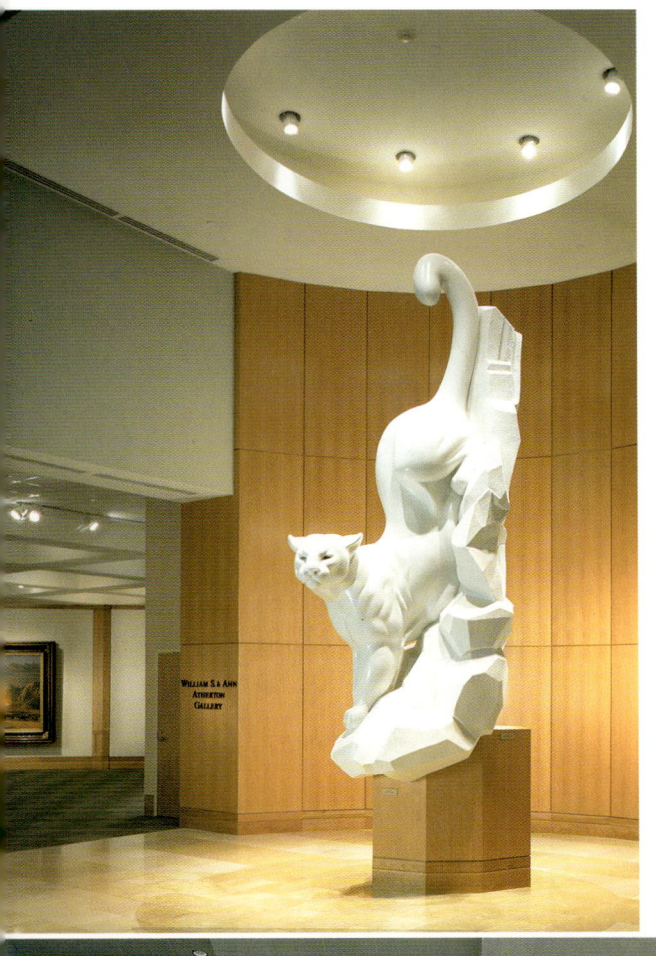

explore a variety of media. A brass re-creation of the work adorns the Museum's entrance gates.

The architects included pragmatic features to ensure that the functionality of the new space would match its aesthetic achievement. Such features include a 1,200-seat banquet facility, administrative offices, collection storage, seminar classrooms, an orientation theater and an expanded museum store. In addition, the architects met all technical guidelines and restrictions, while emphasizing innovation and user specificity. These considerations were addressed in areas such as lighting, heating/cooling and ventilation, acoustics, security, maintenance, graphics, colors and finishes. All standards were met for humidity levels, dust control, fire protection and the American Association of Museum's policies on art display, assuring the greatest possible flexibility for a museum capable of almost any type and size of display. The vision for this updated facility echoes the vision that spurred westward expansion in the 19th century: a desire for more, a dream of the future and a readiness to explore the possibilities.

FACING PAGE:
THE NEW ATRIUM HOUSES ONE OF THE MUSEUM'S MOST SPECTACULAR SCULPTURES, "END OF THE TRAIL," BY JAMES EARL FRASER.

THIS PAGE
ABOVE:
"CANYON PRINCESS" BY GERALD BALCIAR, A TWICE LIFE-SIZE MARBLE SCULPTURE OF A FEMALE COUGAR DESCENDING A CANYON WALL, STANDS 18 FEET TALL AND WEIGHS 6,100 POUNDS. THE MUSEUM WAS REQUIRED TO IMPLEMENT SPECIAL FOUNDATION AND ROOF-FRAMING DETAILS TO ACCOMMODATE THE PIECE.

LEFT:
THE FACILITY FEATURES A 1,200-SEAT BANQUET HALL.

MUSEUM OF WESTERN ART
DENVER, COLORADO

The 25,000-square-foot building was constructed in 1880 as the Brinker Collegiate Institute, the first coeducational college west of the Mississippi River. Having changed hands several times, it became the Richelieu Hotel in 1889, and then a classy casino and bordello until 1904, when such activities were outlawed. It was renamed the Navarre after Henry of Navarre, the 16th-century French king. In 1983, William Foxley purchased the building, which had become a designated city landmark listed on the National Register of Historic Places.

Foxley chose to use the space for exhibition of his large, private western art collection, which comprised over 125 paintings and sculptures. But the building required extensive restoration and adaptation in order to create a space capable of enhancing both the art and the visitor's viewing experience.

Fentress Bradburn's design solution integrates aspects of the building's original character into a more contemporary space. While the historic nature of the Navarre is most pronounced in the front lounge area, with finishes and period furniture that enhance its turn-of-the-century Victorian character, the rest of the facility boasts clean white walls. A glass-enclosed stairway within the core separate the building vertically into two distinct sections: a 20th-century museum

THE GLASS PANES OF THE ENCLOSED STAIRWAY PAY HOMAGE TO THE BUILDING'S HISTORICAL ROOTS.

48 | MUSEUMS+THEATERS MUSEUM OF WESTERN ART

MUSEUM OF WESTERN ART **MUSEUMS + THEATERS** | 49

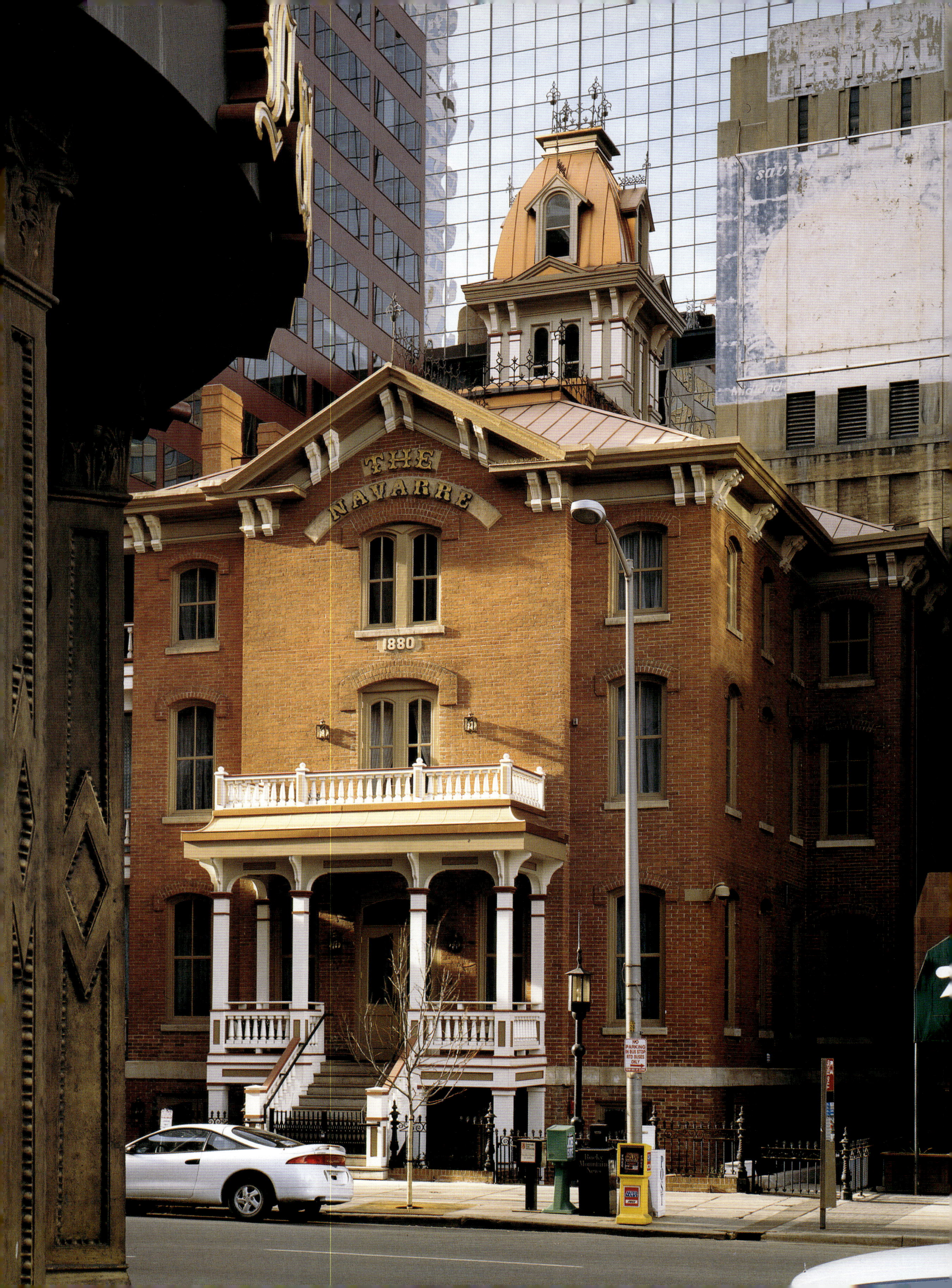
TERMINAL
THE
NAVARRE
1880

and its 19th-century anteroom. However, elements including the eggshell-colored mullion grid, which is applied throughout the gallery spaces, blends historical and modern, as it is reminiscent of the historical applications of glass paning.

The interior circulation plan routes patrons to the uppermost gallery floor, down the glass-enclosed stairway beneath the cupola space and horizontally through each gallery floor. By placing the gallery stair directly beneath the cupola, Fentress Bradburn took advantage of this historical focal point and its abundant natural light for the museum's major vertical element.

An opening between levels two and three establishes continuity between the two galleries and allows the second floor sculpture platform to be viewed laterally as well as from above. The two-story opening also creates a monumental public display space and, at the same time, preserves an intimate scale for patrons to view paintings.

A two-foot space between the interior and exterior walls was an innovative solution to create a controlled environment. The space became a plenum for the air circulation system, which directed airflow to the viewer and away from the art.

FACING PAGE
FENTRESS BRADBURN ADDED THE PORCH AS THE FINAL ELEMENT IN THE RESTORATION PROCESS BEGUN BY GOULD EVANS

THIS PAGE
HISTORIC PHOTOS.

MUSEUM OF WESTERN ART **MUSEUMS+THEATERS** | 51

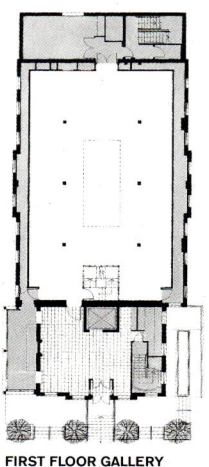

FIRST FLOOR GALLERY

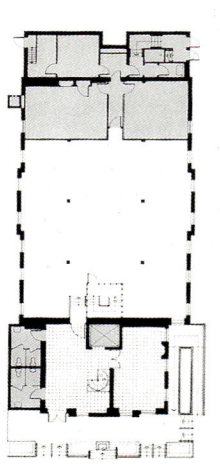

THIRD FLOOR OFFICES

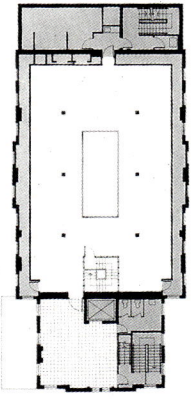

SECOND FLOOR GALLERY

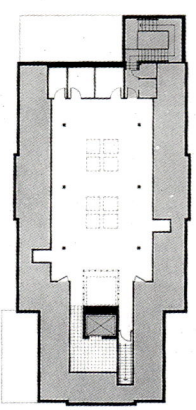

FOURTH FLOOR OFFICES

THIS PAGE
THE CUPOLA PROVIDES FILTERED, NATURAL LIGHT TO EACH FLOOR THROUGH THE GLASS-ENCLOSED STAIRWAY.

FACING PAGE
AN OPENING BETWEEN THE MUSEUM'S TWO GALLERY FLOORS ALLOWS LATERAL AND VERTICAL VIEWING OF THE BRONZE SCULPTURES.

52 | MUSEUMS + THEATERS MUSEUM OF WESTERN ART

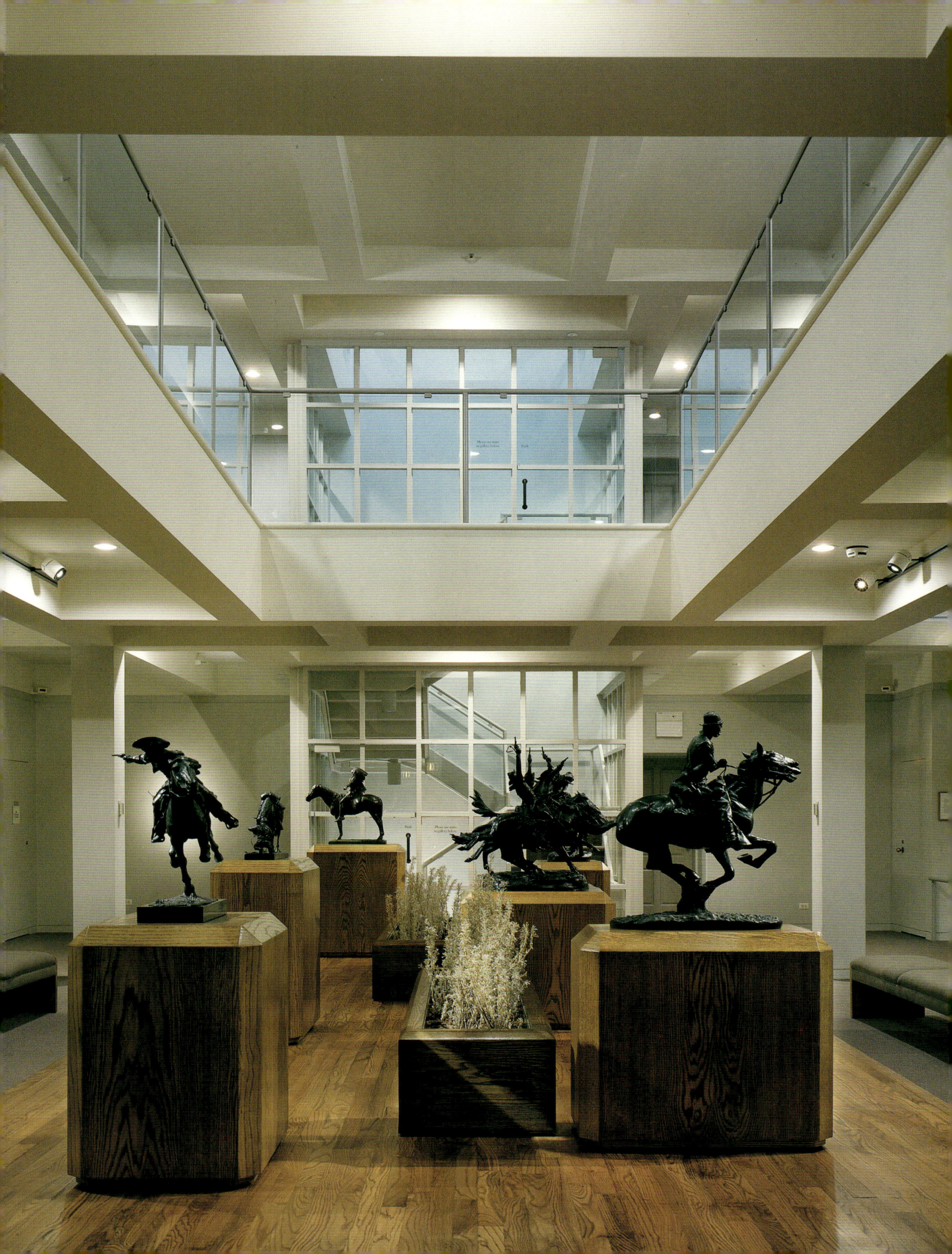

54 | **MUSEUMS + THEATERS** BLACK AMERICAN WEST MUSEUM

BLACK AMERICAN WEST MUSEUM AND HERITAGE CENTER
DENVER, COLORADO

The Black American West Museum and Heritage Center is a real life example of a community dream come true. Dr. Justina L. Ford's house, which was built in 1890, was saved from demolition after a wrecking crew had partially destroyed a sidewall. The 3,000-square-foot home was purchased with public funds and moved to its present site in 1984. Dr. Ford was Denver's first black female doctor and the house was transformed into the Black American West Museum in her memory.

Fentress Bradburn worked to restore the house to its 1912 appearance, accommodating current code requirements and the change from a mid-block to a corner lot site. The exterior was restored, which included reconstruction of the porch, stone base, windows and doors. The exterior walls were structurally tied back together and painted in the original color scheme. Building equipment and a handicapped-accessible ramp were located on the less visible west side in a slot of space between the museum and an adjacent house.

Fentresss Bradburn maintained the existing interior space layout with minor modifications. Economical finishes and furnishings were installed in the spirit of the original design, while also providing flexible exhibit and meeting space. Complementary wall moldings were added in most exhibit rooms for flexibility of hanging exhibits. The firm helped to retain the memory of Dr. Ford with a permanent exhibit of her office.

The museum has become a community center and educational resource which celebrates African-American history and promotes opportunities for African-American people on a local and national scale. The Black American West Museum and Heritage Center has grown to become one of the most comprehensive sources of historic materials about African-Americans in the West.

THIS PAGE AND FACING PAGE
THE EXTERIOR AND INTERIOR OF THE BUILDING WERE FULLY RESTORED TO THE TIME OF DR. FORD'S OWNERSHIP.

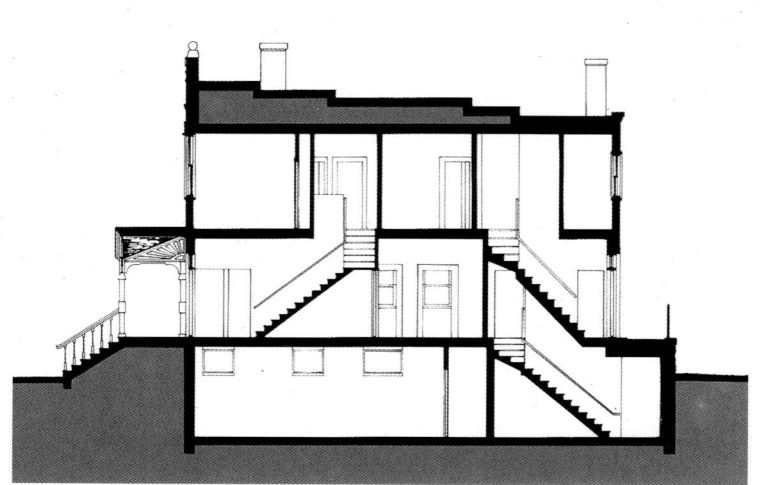

CROSS SECTION

FACING PAGE
TOP:
PRE-RESTORATION CONDITIONS

BOTTOM:
CROSS-SECTION

THIS PAGE
ALL OF THE ELEMENTS, FROM CROWN MOLDINGS TO THE DENTIST CHAIR, WERE EITHER RESTORED OR RECREATED FROM PHOTOGRAPHS.

THIS PAGE
AN UNUSUALLY SHAPED RECTILINEAR ATRIUM WELCOMES AND ORIENTS PATRONS.

FACING PAGE
AT 180 FEET TALL, THE ATRIUM PAYS TRIBUTE TO THE SKY.

58 | **MUSEUMS+THEATERS** LEGACY OF FLIGHT

LEGACY OF FLIGHT
SPRINGFIELD, MISSOURI

The Legacy of Flight is designed to chronicle the history of aviation, from the first operational aircraft to spaceships and hang gliders. The goal of Fentress Bradburn's design is to bring to life the unusual and intriguing program proposed by DMCD, a New York exhibit design firm.

The iconic landmark feature of the building will be an unusually shaped rectilinear glass atrium of heroic scale. The atrium celebrates the sky and expresses the soaring spirit of flight that is detailed inside.

Visitors approach the museum through a grand welcoming plaza to enter the atrium, which is 180 feet high and 150 feet across. Hanging from the ceiling is a large replica of the International Space Station. A glass elevator transports visitors to the mezzanine level, where they can board a roller coaster that travels the entire perimeter of the building.

The facility encompasses almost 300,000 square feet and houses an expanding collection of vintage aircraft, from Kitty Hawk through World War II, as well as interactive simulators that will take visitors all the way from first flight to the experience of space travel. An anticipated 2,000 people per day will pass through the facility.

The main exhibits are a scenic re-creation of an aircraft carrier at dockside, a B-17 crash diorama, an interactive World War I-era observation balloon and simulators that re-create such experiences as hang gliding and the London Blitzkrieg. Other attractions include a carousel in the children's play area, a memorial chapel and vintage aircraft displays under the hangar-inspired arched roof of the main gallery. The building also features a 250-seat auditorium, a 5,000-square-foot shopping arcade, a 600-seat food court, a 100-seat English pub and a rotating orientation theater.

60 | **MUSEUMS+THEATERS** LEGACY OF FLIGHT

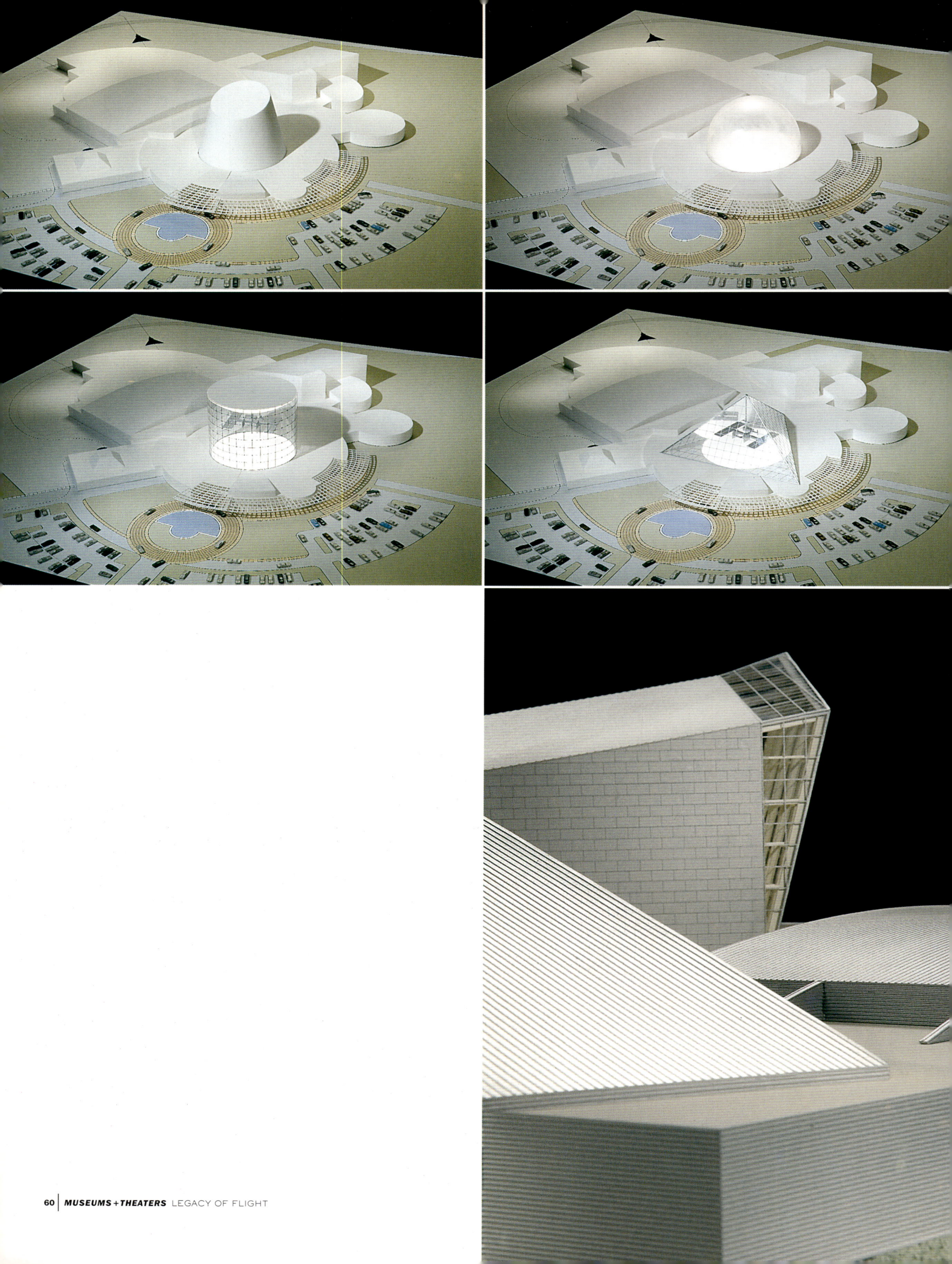

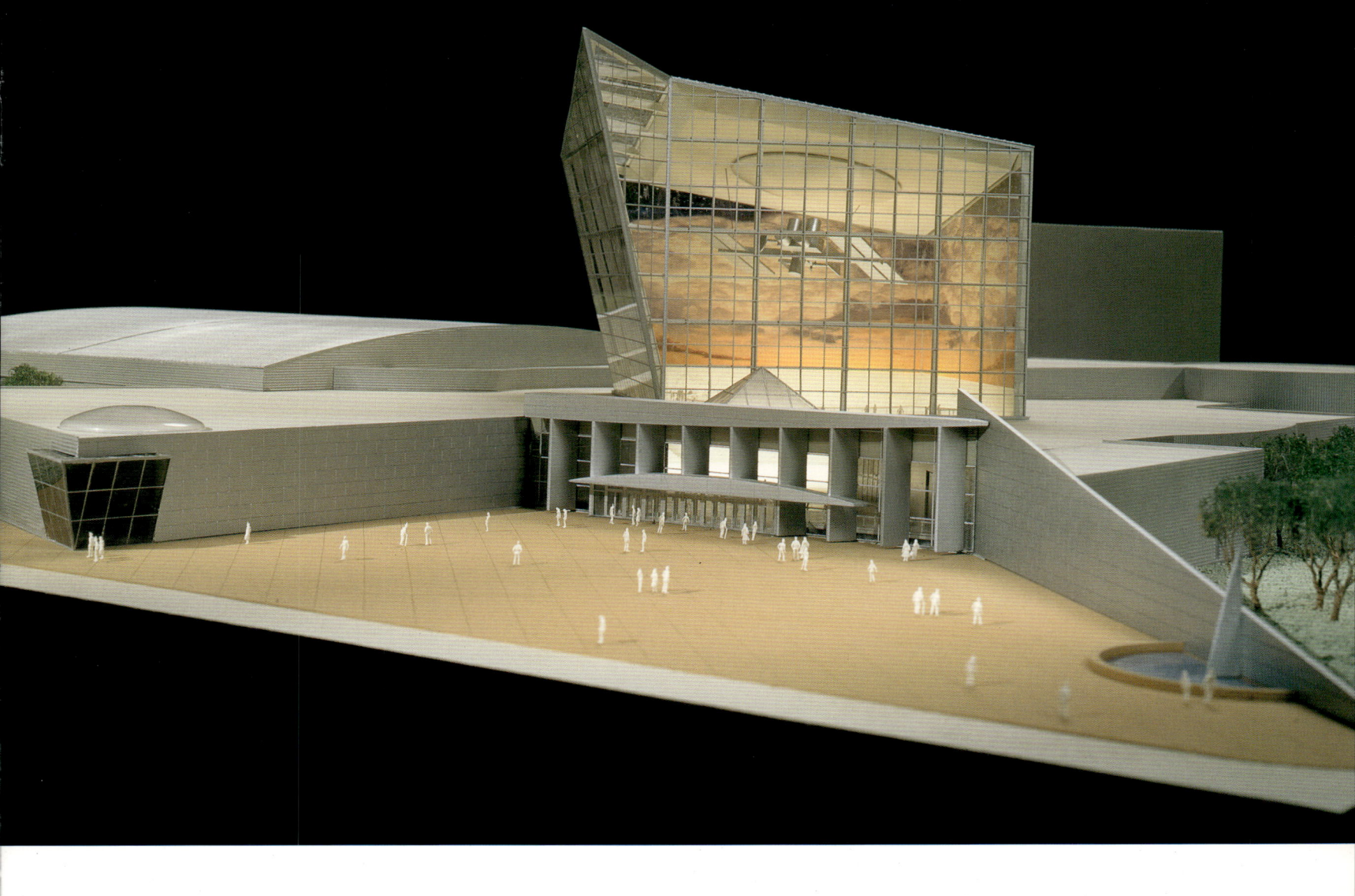

FACING PAGE
TOP:
CONCEPTUAL DESIGN MODELS ILLUSTRATE THE DESIGN EVOLUTION PROCESS.

BOTTOM:
VARIED ROOFLINES SPEAK OF IMAGINATION AND INNOVATION.

THIS PAGE:
VIEW UPON ARRIVAL.

LEGACY OF FLIGHT **MUSEUMS + THEATERS** | 61

PEERY'S EGYPTIAN THEATER ORIGINALLY OPENED IN 1924 AND WAS REFURBISHED 70 YEARS LATER.

Fentress Bradburn designed the new David Eccles Conference Center and completed the renovation for Peery's Egyptian Theater as part of Ogden, Utah's downtown revitalization plan. Modeled after King Tut's Tomb, the renewed theater houses a multitude of events, including Utah's Musical Theater. Peery's Egyptian Theater worked with the city for 12 years to raise desperately needed funding for its renovation and, ultimately, the addition of a conference center. Both the theater and the conference center needed space for live theatrical productions and cinema. Located within the project is a 95,000-square-foot conference center, 40,000 square feet of performing arts and offstage support space and a 15,000-square-foot ballroom. The performance auditorium, with 867 seats, was restored to complete the facility.

Fentress Bradburn led a collaboration between Sanders

PEERY'S EGYPTIAN THEATER and THE DAVID ECCLES CONFERENCE CENTER
OGDEN, UTAH

Herman, the local associate architect, and a marketing research firm, Hammer, Siler, George Associates, to produce a feasibility study for the project. The 18-week process, which included two five-day workshops and four public meetings with various interest groups, assessed the functional programmatic requirements for the facility. Results from the study identified the need for clear and efficient way-finding devices and circulation paths, easy to understand signage for meeting and conference rooms and restrooms, and a building that functionally and aesthetically combined the county conference center with the performing arts complex.

A large ballroom is located on both floors of the conference center. The design allows this ballroom to convert easily into five, fully self-contained areas for smaller groups

THE DAVID ECCLES CONFERENCE CENTER BORROWS EGYPTIAN MOTIFS FROM PEERY'S EGYPTIAN THEATER.

THIS PAGE

ABOVE: RESTORATION OF THE THEATER FOLLOWED SEVERAL YEARS OF FUND-RAISING AND COLLABORATIVE WORK, BY THE THEATER AND THE CITY OF OGDEN, UTAH.

RIGHT: NORTH SECTION OF PEERY'S EGYPTIAN THEATER (ABOVE). NORTH SECTION OF THE DAVID ECCLES CONFERENCE CENTER (BELOW).

FACING PAGE: A PYRAMID-SHAPED CLERESTORY BRINGS LIGHT INTO THE TWO-STORY-HIGH LOBBY OF THE DAVID ECCLES CONFERENCE CENTER.

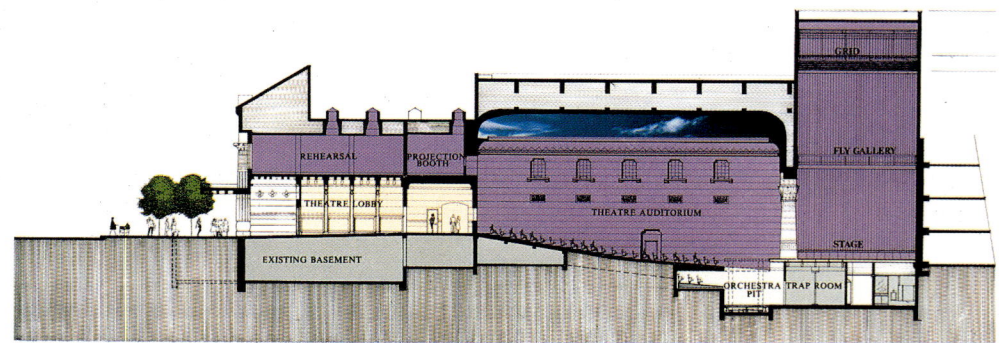

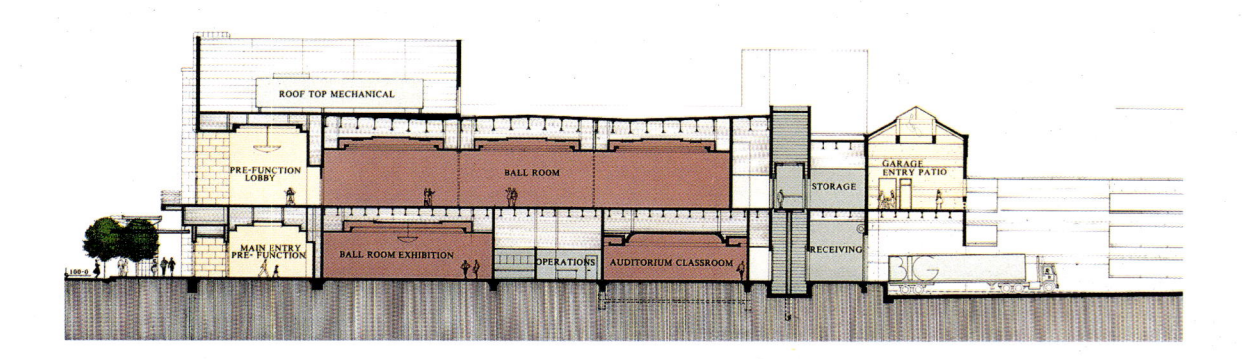

64 | MUSEUMS + THEATERS   PEERY'S EGYPTIAN THEATER AND THE DAVID ECCLES CONFERENCE CENTER

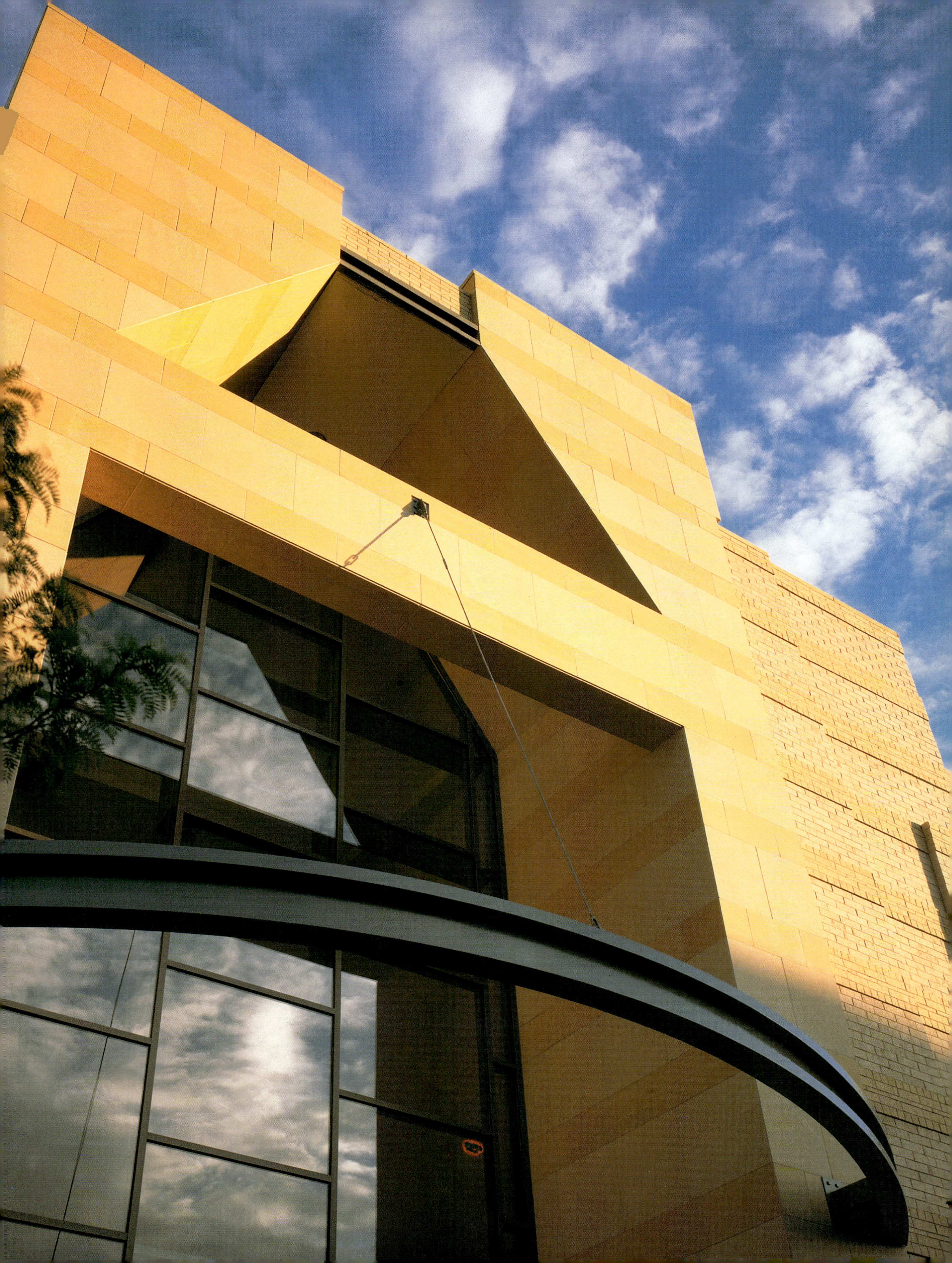

ABOVE LEFT:
EGYPTIAN DETAILING WAS RESTORED ON THE COLUMNS AND LINTEL, AS WELL AS ON THE CROWN MOLDING.

ABOVE RIGHT:
ART DECO DETAILING WAS RESTORED IN THE ORIGINAL THEATER BOX OFFICE AREA.

RIGHT:
HIEROGLYPHICS AND OTHER EGYPTIAN-INSPIRED IMAGERY ADORN BEAMS AND THE ORNATE COFFERED CEILING OF THE THEATER.

and individual needs, such as catering. Each space is equipped with an individual acoustical system. This feature permits a multitude of activities to coexist without disturbing one another. The Executive Training Laboratory includes a multimedia training center, fully wired for the computer and audio-visual requirements of both large and small groups. A wall-sized pull-down screen allows this laboratory to accommodate almost any presentation.

When Peery's Egyptian Theater opened in 1924, it was considered a state-of-the-art movie palace, as much an event as the movie itself. With the growth of suburbs and the advent of the multiplex in the 1980s, Peery's eventually deteriorated. With the aid of Fentress Bradburn, the theater was renovated and reopened in July 1996. Restorative efforts aimed for a modern-day re-creation of the original Egyptian Theater, complete with the famous atmospheric ceiling, elegant side balconies and detailed proscenium arch. The exterior retains many original details, while elements of surprise and innovation were added. The original terra-cotta exterior has been refurbished, the papyrus-texture columns have been enhanced with vibrant hues and the six original Egyptian figurines still line the outside of the building. The performance stage, featuring a hydraulic orchestra pit and fly gallery, has been considerably enlarged. The lobby has been expanded from its original form, complete with a replica of the 1924 box office. A new gallery area to the south allows audience members to mingle during intermissions.

To aesthetically blend the Eccles Conference Center with Peery's Egyptian Theater, elements of the theater's original design were recalled in profile and form. The asymmetrical, curvilinear design of the two-toned, sand-colored walls, along with the cut-stone shape and texture of the theater's exterior, are subtly echoed in the conference center. Combinations of local sandstone, pre-cast concrete and curtain walls complete the structure. The strategically recessed bands of horizontal brick simulate Egyptian pyramid design elements, while blending the two buildings into one. On the interior, wrought-iron railings emulate Egyptian papyrus reeds, the elevator doors feature Art Deco detailing and strategically designed ceilings allow indirect lighting to guide patrons between the theater and the conference center.

ABOVE LEFT:
THE STAIRWAY TO THE SECOND FLOOR OF THE CONFERENCE CENTER RECALLS THE ELEGANT THEATER DESIGN IN A MUTED FORM.

BELOW LEFT:
BLACK COLUMNS AND OTHER DETAILS SIGNAL THE CONFERENCE CENTER'S CONNECTION TO THE THEATER.

ABOVE:
THE CONFERENCE CENTER IS EQUIPPED WITH STATE-OF-THE-ART TRAINING FACILITIES.

THE AUDITORIUM
COLORADO CONVENTION CENTER PHASE II EXPANSION
DENVER, COLORADO

A 5,000-seat auditorium will be included in the new 2.5 million-square-foot Colorado Convention Center. While the auditorium is designed to functionally accommodate the needs of conventioneers, its rounded shape aesthetically counterbalances the Center's canted, 1,000-foot-long roofline and full-façade glass curtain wall.

The pre- and post-function spaces include the galleria between the street level entrance and the auditorium, as well as the upstairs exterior terrace and interior lobby atrium, which are accessible from the galleria via stairwells and escalators. The Convention Center's operators envision large gatherings for keynote speeches, special evening events and large panel discussions to adjourn from the auditorium to corporate sponsored receptions in the lobby and on the terrace, which have spectacular views to the majestic Rocky Mountains.

After conducting over 100 meetings with various interest groups, flexibility and accessibility were identified as key elements for success. With flexibility in mind, Fentress Bradburn created an auditorium that may be split into three separate spaces, ranging in size from 1,300 seats to 2,400 seats. Partitions will allow the space to be divided into three possible arrangements: the whole house, a small and a large house or three smaller houses. Proper acoustical treatments to the partitions and other surfaces, along with three state-of-the-art audiovisual, acoustical and lighting systems will allow simultaneous events to be held without disrupting one another.

Accessibility was a key determinant in the layout of the auditorium. Two separate bays service the stage and accommodate vehicles including dressing trailers, semi-trailer trucks and catering vans. The facility is equipped with an underground conduit system so that traveling shows wishing

THIS PAGE
THE ROUNDED SHAPE OF THE AUDITORIUM PROVIDES A COUNTERBALANCE TO THE CENTER'S CANTED ROOFLINE.

FACING PAGE
TOP:
UPLIT AT NIGHT, THE ENTIRE CENTER WILL HAVE A DRAMATIC IMPACT ON THE DENVER SKYLINE.

BOTTOM:
STREET LEVEL PLAN

to supply their own equipment can link their cables to the house control positions.

The stage, at 50 feet by 100 feet, may be extended by up to 1,750 square feet through the use of movable panels. These panels may be used in a variety of configurations, including a runway, and store easily in a recess that is flush with the house floor. Both the stage and its expandable panels are made of resilient flooring with a hardboard finish.

An 8,000-square-foot tension grid hangs 34 feet above the staging area. The grid, composed of wire panels, supports stage-lighting fixtures and includes loft wells that support cables for hoisting scenery and props. Above the tension grid is a catwalk and beyond the catwalk is a control catwalk. The entire facility, including all positions on the grid, catwalk and control catwalk, is handicapped-accessible.

COLORADO CONVENTION CENTER PHASE II EXPANSION **MUSEUMS + THEATERS** | 69

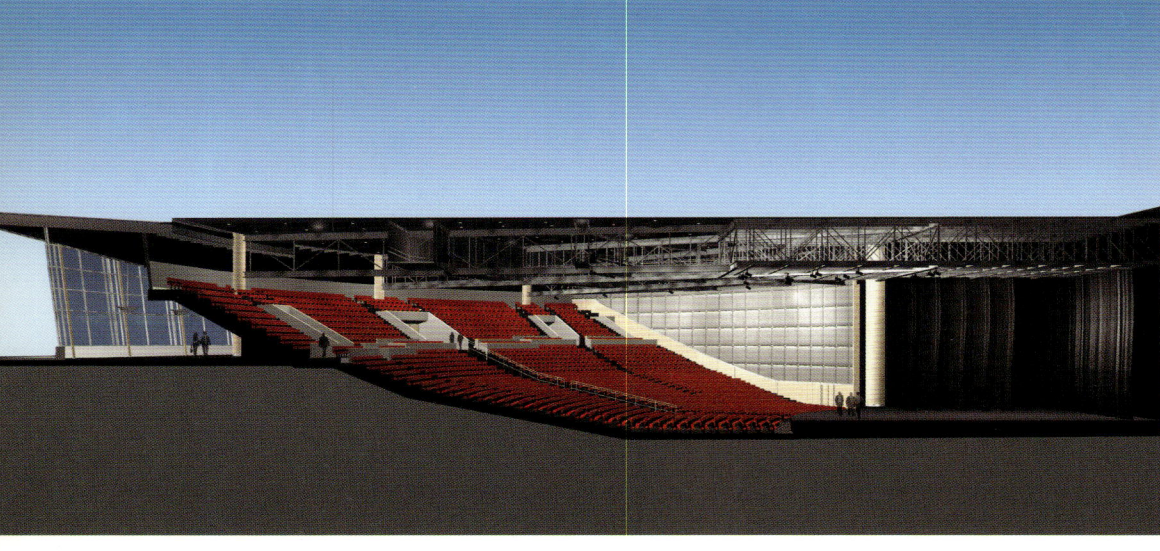

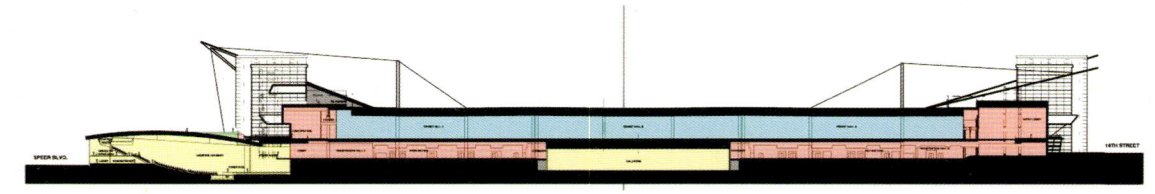

EAST-WEST SECTION WITH AUDITORIUM ON FAR LEFT

70 | *MUSEUMS+THEATERS* COLORADO CONVENTION CENTER PHASE II EXPANSION

FACING PAGE, THIS PAGE
LEFT, CENTER AND RIGHT: VARIOUS SECTIONS

THIS PAGE
TOP: THE LOBBY SERVES AS A PRE- AND POST-FUNCTION SPACE AND OFFERS ACCESS TO AN OUTDOOR TERRACE.

COLORADO CONVENTION CENTER PHASE II EXPANSION   *MUSEUMS+THEATERS* | 71

ARVADA CENTER FOR THE ARTS AND HUMANITIES EXPANSION

DENVER, COLORADO

Fentress Bradburn was selected from 21 applicants to design an expansion for the 25-year-old, 122,000-square-foot Arvada Center, which is home to one of two professional theater companies in Colorado. In addition to indoor and outdoor theater productions, this award-winning Center offers concerts, contemporary art exhibitions, a history museum, an imaginative playground and over 600 classes in the arts and humanities to over 340,000 visitors each year. The Center also hosts nearly 1,100 meetings, banquets, parties, weddings and trade shows each year that range in size from ten to 900 people.

The Arvada Center identified four primary goals for the expansion: create a synergy between the conference and art functions; integrate existing public art elements with new architecture; utilize the expansion to make a strong visual statement; and create an interior environment that makes a positive, lasting impression.

Fentress Bradburn recently completed the programming phase, which identified a need for site improvements and an additional 152,000 square feet. The additional space will accommodate a new 1,000-seat theater and expand administrative and development offices, building operations, classrooms, galleries, the museum, guest services and the performing arts spaces.

FACING PAGE
ARTIST'S CHARCOAL RENDERING OF NEW ENTRANCE.

THIS PAGE
TOP:
ARTIST'S CHARCOAL RENDERING OF ENTRY LOBBY.

BOTTOM:
MASSING MODEL DEPICTING ADDITION IN RED.

CREDITS

ARVADA CENTER FOR THE ARTS AND HUMANITIES EXPANSION
Consultants:
STRUCTURAL
Martin/Martin
LANDSCAPE
Civitas
THEATER
Theater Projects Consultants
AUDIO/VISUAL
Engineering Harmonics
MECHANICAL, ELECTRICAL, PLUMBING, FIRE PROTECTION:
M-E Engineers
FOOD SERVICE
Thomas Ricca
COST
Capstone Planning & Control
CODE
Rolf Jensen & Associates
INFORMATION TECHNOLOGY
Technology Plus
ACOUSTICS
Robert F. Mahoney & Associates
MUSEUM
Southwest Museum Services
FEASIBILITY STUDY
CS&L
TRANSPORTATION STUDY
Trans Plan
LIGHTING
Hefferan Partnership

THE AUDITORIUM, COLORADO CONVENTION CENTER EXPANSION
Associate Architects:
Bertram A Bruton & Associates;
Harold Massup Associates;
Abo Copeland Architecture
Consultants:
STRUCTURAL ENGINEER
Martin Martin; The Sheflin Group
STRUCTURAL DRAFTING
Precision Cadd & Graphics
CIVIL ENGINEER
The Lund Partnership
MECHANICAL, PLUMBING, FIRE PROTECTION
M-E Engineers
ELECTRICAL
BCER
INTERIORS
Compositions
LIGHTING DESIGNER OF RECORD
Socar Engineering
LIGHTING DESIGN
LAM Partnership
MECHANICAL, PLUMBING, DRAFTING
CADCO
URBAN DESIGN, LANDSCAPE, SITE PLANNING
Civitas
SIGNAGE AND GRAPHICS
TKD Design
CODE
Rolf Jensen & Associates
FOOD SERVICE
Thomas Ricca and Associates
ACOUSTICAL DESIGN AND THEATER SYSTEMS
David L. Adams & Associates
AUDIO VISUAL
Shen Milsom & Wilke + Paoletti
VERTICAL CIRCULATION
Lerch Bates & Associates, Inc.
PARKING
Walker Parking Consultants
AUDITORIUM
Semple Brown Design
SCHEDULING, COST ESTIMATION:
Capstone Planning & Control
INFORMATION TECHNOLOGY
Technology Plus
TRAFFIC AND LIGHT RAIL
BRW; Heery International
SPECIFICATIONS WRITER
Carpenter & Associates
SECURITY
HMA Consulting
TESTING
Rowan Williams Davies & Irwin;
CTC-Geotek

BLACK AMERICAN WEST MUSEUM AND HERITAGE CENTER
Consultants:
SURVEY
Zylstra Baker Surveying
STRUCTURAL
Borman Smith Bush & Partners
MECHANICAL, PLUMBING, FIRE PROTECTION
M-E Engineers
TESTING
Goodson & Associates

BUFFALO BILL HISTORICAL CENTER
Consultants:
ARCHITECTURAL SPECIFICATIONS
Carpenter Associates
AUDIOVISUAL and ACOUSTICAL
David L. Adams Associates
CIVIL ENGINEERING and LANDSCAPE DESIGN
Fisher & Associates
COST ESTIMATOR
CTA Architects Engineers
EXHIBIT DESIGN
DMCD
West Office Exhibit Designs
MECHANICAL and ELECTRICAL ENGINEERING
CTA Architects Engineers
SPECIALTY LIGHTING DESIGN
Hefferan Partnership, Inc.
STRUCTURAL ENGINEERING
Richard Weingardt Consultants, Inc.
VERTICAL TRANSPORTATION
Lerch Bates & Associates, Inc.

DRAPER MUSEUM OF NATURAL HISTORY
Consultants:
CIVIL ENGINEER/ LANDSCAPE ARCHITECT
Fischer & Associates
STRUCTURAL ENGINEER
Richard Weingardt Consultants
MECHANICAL/ ELECTRICAL ENGINEER
CTA
COST ESTIMATOR
CTA
KITCHEN DESIGN
Thomas Ricca and Associates
AUDIO VISUAL/ACOUSTICS
David Adams & Associates
SPECIALTY LIGHTING
Hefferan Partnership, Inc.
ELEVATOR
Lerch Bates & Associates, Inc.
EXHIBIT DESIGN
DMCD; Gensler; West Office
EXHIBITION DESIGN SPECIFICATIONS WRITER
Carpenter & Associates

LEGACY OF FLIGHT
Associate Architect:
Wigen Tincknell Meyer & Associates
Consultants:
EXHIBIT DESIGN
DMCD
STRUCTURAL ENGINEER
Robert Darvas Associates
CIVIL ENGINEER
Fishbeck, Thompson, Carr & Huber Inc.
MECHANICAL/ ELECTRICAL ENGINEER
Tower Pinkster Titus Associates
LANDSCAPE
O'Boyle, Cowell, Blalock & Associate
SPECIALTY LIGHTING
Hefferan Partnership, Inc.
KITCHEN DESIGN
Thomas Ricca and Associates
AUDIO VISUAL/ACOUSTICS
David Adams & Associates
SPECIFICATIONS WRITER
Carpenter & Associates
ELEVATOR
Lerch Bates & Associates, Inc.
SECURITY
Shiff
TRAFFIC CONSULTANT
Wade – Trim

MUSEUM OF WESTERN ART
Associate Architect:
John Prosser
Consultants:
STRUCTURAL
Borman Smith & Partners
MECHANICAL, ELECTRICAL
Abeyta Engineering Consultants
EXHIBIT DESIGN
Jack Kurfman

NATIONAL COWBOY AND WESTERN HERITAGE MUSEUM
Consultants:
ACOUSTICAL
David L. Adams Associates, Inc.
ARCHITECTURAL SPECIFICATIONS
Carpenter Associates
CIVIL ENGINEERING
JGVE, Inc.
CONCESSIONS
Tom Shores
COST ESTIMATOR
Jerry Pope
ELECTRICAL ENGINEERING
Garland D. Cox Associates
EXHIBIT DESIGNERS
1717 Design Group
Design Craftsmen, Inc.
FOOD SERVICE CONSULTANT
Thomas Ricca Associates
FOUNTAIN DESIGNERS
The Fountain People
GRAPHIC DESIGN
TKD Designs
HARDWARE
Johnson Hardware, Inc.
LANDSCAPE DESIGN
EDAW-HRV
MECHANICAL/ELECTRICAL ENGINEERING
PSA Consulting Engineers
MECHANICAL ENGINEERING DESIGN
Riegel Associates, Inc.
PAINTER
Wilson Hurley
Duane R. Chartier
SECURITY
Steven R. Keller & Associates
STRUCTURAL and CIVIL ENGINEERING
Richard Weingardt Consultants, Inc.
STRUCTURAL ENGINEERING for TENSILE STRUCTURE
Severud Associates Consulting
SURVEYOR
Topographic Mapping Company
VERTICAL TRANSPORTATION
Lerch Bates North America, Inc.

NATIONAL MUSEUM OF THE MARINE CORPS AND HERITAGE CENTER
Exhibit Design:
Christopher Chadbourne & Associates
Consultants:
CIVIL ENGINEER
Patton Harris Rust & Associates
LANDSCAPE
EDAW
STRUCTURAL ENGINEER
Weidlinger Associates
MECHANICAL, ELECTRICAL, PLUMBING, FIRE PROTECTION
Hankins and Anderson
SUSTAINABLE DESIGN
Architectural Energy Corporation
FOOD SERVICE
Thomas Ricca and Associates
LIGHTING DESIGN
HM Brandston & Partners
AUDIO VISUAL/ACOUSTICS
Shen Milsom & Wilke
SPECIFICATIONS WRITER
Carpenter & Associates
GEOTECHNICAL
Patton Harris Rust & Associates
COST
PMSI
VALUE ENGINEER
Hanscomb

NATIONAL MUSEUM OF WILDLIFE ART
Consultants:
ASSOCIATE LANDSCAPE ARCHITECT
Richard Vangytenbeek
AUDIOVISUAL
David L. Adams Associates, Inc.
CIVIL ENGINEERING
Jorgensen Engineering
ELECTRICAL ENGINEERING
Consulting Engineers, Inc.
FOOD SERVICE CONSULTANT
Thomas Ricca Associates
GEOTECHNICAL ENGINEERING
Chen Northern, Inc.
GROUND-WATER HYDROLOGY
Hydrokinetics
LANDSCAPE ARCHITECT
Civitas, Inc.
MECHANICAL ENGINEERING
M-E Engineers, Inc.
SECURITY
Electronic Design Associates
STRUCTURAL ENGINEERING
Jirsa+Hedrick & Associates
WILDLIFE ASSESSMENT
Biota Research & Consulting, Inc.

PEERY'S EGYPTIAN THEATER and THE DAVID ECCLES CONFERENCE CENTER
Associate Architect:
Sanders Herman Architects
Consultants:
ACOUSTICAL
David L. Adams Associates
ARCHITECTURAL SPECIFICATIONS
Carpenter Associates
CIVIL ENGINEERING
Jones & Associates
CONFERENCE CENTER CONSULTANT
Tom Pickering
ELECTRICAL ENGINEERING
Becherer Nielson Associates
FOOD SERVICE CONSULTANT
Thomas Ricca Associates
GRAPHIC DESIGN
TKD Designs
MECHANICAL ENGINEERING
Colvin Engineering
LANDSCAPE and URBAN DESIGN
Civitas, Inc.
BMA
STRUCTURAL ENGINEERING
ARW Engineers
THEATER DESIGN
Theater Projects
THEATER RESTORATION
Conrad Schmitt Studios

WHITNEY GALLERY OF WESTERN ART
Consultants:
STRUCTURAL
Richard Weingardt Consultants
LIGHTING
LAM

PHOTOGRAPHY AND ILLUSTRATION CREDITS
PATRICK BARTA: 5
CARL DALIO: 22, 23, 38, 39, 58
FENTRESS BRADBURN ARCHITECTS: 4, 5, 7, 13, 14, 16, 35, 36, 38, 39, 43, 52, 56, 57, 68, 69, 70, 71, 72, 73
CURTIS WORTH FENTRESS: 4, 23
JEFF GOLDBERG/ESTO: 13, 14, 16, 17, 18
STEVE HALL/ESTO: 62, 63, 66, 67
LISA HILMER: 6, 7
JOHN HUGHES: 44, 45, 56
TIMOTHY HURSLEY: 6, 7, 10, 16, 19, 44, 45, 46, 47
RON JOHNSON: 4, 5, 7, 20, 21, 22, 26, 27, 37, 54, 55, 57, 59, 60, 61
JASON KNOWLES: 24, 25
ELIZABETH GILL LUI: 42
NICK MERRICK/HEDRICH-BLESSING: 5, 6, 9, 13, 14, 15, 19, 40, 41, 43, 47, 50, 52, 53, 66
JON MILLER/HEDRICH-BLESSING: 32, 33, 34
JOCK POTTLE: 13, 48, 49, 52
ROCKY MOUNTAIN CUSTOM PHOTOGRAPHICS: 28, 29, 30, 31
UNITED STATES MARINE CORPS: 22

ACKNOWLEDGMENTS
JIM BRADBURN, FAIA

Architecture is not created in a vacuum; it takes a team. Fentress Bradburn Architects has enjoyed the support of many people over the years—from clients and staff, to contractors, developers and product suppliers and manufacturers. In large part, it is thanks to the generous and open hearts and minds of these people that we have been able to achieve the success the firm enjoys today.

Without great clients, you can't make great architecture. Unless the client is open to thoughtful innovation, a design firm can only go so far. We have been fortunate to have clients who are looking for a fresh approach to the design of their buildings. These have included such museum entities as the Arvada Center for the Arts and Humanities; Denver Art Museum; Black American West Museum; Buffalo Bill Historical Center; Gulf Canada Resources Limited; Leanin Tree Gallery; Museum of Western Art; National Cowboy and Western Heritage Museum; National Museum of Wildlife Art; Department of the Navy; and the Buffalo Bill Historical Center.

Government agencies may not be thought of as bastions of innovation and creativity, but we have had the pleasure of working with several that were willing to push the envelope in order to create great civic architecture. These have included the City and County of Denver; the State of Colorado; the City of Oakland, California; Clark County, Nevada; the State of California; the Port of Seattle; the State of Washington; and the General Services Administration of the U.S. federal government. We are grateful to have had the opportunity to work with them.

Many of our technological innovations have blossomed as a result of unusual and extensive collaboration with our product suppliers and manufacturers. It has been my particular pleasure to explore new frontiers of materials science with a number of these people. Among others, we owe a debt of gratitude to BirdAir for its work on the fabric roof of Denver International Airport; Indiana Limestone for its post-tensioned limestone spandrels that proved to be an economical solution in office tower construction; ASI for engineering cable-truss systems that facilitate the creation of large glass curtain walls; Tecnomaiera (Italy) for their development of thin reinforced granite flooring at Denver International Airport; and Tejas Architectural Products and Dow Chemical Company for their exploration of four-sided structural silicone insulated glass systems.

Working relationships are so important to the way a project actually comes to fruition. Fentress Bradburn Architects has had the good fortune to work with contractors who are open to new approaches and true partnership. A few of these include Hensel-Phelps Construction Co., PCL, Perini Building Company, Weitz Construction (formerly Weitz Cohen), Gerald Phipps and Turner Construction.

Last, but most importantly, we must acknowledge the tremendous gifts of our staff and their generous contributions of time, effort and creativity to the projects with which we have been blessed. From principals and associates, to veteran staff and interns, Fentress Bradburn has been fortunate to assemble a truly unique group of individuals devoted to producing the very best possible architecture. Curt and I have a deep respect for them and for what they have created for us and for themselves. We thank them and their families, which have at every turn been supportive of their work here. Without this tremendous support, none of this would be possible.